# Heidegger in Russia
# and Eastern Europe

# New Heidegger Research

**Series Editors:**
Gregory Fried, Professor of Philosophy, Suffolk University, United States
Richard Polt, Professor of Philosophy, Xavier University, United States

The New Heidegger Research series promotes informed and critical dialogue that breaks new philosophical ground by taking into account the full range of Heidegger's thought, as well as the enduring questions raised by his work.

**Titles in the Series:**

# Heidegger in Russia and Eastern Europe

Edited by
Jeff Love

ROWMAN &
LITTLEFIELD
—— INTERNATIONAL ——

London • New York

Published by Rowman & Littlefield International Ltd
Unit A, Whitacre Mews, 26-34 Stannary Street, London SE11 4AB
www.rowmaninternational.com

Rowman & Littlefield International Ltd.is an affiliate of Rowman & Littlefield
4501 Forbes Boulevard, Suite 200, Lanham, Maryland 20706, USA
With additional offices in Boulder, New York, Toronto (Canada), and
Plymouth (UK)
www.rowman.com

**British Library Cataloguing in Publication Data**
A catalogue record for this book is available from the British Library

ISBN: HB 978-1-7834-8863-6
     PB 978-1-7834-8864-3

**Library of Congress Cataloging-in-Publication Data**

Names: Love, Jeff (G. Jeffrey), editor.
Title: Heidegger in Russia and Eastern Europe / edited by Jeff Love.
Description: Lanham : Rowman & Littlefield International, 2017. |
    Series: New Heidegger research | Includes bibliographical references and index.
Identifiers: LCCN 2017018145 (print) | LCCN 2017024554 (ebook) |
    ISBN 9781783488650 (Electronic) | ISBN 9781783488636 (cloth : alk. paper) |
    ISBN 9781783488643 (pbk. : alk. paper)
Subjects: LCSH: Heidegger, Martin, 1889-1976— Influence. | Soviet Union. |
    Europe, Eastern.
Classification: LCC B3279.H49 (ebook) | LCC B3279.H49 H3522333 2017 (print) |
    DDC 193— dc23
LC record available at https://lccn.loc.gov/2017018145

∞™ The paper used in this publication meets the minimum requirements of
American National Standard for Information Sciences—Permanence of Paper for
Printed Library Materials, ANSI/NISO Z39.48-1992.

Printed in the United States of America

# Contents

# Acknowledgments

Many people have worked hard to bring this volume together. I would like to thank Ilya Kliger, who helped set the idea in motion. I would also like to thank Ludger Hagedorn of the Institute for Human Sciences (IWM), in Vienna, for his willingness to assist with the volume (and Andrzej Serafin for putting me in contact with Professor Hagedorn). I should also like to thank my colleague Michael Meng, whose advice in designing and preparing this volume has been invaluable. Finally, I owe thanks to Salvador Oropesa, chair of the Department of Languages at Clemson University, for financial support, and Kacie Harris for her help in preparing the final manuscript.

Gregory Fried and Richard Polt were ideal editors: attentive, helpful, and generous.

# Introduction

## A (Counter-) Revolution Delayed

### Jeff Love

The philosophy of Martin Heidegger exerted an extraordinary influence in the twentieth century. Even before the publication of *Being and Time* in 1927, his version of phenomenology had attracted attention from all over the world. As the heir apparent to Husserl in phenomenological circles, Heidegger cultivated a generation of talented students who would introduce his thought to their respective countries, ranging from Argentina to Japan. While the various streams of influence and adaptation of Heidegger's thinking have yet to be fully explored, his influence in Japan, Western Europe, South America, and the United States is fairly well documented.[1] This volume is concerned with contributing to this general exploration in connection with a part of the world that for much of the twentieth century was profoundly hostile to Heidegger's philosophy, largely on political grounds. For if Heidegger's influence was felt in Eastern Europe in the interwar period, particularly in Czechoslovakia thanks to Jan Patočka, the same cannot be said for the Soviet Union. And with the consolidation of Soviet power after the Second World War, it became not merely difficult, but dangerous to occupy oneself with Heidegger's thought, especially given the philosopher's initially enthusiastic support for the National Socialist regime.

\*\*\*

The chapters that follow are devoted, in the best Heideggerian sense, to uncovering and elaborating a somewhat hidden history. The most striking feature of this history—indeed, all the more striking given Heidegger's extremely controversial status now as a philosopher whose association with National Socialism was neither casual nor innocent— is the extent to which Heidegger's thought inspired and continues to inspire emancipatory struggle. It is fair to say that reading Heidegger became a gesture of resistance, first against the authority of the communist state, and second, and for many outside observers much more disquietingly, against the dominance of European thought itself. The two streams of resistance are in fact inextricably linked, in particular in Russia, because the environmental and psychological devastation suffered by the peoples of the communist East made it far easier to connect resistance to communism to resistance to the Western tradition in general as one that culminated not in Social Democracy but in the political repression and brutal exploitation of the environment characteristic of the communist states. In the end, the manifold failures of the communist states invited what we may recognize now as a counterrevolutionary stream of thought whose original association with National Socialism was either attenuated, glossed over in silence, or even reinterpreted as essentially of emancipatory intent. Heidegger became a source of inspiration for both those seeking a new kind of state entirely and those whose nationalist tendencies came far closer to what we might call a renewed fascism.

Heidegger's thought has thus played a strikingly ambivalent emancipatory role in Russia and Eastern Europe, ranging from an attack on the pieties of Marxist dogmatics to what may be the last and perhaps most radical anticolonial struggle: that of Russia against the hegemony of Western thought, particularly as pilloried in the guise of modern American neoliberalism, at once ravenous and vacuous.

***

The present volume traces this history in three parts. The first part examines Heidegger's strong interest in Russia as well as the influence of Russian literature on Heidegger. It begins with Michael Meng's investigation (chapter 1) into the significance of what we might refer to as Heidegger's "Russophilia" with reference to a dialogue Heidegger staged in a Russian prison camp and completed on a very significant date: May 8, 1945, the day of the final unconditional surrender of Nazi Germany. It ends with Alexander Kluge's imagined encounter (chapter 4) between Heidegger and a young Jewish girl whom he seeks to protect from Otto Ohlendorf's brutal Einsatzgruppe D, which killed more than ninety thousand Jews in Ukraine and the Crimea. This imaginary encounter was first published in German in 2004 and appears here in English for the first time.[2]

One of the most notable aspects of Heidegger's interest in Russia was his interest in Russian literature. As Horst-Jürgen Gerigk notes in chapter 2, the young Heidegger had two portraits on his writing desk in 1922, one of Pascal, the other of Dostoevsky. While Heidegger rarely refers to Dostoevsky in print, according to Hans-Georg Gadamer, Heidegger's enthusiasm for Dostoevsky was considerable, and, as Gerigk outlines in some detail, one of their important affinities was a common orientation to eschatological thinking, an orientation to a new, salvific beginning that is as dramatic in Heidegger as it is in Dostoevsky.

*Being and Time* bears witness also to the influence of Dostoevsky's great rival and counterweight, Lev Tolstoy. The famous note referring to Tolstoy's novella *The Death of Ivan Ilyich* in section 51 of *Being and Time* has led to all manner of speculation over the influence of Tolstoy on Heidegger. In chapter 3, Inessa Medzhibovskaya digs deeper to uncover a much broader network of affinities and influences than has hitherto been contemplated. What is more, she explores some of the ways that Tolstoy's virtuosity in expressing different approaches to objects and situations finds a correlate in a radicalized Heideggerian phenomenology.

Chapters 5 through 9, in the second part of the volume, deal with various ways in which Heidegger's thinking was received by three important philosophers who all deserve more international attention than they have had so far: Jan Patočka (1907–1977), Krzysztof Michalski (1948–2013), and Vladimir Bibikhin (1938–2004).

As I note briefly above, Patočka played a crucial role in introducing phenomenology to Czechoslovakia in the interwar period. He was the only one of these three philosophers to have known both Husserl and Heidegger personally, and his influence in Czechoslovakia has been enormous. He played a significant role as an opponent of the Communist regime and died after being brutally interrogated by the secret police. The two chapters included in this volume attempt to provide a broad introduction to Heideggerian elements in Patočka's thought. Josef Moural (in chapter 5) gives an overview of this influence, whereas

Vladislav Suvák (in chapter 6) examines the relation between Heidegger's extremely important essay on truth, "On the Essence of Truth"
(1943), and Patočka. Together the chapters seek to shed light on how
Patočka adapts Heidegger's thought to a renewed Socratism that may
seem to have little to do with Heidegger.

Krzysztof Michalski played a similarly important role in Poland by
developing an openly theologically oriented approach to Heidegger.
Michalski cautions, as Andrzej Serafin points out in chapter 7, that
a Heideggerian theology has to be a most peculiar one since Heidegger's notion of God hardly seems to fit the doctrinal and dogmatic
requirements of any established church. Yet, on this account alone,
Heidegger's investigations may be more genuinely Christian because
they seek to get to the bottom of what a "God" can or must be. The
exploration of deity itself is radical and sets Heidegger against rather
more traditional notions of deity—in this sense Heidegger opens up
new possibilities for a renovated Christianity that have nothing to do
with how Christianity has hitherto been understood or practiced outside
of the initial century after the death of Christ.

This section also presents a text (chapter 8) by Michalski himself,
presented here in English for the first time, a translation that Michalski
personally supervised. This text highlights one of the most important elements in Heidegger's thinking in the communist East: questioning. While
questioning is no doubt also perceived as an affront to accepted ways
of thinking in any context, the fundamental significance that Heidegger
grants to questioning and an unceasing pursuit of questioning had powerful resonance in the closed forum for discussion that prevailed in Eastern
Europe. In Heidegger is found not only questioning but the notion of
reviving a kind of philosophy that did not necessarily have to end up or
be in concordance with ruling Marxist dogma, which in its objection to
dogma of any kind—indeed, even being taken as such on its own—had
considerable significance and exerted an attractive force of its own.

In chapter 9, Michael Marder introduces the thought of Vladimir
Bibikhin by focusing on one of its key features, a thorough reconsidera-
tion of who we are based on the notion of what we consider our own.
What belongs to us? and What does it mean to belong? are simply two
questions raised by Bibikhin's investigations of the difference between
what belongs to us (and why) and what cannot belong to us or resists
us. To draw attention to the fundamental importance of ownership to
modern understandings of the human being as master or owner of the

world, this "maître du monde," identified by another Russian philosopher (Alexandre Kojève), is an important aspect of Bibikhin's thought. Equally important is Bibikhin's exhortation to create a new attitude to ownership by giving oneself in some degree over to what resists appropriation by us, thereby relinquishing the need to possess, to have and command. Here Bibikhin attempts to reject the foundation of property pertinent to both the Soviet state and post-Soviet economism in favor of a new relation to ownership whose political implications remain revolutionary.

Indeed, the political ramifications of Heidegger's thinking, so explosive at the moment, were no less explosive in the communist East. Part 3 of the volume examines these political consequences in Czechoslovakia as they helped to ground the famed "Velvet Revolution" of 1989 and, more immediately, as they play out in modern Russia. Daniel Kroupa's absorbing description (chapter 10) of Patočka's influence on a wide spectrum of intellectuals in Czechoslovakia, before and after his untimely death in 1977, is a remarkable insider's account, since Kroupa played an important role in the liberation of Czechoslovakia from the yoke of Soviet rule in 1989 and the early 1990s. Heidegger acted in these contexts as a voice of rebellion and emancipation, hardly as a representative of Nazism or, to recall Emanuel Faye's memorable title, as the "introduction of Nazism into philosophy."[3]

The impact of Heidegger's thought on Russian politics is far more complicated, and it highlights profound divisions in the Russian attitude to the West. As I point out in chapter 11, the Russian attitude to the West and Western thought has never been free of ambivalence. The two major streams of Heidegger's influence in Russia provide an absorbing outline of this ambivalence. On the one hand, Alexander Dugin draws on Heidegger's critique of metaphysics as a critique of universalism and a support for a totally different attitude to politics (chapter 12). This attitude is totally different because it does not demand a universal hegemon but allows for many differing centers of power and a cultural diversity that resists domination by one way of thinking. Dugin refers to this notion as multipolarity, and it can sound quite attractive unless one considers to what degree it resembles the old segregationist notion of "separate but equal" that justified the maintenance of racial division and conflict in the United States. Moreover, Dugin's attempted recovery of a distinctively Russian *Dasein* is difficult to distinguish from traditional Russian nationalism and imperialism with its belief, stated succinctly by Dostoevsky, that the star of salvation (for the world) shall arise in the East.

Vladimir Bibikhin, surely an antipode to Dugin, seems equally concerned with issues of salvation (chapter 13). Yet this salvation is rather distant from a specifically Russian salvific mission vis-à-vis the rest of the world. Still, Bibikhin seems most concerned with protecting Russia from the dangers of modern consumer society, the kind of capitalism characteristic of the United States, though Bibikhin does not single out the United States as the crucial threat in the world as Dugin does. In his striking article on the difference between *Being and Time* and *The Contributions to Philosophy*, the principal underlying current of thought is the recognition and exploration of the need for a thoroughgoing examination of who we are in contrast to the—potentially easier—submersion in quotidian cares. In this respect, Bibikhin seeks to bring about a moment of self-reflection in the overwhelming dash for personal enrichment and power characteristic of the 1990s and the early part of the new millennium.

The volume ends with the work of one of Bibikhin's closest friends and arguably the most important voice in contemporary Russian philosophy, Sergey Horujy. Chapter 14 provides a brief and anecdotal account of Heideggerian influence in the Soviet Union from one of the key participants. He then gives a brief outline of his "synergistic anthropology," his own thinking as influenced by Heidegger, that draws on the rich Russian religious tradition, and, in particular, Hesychasm, the practice of silence, to offer a new identity for human beings that escapes both rampant consumerism and the dangerous aspects of Heidegger's thought. That thought, for Horujy, is unable to grasp the most terrible crimes of the Nazi regime and thus remains forever complicit with it.

***

A word about the limitations of this volume, two of which seem to me important enough to discuss briefly in this introduction. While Czech, Polish, and Russian responses to Heidegger are amply discussed in this volume, several countries in Eastern Europe are left out. For example, one of Heidegger's important students was Walter Biemel, a Romanian who studied with Heidegger in the crucial years from 1942 to 1944. Biemel remained in Germany and became a well-known professor. While Biemel can no doubt be called a Romanian philosopher, it is evident that he moved almost wholly in the German philosophical sphere and did not feel a calling to create a distinctively Romanian philosophy or to adapt Heidegger to Romanian traditions, as seems to be the case with the main philosophers dealt with in this volume.[4] Moreover, Heidegger had a significant impact on an important Romanian poet who wrote in German, Paul Celan, as well as an important modern Polish poet, Adam Zagajewski. In the case of the former, the relation has been so widely studied elsewhere that it made little sense to include it here; as for the latter, the influence of Heidegger on Polish poetry is a subject worthy of its own volume.

A perhaps more serious omission is that of the important Hungarian Marxist thinker, Georg Lukács, considered by many the leading Marxist thinker of the twentieth century. While Heidegger has had many opponents, few have been as formidable as Lukács, who was well aware of Heidegger quite early on and who carried out a not-so-hidden polemic with his thought. Two works come immediately to mind: Lukács's article from 1949, "Heidegger Redivivus," that took aim at what Lukács considered Heidegger's attempt at rendering his thought acceptable after the nightmarish collapse of the National Socialist regime; and Lukács's immense work *The Destruction of Reason*, which carries on a violent and sustained confrontation with the German idealist tradition and the radical thinking of Nietzsche and Heidegger in particular.[5] Indeed, the very interest in authenticity and the ontological that were for Lukács signs of the destructive character of Heidegger's thinking become sources of inspiration for several of his East European readers like Michalski and Bibikhin.

I have chosen not to include Lukács, however, for several reasons. First among these is the eminence of Lukács himself. There is a far more extensive international literature on Lukács than on any of the figures introduced in this volume. Perhaps more importantly, this volume is dedicated to exploring the lesser-known and most productive aspects of Heidegger's thought in Russia and Eastern Europe, where it has contributed to creating a new kind of thinking. In this respect, the impact of Heidegger on Lukács is different, because it is wholly negative.[6] Lukács encountered Heidegger as an enemy from the outset, and his engagement with Heidegger, though complex, is largely a work of opposition to Heidegger that sought to undermine and eradicate his baleful influence in favor of what has seemed to many to be Lukács's adherence to a kind of high Stalinism. It is no surprise that, as a Marxist, Lukács would seek to counter Heideggerian ideas as forming part of enervating, antirevolutionary bourgeois philosophy. While this is no doubt so, it is also fair to say that Lukács ultimately sought something more than bland assertion of Stalinist orthodoxy: to defend the kind of reason that Habermas later sought to defend as being capable of creating a venue for discussion and the adjudication of disputes that would result neither in the narrow imposition of the prerogatives of one group on another nor alienating reification. Lukács saw the destruction of reason, the dismantling of the tradition of universal reason, not merely as a political gesture intended to support a fascist revolution, but as playing a fundamental role in a thoroughgoing counterrevolution whose end was to eradicate egalitarianism *in toto*. This story, fascinating in itself, also merits a volume of its own.

## NOTES

1. For example, the influence of Heidegger on the philosophers of the so-called Kyoto School is fairly well attested. See Lin Ma, *Heidegger on East-West Dialogue: Anticipating the Event* (New York: Routledge, 2008). How Heidegger was received in the United States was tracked by Martin Woessner's *Heidegger in America* (Cambridge: Cambridge University Press, 2010). Heidegger's influence on the well-known Argentinian philosopher Carlos Astrada is itself well known, as is his influence on the revolution in Iran through the curious figure of Ahmad Fardid.

2. Alexander Kluge, *Cronik der Gefuhle* (Berlin: Suhrkamp, 2004).

3. Emmanuel Faye, *The Introduction of Nazism into Philosophy in Light of the Unpublished Seminars 1933–1934*, trans. Michael Smith (New Haven, CT: Yale University Press, 2011).

4. The more distinctively Romanian voice might be that of Alexandru Dragomir (1916–2002), who published nothing during his lifetime. His work is just beginning to be published in Romanian with a selection of texts made available recently in English. See Alexandru Dragomir, *The World We Live In*, ed. Gabriel Liiceanu and Catalin Partenie (Cham, Switzerland: Springer, 2016).

5. Georg Lukács, "Heidegger Redivivus," *Sinn und Form* 1 (1949): 37–62; *The Destruction of Reason*, trans. Peter R. Palmer (London: Merlin Press, 1980). See also Georg Lukács, *Existentialismus oder Marxismus?* (Berlin: Aufbau Verlag, 1951).

6. Jan Patočka, one of the key figures in this volume, wrote an incisive account of the conflict between Lukács and Heidegger. See Jan Patočka, "Heidegger vom anderen Ufer," in *Ausgewählte Schriften*, ed. Klaus Nellen, Jiří Němec, and Ilja Srubar (Stuttgart: Klett-Cotta, 1991), 556–73.

*Part I*

# HEIDEGGER AND RUSSIA:
# INFLUENCES

## Chapter 1

# Russia in the Age of *Machenschaft*

## Michael Meng

It is possible to provide security against other things, but as far
as death is concerned, we men all live in a city without walls.

—Epicurus

Russia and Germany belong together.

—Thomas Mann

With his own sons missing in Russia and with the Soviet Union in ruins
after Hitler's *Vernichtungskrieg*, Martin Heidegger wrote a dialogue set
in a Russian prisoner of war camp. He dated it May 8, 1945. By that
point, when Hitler's war had finally ended, some 25 million Soviets
had been killed, of whom some 3.3 million were POWs who had died
largely of starvation in Nazi camps. The dialogue momentously speaks
of "desolation" and "evil." Not of the evil wrought by Hitler's genocidal
war but of a different kind of evil: that of the abandonment of Being
by the regime of *Machenschaft*. The evil that concerns Heidegger is the
devastation of the human by technology, or what Heidegger refers to
as *Machenschaft*, before 1945. As the most complete manifestation of
the Western metaphysical contempt for human finitude, *Machenschaft*
threatens to destroy the "essence" of the human as *ho thnētos*, "as the
mortal in distinction to the immortals, the gods."[1]

But Heidegger, no pessimist, believes that where danger lies, there
emerges also that which saves. For Russia, like Germany, might be

3

able to unshackle the yoke of the Western metaphysical banishment of death that has been foisted upon it by Bolshevism. This is how the dialogue begins: "As we were marching to our workplace this morning, out of the rustling of the expansive forest I was suddenly overcome by something healing. Throughout the entire day I meditated wherein this something that heals could rest."[2]

Wherein rests that which heals? It rests in the Russian forest, which carries one into the "open [*ins Offene*]" where one lets oneself be the being that one is, *ho thnētos*. In this "space" of the open, one embraces one's mortality rather than fleeing from it into a determinate world of objects. Letting in the "healing" expanse of the open, of the Russian forest, one becomes free from the metaphysical contempt for indeterminacy and transience that now threatens to destroy *Russentum* as one of the last cultural traditions in the world that has a rooted attachment to the soil and to an appreciation of human fragility.[3]

With this admiration of Russia—of its forests, of its culture, of its respect for human vulnerability—Heidegger shows himself a master at creating metaphors and myths to advance his political revolution against metaphysics; otherwise one might be tempted to characterize him as nothing more than a romantic ethno-cultural nationalist who longs for returning to a "rooted" world freed from spiritless technology and Jewish cosmopolitanism, the peddler par excellence of *Machenschaft*.[4] That Heidegger saw Russia and Germany as the "healing" powers that could save the world from the sickness of the Platonic-Jewish-Christian tradition can hardly be doubted in light of the recently published *Black Notebooks*. But Heidegger is no nostalgic romantic who longs for some lost past or some pure "natural" state. There can be no return to nature for him because there is no nature. "The 'natural' is always historical."[5]

Hardly nostalgic, Heidegger is a revolutionary who looks to the future in calling for the end of philosophy and the preparation for "metapolitics" as the only way to save us from the nihilism of modern technology.[6] His revolution seeks a total overcoming of the Western tradition that has estranged most of us from our essence as mortal beings for the past two millennia with a few exceptions: The Germans and the Russians still cultivate an awareness of death and, thus, it is they who can lay the groundwork for transitioning humanity to a new beginning beyond *Machenschaft*.[7] In 1933 and 1934, Heidegger believed that Nazism could prepare the path for this transition. Though he quickly grew frustrated by the bureaucratic intransigence that his sweeping reforms for the German university faced, he never renounced the "inner truth and greatness" of Nazism as a movement that could confront the tyranny of *Machenschaft*, and he envisioned before and during the Nazi attack against the Soviet Union an alliance of Germany with Russia to combat the technological interpretation of Being.[8] Heidegger prophesized that Germany and Russia could save Europe, if not the world, from the assertion of the modern technological era as the end of history and from its elimination of the human as an imperfect being-toward-death.

Heidegger as prophet? It seems so. But he is a prophet fully aware of himself as such. With considerable deftness and erudition, he recasts traditional concepts such as evil, estrangement, and salvation, employing the clichés of the Western tradition to overcome that exhausted tradition; he foretells the apocalyptic ending of time as dangerously self-destructive, not redemptive or healing in the least. Heidegger is, then, a prophet of the most ironic kind who warns about the ending of time. Specifically, Heidegger plays on three tropes in Western history: the Homeric attachment to soil, the metaphysical notion of "essence [*Wesen*]," and the Christian narrative of salvation. This trinity can be found in the basic narrative he tells about the modern era: Technology has estranged us from our essence as mortal beings, but a rooted community of people, the Germans in alliance with the Russians, can lead us out of this nihilistic evil. Let us hear from the herald himself:

Zerstörung ist der Vorbote eines
verborgenen Anfangs, Verwüstung aber
ist der Nachschlag des bereits entschiede-
nen Endes. Steht das Zeitalter schon
vor der Entscheidung zwischen Zerstörung
und Verwüstung? Aber wir wissen
den anderen Anfang, wissen ihn
fragend.[9]

This passage, poetic and prophetic, foreboding and hopeful, reflects a creative play on the Western salvific tradition. It invokes a sense of mystery and urgency as the world teeters between destruction and renewal. What shall we choose? Should we continue along the path of desolation or discover a hidden path to a new beginning? Whom shall we follow? Plato or Heidegger?

In what follows, I discuss in greater depth Heidegger's political mythmaking in three central parts. The first part examines Heidegger's claim that *Machenschaft* evades mortality, the second part looks at his portrayal of Russia as a salvific force that can free the West from the nihilism of *Machenschaft*, and the third part reveals the political implications of the ostensible "salvation" narrative that Heidegger creates—namely, that Heidegger's critique of technology and his focus on death as one's "ownmost" possibility brings him to reject the universalist and egalitarian tradition that he identifies as originating with Plato. He expresses this animus against egalitarianism in a lucid manner in his discussion of *koinon* as the basis of communism in *Die Geschichte des Seyns*.

Heidegger's "salvation" from the metaphysical tradition involves embracing *Dasein* as the placeholder of the nothing, of affirming the "essence" of the human as having no essence. Death, as one's ownmost possibility, can only be confronted as the possibility of my impossibility, not of anyone else's. To claim differently, to claim human commonality through suffering, Heidegger suggests, is to avoid death as one's ownmost possibility, and, in the case of communism, to legitimize the imposition of a tyrannical regime.

In viewing Russia as a country that, like Germany, still has a vitality and spirituality to it that "the West" no longer possesses, Heidegger stands in a long tradition of German admirers of Russia that stretches from Friedrich Nietzsche to Thomas Mann to Arthur Moeller van den Bruck; the latter, while less known, edited the German translation of Dostoevsky's complete works and imagined a German-Russian fantasy against the West in *The Third Empire* (1923).[10] But while Heidegger has predecessors, his prophetic call for freedom from the tyranny of *Machenschaft* through a German-Russian alliance has no rival in its astonishing challenge to many of the norms we cherish to this day.

\*\*\*

Though Heidegger often insists that he does not oppose technology but merely a certain interpretation of it, one would be hard pressed to find an "authentic" approach to technology in his thought. Quite the contrary, Heidegger declares technology to be evil. This is a strong assertion and wittingly so. By saying "evil," Heidegger seems quite obviously to be alluding to Augustine, that great thinker of evil in Western Christianity, who warns about absorbing oneself in things rather than worshiping God. So too does Heidegger exhort us not to mistake Being for a being, again and again, in various ways, including by employing the less-familiar word *Seyn* and the unusual locution of a crossed-out *Seyn* in his works during the 1930s. In so doing, he appeals to the Christian animus against materiality to gain adherents, as a prophet, yet in a subversive way so as to advance a wholly different kind of salvation—a salvation from the salvific tradition that hypostatizes Being in terms of beings, most obviously Christianity through its God.

The modern take on this hypostatization of Being is *Machenschaft*. The word means simply the "making or producing of things." *Machenschaft* is "the accordance of everything with producibility."[11] Inherently imperialistic and hegemonic, *Machenschaft* threatens to regulate the relations of all beings to each other in a fixed and singular manner. *Machenschaft* discloses the Being of all entities in the world as equally exchangeable resources of measurement and exchange. Any other way of viewing things, ascetic, historical, or otherwise, is excluded by *Machenschaft*. So powerfully hegemonic is *Machenschaft* that it even threatens to turn Dasein into a producible thing or "resource [*Bestand*]."

While the conventional way of explaining Heidegger's concern about *Machenschaft* would be to suggest that he views it as the most profound forgetting of Being (and, in a rather purple phrase, the forgetting of that forgetting), the question begs itself: Why does forgetting matter for Heidegger? For whom does the forgetting of Being mean something? Does the forgetting of Being mean something for rocks, plants, or animals? No, it does not. It means something for Dasein as the being for whom the question of Being matters. Now, some readers might suspect that I am working my way up to making the hackneyed anthropomorphism charge against Heidegger. I am not. To be sure, Heidegger does make Dasein a "guardian" or "shepherd" of Being. But he hardly seeks to enthrone the human, as modern technology so forcefully does with the most withering and enervating of consequences as we shall see. Indeed, it is precisely those consequences that prompt Heidegger's prophetic warning that we save ourselves from technology.

Technology is nihilistic for Heidegger. The hegemony of modern technological mastery reflects the most complete estrangement of the human from its "essence" as a finite being. *Machenschaft* continues the Western metaphysical attempt to overcome the imperfection of the human being by banishing one's relation to death as one's ownmost possibility, on the one hand, and by viewing the actual moment of dying as merely a bureaucratic affair, on the other. In the modern era of *Machenschaft*, dying increasingly takes on a purely technocratic meaning insofar as the human does not die but merely ends or is liquidated as a piece of inventory. Death comes to mean merely the ending of replaceable units; it comes to mean nothing more than the decay or termination of bodily functions equivalent to the cessation of machines.

In its most tyrannical form, *Machenschaft* discloses Dasein as a resource or *Bestand* to be managed and controlled. If Dasein becomes antecedently fixed and finalized in such a manner, then it no longer exists in the world with multiple possibilities open to it. Dasein becomes a widget in a machinelike regime of self-perpetuating repeatability. Sameness ensues in a condition of complete equalization where the disclosure of death as one's ownmost possibility becomes increasingly eliminated. Equalization encourages each of us, we might say, to run away from death as our *ownmost* possibility, one that cannot be shared with anyone else. Hence, we forget the possibility of our impossibility or, when that possibility is disclosed to us, we turn away from it rather than explore it, since we live in an emergency era of needlessness when nearly everything has been rendered manageable, secure, and common. We will soon become, Heidegger fears, Nietzsche's last man, the man who seeks nothing else than to live a long, prosperous, and materially satisfied life that is as secure as possible. Terrified of any kind of disruption, the last man flees into the bourgeois shelter of materialism and forgets his "essence" as a fragile, dying being.

What kind of life is this? Not a life for Heidegger. Heidegger is direct on this point in the *Black Notebooks* when he says that the modern technological era seeks to establish a final regime of material satisfaction in which the animal in the human will be set free in its "full animality." Which is to say that the human will become an utterly servile being compelled solely by the animal desire for self-preservation. The reduction of Dasein to self-preservation will result in its "bestialization."[12] This is so because Dasein will no longer have the capacity to relate to death in any other way than by fear. And if Dasein can only relate to death in a singular and antecedently fixed manner, then it ceases to be Dasein with multiple possibilities open to it. Technology threatens to enslave and eliminate Dasein.

Technology is suicidal. This is quite a foreboding claim by itself. Yet Heidegger goes on to suggest—and here his radicality only heightens—that the elimination of the human by *Machenschaft* is the culmination of the Western metaphysical tradition's pessimistic evasion of mortality and its revengeful contempt for suffering. At least since the rise of Christianity, which is Platonism for the masses, Heidegger suggests, the dominant reaction to suffering and mortality has been avoidance. Revenge against time, against death, has sent us looking for salvation from our essence as *ho thnētos*.

The desire for salvation is key to Heidegger's interpretation of the metaphysical tradition. Salvation promises to save us from what distresses us.[13] What distresses us? Our temporal, finite being distresses us according to Heidegger, who finds an "ontological" relation to death lurking below the surface of everything we do. All our pursuits—work, science, art, politics, history, and so forth—relate to our attitude toward our temporal being, to the nothingness or emptiness that is our essence as beings-toward-death. Our essence is that we have no essence. Habituated as we are to thinking in terms of things, Heidegger provides the example of a jug in *Contributions to Philosophy (of the Event)* to approximate the point he wishes to make about Dasein's nothingness. The jug suggests that form conceals the negative that is its essence. The walls of the jug conceal the pure emptiness of its "inner recess." This inner recess does not arise from the walls of the jug. Rather, the inner recess gives shape to those walls (*Wände*).[14]

The emptiness of the inner recess of the jug is the "essence" of Dasein's Being. The emptiness or nothingness of our lives determines the walls of culture that we construct in the constant strife of turning toward and away from death. We build walls to protect ourselves from our essence as transient, historical beings.

Why is this so? This brings us to Plato, the first great builder of walls in the West that have endured for centuries in Heidegger's view. Death gave birth to Plato's metaphysics, or, put more prudently, a pessimistic reaction to death happened to give birth to the walls that Plato constructed to protect the human from death. Plato's "hostility to the body," in Hannah Arendt's apt formulation, shaped his elaborate metaphysical system.[15] Lest confusion arise here, it bears stressing that Heidegger does not suggest that death drives us in some kind of deterministic manner. Were he to suggest so, then he would have to presuppose the existence of a fixed human "nature" that drives history in a predictable pattern. There is no human nature for Heidegger other than a border, an insufficiency or lack of identity, that is death. Death as our nature undermines the metaphysical notion of nature that seeks to give a determinate identity to the indeterminacy of Dasein's Being. Rather than claiming that human nature moves history in a certain way, Heidegger suggests that Plato's metaphysical creation became dogmatic as Western history unfolded.

Now, if Heidegger denies human nature, then how does he make the claim of historical continuity that he does? He creates it as a *happening* at a specific historical moment through interpretations of the Western tradition in an attempt to overcome the very history he creates; and he thereby prepares, indirectly, for the future possibility of transformation. Always turning back to the past to turn toward the openness of the future, Heidegger, never an ordinary historian, creates histories of the walls that have been put up by the Western metaphysical tradition to dismantle them. Energetic, aggressive, and challenging, his histories nourish the possibility of transformation by revealing that what may appear natural is in fact historically contingent.

Heidegger creates two kinds of histories. One kind provides a sweeping narrative of the history of Being and can be found mainly in the prophetic writings of the 1930s. The other kind of history consists of highly detailed accounts of major thinkers that Heidegger wrote as lectures in the 1920s. The lectures support the broad claims that Heidegger makes in the more prophetic writings. Whereas the style of the first type of history draws on the prophetic tradition, the style of the second appeals to the scholarly tradition that emphasizes careful and dense analysis of primary sources. Both kinds of histories can be interpreted as attempts to persuade readers to accept Heidegger's interpretation of the Western tradition, since by his own admission they cannot claim to be more authoritative than any other narrative. For if the natural is historical, if truth is freedom, then there is obviously no transhistorical standard that can be invoked to declare Heidegger's histories "correct." Heidegger leaves one with agreement or conversion and he does so with all due irony in light of his understanding of truth as freedom: One assents to his interpretation presumably because one finds it to be "correct," even though Heidegger's "open" undermines any notion of correctness.[16] It would seem, then, that Heidegger brings us to a state of ironic irresolution: We circle endlessly in a hesitated state of belief and disbelief. But even fence-sitting is a position that Heidegger seeks to persuade us of affirming, presumably because it is better than Schmittian decisionism—we are better off as Hamlet than

Hitler. Can Heidegger escape the regime of correctness in his effort to save us from the nihilism of metaphysics? If he cannot, then it would be difficult not to view his writings as striving to persuade.[17]

Indeed, the revolutionary view to which Heidegger wishes to gain adherents concerns the metaphysical attitude toward death. Heidegger's central claim *in nuce* is this: Metaphysics seeks salvation from death born of a fearful and nihilistic rejection of the human as an imperfect being. Metaphysics finds human suffering intolerable and turns away from it through imaginations of a perfect world, an evasion of mortality that begins with Plato, who made godlikeness the telos of human existence.[18] But while Plato initiated one's estrangement from one's essence as a mortal being, it was Christianity that affirmed and spread the metaphysical evasion of mortality; and since then little has changed for two millennia. Remarkably resilient, the basic pattern of salvation, while it has taken on different forms in different historical eras, has persisted since the ancient period, in Heidegger's view.

Heidegger's history of salvation can roughly be divided into two periods. The first is the consolidation of salvation into a dogma during the Christian era from roughly Irenaeus to Descartes.[19] Elevating the human as a privileged being worthy of immortality, the Christian apologists made salvation the determinative value of human existence:

> The Being of a being consists in its being created by God. . . . [Christian doctrine] is a question of securing the salvation of individual immortal souls. All knowledge is tied to the order of salvation and stands in service to securing and promoting salvation. All history becomes oriented towards salvation: creation, the fall, redemption, last judgment.[20]

The second period in Heidegger's history of salvation is the drive to master nature through *Machenschaft*. In the modern era, the Christian concept of salvation morphs into a rapacious search to secure and manage the fragility of human life through technology.[21] Modernity takes over the Christian concept of salvation, but pursues it in this world by attempting to make human life as secure as possible. The modern era brings the Platonic pursuit of perfection to earth by seeking to master and control nature to serve humankind's needs:

> What is new about the modern period as opposed to the Christian medieval age consists in the fact that man, independently and by his own effort,

contrives to become certain and sure of his human being in the midst of
beings as a whole. The essential Christian thought of the certitude of
salvation is adopted, but such "salvation" is not eternal, other-worldly
bliss, and the way to it is not selflessness. The hale and the wholesome
are sought exclusively in the free development of all the creative powers
of man. Thus the question arises as to *how* we can attain and ground a
certitude sought by man himself for his earthly life, concerning his own
human being and the world. While in the medieval world it was precisely
the path to salvation and the mode of transmitting truth (*doctrina*) that
was firmly established, now the *quest* (*Suchen*) for new paths becomes
decisive.[22]

Rivaling Marx, perhaps overtly so, Heidegger provides a grand history
of continuity in this passage by boldly claiming that all history since
Plato has been oriented toward salvation. That level of generalization
does not usually make its way into scholarly books, for such generality is not the product of the *homo academicus*, but of the prophet. And
yet, as noted earlier, Heidegger supports his prophetic generalizations
with immense scholarly erudition. He offers a corpus of highly detailed
histories that interact with his broad claims in a way that has yet to be
fully explored.

Let us explore, if very briefly, this creative interplay among Heidegger's texts by considering the central thought that courses through
the passage above: that salvation is a struggle against time. The metaphysical tradition has compelled us to construct all kinds of safeguards
to protect ourselves from our fleeting lives. We tell histories. We build
monuments. We buy things. We flee toward what we consider to be permanent. All of our activities are escapes for Heidegger insofar as they
turn us away from the least permanent, yet the most important "thing"
in our lives: our preciously brief existence in this world. Or, in more
Heideggerian terms, we evade the least concrete aspect of our lives—
the future possibility of our ownmost impossibility—by fleeing into the
ontic realm of beings. We turn everything into a being, even history and
time, which we conceive as a continuous sequence of "seconds" that
can be preserved and narrated. Time and history thought as a "thing"
may be the sturdiest of all the walls we have constructed.

Time is indeed the crucial issue. According to Heidegger, metaphysics views time as a sickness from which we must be healed. *Das Heil*
is the German word for "salvation," and Heidegger plays on this word

to great effect in the above passage. We have to quote the German to see the linguistic play: *die Sicherung des Heils; Heilsordnung; Heilssicherung und -förderung; Heilsgeschichte; das Heile und Gesunde.* The last pairing expresses Heidegger's thought most concisely, since it obviously references the cliché, *heil und gesund*, "safe and sound." While the English conveys the point, the German does so with greater precision with its explicit connection to the body. The verb *heilen* means "to cure or make healthy"; it means *gesund machen.*

To be safe and sound, to make Dasein secure and certain, is the medicine metaphysics offers to the sickness that it has created. The sickness is contempt for time, while the medicine offered is described by Heidegger through a myriad of terms: inauthenticity, *Heilsgeschichte*, anthropomorphism, *Machenschaft*, *Historie*, to name just a few. All of these cures encourage Dasein to shelter itself from the pure ephemerality of time.

This propensity to find shelter can be seen throughout the Western tradition. No matter where Heidegger looks, he sees attempts to find a secure and permanent ground for Dasein: Plato's *idea*, Aristotle's essence, Augustine's eternal life, Descartes's *Ego cogito, ergo sum*, Hegel's philosophy of history. While Nietzsche offers the first break from this derision of time in *The Genealogy of Morals*, he ends up peddling a salvific myth in *Thus Spoke Zarathustra*. Nietzsche fails to overcome metaphysics.

Heidegger sees continuity throughout Western history. Nevertheless, he does see a shift taking place roughly in the modern era, as does Marx. In this respect, one cannot fail to notice the broad parallel between these two otherwise strikingly different thinkers. Something intensifies, grows worse, becomes darker in the modern era for Heidegger. The same is the case for Marx as he demonstrates in his brilliant critique of commodification in *Capital*. But there is a crucial difference between the two, and that difference hinges on their diverging views of the essence of technology. Technology, if oriented toward human emancipation, can be liberating for Marx. The communist utopia of materially satisfied humans requires technology as the condition of its possibility unless the communist utopia is to follow a wholly different model than that of distributing goods to all equally.

Heidegger could not be more different. He opposes the egalitarian ideal that Marx believes is truly human, viewing egalitarianism as a form of nihilism that turns Dasein away from its essence as *ho thnētos*. Moreover, technology is hardly liberating for Heidegger. Dark, tyrannical, nihilistic, technology brings to completion the metaphysical propensity for security in a hegemonic and imperialistic manner. Asserting itself as the only truth of Being, *Machenschaft* orients everything to *gesund machen*. The modern era exploits the fear of death by creating a hegemonic regime of salvation in which everything—art, science, literature, poetry, history—becomes oriented toward securing the preservation of the individual.[23] Everything becomes a thing that serves human needs in the regime of *Machenschaft*. Everything becomes reified, if we want to employ a Marxist concept, even Dasein.

*Machenschaft* brings to nihilistic fruition the metaphysical flight from death into beings—hence, its name, *Machenschaft*, the regime of produced things. And its most important "product" is the modern bourgeois citizen, "the ape of civilization," who lives for nothing else than to make and consume beings[24] and who runs away from death into the world of beautiful homes, nice cars, and fancy suits.

The bourgeois, who might be the telos of history for Thomas Hobbes and ironically perhaps even for Marx, reflects for Heidegger the terrifying culmination of salvation. Utterly absorbed in the everyday world of things and nothing else, the bourgeois threatens to eliminate Dasein either metaphorically by forgetting death almost entirely or literally through technological destruction. The latter Heidegger saw as very much possible. Before the dropping of the hydrogen bomb, he wrote, in 1941, that the last act of the highest consummation of technology would be that "the earth blows itself up in the air and present-day humanity vanishes." This technological destruction of humanity would not be a "calamity, but the first purging of Being of its deepest deformity through the supremacy of beings."[25]

***

When Heidegger wrote these words—very likely in quiet solitude— German soldiers enjoyed no such peace as they marched across Eastern Europe creating destruction of a different kind. The fear of death also played a crucial role in the Nazi explosion of violence during World War II, as Curzio Malaparte understood as few other observers of war have. Traveling across the eastern front, he witnessed Nietzschean toughness in the face of death collapse into a violent and revengeful fear of death:

> I saw the white stain of fear growing in the dull eyes of German officers and soldiers. I saw it spreading little by little, gnawing at the pupils, singeing the roots of the eyelashes and making the eyelashes drop one by one, like the long yellow eyelashes of the sunflowers. When Germans become afraid, when that mysterious German fear begins to creep into their bones, they always arouse a special horror and pity. Their appearance is miserable, their cruelty sad, their courage silent and hopeless. That is when the Germans become wicked.[26]

Heidegger does not confront this violent reaction to the fear of death. He does not confront this German, this human, who lashes out against others in desperate and vicious attempts to overcome the fear of death. Instead, as we have seen, he directs his attention to the technological impulse to overcome suffering that he envisioned Russia and Germany opposing during World War II.

When Hitler and Stalin were allies from 1939 to 1941, as well as during the first months after Hitler broke that alliance and ruthlessly invaded the Soviet Union, Heidegger imagined "a beyng-historical confrontation between Germanness and Russianness" to root out Bolshevism and World Judaism as carriers of the metaphysical sickness of *Machenschaft*.[27] In the *Black Notebooks*, he views Bolshevism as a product of the "occidental-Western modern rational metaphysics."[28] The West is colonizing Russia through Bolshevism, which is turning the country into one large factory of workers and consumers who strive for little else than total comfort. The slavish values of the Nietzschean last man are spreading from the West to Russia, in the guise of "emancipation" advanced by an all-powerful Communist party led by a nefarious "power of the few" that elusively remains "unnamed."[29] *Machenschaft* stops at no national boundaries in its drive to rule the world.

In Heidegger's narrative, the proponents of *Machenschaft* are rootless cosmopolitans who seek to make everything the same throughout the world through "the rule of reason as equalization [*die Vernunfts-herrschaft als Gleichsetzung*]."[30] Among the proponents of *Machenschaft* are Jews whom Heidegger characterizes as carriers of "empty rationality."[31] Just after the Nazi invasion of the Soviet Union,

Heidegger wrote: "The question about the role of *World Jewry* is not a racial one, but rather the metaphysical question about the kind of humanity, which *completely unrestricted* can take over the uprooting of all beings from Being as its world historical 'task.'"[32]

This sentence may seem to those who wish to defend Heidegger as little more than anti-Semitic cliché written in a private notebook by a philosopher who either fell captive to his historical era or became unhinged.[33] If Heidegger capitulated to the opinions of "the they" so obsequiously—if there was one thing clear about the Nazis, it was that they did not like Jews—then we would have to rethink seriously his capacities as a thinker who, on his own terms, resists worldviews.

Joseph Goebbels hardly duped Heidegger, nor did Heidegger go "mad" (unless Platonically mad). On the contrary, Heidegger appeals to an odiously venerable tradition in European history to promote a political agenda of "saving" the West from the metaphysical sickness that has reached cancerous form in bourgeois materialism and technological equalization. Heidegger radicalizes Nazi anti-Semitism to advance his animus against the Western metaphysical tradition: The nihilistic morals of the Jewish slave revolt that culminate in *Machenschaft* are leading to the "uprooting" of Dasein from its way of Being as *Sein zum Tode*. In this respect, "World Jewry" is a figuration of everything that Heidegger opposes, a figuration that he must have assumed would find adherents decades later, when the *Black Notebooks* were scheduled to be published. The *Black Notebooks* are a bet on the future and, in this case, a gruesome bet after the Nazi genocide of the Jews about which Heidegger likely knew something when he wrote these anti-Semitic attacks.

Heidegger's clarion call to overcome the Western tradition demands the elimination of Judaism as one of the crucial historical developments that corrupted the "great" Greek beginning of philosophical wonderment.[34] The elimination of Judaism entails overcoming the "Jewish" attitude toward the world; which is to say that Heidegger targets the "spirit" of Judaism. In so doing, he reorients Nazi anti-Semitism from a racial-biological approach to a metaphysical one: Hitler mistakenly deals with Judaism in a "Jewish" manner, since the Jews have long lived by the racial principle according to Heidegger.[35] This claim brings Heidegger to his most shocking suggestion that the Nazi murder of the Jews is an act of "self-annihilation" as an attack against the body.[36] The Nazi biological attack against the Jewish "race" applies a Jewish solution to a metaphysical problem. One must instead approach the problem of Judaism differently. One must eliminate the Jewish attitude toward the world that transposes the human being into a being uprooted from its Being. Otherwise Judaism will live on in its various mutations as Christianity, *Machenschaft*, and Bolshevism.[37]

Heidegger seeks nothing less than complete change from the course of Western history as it has hitherto unfolded. If this point may be apparent in the sheer radicality of his anti-Semitism and the ambition of his effort to overcome Platonism, then the issue becomes how—or better, where—the Heideggerian revolution will unfold. The revolution must come from Europe, where metaphysics originated, and, specifically, from those nations—namely, Germany and Russia—that still have a rooted relationship to death. If Heidegger's mythic creation of Germans as a distinctive *Volk* burdened with a unique destiny has by now received extensive scholarly attention, less well known is the myth that he invented about Russia as a rooted nation that, either in alliance with Germany or subservient to it, could lead the West out of the abyss of decadent nihilism.

In Russia Heidegger saw a country starkly different from its rivaling power, the United States of America. Despite the forced introduction of *Machenschaft* into Russia through Bolshevism, Heidegger maintained that Russia had not yet been fully colonized by the West, and thus a "post-colonial" rebellion against *Machenschaft* could spring from its soil. "Something healing" could come from the Russian forests.[38]

Heidegger imagines Russia as a country that still has a "rooted source in its soil." Russia still appreciates the "brutality" and "hardness" of life.[39] This portrayal of Russia seems so cliché that it makes Heidegger sound like a garden-variety *völkish* nationalist who repeats the same old Homeric themes of blood and soil. Or worse, it makes him seem puerile. Heidegger did, after all, dress up in peasant costumes. But Heidegger is neither doltish nor ironic with regard to the salvific narrative he creates about Germany and Russia. One can detect a mocking humor in Heidegger often directed toward scholars but never toward philosophy. He has no patience for the Roman mockery of philosophy.[40] Completely serious about what he is doing, Heidegger starts with the familiar to bring us to something less familiar and more radical.

Heidegger starts with the "forests" of Russia to bring us to Leo Tolstoy, whom he famously cites in his discussion of death in *Being and Time*. Tolstoy's *The Death of Ivan Ilyich* depicts, in brilliant and harrowing detail, one man's confrontation with the brutal truth of death. Everything seems so splendid for Ivan Ilyich, who is living the bourgeois paradise: He has the successful career, the beautiful family, the nice house; everything is so safe and sound until one day, while hanging curtains, he falls and injures himself. As the pain grows more and more severe, Ivan Ilyich goes to the doctor, who tells him the shocking news that his time in this world is rushing furiously to an end. In the face of this horrifying prognosis, Ivan Ilyich's world suddenly melts away. The walls that once made his life secure crumble as he comes to view them as nothing other than illusions. "All that you've lived and live by is a lie, a deception, concealing life and death from you," he says.[41] Ivan Ilyich has been evading mortality his whole life until now.

While the theme of the evasion of death is an obvious similarity between Tolstoy and Heidegger, perhaps the even greater philosophical affinity between the two thinkers lies in the profound questions they raise: What is life for? How does one confront one's own death? Can one live without illusions? Although their questions may be similar, Tolstoy and Heidegger nevertheless arrive at different answers to them. The answer for Tolstoy seems to be suggested by Ivan Ilyich's gripping terror, which implies that to live we must evade the fact that our lives will end. We must build shelters to protect ourselves from the terror of death. In contrast, Heidegger tries to imagine a wholly different relationship to death and suffering that affirms human fragility rather than attempting to evade it through shelters of any kind. He beckons us to accept and explore our mortal lot rather than hide from it in salvific myths or attempt to overcome it through technological perfection.

Having said that, Heidegger holds Tolstoy—and Dostoevsky—in immense regard as stewards of a rich Russian tradition that does not turn away from death and suffering but rather recognizes both as the most powerful "facts" of human life. Heidegger respects Russian culture for its bracing affirmation of mortality because confronting pain for him, as for Nietzsche, is a healthy sign of depth. From this perspective, Heidegger's creation of Russia as a "salvific" force goes beyond a few clichés about blood and soil. To be sure, he exploits those clichés. But he also surpasses them to envision an alliance between Germany and Russia that might upend the metaphysical uprooting of Dasein. Bringing together German philosophy with Slavic vitality, he seeks to leap into a new beginning that "restores" the human to its primordial essence as having no essence, that restores the human to nothingness or death:

"Only the human being 'has' the distinction of standing in front of death, because the human being is steadfastly in beyng: death the highest testimony to beyng."[42]

While Heidegger imagined this 1939–1941 German-Russian alliance, he obviously wrote of it with an eye to the future, in awareness that "every significant *thinker* comes too early."[43] Otherwise the decision to publish the *Black Notebooks* decades later makes little sense. If Heidegger looks toward the future, then we ought to do so as well by revealing the political implications of his thought. The political target of Heidegger's animus against *Machenschaft* is the universalistic and egalitarian tradition that he identifies as originating with Plato. Heidegger challenges egalitarianism by suggesting that there is no common ground on which to base an egalitarian community because there is no common experience of death. Death cannot be made equal, since one's own death cannot be exchanged with that of another.[44] To make death a common and exchangeable thing as if it were a commodity is to deny that each Dasein confronts death *on its own*.

***

In Heidegger's sweeping history of Western thought, egalitarianism and universalism originate with Plato, who inaugurates a tradition of thinking that aligns Being with the search for the common aspect or essence of beings, *to koinon*. This tendency to look for the essence of things is evident in that most basic of questions: What is this? This question searches for something permanent and universal—a constantly present "whatness"—that lies in advance of particular things and unites them under a universal idea (*idea*). Plato's idea views beings as having a constantly present and common something in them that "exists" prior to the encounter of experiencing and naming them as what they are.

According to Heidegger, this impulse to locate an essence or "whatness" became the dominant approach to thinking about the meaning of Being in the Western tradition, including for the being who asks about Being. We have long asked: What is the human? *Quae natura sum?*[45] This seemingly simple question, a profoundly theological one, ends up turning us away from our essence as beings-toward-death. The "What?" question searches for a common and permanent essence to Dasein that its Being as a differentially finite being otherwise undermines. Put somewhat differently, Plato's ἰδέα initiates a way of thinking that seeks to establish an antecedently fixed and universal identity to the human being that conceals the negative that is its essence. Plato launches an effort in Western history to establish a stable interpretation of the human being, an effort that Heidegger calls "humanism." At stake in any humanism is protecting the human from its essence as a temporal and transient being; humanism erects walls that seek to shelter Dasein from the vicissitudes and vulnerabilities of time:

> What is always at stake is this: to take "human beings," who within the sphere of a fundamental, metaphysically established system of beings are defined as *animal rationale*, and to lead them, within that sphere, to the liberation of their possibilities, to the certitude of their destiny, and to the securing of their "life." This takes place as the shaping of their "moral" behavior, as the salvation of their immortal souls, as the unfolding of their creative powers, as the development of their reason, as the nourishing of their personalities, as the awakening of their civic sense, as the cultivation of their bodies, or as an appropriate combination of some or all of these "humanisms."[46]

The culmination of this Platonic drive for securing the human being is *Machenschaft* and the culmination of *Machenschaft* is communism, the most all-embracing attempt to transpose Dasein into a universal homogeneous being completely estranged from its essence as *ho thnētos*. Cunningly veiled in the name of liberating the proletariat, communism ends up establishing an imperialistic regime of uniformity that benefits a political elite and forces humankind into one way of viewing the world oriented entirely toward security. Communism brings to fruition the Platonic dream of perfection by creating a final end state of complete regularity and correctness: the last human finds his paradise in communism, where all is safe, sound, and error-free—the paradise of Yevgeny Zamyatin's *We*.[47]

The last human has few burdens, worries, breakdowns; very little disturbs the human at all. Not even death. The last human still dies of course, but the possibility of impossibility barely seems to be burdensome enough to confront and explore, for he or she is utterly absorbed in a society that insists on death as something common to all. Communism brings to completion the "tranquilizing" view of death as universal and egalitarian, a view that can be succinctly captured in the cliché that "everyone dies."[48]

What seems to be impoverished about this egalitarian attitude to death, which reaches its apogee in the technocratic view of death as the mere cessation of bodies as machines? The answer is simple. It evades death as Dasein's ownmost possibility. But why does the evasion of death matter for Heidegger? Here the answer is not so simple. It might matter to him because evading death means evading the Being of Dasein. But this answer only pushes the problem back to asking why Heidegger would wish to insist on Dasein as a distinctively finite and fragile being. While Heidegger's affirmation of finitude could be interpreted as a vain attempt to make an ineluctable burden wondrous, to make human suffering the wellspring of creativity or the target of mockery *à la* Nietzsche, another interpretation might be that death serves as the "ground"—rhetorically speaking—for Heidegger's prophetic intervention in the polis. Working within the philosophical tradition to undermine it, Heidegger's ostensible privileging of taking on the burden of death can be interpreted as an appeal to normativity so as to transition to a new beginning beyond normativity. "If we wish to become what we are," Heidegger writes in 1929–1930, "we cannot abandon this finitude or deceive ourselves about it, but must safeguard it."[49] Heidegger the prophet peddles a dogma to intervene in the polis that Heidegger the philosopher would be disinclined to make, since the philosopher remains disinterested in all positions.

The philosopher views all positions with indifference even regarding which attitude toward death ought to be embraced (the authentic and inauthentic attitudes toward death are equiprimordial for the philosopher). Such is not the case for the prophet, who is hardly indifferent regarding which attitude toward death ought to be privileged. This may sound like Leo Strauss's dyad between poetry and philosophy. But it is not. Strauss pessimistically suggests that only the "few" can stare at the abyss whereas the "masses" need illusions and authorities to shelter them from death.[50] Whereas the few take on the freedom of accepting death, the many fearfully give up their freedom to the Grand Inquisitor in exchange for security and salvation. Heidegger does not share this pessimism. He offers no authority, no salvific myth, no banister to hang onto in Hannah Arendt's memorable phrase.[51] While one might be tempted to suggest that Heidegger elevates the nothing or the open to the status of an authority, it bears stressing that he brings into question why we need authority in the first place.[52] Heidegger's prophecy reveals the truth of death to undermine the need for authority at its very source: the fear of death that the metaphysical tradition has created. The fear of death compels us to seek authority. The fear of death is historical, not natural or incorrigible *pace* Thomas Hobbes. Heidegger holds out the possibility of a transformed attitude toward death in a way that very few thinkers in the Western tradition ever have.

Heidegger wishes to turn us to death so as to free us from the metaphysical evasion of death, to free us from World Judaism, Bolshevism, and Americanism.[53] Heidegger wishes to prepare a transition to a wholly new kind of Dasein that embraces time without revenge or pessimism. Appealing to the salvific tradition in Western history, he creates a history of decline with the promise of renewal through an alliance of German intelligence with Russian vitality.[54] *This renewal hinges on a transformed attitude toward death and time.*

If we accept our transient and solitary essence as dying beings without revenge or pessimism, then we will free ourselves from the need to secure our world and ourselves. We will free ourselves from the need for *any* kind of security or authority at all. What kind of life would this be? Heidegger offers at least two visions of what it would be. One would be to embrace the constant strife or "errance [*Irre*]" of mortality. To live is to err—that is, to turn away from and toward death as one's ownmost possibility. In this vision, Dasein heroically takes on the burden of fighting against death, against Being, in full acceptance that "the almighty sway of Being" will always win.[55] This is the Greek Dasein at the dawn of Western history that appreciates with wonder the limits and uncertainty of mortality.

The other vision appears in the Russian prisoner of war dialogue, which takes place at the apocalyptic twilight of Western history when the German Dasein in a devastated Russia offers not wonderment but "letting be" and "waiting" as transitional bridges to the other beginning that will save us from our darkening era of the burden of not having a burden (*Not der Notlosigkeit*). "Freedom rests in being able to let, not in ordering and dominating," the older man says to the younger man.[56] While letting beings be or *Gelassenheit* may sound peaceful and has been interpreted as such by Hannah Arendt, it involves as much struggle as the first vision, albeit the struggle is of an entirely different kind.[57] Whereas the first version involves a heroic struggle against death, *Gelassenheit* entails a constant struggle to remain open to affirming the burden of death. One lives in the constant strife of letting beings be.

One struggles to release oneself from all salvific efforts to overcome the necessity of death.

One struggles to embrace oneself as death, as nothingness, as time. Or, as Heidegger puts it, one waits. "The human is, as that being which can die, the being that waits [*Der Mensch ist als dasjenige Wesen, das sterben kann, das wartende Wesen*]."[58] Waiting in this respect is of the uncanniest sort: One waits on a possibility like no other in the world. One waits without an object, struggling to remain purely released into the open where one lets beings be the beings that they are rather than managing them as objects for one's use.[59]

To wait for one's own death is to remain open to the pure ephemerality of one's being as time and to become aware of all the various evasions from death that one must engage in to live. Waiting seems to be the philosophical-historical life of constant unsettlement and transformation, a life of perpetual openness to new ways of seeing and thinking about beings in the world released of any need to control and evaluate them.[60] It is a life freed from normativity, authority, morality, routine; it is a life that struggles to be freed from all the structures that spring from the oppressive, fearful reaction to death. It is a dynamically fluid life that belies description, since to describe it would be to bring it back into the metaphysical regime of explanation and determinacy. But perhaps we can imagine something of what Heidegger has in mind by saying what the life of waiting is not: It is not the life of the bureaucrat who wants everything perfectly structured and orderly; it is not the life of the bourgeois who sleeps through life utterly unaware of self other than as a consuming and producing being; and, perhaps most radical of all, it is not the life of history that seeks to recuperate a lost moment of vitality and preserve it in narrative. It is a life that resists the closure and finality of history (*Historie*), of the narrative impulse to persuade oneself that one's being is not temporal.

"I really am more than ephemera, more than death, more than nothingness." This could be the slogan of the metaphysical human being who clings desperately to notions of permanency and commonality that palliate death. Heidegger seeks to save us from this being by creating a writing of philosophical questioning that will challenge our revenge against time and, ultimately, transform us from the last human to Dasein, who embraces, without revenge, the truth that there is nothing to preserve from oneself. Heidegger offers a prophetic call to release oneself from the fear of death and leap into another way of thinking that explores with wonder our lot as the most homeless being in the world (*to deinotaton*). He beckons us to commit ourselves to a narrative creation that weaves between the past and the future but is fundamentally oriented to the opening that is the future, that is time.

***

In the end, Nazism failed Heidegger not only in its fascination with technology or in its processing of death as an exchangeable thing but also in its assertion of a common national "nature" that binds all Germans together into a *Volksgemeinschaft* and in Hitler's ambition to conquer death through the immortality gained by glorious fame on the battlefield. Hitler and his movement ended up embracing precisely what Heidegger opposes by affirming and pursuing salvific myths. Nazism became or always was metaphysical. In either case, Nazism proved not to be radical enough for Heidegger. His purported "resistance" against Nazism after 1933–1934 turns out to be a resistance in favor of a more radical political transformation, a truly revolutionary break from the metaphysical rejection of the human being as *ho thnētos*, a break that will transition to a new beginning beyond the salvific, nihilistic pursuits of technological self-abnegation and totalitarian self-assertion.

While Nazism failed Heidegger, he did not collapse into resignation, as his interest in Russia as a salvific force to liberate us from the metaphysical elixir of salvation affirms. What did he see in Russia? In 1938–1940, Heidegger put it this way: "Russia—that we not assail it technologically and culturally and ultimately annihilate it, but set it free for its essence and open up for it the expanse of its ability to suffer the essentialness of an essential saving of the earth."[61] This one sentence is an epitome of Heidegger's heady view of Russia as one of the last cultural traditions in the world that can resist the imperialism of Western metaphysics. Russia's capacity to resist lies in its "essence" as fundamentally different from the essence of metaphysics.[62] It lies in Russia's vitality. If earlier I understood "vitality" as embracing death, I would like to conclude by gesturing at a different implication of this embrace that may unfold another layer of Heidegger's attraction to Russia. To accept oneself as death or, put somewhat differently, to give oneself over to time without fear, means to embrace a dynamic and open relation to the world that metaphysics seeks to close off, if not eliminate, in reducing all things and relations to them to a commonality. Accepting oneself as unfinished means to open oneself up to phenomenology as a mode of disclosure that disrupts the metaphysical need for commonality, certainty, and correctness. Though Heidegger developed this point at great length in Being and Time and elsewhere, perhaps few others have expressed it more concisely and elegantly than Tolstoy:

> When a ripe apple falls, what makes it fall? Is it gravity, pulling it down to earth? A withered stalk? The drying action of the sun? Increased weight? A breath of wind? Or the boy under the tree who wants to eat it?
>
> Nothing is the cause of it. It is just the coming together of various conditions necessary for any living, organic, elemental event to take place. And the botanist who finds that the apple has fallen because of the onset of decay in its cellular structure, and all the rest of it, will be no more right or wrong than the boy under the tree who says the apple fell because he wanted to eat it and prayed for it to fall.[63]

What makes Isaac Newton's account correct over that of the child's? How can one description be correct over another? Who makes the call? And on what basis? These are precisely the kind of questions that the metaphysical tradition forgets, and they are precisely the kind of questions raised by Tolstoy and, of course, Heidegger, who ultimately sees in Russia a culture with the vitality to question, think, and challenge a tradition that, through the technological pursuit of perfection and commonality, seeks to overcome the differential and incomplete Being of Dasein by rendering everything a resource, everything secure and certain.

## NOTES

1. Martin Heidegger, *Country Path Conversations*, trans. Bret W. Davis (Bloomington: Indiana University Press, 2010), 144.

2. Ibid., 132.

3. Heidegger showed a sustained interest in Russian culture going back to 1908. See Martin Heidegger, *Überlegungen XII–XV (Schwarze Hefte)*, GA 96 (Frankfurt am Main: Vittorio Klostermann, 2014), 148.

4. As I will discuss below, it is hard not to read *Machenschaft* as anti-Semitic. Nefarious, powerful, hegemonic, *Machenschaft* seems to come awfully close to sharing the same kind of odious characteristics that anti-Semites would associate with *Weltjudentum*. And, indeed, Heidegger associates

Jews precisely with the equalizing, transparent, and mechanical worldviews of technology, logic, and mathematics. Jews are carriers of "empty rationality" who yield global influence: "World Judaism, goaded on by the emigrants let out from Germany, is ungraspable everywhere, and it—with all its growing power—doesn't need to take part in any military actions, whereas we must sacrifice the best blood of the best of our people." Heidegger, *Überlegungen XII-XV*, GA 96, 46, 56, and 262. For treatments of Heidegger's anti-Semitism, see Peter E. Gordon, "Heidegger in Black," *The New York Review of Books*, October 9, 2014, and Peter E. Gordon, "Heidegger and the Gas Chambers," *The New York Review of Books*, December 4, 2014; Donatella Di Cesare, *Heidegger, die Juden, die Shoah* (Frankfurt am Main: Vittorio Klostermann, 2016); Marion Heinz and Sidonie Kellerer, eds., *Martin Heideggers "Schwarze Hefte:" Eine philosophisch-politische Debatte* (Frankfurt am Main: Suhrkamp, 2016); Peter Trawny, *Heidegger and the Myth of a Jewish World Conspiracy*, trans. Andrew J. Mitchell (Chicago: University of Chicago Press, 2015). Moreover, some of the letters Heidegger wrote to his brother Fritz have recently been published in *Heidegger und der Antisemitismus: Positionen im Widerstreit*, ed. Walter Homolka (Freiburg im Breisgau: Verlag Herder, 2016), 15–142. This material reinforces yet again Heidegger's enthusiastic support of Nazism and his hostility toward Jews. In one letter, Heidegger recommends that his brother read *Mein Kampf* (21–22). As Marion Heinz argues in a recent interview, one can interpret his recommending the book as support of Hitler's ethnonationalistic, anti-Semitic worldview. See Thomas Assheuer, "Er verstand sich als Revolutionär," *Die Zeit*, March 18, 2015.

5. Martin Heidegger, *What Is a Thing?* trans. W. B. Barton Jr. and Vera Deutsch (South Bend, IN: Gateway, 1967), 39; Martin Heidegger, *Being and Time*, trans. John Macquarrie and Edward Robinson (New York: Harper and Row, 1962), 440.

6. Martin Heidegger, *Überlegungen II–VI (Schwarze Hefte 1931–1938)*, GA 94 (Frankfurt am Main: Vittorio Klostermann, 2014), 115.

7. In the *Black Notebooks* of 1938–1939, Heidegger views "revolution" as an inadequate way of describing the kind of change he envisions as necessary for overcoming metaphysics, since revolution is merely the "appearance of a new beginning of history." Martin Heidegger, *Überlegungen VII–XI (Schwarze Hefte 1938–1939)*, GA 95 (Frankfurt am Main: Vittorio Klostermann, 2014), 53.

8. Martin Heidegger, *Introduction to Metaphysics*, second edition, trans. Gregory Fried and Richard Polt (New Haven, CT: Yale University Press, 2014), 222; Heidegger, *Überlegungen XII–XV*, GA 96, 148. Heidegger expresses his frustration with the bureaucratic resistance to his plans in the first volume of the *Black Notebooks* (GA 94).

9. The passage can be translated as follows: "Destruction is the herald of a/ hidden inception, but desolation/is the grace note of the already decid-/ed end.

Does the age stand already/before the decision between destruction/and desolation? But we know/the other inception, we know it/*questioning*." Heidegger, *Überlegungen XII–XV*, GA 96, 2.

10. While there is very little evidence to document Heidegger's appreciation of Dostoevsky, he had a picture of him on his desk and he cites him in the Nietzsche lecture on European nihilism. See Martin Heidegger, *Nietzsche Vol. IV: Nihilism*, ed. David Farrell Krell, trans. Frank A. Capuzzi (New York: HarperCollins, 1982), 3–4; Heinrich Wiegand Petzet, *Encounters and Dialogues with Martin Heidegger, 1926–1976*, trans. Parvis Emad and Kenneth Maly (Chicago: University of Chicago Press, 1993), 120. For Nietzsche and Mann, see Friedrich Nietzsche, *The Anti-Christ, Ecce Homo, Twilight of the Idols*, ed. Aaron Ridley and Judith Norman, trans. Judith Norman (New York/ Cambridge: Cambridge University Press, 2005), 214; Thomas Mann, *Reflections of a Nonpolitical Man*, trans. Walter D. Morris (New York: Frederick Ungar Publishing Co., 1983), 325.

11. Martin Heidegger, *Mindfulness*, trans. Parvis Emad and Thomas Kalary (London: Continuum, 2006), 12.

12. Martin Heidegger, *Anmerkungen I–V (Schwarze Hefte 1942–1948),* GA 97 (Frankfurt am Main: Vittorio Klostermann, 2015), 41–42.

13. Heidegger, *Überlegungen II–VI*, GA 94, 5. See also Hans Blumenberg, *The Legitimacy of the Modern Age*, trans. Robert M. Wallace (Cambridge, MA: MIT Press, 1985).

14. Martin Heidegger, *Contributions to Philosophy (of the Event)*, trans. Richard Rojcewicz and Daniela Vallega-Neu (Bloomington: Indiana University Press, 2012), 268.

15. Hannah Arendt, *The Life of the Mind* (New York: Harcourt Brace and Company, 1977), 34 ("Willing").

16. See Martin Heidegger, "On the Essence of Truth," in *Basic Writings*, ed. David Farrell Krell (New York: HarperCollins, 2008), 111–38.

17. See Alexandre Kojève, "Tyranny and Wisdom," in *On Tyranny*, ed. Victor Gourevitch and Michael S. Roth (Chicago: University of Chicago Press, 2000), 135–76.

18. The *locus classicus* of this Platonic doctrine is *Theaetetus* 176b.

19. Heidegger lays this specific chronology out in *Überlegungen VII–XI*, GA 95, 3–4.

20. Martin Heidegger, "European Nihilism," in *Nietzsche Vols. 3 and 4*, trans. David Farrell Krell (New York: HarperCollins, 1987), 88–89.

21. It is worth noting that Heidegger does not say "secularization" *pace* Karl Löwith and Jacob Taubes. Rather, he suggests that the modern era, in various forms, "takes over [*übernehmen*]" the Christian concept of salvation. See Karl Löwith, *Meaning in History* (Chicago: University of Chicago Press, 1949); Jacob Taubes, *Occidental Eschatology*, trans. David Ratmoko (Stanford, CA: Stanford

University Press, 2009). For Heidegger's dismissal of the secularization thesis, see Heidegger, "European Nihilism," in *Nietzsche Vols. 3 and 4*, 100.

22. Heidegger, Ibid., 89.

23. Heidegger, *Überlegungen XII–XV*, GA 96, 79; *Anmerkungen I–V*, GA 97, 32.

24. Martin Heidegger, *The Fundamental Concepts of Metaphysics: World, Finitude, Solitude*, trans. William McNeill and Nicholas Walker (Bloomington: Indiana University Press, 1995), 5.

25. Heidegger, *Überlegungen XII–XV*, GA 96, 238.

26. Curzio Malaparte, *Kaputt*, trans. Cesare Foligno (New York: New York Review Books Classics, 2005), 214.

27. Heidegger, *Überlegungen XII–XV*, GA 96, 148.

28. Ibid., 47.

29. Not even Stalin is of the few. Who or what comprises the power of the few? This passage is written in the volume in which Heidegger speaks of "World Judaism." While he never makes the link directly, his identification of an "unnamed few" that has complete control over everything shares an obvious affinity with one of the central anti-Semitic tropes of his era: that Jews secretly control the world. Heidegger, *Überlegungen XII–XV*, GA 96, 149.

30. Martin Heidegger, *Beiträge zur Philosophie*, GA 65 (Frankfurt am Main: Vittorio Klostermann, 2003), p. 54.

31. Heidegger, *Überlegungen XII–XV*, GA 96, 46.

32. Ibid., 243.

33. The latter view—that Heidegger went "mad" or tragically lost his philosophical bearings during the 1930s—was expressed as early as 1949 by Hannah Arendt, one of Heidegger's most important defenders after the war, in a letter to Karl Jaspers where she mocked his "writing Sein with a y" and suggested that he had tragically fallen in the 1930s from his "old standard." In connection with the *Black Notebooks*, this view can be found in David Farrell Krell, *Ecstasy, Catastrophe: Heidegger from* Being and Time *to the* Black Notebooks (Albany: State University of New York Press, 2015); *Hannah Arendt/Karl Jaspers Correspondence, 1926–1969* (New York: Harcourt Brace Jovanovich, 1992), 142.

34. Martin Heidegger, *Der Anfang der abendländischen Philosophie. Auslegung des Anaximander und Parmenides*, GA 35 (Frankfurt am Main: Vittorio Klostermann, 2011), 1.

35. Heidegger, *Überlegungen XII–XV*, GA 96, 56.

36. Heidegger, *Anmerkungen I–V*, GA 97, 20. Moreover, "self-annihilation" *might* be a reference to the technological method the Nazis used to carry out their attack against the Jewish body. But, on this point, we cannot be sure because the quote is too ambiguous and we simply do not know what Heidegger specifically knew about the technological method of killing in Eastern Europe in the summer of 1942 when he wrote these words.

37. In *Contributions to Philosophy* (1936–1938), Heidegger links together in a single sentence Judaism, Christianity, and *Machenschaft* (here in the particular form of Bolshevism) as follows: "Bolshevism is originally Western, a European possibility; the rise of the masses, industry, technology, the dying out of Christianity; insofar, however, as the supremacy of reason, qua equalization of everyone, is merely a consequence of Christianity, which is itself basically of Jewish origin [cf. Nietzsche's idea of the slave revolt in morals], Bolshevism is in fact Jewish; but then Christianity is also basically Bolshevist!" See *Contributions*, 44.

38. Heidegger, *Country Path Conversations*, 132.

39. Heidegger, *Überlegungen XII–XV*, GA 96, 257.

40. Heidegger always denigrates the Romans, and anyone who has read Petronius's "Dinner with Trimalchio" will understand why he does.

41. Leo Tolstoy, *The Death of Ivan Ilyich*, trans. Richard Pevear and Larissa Volokhonsky (New York: Vintage, 2009), 51.

42. Heidegger, *Contributions*, 181.

43. Heidegger, *Anmerkungen I–V*, GA 97, 126.

44. Heidegger bluntly insists on the political implications of death as one's ownmost possibility in *Being and Truth,* trans. Gregory Fried and Richard Polt (Bloomington: Indiana University Press, 2010), 129.

45. Augustine, *Confessions*, vol. II, trans. William Watts (Cambridge, MA: Harvard University Press, 1912), 120.

46. Martin Heidegger, "Plato's Doctrine of Truth," in *Pathmarks*, ed. William McNeill (New York/Cambridge: Cambridge University Press, 1998), 181.

47. Yevgeny Zamyatin, *We*, trans. Clarence Brown (New York: Penguin, 1993).

48. Heidegger, *Being and Time*, 297.

49. Heidegger, *Fundamental Concepts of Metaphysics*, 6.

50. Leo Strauss, "Notes on Lucretius," in *Liberalism Ancient and Modern* (Chicago: University of Chicago Press, 1995), 85. See also Leo Strauss, *Philosophy and Law: Contributions to the Understanding of Maimonides and His Predecessors*, trans. Eve Adler (New York: State University of New York Press, 1995), 35–37 and 111–33.

51. Hannah Arendt, "On Hannah Arendt," in *Hannah Arendt: The Recovery of the Public World*, ed. Melvyn A. Hill (New York: St. Martin's Press, 1979), 336–37.

52. Heidegger has been interpreted as an anarchist by Reiner Schürmann and Peter Trawny. If the open (*das Offene*) is a negative ground or norm (i.e., the authority of the absence of final authority), then he can be interpreted as an anarchist, although not one committed to the communalist agenda that has long defined anarchism in the modern era and that Heidegger would view as a continuation of Christian ethics. But is Heidegger an anarchist? Does he interpret authority metaphysically in terms of absence? If no authority can be

final, then what authority can any have, including the negative norm that has been embraced by a considerable number of philosophers after 1945 from Hannah Arendt to Jacques Rancière? Heidegger seems to move more radically beyond anarchy or normativity in aligning truth with freedom. See Heidegger, "Essence of Truth"; Reiner Schürmann, *Heidegger. On Being and Acting: From Principles to Anarchy*, trans. Christine-Marie Gros (Bloomington: Indiana University Press, 1990); Peter Trawny, *Freedom to Fail: Heidegger's Anarchy*, trans. Ian Alexander Moore and Christopher Turner (Cambridge/Malden, MA: Polity, 2015).

53. This freedom will lead to the "elimination" of *Machenschaft*. See Martin Heidegger, *Die Geschichte des Seyns*, GA 69 (Frankfurt am Main: Vittorio Klostermann, 2012), 21.

54. Or, in Heidegger's words, Russia is the future of the history of the earth that has not yet been freed, whereas Germany's task is to reflect on the history of world. Russia provides the fertile soil that the German thinker as *Pflüger* sows for others to harvest. Like a god, the thinker plants and then vanishes. See Heidegger, *Geschichte des Seyns*, GA 69, 108; Heidegger, *Anmerkungen I–V*, GA 97, 338–39.

55. Heidegger, *Introduction to Metaphysics*, 198.

56. Heidegger, *Country Path Conversations*, 147, 149.

57. Arendt, *Life of the Mind*, 172–94 ("Willing"). See Gregory Fried, *Heidegger's* Polemos (New Haven, CT: Yale University Press, 2000), 84–86.

58. Heidegger, *Country Path Conversations*, 146.

59. Heidegger, "Essence of Truth," 125–27. See also the second version of the lecture in Martin Heidegger, *Vorträge, Teil 1: 1915–1932*, GA 80.1 (Frankfurt am Main: Vittorio Klostermann, 2016), especially 365.

60. See Heidegger, *Vorträge*, GA 80.1, 365.

61. Heidegger, *The History of Beyng*, trans. William McNeill and Jeffrey Powell (Bloomington: Indiana University Press, 2015), 100.

62. Heidegger, *Überlegungen XII–XV*, GA 96, 134.

63. Leo Tolstoy, *War and Peace*, trans. Anthony Briggs (New York: Penguin, 2005), 670–71.

# Chapter 2

# Dostoevsky and Heidegger

## *Eschatological Poet and Eschatological Thinker*

### Horst-Jürgen Gerigk

Es-cha-tol-o-gy

Doctrine concerning the end of the world and the advent of a new world, of the last things, of death and resurrection. [From the Greek *eschaton*, "the utmost, the last," and *logos*, "speech, account."]

—Gerhard Wahrig, *German Dictionary* (1997)[1]

## CHRIST AND HÖLDERLIN AS ESCHATOLOGICAL GUIDES

Both Dostoevsky and Heidegger should be considered in terms of the eschatological foundation of their thinking. In both cases this thinking orients itself toward a concrete figure: For Dostoevsky this figure is Christ, and for Heidegger it is Hölderlin.

Thus, in both cases, the eschatological thinking is oriented toward a human figure, a normative personage who, through his legacy, is meant to determine the future. It is striking that both figures, Christ and Hölderlin, demonstrate a new awareness and outlook toward beings as a whole. In both cases, this new outlook introduces a veritable Archimedean point out of which existing conditions are transformed. However, both Christ and Hölderlin always speak of this transformation in the

31

sense of a transformation of consciousness. This does not bespeak a transformation through violent means.

Dostoevsky wants the state to become a church: an ideal society in the sense of the (Russian) concept of *Sobornost'* (originally the Old Church Slavic translation of the Greek *ekklesia*, "church"). *Sobornost'* signifies the community in Christ.[2] Heidegger, for his part, aims at the "twisting-free" (*Verwindung*) from metaphysics through a stepping out of the forgetfulness of being, and sees such a stepping out as exemplarily realized in Hölderlin's poetry: "What endures, however, the poet founds" (*Remembrance*).[3]

Thus, both Dostoevsky and Heidegger, in conceiving their normative human figures, refer back to a textual corpus: Dostoevsky to the New Testament, and Heidegger to the works of Hölderlin. Through this retrospective turn, both Dostoevsky and Heidegger orient themselves toward their own present, and they do so in the name of the future.

I intend to show how both the poet Dostoevsky and the thinker Heidegger formulated their *work* from out of a fundamental relation to their own particular present. Dostoevsky's five great novels (for which he is best known)—*Crime and Punishment, The Idiot, Demons, The Adolescent,* and *The Brothers Karamazov*—are contemporary novels that have as their themes the societal development of Russia within a single decade (from 1865 until 1875), with *The Brothers Karamazov* (which takes place in 1866) as the recapitulation and summation of the others.

For his part, Heidegger composed the following major works—*Being and Time, Contributions to Philosophy, Mindfulness, Letter on "Humanism,"* and *Insight into That Which Is* (a.k.a. the *Bremen Lectures*: "The Thing," "Positionality," "The Danger," "The Turn")—entirely from out of the spiritual situation of his time. Out of this situation, which had as its center what was then contemporary Germany (1927–1949), Heidegger unfolds his vision of technology and the forgetfulness of being that technology's mounting domination brings about. For Heidegger, technology is *En-framing* (*das Ge-Stell*): "En-framing is the essence of technology. Its positioning is universal. It addresses itself to the unity of the entirety of everything that presences" ("Positionality").[4] And the fact that he appoints Hölderlin as the figurehead of the resistance to the domination of technology can clearly be seen as political: a quotable paradigm in the resistance against "destitute" times. Similarly, Dostoevsky places Christ against the false gods of contemporary Russia.

In both cases, then, the exalted paradigmatic figures have a "national" function: For Dostoevsky, Christ goes to battle against the domination of instrumental reason (whose symbol is the "Crystal Palace"), and Hölderlin, for Heidegger, rages against the authority of "calculative reason." The passages below can be considered Dostoevsky's and Heidegger's respective guiding principles. For Dostoevsky:

> And if somebody were to prove to me that Christ were outside of the truth, and if it were *truly* so that the truth lies outside of Christ, I would rather remain with Christ than with the truth. (Letter to Natalia D. Fonvizina, from February 20, 1854)[5]

And for Heidegger:

> Full of merit, yet poetically
>    do human beings dwell upon this earth. (Hölderlin, "Blooms in lovely blue, the steeple with its metallic vault")[6]

In both cases the national concern immediately becomes universalized. The enemies of Russia are, for Dostoevsky, the enemies of Christ (i.e., Jewry, Catholicism, Islam); and Heidegger's preference for Hölderlin entailed an aversion to Bolshevism and Americanism and even, eventually, to National Socialism—all in the name of the true humanism that, because of "technology," has been forgotten: "It is humanism that thinks the humanity of the human from out of nearness to being" (*Letter on "Humanism"*).[7]

For both Dostoevsky and Heidegger, the transnational aspiration arises out of a national foundation. Both present themselves as prophets who, to be sure, have their own people foremost in mind, but who at the same time formulate a humanistic pretense to their knowledge. Such an intensification oriented toward the "personal"—such an orientation of history toward the prophet who brings relief—doubtlessly belongs to the peculiarity of eschatology. The "art" of the prophet is to remain vague about what *will be*, but to dramatize the defects of what *is*. This vagueness, however, has a peculiar authenticity that arises from the deference given to the not-yet-existing. Where the art truly exists, it is not to be misunderstood as pure rhetoric.

Both Dostoevsky and Heidegger cultivate, each in his own way, a hypnotizing of their readers by means of the "not-yet." The glimpse into the future precedes the occupation with the past, so that the decisive moment of existence is distinguished by an inherent dynamism. Out of the hermeneutic situation of their own present, both the poet and the thinker construe, with an elitist projection of themselves, the world-historical aspirations of their respective target audiences.

## THE DECISIVE MOMENT
## (*DER AUGENBLICK*) OF EXISTENCE

By way of the above considerations, the goal of my exposition has now been clearly identified: to present the fundamentally eschatological attitudes of both Dostoevsky and Heidegger. In both cases this will occur by means of a perspective that leaves behind historical references to their entirely different political contexts. My exclusive concern is to emphasize the striking general similarities that obtain between the "poet" and the "thinker."

Phrased more concretely, my concern is with the eschatological structuring of the "decisive moment" for Dostoevsky and Heidegger. With the concept "decisive moment," I mean the existential moment that protrudes out of everyday dealings and brings the human being into an outstanding relationship to itself: In such a decisive moment, the human being experiences the world and itself under the premise of the uniqueness and unrepeatability of "its" existence. Through this there occurs a stepping out of the "forgetfulness of being."

This decisive moment of existence, which stands out from every-dayness, is fashioned repeatedly by Dostoevsky. In the argument that follows I will turn to Raskolnikov's double murder from the novel *Crime and Punishment*. Never again does Dostoevsky construct the limit situation (*Grenzsituation*) of becoming guilty from the direct, inner perspective of the murderer as he does in *Crime and Punishment*. Only in *Crime and Punishment* do we have a murder (which becomes a double murder) depicted in its preparation and carrying out, all within the horizon of the experience of a murderer. Dostoevsky lets the readers become witnesses to the decisive moment of existence in its complete unfolding. In what follows, I view this unfolding in terms of its eschatological basis.

After this, I will discuss Heidegger's comments concerning the "decisive moment [*Augenblick*]" (*Being and Time*, section 68). The "decisive moment" is defined by Heidegger as the "authentic present," which brings itself about from out of the "authentic future." To the decisive moment belongs "anticipatory resoluteness," with which "the self, thrown into its individuation," returns to itself. Concerning the decisive moment, Heidegger writes: "This term must be understood in the active sense as ecstasy [*Ekstase*]. It means the resolute rapture of Dasein in that which is encountered in the situation as possibilities and circumstances to be taken care of, but a rapture precisely *held* in resoluteness."[8]

The temporality of the "decisive moment" is of interest for the present context. In the "decisive moment," *Da-sein* has a special, "authentic" relation to the future (anticipation) and to the past (recollection). Heidegger later formulates this situation as *Ereignis*: With "Ereignis," Da-sein comes to be thought in relation to being (*Sein*), whereas with the "decisive moment," being is thought in relation to Da-sein. Da-sein is, for Heidegger, a synonym for the human being, whose essence, however, is conceived in novel terms. The concept *Dasein* should capture the human being in its neutrality, independently of sexual or gender specificity and of all ideological determination. "Care," as the "being of Dasein," constitutes the human being in its constant determinateness through "projection" and "thrownness." In the special situation of the "decisive moment," a stepping out of the forgetfulness of being takes place.

The eschatological foundation of the "decisive moment" becomes clear through the following formulation from Heidegger's *Contributions to Philosophy*: "The thoughtful question of the truth of beyng [*Seyns*] is grounded in the decisive moment that bears the transition."[9] Transition means here the overcoming of the "abandonment of being." To clarify, Heidegger adds: "Thus, a long future remains for the decisive moment, supposing that once more the abandonment of beings by being is to occur."[10] Only the decisive moment "sets" the "time of Ereignis." The "aim" of thinking is, for Heidegger, the "seeking of beyng [*Seyns*]," and he names this seeking the "most profound discovery," because "to be *seeker, preserver, guardian*—this means care as the essential feature of Dasein."[11] To set an aim would be premature. Here we reach Heidegger's eschatological ground. The "eschaton," which Heidegger translates as "the last [*die Letze* (sic!)],"[12] is prepared through the "turn [*die Kehre*]." Dasein has to turn toward Ereignis and not, in a state of forgetfulness of being, lose itself to the objects of its concern. "The seeking is itself the goal. And that means: Goals are still too much in the foreground and are still placing themselves before beyng [*Seyn*]—and flooding over what is necessary" (*Contributions to Philosophy*).[13] At stake is to stand "outside of the volubility of 'beings' and their interpretations." Striving is the "preparation toward essential thinking."

Having now brought about some initial contact with Heidegger's considerations, I wish to turn to the "situation" of Raskolnikov, which needs to be analyzed in its own temporality.

## DOSTOEVSKY'S *CRIME AND PUNISHMENT* AS ESCHATOLOGICAL PARADIGM

"*Vive la guerre éternelle*—that is, until the New Jerusalem!"
　　Raskolnikov in conversation with the examining magistrate (*Crime and Punishment*, part III, chapter 5)

"Life had taken the place of dialectic."[14] So reads the decisive sentence from the epilogue of the novel *Crime and Punishment*. In the epilogue, Raskolnikov is on his way toward a "lively life [*lebendigen Leben*]"; however, this way is indeed a long one, and the narrator calls it a "new story."

"Life had taken the place of dialectic": This means that Raskolnikov's basic position toward the world, and toward himself, has changed. To be sure, initially such a change only leads to his sullen silence. The division of his consciousness can only be gradually overcome: He will then be some other and no longer "Raskolnikov" (i.e., the Russian *raskol*, "division"). His name will then no longer suit him.

From the Siberian prison where he must spend eight years, Raskolnikov looks back on his crime, which at this point had occurred one and one-half years ago. This means that everything that Raskolnikov has experienced in the six parts of the novel that precede the epilogue is to be read as a recollection. Raskolnikov recapitulates his crime only after he has leapt into punishment. Through *punishment* Raskolnikov wins back the positive relation to the "lively life" that he had destroyed through his *crime*. The leap into punishment is a leap into the future. The look back, which Raskolnikov carries out from his Siberian prison, gathers the experienced (*das Erlebte*) into an experience (*Erlebnis*). Dostoevsky is surprisingly terse here when it comes to what obtains to

Raskolnikov's reversion to his true conscience, which was abandoned in the maelstrom of the crime. While passages such as the following pervade the novel, the process of remembering designated therein is only hinted at by Dostoevsky: "Later, when he remembered this moment, it presented itself as follows."[15] Indeed, we must assume that Raskolnikov, from within the Siberian prison, recollects still other scenes that haunt him in connection to his crime, without actually recounting them to us. Nevertheless, through these sparse references, the story of Raskolnikov's crime of murder is characterized as a sequence of images passing through his awareness: as an act of self-contemplation within the Siberian prison.

Everything that happens prior, once upon a time in July (comprising the six parts that make up the novel *Crime and Punishment*, with the crime at the end of the first part as the abrupt high point)—all of that happens, so to speak, under the spell of a not-yet, that is, under the spell of the not-yet of Raskolnikov's transformation in the Siberian prison. In a word: Raskolnikov's path through the crime has the character of a conversion experience and is an analogy for the resurrection of Christ, presented in the text itself as the resurrection of Lazarus. After his crime, Raskolnikov suffers a psychosomatic breakdown that brings him, as it were, close to death. With his deed he has murdered his own soul, and by sinking into unconsciousness he undergoes a Lazarus-type experience.

With Raskolnikov's abrupt ascent to the apex of the murder, which *in medias res* becomes a double murder, Dostoevsky displays the limit situation of guilt under the spell of which a perpetrator such as Raskolnikov is shaken such that he, to make the connection to our concern clear, steps out of the "forgetfulness of being." The eschatological foundation of Raskolnikov's crime deserves our utmost attention: For represented as though under a microscope, one finds within Raskolnikov's "personal" situation the state of the Russian commonwealth in the year 1865.

In Raskolnikov a certain unease breaks forth, which could be designated as the unease of Russian culture in general. Raskolnikov sees a lack of freedom all around him owing to financial powerlessness. Everywhere, money is in the wrong hands. And so the pawnbroker Alyona Ivanovna—old, ugly "Helen," who lives with her stepsister—becomes the epitome of the spiritual situation of the time.

It has now been demonstrated how in Raskolnikov's decision to act, his future and past merge together in the present and create the actuality of evil. In the actuality of evil, the world for Raskolnikov is suddenly torn out of the "forgetfulness of being." One may say that in the shock that Raskolnikov suffers through the enacting of his crime, his "I" opens itself to conscience as the "call of care" (Heidegger). It should be remarked that he plans his murder of the pawnbroker on moral, ethical grounds: He wants to release Sonja and Dunja from their financial impotence. Stated in terms of mythology and literary history, he seeks in the pawnbroker the Count of Monte Cristo's treasure chest.

However, the misdeed, which Raskolnikov resists deep down, is placed before the attainment of his goal. Thus, already the *idea* of the deed, under whose fixating spell Raskolnikov confronts us at the onset of the book, is characterized by moral outrage that, however, only recognizes archaic violence as an effective means of implementation and thereby contradicts itself. Raskolnikov lives the contradiction pertaining to his decision, and it is in accordance with this contradiction that Dostoevsky the author gives Raskolnikov his name: the division of the self.

With the fulfillment of the act, this divided self becomes "objective." Above all, the deed, as it is brought to completion, carries with itself something that could not be foreseen and is profoundly undesirable: the unplanned murder of Lizaveta. While Raskolnikov "experiences" in a direct, corporeal way the paradox of a crime motivated by moral outrage—namely, as a flulike infection that, following the deed, leads to disorders of consciousness followed by several days of unconsciousness—he arrives at the "decisive moment" of "authentic existence." Understandably, Raskolnikov's outrage consists in a reaction to the situation in which he finds himself, and leads him to justify robbery and murder by means of calculative reasoning: "Beat her to death and take her gold. . . . For one life, a thousand lives rescued from rot and decay. One death, and for this a hundred lives—it's simple arithmetic."[16]

This is Raskolnikov's justification for his crime in rational and altruistic terms; it is a justification that one month prior, at the outset of the action of the novel, he randomly overhears while sitting in an unassuming bar in which a student offers such a justification to the person (an officer) sitting next to him. Moreover, half a year prior Raskolnikov drafted an essay entitled "Concerning Crime" in which he pleaded, in rational/egotistical terms, for special privileges for exceptional human beings.

In summary, an infectious problem runs rampant in Raskolnikov; it unfolds into the concrete plan to rob and murder the pawnbroker Alyona Ivanovna and, at the outset of the novel, dominates his consciousness. This means that Raskolnikov has a divided awareness of himself; the affirmation and negation of the pending misdeed interlock with one another. The result is an oscillation between affirmation and negation of his own resoluteness to commit the desired robbery and murder of the pawnbroker. The plea of conscience simmers beneath the will to commit the crime. And as the resoluteness prevails, every step that Raskolnikov takes becomes an infringement upon the moral insight that has swelled to the extreme. In a word, a premeditated murder is committed here in concert with the highest moral *sensorium*, with a second, unplanned murder spontaneously added to it in order to eliminate the only witness.

The horrendousness that takes place in this way before the eyes of the reader and from the point of view of the killer, along with the actuality of the evil irrevocably produced, pierces through all everydayness. Raskolnikov, wide awake, comes to stand within Ereignis. Entirely consumed by action—namely, in the maelstrom of care—the ice-cold exhilaration of evil throws him back to his authentic self. Within the lightning flash of the double murder, which due to the second victim intensifies into something unimaginable, Raskolnikov finds himself in the midst of the decisive moment.

The relation of the murderer to himself during the murdering "consists" in both moral insight and an accompanying and overflowing will toward evil for its own sake. One could also say that Raskolnikov, with open eyes, forcibly mistreats his own soul.

Thus, just as his disposition toward the crime prompts Raskolnikov to seek various rationalized justifications, his execution of it at the crime scene prompts the pretexts with which it was draped to withdraw: The shock of the entire spiritual and bodily "apparatus" (in Schiller's sense) now works "conscientiously," so that all the superficial rationalizations of what has happened peel away. What remains behind is the naked will toward evil.

The event of salvation that is presented in *Crime and Punishment* has its lowest point (nadir) in the execution of the crime and its highest point (zenith) in the acceptance of "punishment" as a form of atonement. This high point, while being deferred into the future, nevertheless effects all that occurs in the present. The essential feature of the event of salvation—that the *future* as promise merges with the *past* of completed experience into the dynamic *present*—remains fully in force even where a subject destroys his salvation through the freedom of his selfishness. Phrased otherwise, the madness of arrogance can actually cause the subject to fall out of the force field belonging to the event of salvation. However, the event of salvation is not thereby thoroughly revoked; rather, it is confirmed. The character, who is in the wrong, has his attention drawn to this automatic process by the caution light of his psychosomatic shock.

I would thus like to make the following claim, already with an eye toward the ensuing elucidation of Heidegger's "eschatology": In the Ereignis of the execution of his crime, Raskolnikov experiences the "turn [*Kehre*]." In other words, as he kills he acts entirely as "subject," but through his vital contact with the actuality of an evil that he himself manufactured, he comes to be gripped by a supra-individual, trans-subjective power, in the thrall of which he experiences his forgotten "participation" in the world of morality. He opens himself up to this world of morality in order to find himself as a "moral person." The last sentences of the book read: "But here begins a new story, the story of the gradual renewal of human beings, of the slow crossing from one world into another, of the discovery of a new, heretofore wholly unknown reality. It could be the theme of a new story—our present story, however, has come to an end."[17]

This movement of transition by which Raskolnikov is presented to us serves as the model of all five of Dostoevsky's great novels, and is also thereby the model of the eschatology presented therein. Indeed, Dostoevsky essentially wrote only a single book that remained unwritten as such but was disaggregated into five separate books, the first of which—*Crime and Punishment*—demonstrates the basic schema of each of the others. Through the Ereignis of his crime, Raskolnikov moves from his isolation into participation in "another" world. What this means "artistically" shall now be clarified in detail.

It is immediately clear that *Crime and Punishment* also serves as the eschatological model for Dostoevsky's final novel, *The Brothers Karamazov*. Here, it is Dmitri Karamazov upon whom the weight of suffering rests. He is found guilty of patricide owing to the fact that he publically wished it and sowed the traces of his sentiment all too clearly, thus allowing another person, Smerdyakov, to slip into his role; and thus, from the point of view of the court, all evidence points toward

Dmitri's guilt. Dmitri is also led from the isolation of arrogance into participation in "another" world, just as was the case with Raskolnikov. In Dmitri, the "turn" occurs as he recognizes his decisive role in the murder of his father.

Of the three intervening novels, it is *The Adolescent* that most clearly exhibits the same "event of salvation" that one finds in *Crime and Punishment*; yet, in this case, there is no crime, for the self-discovery of the nineteen-year-old title character occurs instead in his passage through the hell of puberty. In the interval between *Crime Punishment* and *The Adolescent*, *The Idiot* and *Demons* appear to depart the most from the basic pattern. The event of salvation is present in them only *ex negativo*: as the revelation of the reasons for demise within a hopeless situation. In *the Idiot*, Prince Myshkin—the "complete and beauteous man"—loses his mind in the face of (Russian) reality; and in *Demons*, Stavrogin's creation, the result of a creative nihilism, obliterates itself entirely in the sense of its conjurer, who in the end hangs himself with a silk cord. Through his premise concerning human beings, which takes account only of their *intelligible* but not *empirical* realities, Dostoevsky demonstrates that the immoral is not livable for moral human beings. When, through contamination, the immoral comes to dominate within the human being, it can only be destructive.

It should be observed that the extreme model presented in *Crime and Punishment*, of a main character awakened through a spiritual shock to the buried remnants of the good and its cultivation, also anchors Dostoevsky's four subsequent novels. In each case a certain distance (*The Idiot*, *Demons*) or nearness (*The Adolescent*, *The Brothers Karamazov*) to the ideal of a moral community demonstrates the search for a sustainable identity. Dostoevsky expresses this situation through the *absence* of a corporeal father for Raskolnikov and Myshkin and the gradual *appearing* of a spiritual father for Stavrogin and Arkady Dolgoruky. In *Demons*, Bishop Tikhon, to whom Stavrogin addresses his "confession," serves the function of a spiritual father. Arkady, in *The Adolescent*, makes his stepfather into a spiritual father—a pilgrim—who after a long journey dies in Petersburg, but not without having left his "son" with Christian inspiration. Only in *The Brothers Karamazov* do the *spiritual* father, in the form of the elder Zosima, and the *corporeal* father, in the form of Fyodor Karamazov, come to prominence, by confronting each other in a prolonged conversation early in the novel (book II, chapter 2).

All of the above-named considerations regarding Dostoevsky's five great novels operate on that level of meaning that within the "fourfold exegesis" constitutes the "allegorical" sense: history, as the story of a people, understood as a story of salvation or more precisely as prefiguration for the event of salvation.

If *Crime and Punishment* is thus understood as the model of the event of salvation in Dostoevsky's sense, we see that the subsequent four novels—*The Idiot, Demons, The Adolescent*, and *The Brothers Karamazov*—are the chronological continuation of that model, for they span the development of Russian society from 1865 until almost the middle of the 1870s. *The Brothers Karamazov* is set in the year 1866 and is meant to recapitulate the epoch of the three preceding novels. The model is also varied, according to the proximity of each particular narrated present to the event of salvation. Thus, the conclusion of *The Adolescent* is optimistic while, by the end of *Crime and Punishment*, Raskolnikov has still not found a way out of his silence. However, Arkady, the adolescent, certainly did not have to go through the hell of a criminal offense like Raskolnikov did, in order to desire the "moral condition" in Schiller's sense.

Dostoevsky was confronted with the task of taking the pulse of the lived present for symptoms of salvation—that is, of examining the history of Russia between 1865 and 1875. At stake for him was the detection and depiction of certain trends within the "news of the day," trends that could be put to positive use regarding his image of the human being. His utopian thought understands itself to be deeply indebted to reality. Indeed, for him the task of the author is to reveal, through the course of events, the rationality that lies hidden from the uninitiated and to highlight the visible irrationality that, despite being readily discernible, often remains unrecognized. For Dostoevsky, insight into what *is* means to think eschatologically.

My argument concerning Dostoevsky now comes both to its end and also its goal, for Dostoevsky's eschatological foundation, according to all the rules of his art, is transposed into characters and actions, that is, into *situations*. As I have already highlighted, the situation of Raskolnikov with its reality-producing enactment of the murder, which *in medias res* becomes an unplanned double murder, is the most detailed account of a perpetrator's state of conscience in all of Dostoevsky's works.

Now it is time to consider Dostoevsky's narrative technique in its integration of the past and future within the situation evoked as the present by Raskolnikov. Here we are confronted with a model depiction of conscience on both the level of the story's *content* and its *formal* characteristics. Regarding the content, it is a model *exemplum* because human conscience is brought to its fullest realization by way of the mental disturbance of a highly sensitive and moral young man who plans a brutal robbery and murder; regarding the formal characteristics, it is a model *exemplum* because the imaginary narrator deployed by Dostoevsky autonomously dramatizes the plot. This means that something is being simultaneously revealed and hidden from the reader. The narrator neither simply maps the activity of his hero's conscience, nor does he make use of the knowledge he actually has. Although he narrates with knowledge of the resolution of the story, he immerses himself so completely into Raskolnikov's conscience that the character's embeddedness in the present provides the fundamental orientation of the story. In a word, Raskolnikov's thoughts, dreams, and actions are depicted *in their execution*. Through the artistic realization of this "situation," the intellectual effort of Dostoevsky is realized in *Crime and Punishment*. The title of the novel thus reveals itself to be programmatic shorthand for an event of salvation, as understood by Dostoevsky.

## HEIDEGGER'S *TURN*: EVENT AND THE DECISIVE MOMENT

Being itself is, as fateful, eschatological. (Heidegger, "The Saying of Anaximander")

Crisis, catastrophe, and crime are the keywords by which the typical moments of self-discovery within Dostoevsky's novels are recognized. The stepping out of everydayness occurs suddenly and is a "limit situation" (in Karl Jaspers' sense). As the poet of the corrupt conscience, Dostoevsky is obsessed with the limit situation of guilt.

Heidegger's term for the stepping out of the forgetfulness of being through Ereignis is "turn." The turn, according to Heidegger, happens "abruptly." The concept thus designates the *sudden* stepping out of the forgetfulness of being into the "clearing of the essence of beyng

[*Seyns*]" ("The Turn").[18] Despite the extreme generality of this concept, it remains tied to the "danger" that threatens human beings through "technology." Thus, it may appear as if the "turn" is something unique that only arises through contact with technological apparatus. However, for Heidegger, neither "technology" nor the "turn" is unique. To the contrary, the forgetfulness of being is explained on the basis of "care" as the "being of Dasein." Care as concern finds its most spectacular expression in technology, that is, in the exploitation of the device, the *machine*, that works toward the mastery of nature in the service of human beings.

The "calculative understanding" provoked by technology asserts its dominance: What is encountered as "world" is now only viewed in terms of its usefulness. Heidegger sees the opposite of such an attitude in "the poetic." The poetic is for Heidegger that which "prevails throughout all art of the beautiful." Because art is also dependent upon technology (Greek *tekhnē*), the realm of art is related to the essence of technology, even though the former does not manufacture useful objects but instead opens a world. The "essence of art" and the "essence of technology" are to be thought of in terms of the condition for the possibility of truth. Thus, just as "the whole business of aesthetics" prevents the essence of art from being considered,[19] the essence of technology does not lie in it being simply a tool (that can either be adopted or not) by means of which human beings configure the world to their advantage. Both art and technology have to do with the "truth of being." However, this state of affairs continually veils itself through the activities that arise around art and technology.

Heidegger emphasizes that this concealing of the actual state of affairs should not be seen as a consequence of sheer neglect, but rather as historically (*geschichtlich*) conditioned. This concealing becomes visible now only through Heidegger's own philosophy, which in turn has its own historical (*geschichtlichen*) place that Heidegger does not control but can nonetheless consider and bring to language. Therefore, Heidegger attempts to think the "turn" by which "the truth of the essence of beyng [*Seyns*] enters into that which is."

"Art" and "technology" are thus experienced in their true essences as the realms that enable human beings "to dwell" upon this earth. Literally he says: "Perhaps we stand already in the forward-projecting shadow of the advent of this turn. When and how it will occur historically [*geschichtlich*], nobody knows. But it is not necessary to know such a thing. Knowledge of this kind would be extremely pernicious to human beings—for it is the essence of the human being to be the one who awaits the essence of beyng [*Seyns*] while thoughtfully guarding it."[20] What Heidegger prepares in terms of thought, Hölderlin had already expressed poetically. For Heidegger, Hölderlin is that poet who has already poetized out of the Ereignis of the turn. "Full of merit, yet poetically do human beings dwell upon this earth." Heidegger repeatedly wrote programmatic elucidations of these lines.[21]

In *Contributions to Philosophy* Heidegger speaks of the "future ones" of the "last god." These "future ones" are determined by "surmising and seeking." They are small in number, comprised of the "essentially inconspicuous, to whom belongs no public sphere." These "future ones" are "the only ones that being (the leap) approaches as Ereignis, appropriating them into Ereignis and authorizing them to harbor its truth." And then Hölderlin is distinguished from among them: "Hölderlin, coming from far away, is hence their most futural poet. Hölderlin is the most futural because he approaches from the greatest distance and in this way *traverses* and transmutes what is greatest."[22] The following passage from Heidegger's *Elucidations of Hölderlin's Poetry* deserves emphasis:

> Hölderlin poetizes the essence of poetry, but not in the manner of a time-lessly valid concept. This essence of poetry belongs to a determinate time. However, not in such a way that it conforms to this time as something already existing. Rather, by founding the essence of poetry anew, he determines a new time. It is the time of the gods who have fled and of the god to come. It is the destitute time, because it stands in a double lack and double nothing: it stands in the no-more of the gods who have fled, and in the not-yet of the one to come.[23]

Heidegger appeals to Hölderlin, just as Dostoevsky appeals to Christ. Hölderlin was the most futural of all futural ones; however, he was also already there—just like Christ.

Anticipating the turn as "awaiting" (in the sense of attending) "the essence of beyng [*Seyns*]"[24]—what does that mean? It means that reference is not being made to something that is still to come but not yet here; rather, it means that what is to come, as the promise that already shapes the present, is already here. "So be it! So be it!" reads Dostoevsky's formula for the transformation of reality here and now (from *The Brothers*

*Karamazov*, book II, chapter 5), although the monks in the cloister who utilize this formula do not realize its present-day significance.

## REALIZED ESCHATOLOGY

"Realized eschatology" is the view that states analogous to the traditional after-death states occur in our present life—e.g., God's judgment on the past is a feature of life on earth. Scholars have found strains of realized eschatology, as well as traditional eschatology, in the New Testament; a few very radical theologians defend only realized eschatology.

—*The Oxford Companion to Philosophy* (1995)

When Dostoevsky and Heidegger think "eschatologically," it means in both cases that the *promise* (eschaton) determines the present as *remembrance* (past) and *anticipation* (future). The present as "awaiting" is therefore the experiencing of being in the "decisive moment." *This* decisive moment should not be misunderstood as "lived experience" in the sense of a sentimental personal experience. It is, rather, entirely consumed by the "call of care" (Heidegger), experienced as authentic relation to self—and this same determination holds for the *limit situation of guilt* in the books of Dostoevsky. Christ and Hölderlin as the figures who reflect the future signify in each case, for Heidegger and Dostoevsky, the lived—that is, the experienced and, therefore, accessible—*eschaton* of the decisive moment.

In a word, in both cases we have a "realized eschatology." Not someday, at the end of all time, does "the last" occur, but here and now. Said more concretely, for Dostoevsky, the "resurrection" is not to be found after death, but rather here and now in the "turn." In *The Brothers Karamazov*, the stench of the dead elder Zosima puts the seal on the fact that his *feud* was with the resurrection: His moral conduct was in the spirit of a "lively life." In Dostoevsky's world, resurrection is not an empirical fact but a fact of reason. And for Heidegger, the "turn" is not an Ereignis of measurable time that has a particular date on which it occurs and which one can predict; rather, the Ereignis of the "lightning flash," which each time strikes us "abruptly" in our Dasein and leads us to take a "step back," is that by means of which we step out of the "forgetfulness of being." The step back is not a regression, but a withdrawal into releasement (*Gelassenheit*) before that which occurs (*sich ereignet*).

This is precisely what is meant when Heidegger, in his statements in *Mindfulness*, sets himself off from all "eschatology." The "relief from beings" as "the shift into the question of the most question-worthy" has a prehistory. From out of this prehistory we are directed "into what is to be inquired about." As Heidegger puts it: "The futurity of this prehistory is the *interior* of the constant attuning of the determination of the grounding of the truth of beyng [*Seyns*]—entirely different from every kind of 'eschatological' posture, which is *not* attuned to grounding but rather to holding out for an 'end-time,' and which already has as a presupposition a complete forgetfulness of being. All 'eschatology' subsists on a belief in the security of a new situation" (*Mindfulness*).[25]

To be sure, such differentiation is only necessary for Heidegger because the similarity between the "eschatological" attitude and his "awaiting" Ereignis jumps inevitably to mind. But what did he have in mind when he spoke of "belief in the security of a new situation" in order to characterize "every kind of 'eschatological' attitude"? It must have been the merging of all into a national community, however that is to be defined, amid integrated "technology." (*Mindfulness* was written in the years 1938 and 1939.)

Heidegger wanted the awaiting of Ereignis to be understood as distinct from any concession to modernity. His objection against typical "eschatology" is as follows: "But in the fore-thinking of being-historical thinking, the grounding ground of *Dasein* is this itself, the questioning of beyng [*Seyns*]" (*Mindfulness*).[26] However, this applies also for the eschatology of the New Testament, even though Heidegger would object that the Christian awareness cannot be a philosophical one. "The hour of beyng [*Seyns*] is not the object of a faithful awaiting."[27]

In summary, Heidegger's objection to existing eschatologies does not free his thinking from itself having an eschatological foundation, but rather marks it as a "realized eschatology": "The seeking itself is the goal," as Heidegger remarks laconically in his *Contributions to Philosophy*. In his essay "The Saying of Anaximander," Heidegger speaks of the "eschatology of being" and explains: "Being itself is, as fateful, eschatological." Additionally: "If we think out of the eschatology of being, then we must one day await the former dawn in the dawn to come and learn today therefore to consider the former from there."[28]

I would like to argue that Dostoevsky would have immediately subscribed to one particular line of Hölderlin's poetry on which Heidegger placed emphasis: "What you seek, it is near, it already encounters you."[29] With this line, the meaning of "realized eschatology" becomes clear. Traditional eschatology states that after death follows the resurrection, and after the resurrection follows the judgment of our worldly deeds and the ruling of God over whether we, on the basis of these deeds, go to heaven or hell. But "realized eschatology" says that in our life here and now, the decision has already been made whether we *are* in heaven or in hell. It has been made on the basis of our behavior as intelligible actors, behavior that has immediate psychosomatic consequences.

Expressed otherwise, "hell" for Dostoevsky is not otherworldly, but is rather an attunement here and now, established through deliberate and freely chosen evil thoughts out of which the actuality of evil arises. "Resurrection" is the agent's stepping out of hell through the leap into punishment; but it is also the abrupt refraining from an unplanned misdeed, which Dmitri in *The Brothers Karamazov* presents to us as he resists murdering his father and instead runs off. Several times Dostoevsky presents us with a suicide victim who remains in his hell: Svidrigailov in *Crime and Punishment*, Stavrogin and Kirillov in *Demons*, Smerdyakov in *The Brothers Karamazov*. All four are psychosomatically shaken. Suicide is disrupted resurrection in the here and now—that is, disrupted resurrection into the "lively life."

Analogous considerations regarding the stepping out of the forgetfulness of being are carried out in Heidegger's thinking. The Ereignis here and now, which "abruptly" brings about the decisive moment, can take place at any time: future and past encounter one another in the present. Macrostructures of temporalization [*Zeitigung*] realize themselves, in concentrated form, in the fulfilled now. With this, is traditional eschatology, which is concerned with an entire community—indeed, with a historical humanity in its development toward a goal—annulled? At any rate, one finds both with Dostoevsky and Heidegger arguments for an eschatology in the so-called traditional sense, even though it is realized eschatology that emerges more emphatically.

In order to make this emphasis clear, the "epiphanies" of James Joyce ought to be considered in their fundamental-ontological basis. There, too, "faithful waiting" is lacking. And when Dostoevsky insists upon the "lively life," he thus means that life is immanently meaningful as the condition for the possibility of all genuine piety. To the extent that Dostoevsky cannot be considered a "theologian," Heidegger cannot, for his part, be considered an "atheist." Both have in common the unassailable orientation toward the world of life in its immediacy of being. Poet and thinker coincide in both cases: Dostoevsky's novels subsist on the confrontation of various conceptual worlds; and Heidegger's thinking appeals centrally to Hölderlin's poetry. Indeed, Heidegger programmatically formulates it thusly: "Thinking is the primal poetry which comes before all poesy. . . . All poetry is, in its ground, a thinking" ("The Saying of Anaximander"). Additionally, he writes: "*The poet* gives the question of being to thinking/for its step back/the guiding words" (*Thoughts*).[30]

## CONCLUSION

To conclude my reflections on eschatology in Dostoevsky and Heidegger, which seen as a whole are merely the beginning of an outline, the most obvious commonality bears emphasis once again: Where Dostoevsky speaks of the "Crystal Palace" of the 1852 London World Fair,[31] Heidegger speaks of "technology" which he designates with his characteristic term "En-framing." In both cases, the soul is taken into account regarding the technological age. Dostoevsky prefers to remain with Christ rather than with a calculative truth, while Heidegger adopts Hölderlin's insight as a campaign slogan: "Full of merit, yet poetically do human beings dwell upon this earth." The Crystal Palace and En-framing mean one and the same: the endangering of originary dwelling.

Dostoevsky's oeuvre, like Heidegger's, is propelled by the cool ambition of the professional to continually make clearer what determines the originary insight from out of which all that can be said issues forth. The working out of this movement of thought was the sole aim of the considerations presented here.

Contemporary history is not taken into account here, for otherwise the patriotic and deeply nationalistic use made by the "poet" and the "thinker" of their respective guiding figures would have necessitated a critical, ideological analysis. Above all, this analysis would have to show that Hölderlin and Christ provide, generally speaking, all that for which a demagogue could wish. In short, Dostoevsky and Heidegger were considered exclusively in light of the claim made by their self-image—on the pedestal that they erected for themselves. To question, however, means to tear down, and that would be a different task altogether.

## POSTSCRIPT

In his monograph, *Encounters and Dialogues with Martin Heidegger: 1929–1976*, Heinrich Wiegand Petzet reports on works of Russian literature that especially attracted Heidegger's attention. He states:

> For a long time, a picture of Dostoevsky graced Heidegger's work table—like an homage to the Russian poetic genius. He was familiar with Russian literature; Tolstoy's *The Death of Ivan Ilyich* is mentioned at an important point in *Being and Time*, and he loved Goncharov's *Oblomov*, whose humorous pages he could recount with pleasure, but not without giving one a sense of how seriously he took the hidden world angst of this character.[32]

Petzet mentions this in connection with a 1967 meeting between Heidegger and the young Russian poet Andrei Vosnesensky. Born in 1933 in Moscow, Vosnesensky had been invited to Munich to read his poems in 1967 by the Bavarian Academy of Fine Arts, of which he was a member. When he found out that Heidegger was also a member of this Academy, he made known his wish to meet the famous philosopher. And so it came about: In Heidegger's writing room in Zähringen the two met for a conversation. The translator Alexander Kaempfe had to assist, for communication was in French and English; Heidegger did not speak Russian, and Vosnesensky did not speak German. But there was more. During Vosnesensky's reading in the lecture hall at the University of Freiburg, Heidegger sat in the first row and felt himself to be in living touch with the authentic Russia.

Concerning Dostoevsky, it should be remembered that his complete works, including his journalistic writings, were first published in German, translated by E. K. Rahsin, between 1906 and 1919 by the Piper Publishing House in Munich.[33] As a result, reading Dostoevsky became positively fashionable in Germany, and Heidegger clearly took part in the trend.

On October 28, 1918, Heidegger wrote to his wife from Nouillion-pont (near Verdun), where he had become involved at the front weather station: "And then if you could be so kind and find out if there is an edition of Dostoevsky's *The Brothers Karamazov*, the books are all in good hands here." And on June 28, 1920, he wrote to his wife again, this time from Messkirch: "I am once again taking great pleasure in the *Heimat*, the meadows and fields, and slowly I am beginning to sense what it means to be rooted. It really only became clear to me in reference to Dostoevsky."[34]

Concerning the rootedness testified to here and its connection to the worldview of Dostoyevsky, Heidegger later argues much in the same vein when it comes to the overcoming of European nihilism.[35] He cites Dostoevsky's foreword to the "Pushkin Speech" and references the translation by E. K. Rahsin. In Nietzsche's nihilism, Heidegger sees the announcement of new and different values, an intention he also posits as belonging to Dostoevsky's "Pushkin Speech," specifically in the characterizations of Aleko (*The Gypsies*) and Onegin (*Eugene Onegin*), whose nihilism points toward new and different values in the future.

Based on my essay, "Dostoevsky and Heidegger" (2010), Ulrich Schmid (University of St. Gallen) published his essay "Heidegger and Dostoevsky: Philosophy and Politics" in the journal *Dostoevsky Studies: New Series* and came to this conclusion: "Both deeply believed in the historical mission of their people."[36]

Translated by Julia Goesser Assaiante
and S. Montgomery Ewegen

## NOTES

1. All translations are those of Julia Goesser Assaiante and S. Montgomery Ewegen. For ease of reference, we have included bibliographic references to standard English translations of Heidegger's texts.

2. Cf. Ernst Benz, *Geist und Leben der Ostkirche* (Hamburg: Rowohlt, 1957), 128.

3. Friedrich Hölderlin, "Andenken," in *Hölderlin's Gesammelte Werk*, ed. Hans Jürgen Balmes (Frankfurt am Main: Fischer Taschenbuch Verlag, 2008), 108.

4. Martin Heidegger, "Das Ge-Stell," in *Bremer und Freiburger Vorträge*, GA 79 (Frankfurt am Main: Vittorio Klostermann, 1994), 40. Translated as

"En-framing," in *Bremen and Freiburg Lectures: Insight into That Which Is and Basic Principles of Thinking*, trans. Andrew Mitchell (Bloomington: Indiana University Press, 2012), 38.

5. This sentence's figure of thought, so characteristic of Dostoevsky and later found in his *Demons* (1871–1872, part II, chapter 1, paragraph 7), is also to be found in Cicero's *Tusculan Disputations*: "I would truly rather err with Plato—and I know in what esteem you hold that man—than to think the truth with them (the Pythagoreans); [*Errare mehercule malo cum Platone, quem tu quanti facias scio et quem ex tuo ore admiror, quam cum istis vera sentire*]," *Tusculanae disputationes* 1.17.39. At stake here is the immortality of the soul, as asserted by Plato. The same thought can be found in Cicero's *Cato the Elder on Old Age*: "Should I be in error to think that the soul of the human is immortal, then I gladly err [*Quodsi in hoc erro, qui animos hominum immortales esse credam, libenter erro*]," *Cato maior de senectute*, 23.86.

6. See Wilhelm Friedrich Waiblinger, *Phaeton* (Stuttgart: Verlag von Friedrich Franckh, 1823), 260–61. Phaeton's last notes ("Blooms in lovely blue, the steeple with its metallic vault"). Reprint of the first *Nachdruck* (Dresden: Schwäbische Verlagsgesellschaft, 1920). In his essay, "Hölderlin and the Essence of Poetry," Heidegger calls "In lovely blue" a "great and at the same time uncanny poem," and counts "Full of merit, yet poetically human beings dwell upon this earth" among the five sayings by Hölderlin that are most important to him. See Martin Heidegger, *Erläuterungen zu Hölderlins Dichtung*, GA 4 (Frankfurt am Main: Vittorio Klostermann, 1981), 33 and 42. Translated as "Hölderlin and the Essence of Poetry," in *Elucidations of Hölderlin's Poetry*, trans. Keith Hoeller (Amherst, NY: Humanity Books, 2000), 59. In his edition of the *Collected Poems of Hölderlin* (Bad Homburg: Athenäum, 1970), 462, Detlev Lüders categorizes "In lovely blue" as "dubious." This is relevant to the editorial circumstances behind Heidegger's image of Hölderlin, which is based on Norbert von Hellingrath's "historical-critical edition."

7. Cf. Martin Heidegger, "Brief über den Humanismus," in *Wegmarken*, GA 9 (Frankfurt am Main: Vittorio Klostermann, 1976), 342–43. Translated as "Letter on Humanism," in *Pathmarks*, ed. William McNeill (Cambridge: Cambridge University Press, 1998), 261.

8. Cf. Martin Heidegger, *Sein und Zeit*, GA 2 (Frankfurt am Main: Vittorio Klostermann, 1977), 447. Translated as *Being and Time*, trans. John Macquarrie and Edward Robinson (New York: Harper and Row, 1962), 387.

9. Cf. Martin Heidegger, *Beiträge zur Philosophie (Vom Ereignis)*, GA 65 (Frankfurt am Main: Vittorio Klostermann, 1989), 20. Translated as *Contributions to Philosophy (of the Event)*, trans. Richard Rojcewicz and Daniela Vellega-Neu (Bloomington: Indiana University Press, 2011), 18.

10. Heidegger, *Beiträge*, GA 65, 20; Heidegger, *Contributions to Philosophy*, 18.

11. Heidegger, *Beiträge*, GA 65, 18; Heidegger, *Contributions to Philosophy*, 16.

12. Translator's note: the (sic!) was provided by the author to indicate Heidegger's peculiar spelling of the word *die L etze* (which is more commonly *die Letzte*), and we reproduce it here.

13. Heidegger, *Beiträge*, GA 65, 18; Heidegger, *Contributions to Philosophy*, 16.

14. F. M., Dostoevskii, *Polnoe sobranie sochinenii* 30 vols. (Leningrad: Nauka, 1977–1990) Volume 6, 422. *Crime and Punishment*, Epilogue, Chapter 2.

15. Ibid., 270; Part 4, Chapter 6.

16. Ibid., 53; Part 1, Chapter 6.

17. Ibid., 422.

18. Martin Heidegger, "Die Kehre," in *Bremer und Freiburger Vortäge*, GA 79 (Frankfurt am Main: Vittorio Klostermann, 1994), 73. Translated as "The Turn," in *Bremen and Freiburg Lectures*, trans. Andrew Mitchell (Bloomington: Indiana University Press, 2011), 69.

19. Martin Heidegger, "Die Frage nach der Technik," in *Vortäge und Aufsätze*, GA 7 (Frankfurt am Main: Vittorio Klostermann, 2000), 36. Translated as "The Question Concerning Technology," in *The Question Concerning Technology and Other Essays*, trans. William Lovitt (New York: Harper and Row, 1977), 116.

20. Heidegger, "Die Kehre," GA 79, 71; Heidegger, "The Question Concerning Technology," 41.

21. Cf. Heidegger, "Hölderlin and the Essence of Poetry," in *Elucidations*; "Concerning the Essence of Poetry," in *Hölderlin's Hymns "Germania" and "The Rhine,"* GA 39, trans. William McNeill and Julia Ireland (Bloomington: Indiana University Press, 2014), section 4; and "'. . . dichterisch wohnet der Mensch . . . ,'" in *Vorträge und Aufsätze*, GA 7 (Frankfurt am Main: Vittorio Klostermann, 1951). Translated as "'. . . Poetically Man Dwells . . . ,'" in *Poetry, Language, Thought*, trans. Albert Hofstadter (New York: Harper and Row, 1971).

22. Heidegger, *Beiträge*, GA 65, 401; Heidegger, *Contributions to Philosophy*, 318.

23. Heidegger, *Erläuterungen*, GA 4, 47; Heidegger, *Elucidations*, 64.

24. Heidegger, *Elucidations*, 71.

25. Martin Heidegger, *Besinnung*, GA 66 (Frankfurt am Main: Vittorio Klostermann, 1997), 248. Translated as *Mindfulness*, trans. Parvis Emad and Thomas Kalary (London: Continuum, 2006), 216.

26. Heidegger, *Besinnung*, GA 66, 245; Heidegger, *Mindfulness*, 216.

27. Heidegger, *Besinnung*, 245; Heidegger, *Mindfulness*, 217.

28. Martin Heidegger, "Der Spruch des Anaximander," in *Holzwege*, GA 5 (Frankfurt am Main: Vittorio Klostermann, 1977), 327. Translated as "The

54       *Horst-Jürgen Gerigk*

Saying of Anaximander," in *Off the Beaten Track*, trans. Julian Young and Kenneth Haynes (Cambridge: Cambridge University Press, 2002), 247.

29. Cf. Friedrich Hölderlin, "Heimkunft. An die Verwandten," in *Gesammelte Werke*, ed. Hans Jürgen Balmes (Frankfurt am Main: Fischer Taschenbuch Verlag, 2008), 140.

30. Heidegger, "Anaxamander," GA 5, 328–29; and Martin Heidegger, *Gedachtes*, GA 81 (Frankfurt am Main: Vittorio Klostermann, 2007), 38.

31. In his 1864 book *Notes from the Underground*, Dostoevsky brings a polemic against Nikolay Chernyshevsky, whose 1863 novel *What Is To Be Done?* lauded the Crystal Palace from the London World's Fair as a symbol of positive societal progress.

32. Heinrich Wiegand Petzet, *Encounters and Dialogues with Martin Heidegger 1929–1976* (Frankfurt am Main: Societätsverlag, 1983), 128.

33. See Christoph Garstka: *Arthur Moeller van der Bruck und die erste deutsche Gesamtausgabe der Werke Dostojewskijs im Piper-Verlag 1906–1919*, vol. 9 of the series Heidelberger Publikationen zur Slavistik, foreword by Horst-Jürgen Gerigk (Frankfurt am Main: Peter Lang, 1998). This is an inventory of various prefaces and introductions by Arthur Moeller van der Bruck and Dmitry Merezhkovsky that makes use of the unpublished letters of the translator E. K. Rahsin, with extensive bibliography.

34. See Martin Heidegger and Gertrud Heidegger, *Briefe Martin Heideggers an seine Frau Elfride 1915–1970* (Munich: Deutsche Verlags-Anstalt, 2005), 75 and 106.

35. See Martin Heidegger, *Nietzsche: Der europäische Nihilismus*, GA 48 (Frankfurt am Main: Vittorio Klostermann, 1986), 1 and 2.

36. Ulrich Schmid, "Heidegger and Dostoevsky: Philosophy and Politics," *Dostoevsky Studies: New Series* 15 (2011): 46.

*Chapter 3*

# Tolstoy and Heidegger on the Ways of Being

Inessa Medzhibovskaya

## 1889: THOUGHTS IN THE FOREST (TOLSTOY'S ONTOLOGY BY WAY OF INTRODUCTION)

It is 1889. On September 26 of that year, Martin Heidegger would be born at Messkirch in Baden. Tolstoy was in a bad mood at the start of 1889: The publication of his major philosophical work, *On Life*, which it had taken him a year and a half to write and edit, was halted by the authorities on grounds of blasphemy. Its thirty-five chapters and three appendices proposed that we can only find happiness and become its carriers if we follow the guidelines of what Tolstoy terms "reasonable consciousness," the tool for knowing the world, for acting in it ethically, and for serving the causes of unselfish love. Tolstoy made a presentation titled "The Concept of Life," which was the emerging version of *On Life*, on March 14, 1887, at the Moscow Psychological Society, Russia's first professional philosophical society affiliated with Moscow University. The talk was reviewed in the press and consolidated a circle of admirers and opponents, confirming Tolstoy's stable reputation as an iconoclast. On November 25, 1888, Tolstoy noted in his diary: "If Christ arrived and submitted the Gospels for publication, the ladies would attempt to get his autograph and nothing more. We should stop writing, reading, talking, we should *act*."[1] But how?

Taking long walks in the groves, alleys, and thickets of his vast estate at Yasnaya Polyana in the summer and fall of 1889, Tolstoy summarizes the state of his ontology in the notebooks he carries along on his walks. Later in the day, he transfers short phrases to longer meditations and observations into the pages of his diary.

On the day of Heidegger's birth, he writes:

14 September 1889[2] what is His Will remains a mystery to us forever. And this must be so. There could be no life, eternal life had the goal that we are striving for were clear to us and henceforth were finite [*konechnaia*]. The signs that we are living according to His will and not against it are given quite indubitably to us, similarly or even more indubitably than they would be for a horse that the reins allow running only in one direction. The first, main, undoubtable sign, which we tend to neglect, is the absence of spiritual suffering (as in a horse, the absence of the feeling of pain from the bit). If you are experiencing complete freedom not violated by anything then you live according to God's will. The other sign, which is a test of the first, is that love of people is not violated. If you are not feeling hostility towards anyone and know that no evil thoughts are felt towards you, you are in God's Will. The third sign, which, again, is testing the first and the second, is spiritual growth. If you are feeling that you are becoming more spiritual, that you are subjugating your animal [self], you are in the will of God.[3]

The entry for September 15 reads: "I was thinking: To be joyous! Joyous! The cause of life and its purpose—joy!"[4] The entry on September 16 compared a man with a stone, the foundational unit in the structure of being: "I remember this about a stone: A stone cannot become harmful, it cannot even become useless . . . But a man can be harmful; can be useless."[5] And so it continues, day after day, years before 1889 and years after: Economics, politics, Tolstoy's reading list, his searches for hope, his encounters, conversations of the day, and, most importantly, his thoughts about the experience of being alive and its hardships as well as delights, are records of his experience of being. Age does not date their intensity or their unparalleled force and clarity. The entry made on December 27, 1889, may be the closest description that year of being cornered into despair by "the they," in anticipation of Heidegger's forthcoming theory of Dasein:

It is difficult because of the lie of the life around me and because I cannot find a device with which to point out their delusion without insulting them. . . . I am ashamed of this insane expenditure amid poverty. I was thinking today while out on a walk: Those who assert that this world is a vale of tears, the place of testing and so on, and that there is the world of bliss, are as if asserting that the whole infinite Divine world is most beautiful and that life is most beautiful in the whole wide world, except for in one place and time, namely where we live. A strange accident that would be![6]

Until the early spring of 1889, Tolstoy was still in Moscow where his family was spending the winter. A visit of several philosopher friends who smoked cigars, gossiped about Jubilee sessions and festschrift collections, and enjoyed their dinner with fine wine depressed Tolstoy with their "philosophical chatter": "Terrible hypocrites, scribes, and harmfully-mean ones."[7] The following day he grumbled some more: "Main thing, their brains are busted."[8] When the first issue of the first professional philosophical periodical in Russia was brought to Tolstoy on November 2, 1889, with pride by its editor, Philosopher Nikolai Grot,[9] Tolstoy recorded his impressions late at night about the contents and the defining tones of the issue: "Have been reading Grot's journal. [ . . . ] How much labor spent! The entire journal is a collection of articles lacking in thought and clarity of expression."[10] The task of philosophy, as Tolstoy views it, is to explain the meaning of life in a language that is figuratively clear and vivid.

The image of the horse set out in the September 14 diary entry on Heidegger's birth date was featured also in Chapter XVI of *On Life*, "The Animal Individuality is the Tool for Life."[11] The unruly and reluctant horse is broken down into obedience by the routines of its duties, painful as they are.[12] This image is of course quite familiar to everyone raised in the fold of German culture, from Goethe's *Sorrows of Young Werther* (1774), this hallmark of the discontent of modernity written in the form of letters to a forever silent "Wilhelm," and thus a quasi-diary. Consider August 22 in part I:

It is a disaster, Wilhelm, my active powers have deteriorated to a restless indifference, I cannot be idle and yet I can't do anything, either.[ . . . ], when I think about it again, and remember the fable about the horse that, impatient with its freedom, lets itself be saddled and bridled and is ridden to ruin, I don't know what I should do—and, dear friend, is not perhaps my longing to change my circumstances an inner, restless impatience that will pursue me wherever I go?[13]

How close are these thoughts also to those jotted down by Nietzsche a few months earlier in his "late notebooks" ending in August 1888, in the twilight days of his sane life. Nietzsche speaks of the "will to power as life" necessary for the revival from the fruitlessness of Werther-like restless impatience that can only be realized through our desire for conquest and destruction, without regard of "pleasure and unpleasure."[14]

Tolstoy starts a few Nietzschean-like initiatives to reform life in 1889. Several momentous albeit unfinished drafts attempt to clarify the relationships between authentic and false disclosure. Art should reveal the light of life hidden in the everyday: "A true work of art is a revelation of a new way of knowing life which is taking place in the soul of an artist in accordance with laws incomprehensible to us, but which, by way of expressing itself, lightens up the path which humanity is walking."[15]

Although it begins on a Nietzschen note of destruction, "Carthago delenda est"—a sketch so entitled—is a figural model of the movement of being toward improvement: "The life, that form of life that we, Christian nations, live delenda est, should be destroyed." "I have been saying and will continue saying this until it is destroyed."[16] It should not be destroyed in the sense of elimination, but rebuilt so as to ensure that all parts of its movement are proportionate:

The old form of life is holding up as a tree whose shoots are alive, but which itself seems alive only because the rot eroding it has not yet passed through the core of the trunk. [. . .] If one were to imagine progress as a movement of a quadrangle by means of two straps attached to the two angles at the front then our state is akin to the position that a body would reach if one side of it were to advance incommensurably with the other. There is nothing else to be done than to move the edge that had fallen behind forward so that it catches up with the other edge. The delusion of short-sighted people is natural: they see the irregularity of a position and, in order to rectify it, are willing to push back the advanced edge. But this is impossible. The edge that has moved ahead is reasonable consciousness—and this is the highest force in humankind, and therefore there is no such power that could set it back. One thing remains: to get reality to move forth in keeping with consciousness. Humankind moves only in this way: a step of consciousness, a step of practical activity, which actualizes a new step of consciousness. There are times indeed when reality is apace with consciousness (it appears that this used to be true for a half of the past century), and then there are times just as they are now, when consciousness has stepped forward far ahead, and is not corresponding to life.[17]

The most Nietzschean of the 1889 drafts is not "Carthago delenda est," but a draft called "An Appeal" [*Vozzvanie*], a result of hearing a prophetic voice calling on Tolstoy over a chorus of voices of temptation. A prophetic voice is instructing him to become a leader of humanity who would lift it out of the mire of its worst delusions and suffering: "And everywhere the same: people are suffering, experiencing torments, while trying not to see that this life is insane."[18] The loudest of the dissenting voices impresses this on the sleeping prophet: "Do not think! If you start thinking you will see that this life is worse than nonexistence."[19] But think he must; thought is all the power that he has for enduring life and inspiring others.

Even at this initial approach, themes and questions common to Tolstoy and Heidegger are obvious: anxiety about life and its disordered condition and the very burdens of existing, and desperation about the oppression of the social environment and the disproportionate advance of machinery and technology. What is a place in this for philosophizing, and how to express these yearnings for philosophical thought and action? It appears necessary to explain the connection between Tolstoy and Heidegger on a broader substantive and methodological basis than has been done so far. The questions found at the opening of the notorious and ominous *Schwarze Hefte* inscribed "M.H.," started by Heidegger in 1931 and at last released in 2014 and 2015, already sound familiar to us after the initial perusal of Tolstoy's thought trajectories in 1889, the year when Heidegger was born: "What should we do? Who are we? Why should we be? What are beings? Why does being happen? Philosophizing proceeds out of these questions upward into unity."[20]

In pondering Heidegger's *Ponderings*—the "Überlegungen" and "Anmerkungen" in the *Schwarze Hefte*—Jeff Love notices a common approach with Tolstoy, a habit of mixing in politics, casual observations, and philosophical problematic that "show[s] a remarkable similarity."[21] Whether or not the common ring of terms and the approximate sound of their concerns are members in the same philosophical and intellectual family remains to be discussed. This is the goal of the present chapter.

## TOLSTOY AND HEIDEGGER: PREVIOUS APPROACHES

**"L.N. Tolstoi hat in seiner Erzählung 'Der Tod des Iwan Iljitsch' das Phänomen der Erschütterung und des Zusammenbruchs dieses 'man stirbt' dargestellt."[22]**

So far, the reading of Tolstoy and Heidegger has been restricted to the discussion of Heidegger's footnote to Tolstoy, the sole reference he is known to have made to Tolstoy in his published work: in paragraph 51 of division 2 of *Sein und Zeit*. The comparisons are usually conducted narrowly, by trying to find in the text of Tolstoy's famous novella those elements of Heideggerian philosophy that must have prompted him to his moment of recognition. These are frequently hermeneutic exercises focused on identifying an analogy or a parallel between a literary and a philosophical text and between a literary and philosophical genre. They are also attempts to understand Tolstoy's evasively "realist" text, rich in otherworldly, philosophical, and religious semiology, through a rigid terminological explanation. To remind, *DII*[23] has a puzzling reverse structure in addition to containing a host of enigmatic, nonrealist imagery. The story begins with an announcement of Ivan Ilyich's untimely death and with a display of his pleased-looking but reproachful corpse at his wake, in chapter 1. From chapter 2 through the final chapter 12, the novella operates on a "dual time" schedule, one external ("clock-face time"), the other internal (the time of Ivan's thoughts, suffering, and spiritual breakthroughs), and it ends on the words "and died" when Ivan completes his final physical stretch while already in flight toward his tunnel of light. The evaluations are split therefore in deciding whether *DII* is an illustration of, or an attestation to, Heidegger. Some intimate that Heidegger exhibited "reticence" in giving Tolstoy's novella only a footnote because he owed him more. Others insist that Heidegger should have acknowledged Tolstoy's coauthorship.

A good beginning to the discussion is provided by Elisabeth Feist Hirsh (1978).[24] She pays attention to the uncommon linguistic charisma of Heidegger's narrative. Tolstoy's inclusion helps Heidegger to enunciate how "everydayness turns 'the courage to face death with anxiety' . . . into fear of an approaching event," and how "authentic existence has the courage to live with the nothing inherent in Dasein."[25]

The second critic to comment on the footnote in detail is Alan Pratt (1992): "In the death analytic, . . . Heidegger . . . mentions neither the poet nor the philosopher [neither Rainer Maria Rilke nor Karl Jaspers, the traces noted by critics at once] but references only Leo Tolstoy's 'The Death of Ivan Ilyich,' significantly the only prose fiction work mentioned in *Being and Time*. Clearly Tolstoy's novella made a lasting impression on Heidegger because in it he could find dramatically illustrated most of the characteristic behaviors and evasive attitudes uncovered in his own phenomenology of death. 'The Death of Ivan Ilyich,' then, is an illuminating supplement—specific, personal and emotional—to what Heidegger universalized in his philosophy."[26] The quoted passage comprises the quintessence of Pratt's argument.

The third critic is Robert Bernasconi (1990). He gives Tolstoy's literary attestation a high pass, but with illuminating caveats: "The footnote seems straightforward enough. It would appear to invite a reading of Tolstoy's story which would serve to illustrate Heidegger's account of the phenomenon of everyday Being towards-death."[27] Bernasconi's essay opens the volume titled *Philosophers' Poets,* which must be intended as a compliment: Bernasconi hands the laurel of Heidegger's poet to Tolstoy and not Hölderlin or Rilke or Trakl (Heidegger's all-time favorites). Bernasconi is the first to acknowledge that this is not the point: There is a discomfort with a sense of ownership of literature by philosophy and with the word "attestation" itself. He implies that Levinas rather than Heidegger should have made the reference: "The crucial transformation in Ivan's relation to his own death comes when he is, in Levinas's phrase, 'liberated from the egoist gravitation.' . . . But decisions for and against rival philosophical interpretations of a story cannot be made on the basis of a few details. It would be necessary to attempt a sustained Levinasian reading of 'The Death of Ivan Ilyich'. But to what purpose? And what does it mean to call a reading of a story after the name of a philosopher? Valuable though it might be to explore such a reading on some other occasion, in the present context it would distract from the question of the character and legitimacy of a philosophical reading of literature."[28] Just as Ivan Ilyich's death proved a matter of inconvenience (memorably, Petr Ilyich, his friend, thinks that Ivan Ilyich "arranged the affair stupidly" [*glupo rasporiadilsia*]), so a literary intervention inconveniences philosophy, clarifying as it does, a few moments of its density: "Is there not here a basis for an understanding of the violence literary examples perform within philosophy? Such examples—and all examples are in a sense literary—destroy the autonomy and integrity of the philosophical text."[29]

Bernasconi's essay is the second-longest exploration after the splendid and thorough comparison of Tolstoy's text with Heidegger's term "being-toward-death" performed by Natalie Repin in 2002. Repin writes: "The footnote amounts to Heidegger's unequivocal recognition of Tolstoy's successful comprehension of the question of death, a recognition that has proved not easy to gain."[30] Again, we notice that Tolstoy is the complimented party:

> Heidegger makes it possible for us to understand Tolstoy better, if only in return for Tolstoy's inspiring Heidegger to create his conception. [. . .] It is Tolstoy's uniquely sophisticated understanding of death that maintains readers' interest in this particular work, considered important even today on philosophical, not only artistic, grounds. To that effect, however, Heidegger's interpretation of death is essential in that it mediates, accommodates, and augments Tolstoy's philosophical relevance, for the former may be viewed as both an inadvertent elucidation of the latter and an incentive to its reappropriation. This, then, is a possible version of what could be retrieved from the reticence of Heidegger's footnote, of how its silence may sound.[31]

There is perhaps nothing wrong about being right, yet again anachronistically. Repin thinks it is important to keep reading Tolstoy and Heidegger together, but she points to a departure of Tolstoy from Heidegger, a paradoxical lapse of an originator from his successor, despite their similarity.

Likewise sophisticated is an excellent piece by A. G. Zavalyi (2010).[32] He thinks that what attracts us to the comparison is a set of unknowables about being-toward-death dealt with by Tolstoy and Heidegger: a chronological one (when?) and a meaningful one (why?). But in addition to the similarities apportioned by Tolstoy and Heidegger to the description of absolute abandonedness, and loneliness in the affirmation of the authentically existential at the price of losing one's life, Zavalyi underscores the differences between Tolstoy and Heidegger.[33] The more a human being is dissolved in others, according to Tolstoy, the more illusory is his death: "Only in this way can death lose its ontological substantiality."[34] In the end, Tolstoy denies death its primacy and its ontological rights and thus wrongs Heidegger.

Finally, William Irwin (2013) thinks that Heidegger's debt to Tolstoy is larger than a single footnote can express. He feels that an entire edifice of *Sein und Zeit* is dependent upon Tolstoy's novella: "It is tempting to describe 'The Death of Ivan Il'ich' as an excellent illustration of some major elements of *Being and Time*, but that would not be accurate. More properly, Heidegger owes a debt of inspiration to Tolstoy, a debt not fully repaid by the single footnote to 'The Death of Ivan Il'ich' in *Being and Time*.[35] Ivan's initial denial turns to resoluteness [*Entschlossenheit*] "The call of conscience [*Ruf des Gewissens*]" "that can reorient Dasein" and that has brought itself back from falling, allows us to see Ivan's fall through the black sack as one such reorientation.[36] But of course Heidegger's conception of authenticity does not fit in well with Tolstoy's denial of death, and Weil chooses not to attend to this aspect at all: Is resolution all that makes Ivan "saved" or simply "safe to die" authentically?

And thus one critic, Bernasconi, thinks that despite similarities, a comparison of two generically dissimilar masterpieces visits violence unto either. Two critics, Repin and Zavalyi, decide that Tolstoy and Heidegger disagree: Tolstoy denies mortality while Heidegger depends on positing it as a ground of his philosophy. Yet both critics think that reading them side by side is useful. Three critics, Pratt, Repin, and Irwin, decide that Tolstoy provides a dramatically vivid illustration to Heidegger's densely phrased philosophy. Repin calls this illustration a case of laudable and precocious foresight, which keeps *DII* relevant. Zavalyi thinks that a comparison is only good if held at a point level with two aspects of questioning, the "when" and the "why."

While many particular insights offered in these excellent pieces of comparative work will remain important, their conclusions are inconclusive at their own insistence. The appearance of the footnote remains mysterious and explicable only on a vaguely suggestive level because a novella is not a philosophical piece. Notably, two eminent companions to *Sein und Zeit*, one by Michael Gelven and another by Stephen Mulhall, do not even mention the footnote.[37] Instead, in commenting on paragraph 51, Gelven draws upon the mastery of Dostoevsky: "Few accounts in literature can match the phenomenological power with which Dostoevsky focuses attention on the terrible certainty of ceasing to be."[38]

Thus, we do not yet have a substantive explication of the pull and draw of Heidegger and Tolstoy as thinkers. Does the footnote point to Tolstoy's unique role in the text of *Sein und Zeit*? How does it fare in comparison with other footnotes in Heidegger's book? What are the exact location and function and context of the footnote in Heidegger's text and in the overall picture of the book's argument? What could Heidegger's sources and inspirations have been more concretely?

## THE FOOTNOTE

Heidegger's footnote sounds nothing like Wittgenstein's illumination, "a profound change of personal outlook" upon his discovery of Tolstoy's *Gospel in Brief* at the front of World War I.[39] The footnote looks like a familiar presence, and a decision to credit Tolstoy in this way seems either a matter of haste in which the book was written to meet the deadlines for Heidegger's tenure dossier at Marburg, ultimately unsuccessful, or a matter of shame because it had to be acknowledged somehow, so much was owed it, but it has already too deeply inhabited Heidegger's thought. It was too late to disown or repurpose it.

This is what occurs exactly in paragraph 51, "Being-Toward-Death and the Everydayness of Dasein," which states at the beginning: "Idle talk must make manifest in what way everyday Dasein interprets its being-toward-death. Understanding, which is also always attuned, that is, mooded, always forms the basis for this interpretation. Thus we must ask how the attuned understanding lying in the idle talk of the they has disclosed being-toward-death."[40] "One dies [*Man stirbt*]" is a tranquilizing linguistic trick of everydayness to an event that "belongs to no one in particular."[41] Thus Tolstoy, in the context of what Heidegger is talking about, has done away with the "cultivation of such a superior indifference."[42] Before Heidegger makes this point about estrangement of death from the modern everyday as a tactic for its tranquilization and sanitization, he cites Tolstoy. This is how it happens:

> The evasion of death which covers over dominates everydayness so stubbornly that, in-being-with-one-another, those "closest by" often try to convince the one who is "dying" that he will escape death and soon return again to the tranquilized everydayness of his world taken care of. This "concern" has the intention of thus "comforting" the "dying person." It wants to bring him back to Dasein by helping him to veil completely his ownmost nonrelational possibility. Thus, the they provides a *constant tranquilization about death*. But, basically, this tranquilization is not only

for the "dying person," but just as much for those "comforting him." And even in the case of demise, the carefreeness that the public has provided for itself is still not to be disturbed and made uneasy by the event. Indeed, the dying of others is seen as a social inconvenience, if not a downright tactlessness, from which the public should be spared.[43]

Immediately after the sentence explaining that the public should be spared the tactlessness and inconvenience of the dying of others, Heidegger inserts his footnote numbered "12": "12. L.N. Tolstoi in his story 'The Death of Ivan Ilyich' has portrayed the phenomenon of the disruption and collapse of this 'one dies.'"[44]

Heidegger's footnote thus refers Tolstoy's novella not so much to the analytic of one's own existential confrontation with dying, but to human indifference to death, to heartless indifference to the suffering of others, to the estrangement of death from the dying and from their own experience. Anxiety, the correct mooding of one's behavior toward death in existential terms, is not connected with Tolstoy's example, but with other examples that Heidegger cites in footnotes 9, 10, 11, and 13 that reference paragraphs 26, 27, 38, and 40, the earlier sections in *Sein und Zeit*, which would have had a closer relation to the customary range of comparisons between Tolstoy's novella and Heidegger's most famous terms ("Dasein with others," "Self and the they," "curiosity," "chatter," "inauthenticity," "falling prey," "thrownness," and "the attunement of anxiety" among them).

This is very curious, and the curiosity increases, in a way far from idle as described in paragraph 36, when one goes on reading what Heidegger has to say about estrangement and about the cultivation of superiority in the paragraphs that follow.

But along with this tranquilization, which keeps Dasein away from its death, the they at the same time justifies itself and makes itself respectable by silently ordering the way in which *one* is supposed to behave toward death in general. Even "thinking about death" is regarded publicly as cowardly fear, a sign of insecurity on the part of Dasein and **a gloomy flight from the world.**[45] *The they does not permit the courage to have anxiety about death.* The dominance of the public interpretedness of the they has already decided what attunement is to determine our stance toward death. In anxiety about death, Dasein is brought before itself as delivered over to its insuperable possibility. The they is careful to distort this anxiety into the fear of a future event. Anxiety, made ambiguous as fear, is moreover taken as a weakness which no self-assured Dasein is permitted to know. What is "proper" according to the silent decree of the they is the indifferent calm as to the "fact" that one dies. The cultivation of such a "superior" indifference **estranges [*entfremdet*] Dasein from its ownmost nonrelational potentiality-of-being.**[46]

Unlike the term *Verfremdung*,[47] the making something familiar look unfamiliar, that had already been widely practiced across Germany and originated in the theatrical-literary installations of Erwin Piscator and Bertolt Brecht, *Entfremdung* is a Hegelian and Marxist term that more literally means "alienation." Its appearance in the description of Ivan's flight from death into the light of deliverance is quite stark. Heidegger makes it sound as if a romantically hued "gloomy flight from the world" should be privileged over the bourgeois "entangled," "everyday being-toward-death" that is a "constant flight from death." Such an entitlement to a flight from death should be expropriated from the well-off, protected everyday. Only a "gloomy flight from the world" is the liberation of Dasein. Dasein in this presentation is something like a waking-up proletarian still not fully aware of its "ownmost nonrelational potentiality-of-being." It has nothing to lose but its chains, but it will take possession of the historical world. It would be silly to argue that Heidegger nourishes any proletarian-Marxist sympathies. The early National Socialist sympathies might be a closer link. Both ideologies accuse their opponents of using tranquilization tactics. Let us look further at how the quotation unfolds:

Temptation, tranquilization, and estrangement, however, characterize the kind of being of *falling prey*. Entangled, everyday being-toward-death is **a constant flight from death**. Being *toward* the end has the mode of *evading that end*—reinterpreting it, understanding it inauthentically, and veiling it. Factically, one's own Dasein is always already dying, that is, it is in a being-toward-its-end. And it conceals this fact from itself by reinterpreting death as a case of death occurring every day with others, a case that always assures us still more clearly that "one" is "oneself" still "alive." But in this entangled flight *from* death, the everydayness of Dasein bears witness to the fact that the they itself is always already determined as *being towards death*, even when it is not explicitly engaged in "thinking about death."[48] *Even in average everydayness, Dasein is constantly concerned with its ownmost, nonrelational, and insuperable potentiality-of-being, even if only in the mode of taking care of things in a*

*mode of untroubled indifference (Gleichgültigkeit) that opposes the most
extreme possibility of its existence.* The exposition of everyday being-toward-death, however, gives us
at the same time a directive to attempt to secure a complete existential
concept of being-toward-the-end, by a more penetrating interpretation in
which entangled being-toward-death is taken as an evasion *of death. That
before which* one flees has been made visible in a phenomenally adequate
way. We should now be able to project phenomenologically how evasive
Dasein itself understands its death.[49]

And so to not fall prey, to not be a victim, a martyr, or a degenerate
abettor to the power of the they, the entangled Dasein should disentan-
gle, liberate itself, and establish itself in one's "ownmost, nonrelational
way."

When Heidegger wants to tune thoughts about death to the right
nonrelational "mood," he is far from wanting to make an existential
allegory out of it. Another habilitation thesis, to become a famous
book, was not accepted for a tenured university bid in the same year:
. Walter Benjamin's *Ursprung des deutschen Trauerspiels* (written in
1925, it would be published in 1928). Benjamin's book discusses the
corpse as the melancholy emblem of the ruin. It speaks of the allegorical soullessness of history built off the mood of pensive and mournful
martyrdom. Benjamin's erratic Hegelianism voices its concern about
the allegorization of Physis, about leaving the character-imprint on a
corpse, rendering it *immerlich* ("immediately eternal").[50] Everything
passes and everything has its fate. Benjamin's discussion deals with the
survival of the everyday through the historical dialectic in which every
snowflake that melts and every building that still stands have their own
unrepeatable character. True, their loss is inevitable, but it is redeemed
in the transgredient principle of their uniqueness that will continue in
their successors without being carved in stone. Everything ordinary is
simultaneously extra-ordinary because it will die.

Heidegger's debt to Hegelianism is a key element of division 2. At
this point, we should not forget that *DII*, an emblematic story and thus
a history of a man whose life is "most simple, most ordinary and therefore most terrible,"[51] is referenced by Heidegger in the first chapter of
division 2—that is, closer to the opening of "Dasein and Temporality,"
which begins, like Tolstoy's novella, with an analytic of Dasein. Division
2 then leads us toward salvation at the end of the book through history,

through "the occurrence of the world in its essential existent unity with Dasein."[52] Natural history, buildings and institutions, and nature "colonized" in the countryside and on battlefields or as a site of a cult: Just like a human body, these entities are not mere accompaniments to the "inner" history of the soul.[53] This is the material in Hegel's *Lectures on the Philosophy of Religion.* With the last gods prayed to in the organized religious cults dead or in ruin, is Spirit our God, or Light? A God, anything?

Dasein is a construction of one's own inherited possibility. It needs not be told why it exists and wherefore. As Heidegger puts it, "Only a being that is essentially futural in its being so that it can let itself be thrown back upon its factical there, free for its death and shattering itself on it, that is, only a being that, as futural, is equiprimordially having-been, can hand down to itself its inherited possibility, take over its own thrownness and be in the moment for 'its time.' Only authentic temporality that is at the same time finite makes something like fate, that is, authentic historicity, possible."[54]

Is this inherited possibility shared by Tolstoy's Ivan with other literary characters and artists named by Heidegger in *Sein und Zeit*? To understand the footnote to *DII* and its location within Heidegger's text, it is most illuminating to observe how Heidegger lists his other literary debts in the footnotes of *Sein und Zeit*. He owes one of his key terms, Care, to Goethe. The character of Care appears in the final scenes in act 5 of *Faust II.* She is one of the Four Gray Women (Want, Debt, Care, Distress) appearing before Faust when he gazes at the sky from his balcony at the last stroke of midnight. Only Care enters the palace and tells Faust to take her appearance for an affirmation of the nearing of his death. He is reluctant: What need has he to float into eternity? But Care would not leave, explaining that this is her proper place. Care: "Once I make a man my own, / nothing in this world can help him."[55] The vengeful "companion-cause of fear," she whispers to Faust that it is his time at last, breathes death into him, and vanishes. Faust is blinded and left to the company of Mephistopheles and Lemures. As we know, from this grip of darkness and night, Faust's soul will be taken back to light, by the choir of heavenly spirits who are carrying him on his final flight from earth.

This flight to the sky and toward light is not the gloomy flight of liberation taking place in *Sein und Zeit*. Heidegger brings in Goethe first, in support of his position that as an ontological construction, his Dasein is "well grounded and has been sketched out beforehand in elemental ways."[56] Heidegger explains that Goethe's source of Care is contained in Hyginus's medieval remake in Latin of the argument between "care" [Cura] and Jupiter [Job] about what to name humankind, "spirit" or "earth." Saturn, the god of the Night, is called in to adjudicate the dispute and to deliver his solution: "Let it be called 'homo,' for it is made out of humus (earth) [homo vocetur, quia videtur esse factus ex humo]."[57] In footnote 5, Heidegger lists Goethe's source: an obscure scholar, a "K.Burdach" by name who wrote an article that had established Goethe's source. "Faust und Sorge." Deutsche Vierteljahress-chrift fur Literaturwissenschaft und Geistesgeschichte I (1923).[58] Heidegger thus turns Goethe, not himself, into a borrower. He cites Goethe's and not *his* own sources of information.[59]

Heidegger's other important moment of citation impropriety is the short shrift that he gives in *Sein und Zeit* to Kierkegaard's existentialist interpretation of the Moment of decision, of the orientation of one's flight and its authorship.[60] An especially revealing casualty of Heidegger's short-changing is Georg Simmel. For not only did Simmel write about Tolstoy in connection with the necessity to individualize and de-universalize the impersonality of unhappiness and grief, he also fastened the discussion of such processes on the example of Caius. Caius, of course, is the logical Everyman who helps Ivan Ilyich to determine that "he is not Caius, but Ivan Ilyich" and to commit the very disruptive operation with ontic logic with its refrain of comfort, "one dies," because "Caius dies" that interests Heidegger.[61]

On Simmel, Heidegger writes only this in footnote 6 of "How the Existential Analysis of Death Differs from Other Possible Interpretations of this Phenomenon" when he discusses the inability of the preceding ontologies of life to recognize its connection with death: "Recently G. Simmel has also explicitly related the phenomenon of death to the definition of 'life,' however without a clear separation of the biological and ontic from the ontological and existential problematic."[62] And he names precisely "Vier metaphysische Kapitel" (Four Metaphysical Chapters) in Simmel's book, *Lebensanschauung* (1918).[63]

But Heidegger also once confessed to Gadamer: "Simmel's Four Metaphysical Chapters were of fundamental significance for my introduction to philosophy." This must have been especially in relation to conceptions of death and temporality extracted, again, thanks to Tolstoy, in the projection of Dasein and its possibilities.[64]

In the fourth essay, "The Law of the Individual," Simmel relies on his earlier work on social differentiation (*Über soziale Differenzierung*, 1890), to suggest that shared beliefs result in the downfall of mental activity. This is of course the claim of Heidegger about the ruinance caused by the they:

> Thus Tolstoy observes in one passage: "all happy people are as such similar to one another"—as though there were ultimately only *one* happiness, which is also Kant's view—"but the unhappy are each unhappy in their special way." This can only hold if one confuses happiness with its typical causes with riches, social position, successes, "possession" of a beloved person; then it is admittedly something pretty much the same: these goods can be brought under a few very general and qualitatively ratable concepts. However, if one asks, not about the external causes of happiness, but rather about happiness itself, about its subjective actuality (Tatsächlichkeit), then it is just as individual and incomparable as life itself, whose momentary excitement and beauty it forms. Simply because suffering cannot be traced back to any such visible external causes— because it often consists only in a lack, in disappointment, a decline—it seems to flow more from the inner, specific essence of the individual than does the happiness that in actuality abides there to no less extent. To the contrary, happiness is for the most part something much more delicate, indefinable and dependent on the favorability of unusual combinations, that it strikes me in much greater measure as something special, individual, and so to speak accidental than does unhappiness, which can be brought about by much more frequent elements always existing, so to speak, in the air.[65]

Simmel takes issue with Kant's "universality of moral" that seems to him to have its root in a "typical tendency towards harmony of values."[66] For Simmel, there can be no ontic sameness within the most diverse life courses: "How may I conclude, from the mortality of all men and the manhood of Caius, that he too will die, for the former premise is only valid when I am already certain of the mortality of Caius?"[67] Simmel is not very knowledgeable about the details of Tolstoy's ontology, and he is making his analogy between Tolstoy and Caius taking the opening sentence of *Anna Karenina* for his cue. Still, the importance of a prompt to Heidegger in a book that spoke of humankind's relation to mortality and, for the most part, of its sacrifices to commonality is hard to overestimate.

Yet Heidegger's arguably most important source on Tolstoy is left unacknowledged altogether. His idea about the role of Tolstoy in the interpretation of Dasein must have been informed by Max Weber. In his renowned "Science as a Vocation," Weber spoke, as we all know, of the "disenchantment of the world," characterizing the times overwhelmed by rationalization and intellectualization on the one hand, and the retreat of the most sublime values "from public life into the transcendental" realm, on the other.[68] These are the times for the advance of a new savagery. It is not as readily remembered that Tolstoy's vision of death and its disappearance from the mortal eye of the modern human helped Weber steer his interpretation of the times.

The savage knows what he does in order to get his daily food and which institutions serve him in this pursuit. The increasing intellectualization and rationalization do *not,* therefore, indicate an increased and general knowledge of the conditions under which one lives. It means something else . . . intellectualization brings disenchantment. Do science and progress have any meanings that go beyond the purely practical and technical? You will find this question raised in the most principled form in the works of Leo Tolstoy. He came to raise the question in a peculiar way. All his broodings increasingly revolved around the problem of whether or not death is a meaningful phenomenon. And his answer was: for civilized man death has no meaning. It has none because the individual life of a civilized man, placed into an infinite "progress," according to its own imminent meaning should never come to an end; for there is always a further step ahead of one who stands in the march of progress. And no man who comes to die stands upon the peak which lies in infinity. Abraham or some peasant of the past, died "old and satiated with life" because he stood in the organic cycle of life; because his life, in terms of meaning and on the eve of his days, had given to him what life had to offer; because for him there remained no puzzles he might wish to solve; and therefore he could have had "enough" of life. Whereas civilized man, placed in the midst of the continuous enrichment of culture by ideas, knowledge, and problems, may become "tired of life" but not "satiated with life." He catches only the most minute part of what the life of the spirit brings forth anew, and what he seizes is always something provisional and not definitive, and therefore death for him is a meaningless occurrence. And because death is meaningless, civilized life as such is meaningless; by its very "progressiveness" it gives death the imprint of meaninglessness. Throughout his late novels one meets with this thought as the keynote of the Tolstoyan art.[69]

Tolstoy's *memento mori* allowed Weber to impress on his audience the idea of a unique value of each human finitude, caught as it is in the horrible slaughter of the war years, and losing individuality in the scientism and dehumanization of technology. Weber then switches the discussion to Tolstoy's rejection of progress and his rebellious "flight" into the future of history from the deadened past of a self-escheated culture: "What stand should one take? Has 'progress' as such a recognizable meaning that goes beyond the technical, so that to serve it is a meaningful vocation? The question must be raised. But this is no longer merely the question of man's calling for science, hence, the problem of what science as a vocation means to its devoted disciples."[70]

Most biographers of Heidegger agree on Weber's impact on the young Heidegger. According to Rüdiger Safranski, Heidegger was present at Weber's lecture in Munich in 1917.[71]

## THE GERMAN TOLSTOY DURING HEIDEGGER'S PHILOSOPHICAL FORMATION

Richard Wolin credits the staggering success of *Sein und Zeit,* which "fundamentally recast the terms of philosophical thought" to its no less impressive list of contributing influences: "Kierkegaard, Nietzsche, and Dilthey (not to mention literary sources as diverse as Tolstoy, Dostoevsky, and Rilke)."[72] The instructional power of the Russian classics on German youths of the turn of the century and the early twentieth century was hard to deny. In his memoir, the writer Klaus Mann, son of Thomas Mann, reminisced about family nights spent reading Tolstoy: "'Well, you'll find a place to sit somewhere,' Father said, confident and distraught. Whereupon he seated himself in the huge armchair, next to the floor-lamp. And then the great entertainment began. His favorites were the Russians. He read to us 'Cossacks' by Tolstoy and the strangely primitive, childlike parables of his latest period. . . . Sometimes he had to interrupt his lecture for a minute or so, all shaken and overwhelmed by his nervous delight."[73] The young Klaus was especially impressed with Tolstoy's obstinate urge to escape fame:

The imprisoned giants—but why don't they want to escape? [. . .] Small wonder that Tolstoy groans: he carries huge pieces of stone from one corner of the dingy room to the other, to punish himself. [. . .] Sometimes he falters and stands motionless for a minute, absorbed in prayers; looking like a very old Russian peasant, or a weather-worn piece of rock. "Let me be simple, my Lord!" mumbles the illustrious old man. "I abominate my fame, my talent, my work. I loathe literature. I disapprove of *Anna Karenina*. I don't want to be Homer. I want to be a peasant. Oh Lord! Let me do a peasant's useful, primitive work!" And he continues to carry the heavy stones.[74]

The theme of Tolstoy's existential flight was powerfully impressed upon the German philosophical imagination. Gustav Shpet, one of Husserl's favorite students before Heidegger, ends his phenomenological study *Iavlenie i smysl* ([Phenomenon and Meaning] 1914), on a paean to experience and expression, which would of course become Heidegger's key terms (*Erlebnis*, *Erfahrung*, and *Aussage*): "A flight from the world is thinkable only as a flight from that world which is familiar, from that life which we have lived through emotionally. Who has experienced nothing will gain nothing from an escape from the world. Life away from society in communion with nature and in the lonely company of one's thoughts cannot lead to a world any other than the one possessed by an animal."[75]

In the philosophical etudes written from 1916 to 1919, Shpet commented on Tolstoy's flight specifically in connection with the homelessness of philosophy. A philosopher has no dwelling: The greatest value of philosophy is its freedom.[76] It is in this sense that Shpet also uses Tolstoy's term, "reasonable consciousness" or *razumenie* by adding a vowel signifying the phenomenological way of making sense of it, *urazumenie*. From the same point of gaining understanding through flight, Shpet interprets Tolstoy's departure, which to Shpet is an example of an actualization of his ownmost humanity.[77]

Tolstoy's flight from home at age eighty-two and his death two weeks later at a provincial way station, Astapovo, was covered by media the world over and could not have passed unnoticed by a then twenty-one-year-old Heidegger. Tolstoy is discussed routinely in the German philosophical press in the years of Heidegger's tender youth and young adulthood. There was a strong strand of German scholarship that included him in the Schopenhauer school of thought and linked his philosophy of life to Wagner, Feuerbach, Eduard von Hartmann, Nietzsche, Paulsen, and Wundt. Another strand of thought strongly associated Tolstoy with Nietzsche. Notable here is Grot's essay on

Tolstoy and Nietzsche. Published originally in Russian in 1893, it appeared in a Berlin edition in German in 1898.[78] The basic difference between the two anarchist thinkers in Grot's interpretation is the question of their disobedience or obedience to the higher law. Nietzsche disobeyed it, but Tolstoy obeyed. And thus, for Nietzsche, more evil promised more good; but for Tolstoy, the decrease in evil expanded the realm of good.

Yet another version of Tolstoy was propagated in Germany: He was a Homer of our time. But he was not a happy Greek, happy in war and in love, at the feasts of life or in pursuance of arête, eunoia, and phronēsis. As Walter Benjamin put it in 1916, the happiness of the ancient man was over forever: "The agon—and this is a deep-rooted meaning of that institution—accords to each the measure of happiness which the gods have decreed for him. But, again, was there room here for the empty, idle innocence of the unknowing with which modern man conceals his happiness from himself?"[79]

On the question of Tolstoy's alleged Greekness, Georg Lukács's *Theory of the Novel* (1920) makes one of its central claims, namely that Tolstoy's novels are the only modern epics approximating the totality of Nature, but, fully aware of the dualism of modern life, they attempt to destroy institutions.[80] Tolstoy shows that nature is alive inside humankind but, when it is lived as culture; it reduces humankind to the lowest, most mindless, most idea-forsaken conventionality."[81] The third layer of reality reveals itself in Tolstoy's description of the *experiences of dying*: "At very rare, great moments—generally they are the moments of death—a reality reveals itself to man in which he suddenly glimpses and grasps the essence that rules over him and works within him, the meaning of life. His whole previous life vanishes into nothingness in the face of this experience."[82] "Going outside and beyond culture has merely destroyed culture but has not put a truer, more essential life in its place."[83] According to Lukács, no flight occurred; Tolstoy remained in the world he created, hard as he tried to take a flight from it.

And there was no flight of Tolstoy's into the future according to Oswald Spengler as well—even if this flight were to be regarded as a revolutionary act. The future belongs to the Russia of Dostoevsky, a saint akin to the "the Apostles of primitive Christianity," and not to Tolstoy, "a Petrine revolutionary."[84] Spengler added his regret that Goethe's age was over and lost to the occult version of Dostoevsky's Russia that proved irresistible. (Note that Dostoevsky was most surely associated with this irrationalism, not Tolstoy.) Thomas Mann's seminal "Goethe und Tolstoj" (1922) proposed to consider Goethe a winner over Tolstoy for Germany, a healthier and more necessary modern Greek, a universal man and a standard for culture. Germany had to choose between the two destinies opening up before it: "communistic" and "humanistic." Mann suggests that he is far from proposing "to dwell upon German fascism." To follow after Tolstoy would lead Germany into following a "folk-barbarian" future. And thus, instead of patterning herself "upon Tolstoy's pedagogic bolshevism," it should pattern itself on Goethe's "hedonism of the general humanistic ideal."[85]

But this was still an aestheticism about life, and Tolstoy was believed by many in Germany, most famously by Ernst Bloch (1918), to be its mystic and utopian.[86] Where was its truth? It could not be in the opposite, in the irrationalism and the shamanism of the occult associated in Germany most closely with Dostoevsky, or with Tolstoy, whose flight was never confused with bourgeois escapism. *Pace* Leo Lowenthal, "German bourgeois escapist literature" embraced Dostoevsky more gladly: "The reception of Dostoevsky's works illuminated significant idiosyncrasies of German society in a time of total crisis . . . infatuation with the so-called irrationalism of the artist; the alleged mystery in the life of the individual; the wallowing in the 'dark regions of the soul,' the glorification of criminal behavior—in short, indispensable elements that were later incorporated into the psychological transfiguration of violence by National Socialism."[87] The young Heidegger is not fond of irrationalism and the occult.[88] He is interested in medieval mysticism, which was flattened in Wilhelm Wundt's posthumous memoir, released just when the young Professor Heidegger was compiling his notes on the phenomenology of religious experience that he already was teaching at Freiburg.

In 1920, when a very old Wilhelm Wundt had at last died, his memoir with a very phenomenological-existential title, *Erlebtes und Erkanntes*, went to print. Its fifty chapters covering the period through 1886 supported the Germanic-nationalist ideal of existentialism. The book warned Germans about their hunt for external power and competition for material goods: Instead of applying themselves to attaining the goal of becoming the leading power among the cultural peoples, they were being unfaithful in their decadent self-isolation to the ideal of their predestined world state [*Weltstaat*].[89]

Lest we be happier with casting anchor in Schopenhauer's friendly harbor, also in 1920 Freud bypassed geopolitical matters and pressed, in "Beyond the Pleasure Principle," for a patient waiting in the disclosure of the mysteries of life and death that Wundt's generation had so thoroughly explored.[90] We did not succeed in disclosing the mystery of life's beginning: "The attributes of life were at some time evoked in inanimate matter by the action of a force of whose nature we can form no conception."[91] We can only say with certitude that life has a limit in the physical sense: "The fact that there is a fixed average duration of life at least among the higher animals naturally argues in favor of there being such a thing as death from natural causes."[92] Through our persistent decisionism rather than patient questioning, "we have unwittingly steered our course into the harbor of Schopenhauer's philosophy. For him death is the 'true result and to that extent the purpose of life,' while the sexual instinct is the embodiment of the will to live."[93] Moreover, in a final argument predicting the gloom of *Civilization and Its Discontent* for the 1930s, Freud warned that we must either "be patient and await fresh methods and occasions of research."[94] Or perhaps we should desist: "We must be ready, too, to abandon a path that we have followed for a time, if it seems to be leading to no good end."[95]

Heidegger's formative years display the impact of these influences and explain the trajectory of his developing ontology on the way to the Tolstoy footnote. Until 1933, he did not desist in his questioning of being. However, even his earliest works both explain what would lead him to the footnote as well as explain why he never again named Tolstoy in his work, either negatively or positively. And that was because he embraced Wundt's idea of Dasein as a Germanic *Weltstaat* over the rich humanistic and scientific signification of the term in the tradition of German culture, as used by Kant, Hölderlin, Hegel, Feuerbach (in his *hier und da*) and especially in its meaning of "enduring the hardships of Being [*die Schwere des Daseins zu ertragen*]" immortalized by Schiller.[96] As we have already witnessed from the examples in *Sein und Zeit*, in his ambitious aspiration for the role of the *Führer* of the philosophy of being, Heidegger is not too good about revealing the sources of the philosophical valuables he had borrowed. A good example here is Bergson, whom he only denies. It is true that he cannot agree with Bergson's concept of "duration" during the revision of and departure from the phenomenological approach of Husserl. But he owes a debt to Bergson's idea that only the fundamental self is free.[97]

What prevented Heidegger from pursuing Tolstoy further in the same fashion as he pursued the study of Kant, Hegel, Nietzsche, Schelling, pre-Socratics, and Hölderlin—to the advantages of steering his sinking Dasein in the times of the historical catastrophe and the three decades that he was to live after it—was his inability to come to terms with the other precepts on Tolstoy that he had heard from Weber. The first of Weber's lessons on Tolstoy that Heidegger did not take heed of is a deep-rooted sarcasm about the possibility of acquiring existential experience from petty university prophets who, "in their lecture rooms," are grievously unaware of the decisive state of affairs in the world: "The prophet for whom so many of our younger generation yearn simply does not exist."[98] That is, if "Tolstoy's question reccurs to you: as science does not, who is to answer the question: 'What shall we do, and, how shall we arrange our lives?' or, in the words used here tonight: 'Which of the warring gods should we serve? Or should we serve perhaps an entirely different god, and who is he?' Then one can say that only a prophet or a savior can give the answers."[99] The second precept on Tolstoy's wisdom not taken away by Heidegger from Weber is that even in our worst ascetic travails, we can be happy.[100]

In his early lecture courses, Heidegger is the closest to Weber and Tolstoy. Consider his "Introduction to the Phenomenology of Religion, Winter Semester 1920–1921"[101] in which Heidegger explores the connection between factical life and history: "The historical through the distancing from a particular, present, word-orienting standpoint opens the eyes to other life-forms and cultural ages."[102] The making factical of one's life experience may require "radical self-extradition" from culture, a flight.[103] The situation of Dasein enacts historical understanding, reveals its limits and diversity. In the summer semester 1921, he explores Augustinian "curare," the "Being Concerned" as the basic character of factical life. "What am I?" asks Heidegger in his reflections on Augustine. "I have become a question to myself. What do I love?"[104] "The human being is placed before a decision" and his anxiety in the early Heidegger is caused by his inability to choose between sin or virtue.[105] The "living unity of sense of living being," he cannot do without the sense-structure of consciousness as "historical," "the requirement of . . . the specific worldliness of the sphere of experience concerned as a religious one."[106] The phenomenological experience of "having-become" (*Gewordensein*), the idea of "Having-become-from-elsewhere" is, therefore, no characterization of the "I" as opposed to the consciousness of fulfilled moment. The pure "I" is rather the possibility (not logical, but vocational) of "the being-historical of a fulfilled consciousness."[107] In these evocations of the spiritual "possibility" of living consciousness, Heidegger is the closest to Tolstoy (and Weber). But a departure is beginning already in his concern for the "greekanizing of the Christian life-consciousness," sounded in *Phenomenological Interpretation of Aristotle: Initiation into Phenomenological Research* delivered in 1921 to 1922 at Freiburg.[108] Under the influence of his Nietzsche, of "being alive in life itself,"[109] he is swayed by the easiness of Aristotle who suggests looking up to the universals and moving away from oneself. Heidegger decides that this would lead one toward decline, toward irremediable guilt, into a carefree eudemonic haziness.[110] It is here that he posits Angst and Care as his permanent requirements. The Johannine and Augustinian "lux lucet" are also rejected: They are the "light of something that does not shine."[111] Careful thought is not an empathetic thought, but the thought filled with existential Care, the thought of the "relucent": To become factical, life looks away from itself.[112]

Following his transfer to Marburg, Heidegger explores the possibilities of preaching his emerging version of phenomenology to the initiated from the academic podium. Like Nietzsche before him and Weber himself, he sees severe limits. Research is questioning, but the circumstances of ex cathedra lecturing are not a good point of access as long as the evils of cowardice, docility, and convenience that govern the behavior of salaried professors remain in force. Genuine skepticism or apophatic modesty do not attract him. In *Introduction to Phenomenological Research* read at Marburg, 1923 to 1924, Heidegger chooses pheugo over logos: "I am genuinely free if I go towards what I understand," but "res cogitans" owes its birth to traditional ontology because "there is no securing truth in a simple relation to the already known."[113] It is here that Heidegger elaborates the conditions of the "gloomy flight," the flight that eschews flying toward light and the definitiveness of truth: "The structure of being of existence lies in the structure of distorting. We intend to do this by conceiving more incisively what can be gathered from the specific movement of being as being-on-the-run from [*Auf-der-Flucht-sein*, "taking flight in the face of"] itself [. . .] existence's being (in the sense of the manner of being of care about certainty) flees in the face of itself with respect to being known, with respect to its being interpreted. Being in the sense of *being-in-a-world* means *being-uncovered*, standing *visibly* in a world. It is in the face of uncoveredness of existence that *care takes flight*."[114]

But fly he does not. The most lamentable result of his disobedience to Weber is an attempt to create, out of these insights, a sacerdotal aura of a preacher, a new shepherd of Being. We know too well how this ends, in the secular Nazified branch of onto-theology that, as Lyotard points out, "completely miss[es] the intelligence of the Kantian ethics,"[115] and, as Derrida points out, avoids all that is ethically spiritual, and the word "spirit" itself.[116] Heidegger's Hegel lecture course in 1934–1935 is a scandal of the misuse of spirit placed in the service of the *Führerstaat*, and a sacrifice of philosophy's autonomy of questioning.[117] Martin Heidegger, the Nazi-appointed Rector of Freiburg in 1933, is someone, Lyotard reminds us, for whom "the questioning of being becomes a conversation on the 'destiny' of historico-spiritual people."[118] Unsurprisingly, the Fichte of 1933[119] unfolds a threefold mission of the National Socialism–led Bildung, in which learning (or knowledge) trails behind at a distant third position after military service and labor.[120] Heidegger's evasive attempts at rectification are well known. When pressed on the "three services" in an interview with *Der Spiegel* (1966), he retorted, "If you read carefully, you see that although 'Knowledge Service' is third in order, it's first in significance. But you have to be aware that Work and Defense, like all human actions, are grounded in and illuminated by knowledge."[121]

His thought capitulated not only to "a God" of technology to which he accorded the mystic power that moves us and that effectively "ends" philosophy, but also to the unreflective primitiveness of plant life. He leads us back down the ladder of Aristotelian plant-animal-rational animal. *Gelassenheit* (1959) is a great invitation to "keep meditative thinking alive." The trick is to "strike new roots" in the process of the releasement into the soil of the open. And he directs attention to "the truth of what Johann Peter Hebel says should be renewed: We are plants which—whether we like to admit it to ourselves or not—must with our roots rise out of the earth in order to bloom in the ether and to bear fruit."[122] Reverting progress back to plant life as a solution to redeeming human nature is capitulation. No wonder Heidegger's name never once is mentioned in Hannah Arendt's *The Human Condition*. Tolstoy's "The Root of All Evil [*Koren' zla*]" (1898) is a vivid counterpart to this withdrawal. Our calamitous situation will continue, he writes in this protest against an unthinking submission and tolerant plantlike existence, if we do not uproot the source of evil: injustice, exploitation, inactivity.[123]

The solidity of one's position is tested in whether or not one is willing to recant. In 1889, the year of Heidegger's birth, Tolstoy started writing *Resurrection*, his last long novel. Its early chapters contain scenes in a prison chapel where convicts are forced to take communion and pledge allegiance to the crown before their sentencing, to bow to the icons of the Mother of God and of Christ the Judge. These scenes, expurgated from all published editions of the book before 1917, were an official pretext for Tolstoy's excommunication from the Russian Orthodox Church by the decree of the Holy Synod of Russia in 1901. Tolstoy refused to recant and said this in his public statement about the decree:

> What I believe is this: I believe in God, whom I understand as spirit, and in Love as the beginning of everything. I believe that He is within me and I am within Him. I believe that the will of God is most clearly and understandably expressed in the teachings of the man called Christ, but I consider it the greatest of blasphemies to look on this man as God and to pray to Him. [. . .] Whether or not these beliefs of mine offend, grieve or tempt anyone, whether or not anyone dislikes them or finds them a hindrance, I am no more able to change them than I am able to change my own body. [. . .] Truth corresponds for me to Christianity as I understand it. And I hold to this Christianity; and in so far as I hold to it I live calmly and joyfully, and calmly and joyfully approach my death.[124]

Neither Heidegger's "Letter on Humanism" nor the stony gaze he gave to Bultmann nor his silence to Marcuse in response to exhortations to call himself to account can cover up his evasiveness of the matter. This is not a principled refusal to recant as the one witnessed above. Even the less ominous questions in his *Ponderings* about being and whether to spell it "sein" or "seyn" lose their charm after 1933, and especially during and after the Holocaust and Nuremberg.[125]

Tolstoy's ontology, in contrast, spells humanism and a nonviolent defense of fundamental human rights. He repudiates the state and all encroachments on the autonomy of the individual to choose and decide. He hates dictators and "leaders" of all stripe and is ashamed if he might ever have seen himself in such a role even in a bad dream. Tolstoy adheres to Kant's "second question," "What should we do?" and lives by the light of the Johannine logos, which he translates as *razumenie*, or "reasonable consciousness," a form of practical phenomenology exercised on earth for we are *sent* into the world to expand the sphere of good rather than thrown there to writhe in the boredoms of our *Angst.*

Even the graphs that they would sketch of being from time to time are completely dissimilar. In Heidegger, Being and Man are always forked sideways or crossed through (dispatched) in his fourfold structures.[126] In Tolstoy, Being and Man form parallel lines, where one existential sequence is continuous with another. So are Tolstoy and Heidegger comparable at all?

## THE SACERDOTAL AND THE ANECDOTAL: THE TALE OF THE TWO ONTOLOGIES AND THEIR CRITICS

On the sacerdotal yet ironic note of Weber's unheeded warning we proceed to the conclusion of this long investigation. It is true that Tolstoy's and Heidegger's questions about being and their questioning of being sounded in tune, at least in the earlier Heidegger. Although Heidegger does not notice that Ivan's is a flight toward light, Heidegger's footnote pays tribute to Ivan's "gloomy flight" away from falling prey, from the grip of Care. The theme of a flight into the freedom of authenticity away from the ontic falsehood of "the they" per se and in defiance of Aristotelian logic is one strong point of connection between the younger Heidegger and Tolstoy.

Their second point of connection is a dissatisfaction with the modern state of philosophy, which prompts Heidegger to revamp the tradition of the nineteenth century and to revise the philosophy of his teachers, Husserl and Scheler. We are ourselves the entities to be analyzed since the essence of Dasein lies in its existence, as the beginning sections of *Sein und Zeit* so refreshingly and memorably declaim. Tolstoy formulated the existential burden of explaining our situation and action in a comparable way in "What is Religion and In What Consists Its Essence": "Philosophy should make itself liable to one question: What shall I do?"[127] But even when it did so on rare occasions through the effort of Spinoza, Rousseau, Kant, and Schopenhauer, their answers came in admixed with useless professorial prattle. Since Hegel, the question is replaced with "What is?" and in this manner it develops in all evolutionary theories. The "boyish posturing of a half-mad Nietzsche" in the latest stage has nothing integral or significant to say except for fragmentary asides and immoral ditties lacking in substance.[128] Heidegger would not quite agree to the latter part, but Tolstoy has an excuse of an ongoing questioning. His notebook of November 1900 states: "Any philosophy is a teaching about what to do. Nietzsche."[129]

The third point of connection between Tolstoy and Heidegger is their fondness for their own nontraditional, philosophical idiom. Rich in neologisms, the use of parables and poetry, and live imagery, it is a creation of what Richard Rorty called "conversational philosophy."[130] In this regard, Heidegger was drawn to Nietzsche, whose parables he discusses frequently and with admiration in his Nietzsche course cycle (1938 to 1940) and in his lectures, commentary, and assignments to students on *Untimely Meditations*. Despite his criticism of Nietzsche's ethics, Tolstoy includes heavily edited selections from Nietzsche's *Thus Spoke Zarathustra,* on account of their stylistic brilliance, for a weekly assignment in *The Cycle of Reading*, his late-career collection of aphorisms.

The fourth point of coincidence between Tolstoy and Heidegger is their caution against humankind's increasing overdependence on technology accompanied by the desecration of the earth.

The fifth point on which they agree is an utter impossibility to live or exist without a stance toward being, whether one hopes to find meaning in it or not.

The devil is in the details. Even a gentle fleshing out of these agreements yields more disagreements than can be meaningfully explained in a single chapter. I will therefore make recourse to several powerful critiques that respond to the problems I have already raised. Karl Löwith thinks that Tolstoy and Heidegger are rather similar examples of "an unequivocally nihilistic occurrence, namely the destining of Being that 'the suprasensible world, the Ideas, God, the moral law, the authority of reason, progress, the happiness of the many, culture, civilization, and their formative energy forfeit and become null.'"[131] Löwith quotes a lengthy passage from an unidentified text by Tolstoy: "In 1910, in the last year of his life, Tolstoy wrote the following radical critique of European civilization, which according to him is now corrupting not only Europe but also Africans, the Indians, the Chinese, and the Japanese." This text decries the telegraphs and the machines, railroad transportation, university diplomas and hairdressers, all these token sides of so-called civilization that cover up the betrayal of "what is most important in their lives, [. . .] an understanding of life itself, [. . .]

religion."[132] The text in question is Tolstoy's *On Insanity* (*O bezumii*),[133] which is no mere refutation of civilization, but an attack on pessimism, suicide, asylums, prisons, capital punishment, colonial oppression, and militarism. This text explains that to make our being healthy again, we need to keep the advance of civilization in step with basic human needs, the basic conditions of their happiness, the basic condition of their reasonable consciousness. If the theme sounds familiar, it should be: *On Insanity* is none other than a completion of the drafts of "The Address [*Vozzvanie*]" that Tolstoy started in the year of Heidegger's birth. He also completed *Carthago delenda est* in 1898, one of his most famous antimilitarist texts, published widely in many languages as soon as it was completed. But an interim version, drafted in 1896, contained a comparison of Russian and German militarism and decided the former was worse: It emboldened men wearing uniforms and carrying arms to conduct or perpetrate Jewish pogroms.

Georg Lukács makes only an indirect comparison between Tolstoy and Heidegger, but at around the same time, in 1937. He displays a greater sense of historical sensitivity than Löwith as to the difference between the two. Lukács thinks that a historical "calling to account" is portrayed "most epically . . . in Tolstoy's short story masterpiece, 'The Death of Ivan Ilyich,'" to which no "imperialist decadence" can offer a match in the intensity of its historical sense.[134] Heidegger's "epistemological hocus-pocus with Being and Dasein," on the other hand, is said to be "no more than the ideology of saddest philistinism, of fear and trembling, of anxiety," in "the crisis period of imperialism" of which Spengler also is a symptom, and in which real history is disparaged as "inauthentic."[135] So thinks Hannah Arendt in her diary entries, her *Denkentagebuch* of 1953, in an observation known as "Heidegger the Fox." In her bitterly playful description, having no sensitivity whatsoever for the historical traps on the ground of real life, her teacher-fox missed the real meaning of all the wounds on his tattered fur. No, he preferred to stay trapped in his burrow, luring others in: "Come here, everyone: this is a trap, the most beautiful trap in the world."[136] She continues, "Everyone except our fox could, of course, step out of it again. It was cut, literally, to his own measurement. But the fox who lived in the trap said proudly: 'So many are visiting me in my trap that I have become the best of all foxes.' And there is some truth in that, too. Nobody knows the nature of traps better than one who sits in a trap his whole life long."[137] Two years later, Arendt finds in the "melancholy haphazardness" of Heidegger's temporalizing of Dasein "perplexities" posed by the "vita activa." Heidegger's temporality could never really reconcile itself with the demands of reality, as Hegel would have it; he simply capitulated.[138]

There is a difference between this fox and Isaiah Berlin's presentation of Tolstoy in the double image of a fox and a hedgehog. For according to Berlin, Tolstoy the fox knew every single thing in the world and about the world, but pretended to know only one, his moral-didactic dicta about life. Berlin finds a problem with this posturing, seeing in it a potential totalitarian threat to liberal democracy.[139]

Emmanuel Levinas finds nothing comic in Heidegger's Dasein: It is bound by a bond of anxious care only to itself: "Heidegger's sociality is completely found in the solitary subject. The analysis of Dasein, in its authentic form, is carried out in terms of solitude" and Heidegger's "situation" is not a situation of an ethical "face-to-face."[140] Levinas praises Tolstoy for depriving the "I die" of its grave seriousness, for maintaining its expression in the moods of the tragicomic: "No doubt nothing is more comical than the concern that a being has for an existence it could not save from its destruction, as in Tolstoy's tale where an order for enough boots for twenty-five years is sent by one that will die the very evening he gives his order. That is indeed as absurd as questioning, in view of action, the starts whose verdict would be without appeal. But through this image one sees that the comical is also tragic, and that it belongs to the same man to be a tragic and a comical personage."[141] His example is not *DII*, but "What Do Men Live By? [Chem liudi zhivy?]" (1885). However, one can find similar and even more numerous comic notes in Tolstoy's novella, not to mention his other parable on death of the same period, "How Much Land Does a Man Need?" (1885).[142]

In a similarly open-minded fashion Tolstoy and Heidegger stand to be compared in Vladimir Bibikhin's lectures and writings of the late 1980s and the early 1990s. Bibikhin thinks that Tolstoy's is a vivid example of "practical phenomenology [prakticheskaia fenomenologiia]."[143] He takes one of Tolstoy's forest walks (October 11, 1906) and observes that in the sequence "thought-word-deed" Tolstoy does not even notice that he commits an immediate substitution. "It happens by itself," and Tolstoy is fine with letting them occur in the order they occur, without privileging one over another.[144] Tolstoy's phenomenological triptych uncovered by Bibikhin is certainly comparable to Heidegger's

"Building-Dwelling-Thinking," but here the sequence is strict and irreversible. This is because Heidegger's approach to the clarification of the existential situation is by "grabbing it" (*greifen*) and enclosing it into a concept (*Begriff*), Bibikhin claims.[145] We are reminded of the example of ownership of being through history in a similar metaphor used by Heidegger in *Sein und Zeit* and of the refusal of Tolstoy to "grab" and "destroy" in his variants of *Carthago*.

There is on the frontispiece of one of the first appearances of the documents associated with the Heidegger controversy—the American edition of Heidegger's writings and speeches of the years of the rectorate—an epigraph from "Count Leo Tolstoy": "There is a yellowish grey wolf, who, winters, joins the pack, roaming the icy tundras of Siberia, sparing neither man, animal, nor child. In the heat of the summer, however, when the brush is dry and lifeless, he crawls into the peasant's backyard, licking his hands, whining for food. Such is the nature of man and the brevity of memory that the peasant feeds the bloody tooth of this rapacious beast."[146] This is a fake quote, a remnant of war propaganda rhetoric. It is tempting to think that the rectorate and Nazi-party membership were the fake periods of Heidegger's philosophy. Although the quote is a fake too, Tolstoy, like no other companion, may afford the clarity necessary to separate the authentic from the inauthentic within Heidegger's thought projects and philosophy—just as the footnote itself may have helped Heidegger to separate potentials of the authentic from the inauthentic types of dying in his thinking and building and being.

## NOTES

1. L. N. Tolstoy, *Polnoe sobranie sochinenii L. N. Tolstogo,* vol. 50, ed. V. G. Chertkov et al. (Moscow: Izdatelstvo Khudozhestvennaia literatura, 1928–1958), 5. All translations into English from this edition are mine.

2. All dates in Tolstoy's diary are from the Julian calendar used in Russia until 1918. September 14, 1889, Julian-style, corresponds to Heidegger's birthday on September 26, Gregorian-style.

3. Tolstoy, *Polnoe sobranie sochinenii,* vol. 50, 142–43.

4. Ibid., 143.

5. Ibid., 144.

6. Ibid., 194.

7. Ibid., 20–21.

8. Ibid., 21.

9. I cover Grot's participation in Tolstoy's life since 1885 in Inessa Medzhibovskaya, *Tolstoy and the Religious Culture of His Time: A Biography of a Long Conversion* (Lanham, MD: Lexington Books, 2008).

10. Tolstoy, *Polnoe sobranie sochinenii*, vol. 50, 172–73.

11. Tolstoy, *Polnoe sobranie sochinenii*, vol. 26, 366.

12. I discuss the connection in detail in Inessa Medzhibovskaya, "Introduction: Tolstoy's *On Life* and Its Times," in *Tolstoy's* On Life *and Its Times*, ed. Inessa Medzhibovskaya with a new translation of the text of *On Life* co-translated with Michael Denner (Evanston, IL: Northwestern University Press, forthcoming).

13. Johann Wolfgang von Goethe, *The Sorrows of Young Werther*, trans. Burton Pike (New York: Modern Library, 2005), 60.

14. See notebook 14 [174] in Friedrich Nietzsche, *Writings from the Late Notebooks*, ed. Rüdiger Bittner, trans. Kate Sturge (Cambridge: Cambridge University Press, 2003), 264–65.

15. These drafts of 1889–1891 are the beginnings of the future *What Is Art?* and they are first taking shape in a sketch "Ob iskusstve" [On Art; 1889; 30: 213–15 (30: 225)].

16. Tolstoy, *Polnoe sobranie sochinenii*, vol. 27, 534.

17. Ibid., 534–35. Tolstoy was dissatisfied with what he wrote and decided to revisit the analogy later. See the concluding part of this chapter.

18. Ibid., 531.

19. Ibid., 533.

20. Heidegger writes these questions in a column. These are his October 1931 "Intimations x Ponderings (II) and Directives," in Martin Heidegger, *Ponderings II–VI: Black Notebooks 1931–1938*, trans. Richard Rojcewicz (Bloomington, IN: Indiana University Press, 2016), 5.

21. As Jeff Love aptly remarks, "Heidegger's *Black Notebooks* open with the following questions: 'What should we do? Who are we? Why should we be? What is a being? Why does being happen?' . . . There is in these questions as well as in the tentative, experimental structure of the *Black Notebooks* strong similarities with Tolstoy's diaries. And, since the *Black Notebooks* are in a sense philosophical diaries, an unconventional format mixing politics, history, philosophy, they not only show a remarkable similarity, but seem to pursue something akin to . . . Tolstoy: a new medium in which the seeking is more important than the goal." Jeff Love, "Nominalist Tolstoy?" *Tolstoy Studies Journal* 27 (2015): 94–95.

22. Here is one good translation: "L. N. Tolstoy in his story 'The Death of Ivan Il'ich' has portrayed the phenomenon of the disruption and collapse of this 'one dies.'" Martin Heidegger, *Being and Time*, trans. Joan Stambaugh (Albany: State University of New York Press, 1996), 409.

23. To avoid confusion, I will henceforth abbreviate the long title of Tolstoy's novella to *DII*. Ivan Ilyich will continue to be a reference to the title character of Tolstoy's work.

24. Elisabeth Feist Hirsch, "The Problem of Speech in 'Being and Time,'" in *Heidegger's Existential Analytic*, ed. F. Ellinston (The Hague: Mouton Publishers, 1978), 159–78.

25. Ibid., 171.

26. Alan Pratt, "A Note on Heidegger's Death Analytic. The Tolstoyian Correlative," *Analectica Husserliana* 38 (1992): 297–304.

27. Robert Bernasconi, "Literary Attestation in Philosophy: Heidegger's Footnote on Tolstoy's 'The Death of Ivan Ilyich,'" in *Philosophers' Poets,* ed. David Wood (London and New York: Routledge, 1990), 7.

28. Ibid., 19.

29. Ibid., 31.

30. Natalie Repin, "Being-Toward-Death in Tolstoy's *The Death of Ivan Il'ich*: Tolstoy and Heidegger," *Canadian-American Slavic Studies* 36, nos. 1–2 (2002): 101.

31. Ibid., 131–32.

32. A. G. Zavalyi, "Kategoriia smerti u Tolstogo i Heidegger'a," in *Lev Tolstoy i Vremia,* ed. N.A. Amel'ianchik (Tomsk: Izdatelstvo TGU/Ivan Morozov, 2010), 210–20. Translation of the Russian is mine.

33. Ibid., 211–13.

34. Ibid., 215.

35. William Irwin, "Death by Inauthenticity: Heidegger's Debt to Ivan Il'ich's Fall," *Tolstoy Studies Journal* 25 (2013): 15.

36. Ibid., 21.

37. Michael Gelven, *A Commentary on Heidegger's* Being and Time, revised edition (DeKalb, IL: Northern Illinois University Press, 1989); and Stephen Mulhall, *Routledge Philosophy Guidebook to Heidegger and Being and Time,* second edition (London and New York: Routledge, 1996/2005).

38. Gelven, *A Commentary*, 141.

39. A. C. Grayling, *Wittgenstein. A Very Short Introduction* (New York: Oxford University Press, 1988/2001), 8.

40. Martin Heidegger, *Being and Time,* a revised edition of the Stambaugh translation, trans. Joan Stambaugh, revised and with a foreword by Dennis J. Schmidt (Albany, NY: SUNY Press, 2010), 242.

41. Ibid., 243.

42. Ibid., 244.

43. Ibid., 243–44.

44. Ibid., 244.

45. Emphasis in bold is mine to distinguish it from Heidegger's emphasis in italics.

46. Ibid., 245.

47. The German *Verfremdung* is a cultural borrowing, a derivative of Victor Shklovsky's term *ostranenie* ("defamiliarization") coined in 1916–1917.

48. It should be noted that "Being toward death" and "thinking about death" are not the same and one does not obligate the other.

49. [Fn. 13; cf., with regard to this methodological possibility, what was said about the analysis of anxiety, par 40,] Ibid., 244–45.

50. "Die Allegorisierung der Physis kann nur an der Leiche sich energisch durchsetzen." Walter Benjamin, *Urpsrung des deutschen Trauerspiels*, ed. Rolf Tiedemann (Frankfurt am Main: Suhrkamp, 1974), 193.

51. The famous and enigmatic beginning of chapter 2 in *DII*. It is here that we get to know Ivan Ilyich after we have seen his corpse and have been to his wake and before his "falls" ill and "flies" to light through dying.

52. Heidegger, *Being and Time* (2010), 370.

53. Ibid., 369.

54. Ibid., 366.

55. Johann Wolfgang von Goethe, *Faust I and II*, in *Goethe: The Collected Works*, vol. 2, ed. and trans. Stuart Atkins (Princeton, NJ: Princeton University Press, 1984): 287–88; lines 11,445–50; 11,457–59.

56. Heidegger, *Being and Time* (2010), 190–91.

57. Ibid.

58. Ibid.

59. Immediately afterward, without quoting the scenes in Goethe's *Faust* proper, Heidegger cites in the next footnote (number 6) "Das Kind der Sorge," a poem written by Goethe's teacher, Johann Gottfried Herder. Goethe is invoked next within the context of Heidegger's dispute with Ranke and Kant about time. He takes Ranke's cue that scientific history derives knowledge "from hidden sources," and is part of the autochtonic questioning of Dasein (ibid., 381). And again, Heidegger does not quote *Faust* directly, but paraphrases Dilthey on the question of the same ongoing dispute between Nature and Spirit (ibid., 381). In the same fashion, Heidegger makes passim references to Homer, Aristotle, Kierkegaard, Nietzsche, and Simmel.

60. When Kierkegaard speaks of "temporality," he means human being's being-in-time. Time as within-time-ness knows only the now, but never a moment. But if the moment is experienced existentially, a more primordial temporality is presupposed, although existentially inexplicit. In relation to the "Moment," cf. Karl Jaspers, *Psychologie der Weltanschauungen*, third edition (Berlin: Julius Springer, 1925), 108ff. and the "referat Kierkegaards," 419–32; Heidegger, *Being and Time* (2010), 323. On the important relationship of Kierkegaard to Tolstoy's portrayal of Ivan's flight, see Medzhibovskaya, *Tolstoy and the Religious Culture*, 321–23.

61. A lengthy discussion of this connection with the use of J. G. C. C. Kiesewetter's and Kantian books on logic is found in chapter 11 of Medzhibovskaya, *Tolstoy and the Religious Culture,* 295–332.

62. Heidegger, *Being and Time* (2010), 239. The other two mentions of Simmel in the book are similarly unappreciative brief comments about his failure to establish an existential theory of historicity. Heidegger, *Being and Time* (2010), 375, where history is "an object of a science," and in II–VI, 80, in the section "Time Taken Care of and Within-Timeness" where Simmel's work is named only to prompt that his work on "the connections between historical numeration, astronomically calculated world time, and the temporality and historicity of Dasein need further investigation"; Heidegger, *Being and Time* (2010), 418.

63. Ibid.

64. Hans-Georg Gadamer, "Erinnerungen an Heideggers Anfänge," *Dilthey-Jahrbuch* 4 (1986/1987): 13–26. Donald N. Levine and Daniel Silver, "Introduction," in Georg Simmel, *The View of Life,* trans. John Andrews and Donald N. Levine (Chicago: University of Chicago Press, 2010), xxvi.

65. Simmel, *The View of Life,* 116.

66. Ibid.

67. Ibid.

68. Weber's "Science as a Vocation" was a lecture initially given by him in 1917 at Munich University. Max Weber, *From Max Weber: Essays in Sociology,* trans. and ed. H. H. Gerth and C. Wright Mills (New York: Oxford University Press, 1946), 155.

69. Ibid., 139–40.

70. Ibid., 140.

71. Rüdiger Safranski, *Martin Heidegger Between Good and Evil,* trans. Ewald Osers (Cambridge, MA: Harvard University Press, 1998), 90.

72. Richard Wolin, *Heidegger's Children. Hannah Arendt, Karl Löwith, Hans Jonas, and Herbert Marcuse* (Princeton, NJ: Princeton University Press, 2001), 16.

73. Klaus Mann, *The Turning Point: The Autobiography of Klaus Mann* (New York: Markus Wiener Publishing, 1984), 57.

74. Ibid., 222.

75. G. G. Shpet, *Iavlenie i Smysl. Fenomenologiia kak osnovnaia nauka i ee problem* (Tomsk: Vodolei, 1996), 178.

76. G. G. Shpet, *Filosofskie etiudy,* ed. A. A. Iakovlev (Moscow: Progress, 1994), 177.

77. Ibid., 335.

78. The German translation of N. Grot's *Nietzsche und Tolstoi,* trans. Alexis Markow (Berlin: Hugo Stenitz Verlag, 1898) was based on N. Ia. Grot,

*Nravstvennye idealy nashego vremeni: Friedrich Nietzsche i Lev Tolstoy.* Voprosy filossofii i psikhologii pod red professor N. Ia. Grota, fourth year, book 16, January 1893 (Moscow: Kushnerev and Co, 1893), 129–54.

79. Walter Benjamin, "The Happiness of Ancient Man," in *Walter Benjamin, Early Writings.* 1910–1917, trans. Howard Eiland et al. (Cambridge, MA: Harvard University Press, 2011), 230.

80. Georg Lukács, *The Theory of the Novel: A Historico-Philosophical Essay on the Forms of Great Epic Literature,* trans. Anna Bostock (Cambridge, MA: MIT Press, 1971), 144.

81. Ibid., 148.

82. Ibid., 149.

83. Ibid., 151.

84. Oswald Spengler. *The Decline of the West,* trans. Charles Francis Atkinson, ed. Helmut Werner (New York: Vintage Books, 2006), 81, 273–74.

85. Thomas Mann, *Goethe und Tolstoi: Vortrag, zum ersten Mal gehalten September 1921 anläßlich der Nordischen Woche zu Lübeck* (Aachen: Verlag "Die Kuppel," Spiertz, 1923). I am quoting from the English translation of this text, "Goethe and Tolstoy," in *Thomas Mann, Three Essays,* trans. H. T. Lowe-Porter (New York: Knopf, 1929), 134–36.

86. Ernst Bloch, *Geist der Utopie.* I am making references to the English translation: Ernst Bloch, *The Spirit of Utopia,* ed. and trans. Anthony A. Nassar (Stanford, CA: Stanford University Press, 2000), 245, 298.

87. Leo Lowenthal, *Critical Theory and Frankfurt Theorists. Lectures-Correspondence-Conversations* (New Brunswick, NJ, and Oxford: Transaction Publishers, 1989), 120–21.

88. As Heidegger put it in *Sein und Zeit,* "When irrationalism, as the counterplay of rationalism, talks about the things to which rationalism is blind, it does so only with a squint." Heidegger, *Being and Time* trans. John Macquarrie and Edward Robinson (New York: Harper and Row, 1962), 136.

89. Wilhelm Wundt, *Erlebtes und Erkanntes* (Stuttgart: A. Kröner, 1920), 390.

90. Sigmund Freud, "Beyond the Pleasure Principle," in Sigmund Freud, *The Essentials of Psycho-Analysis,* trans. James Strachey (London: Vintage Books, 2005), 197–217; 218–68.

91. Ibid., 246.

92. Ibid., 251.

93. Ibid., 256.

94. Ibid., 268.

95. Ibid.

96. This phrase from act 1, scene 8 of Schiller's "Die Braut von Messina" is mentioned by Freud ("Beyond the Pleasure Principle," 251). Because Freud mentions Fechner in this essay, he must also have in mind Fechner's famously mischievous book, Gustave Theodor Fechner, *Das Büchlein vom Leben nach*

*dem Tode* (1836; sixth edition, 1906). In it Dasein reappears multiply and in many variations such as "künftiges Dasein," "Jetziges Dasein," "Das neue Dasein," "Ganzes Dasein," "Wurzel alles Daseins," "Anknüpfungspunkte ihres Daseins," "Nun greifen aber alle Daseinskreise, welche das Leben der jenseitigen Gesichter tragen," and so on. Plagiarism it is not, perhaps, but arrogant pride in claiming a discovery already made.

97. Henri Bergson, *Time and Free Will: An Essay on the Immediate Data of Consciousness,* trans. F. L. Pogson (Mineola, NY: Dover Publications, 1913/2001), 231–32. Translated from the original *Essai sur les données immédiates de la conscience* (1889).

98. Weber, *From Max Weber,* 152–53.

99. Ibid.

100. See Weber's "Religious Rejections of the World and Their Directions" in which Weber speaks of a "naïve enthusiasm for the diffusion of happiness" so ubiquiitous in Tolstoy's early work that can be found in its ascetic counterpart in his later work and thought (ibid., 348–49).

101. Martin Heidegger, *The Phenomenology of Religious Life,* trans. Matthias Frisch and Jennifer Anna Gosetti-Ferencei (Bloomington, IN: Indiana University Press, 2010), 3–111.

102. Ibid., 25–26.

103. Ibid., 28–30.

104. Ibid., 183.

105. Ibid., 210.

106. Ibid., 246.

107. Ibid., 251.

108. Martin Heidegger, *Phenomenological Interpretation of Aristotle: Initiation into Phenomenological Research,* trans. Richard Rojcewicz (Bloomington, IN: Indiana University Press, 2008), 6.

109. Ibid., 65.

110. Ibid., 81.

111. Ibid., 56.

112. Ibid., 96. See Heidegger's rumination on the "care-full deliberation" in his appendix to *Phenomenological Interpretation,* 139.

113. Martin Heidegger, *Introduction to Phenomenological Research,* ed. and trans. Daniel O. Dahlstrom (Bloomington, IN: Indiana University Press, 2005), 85–88; 111.

114. Ibid., 218.

115. Jean-Francois Lyotard, *Heidegger and "the Jews,"* trans. Andreas Michel and Mark Roberts (Minneapolis: University of Minnesota Press, 1990), 84.

116. Jacques Derrida, *Of Spirit: Heidegger and the Question,* trans. Geoffrey Bennington and Rachel Bowlby (Chicago and London: University of Chicago Press, 1987).

117. As Susanna Lindberg observes, "Führerprinzip is contrary to Heidegger's own thinking of being because it makes questioning impossible." See "Hegel in 1933," in Martin Heidegger, *On Hegel's Philosophy of Right. The 1934–1935 Seminar and Interpretive Essays*, trans. Andrew J. Mitchell, eds. Peter Trawny, Marcia Sa Cavalcante Schuback, and Michael Marder (New York: Bloomsbury, 2014), 30. In the same volume, see also an illuminating essay by Richard Polt, "Self-Assertion as Founding," 67–82.

118. Jean-François Lyotard, *The Postmodern Condition: A Report on Knowledge*, trans. Geoff Bennington and Brian Massini (Minneapolis: University of Minnesota Press, 1984), 37.

119. I mean Fichte's speeches to the German nation during the Napoleonic Wars in 1813. Johann Gottlieb Fichte, *Addresses to the German Nation*, ed. Gregory Moore (Cambridge: Cambridge University Press, 2008).

120. See Martin Heidegger, *German Existentialism,* trans. Dagobert D. Runes (New York: Wisdom Library, 1965), 13–19.

121. Martin Heidegger, "'Only a God Can Save Us Now': An Interview with Martin Heidegger," trans. David Schendler, *Graduate Faculty Philosophy Journal* 6, no. 1 (1977): 9.

122. Martin Heidegger, *Discourse on Thinking*, trans. John M. Anderson and E. Hans Freund (New York: Harper and Row, 1975), 56–57.

123. Tolstoy, *Polnoe sobranie sochinenii,* vol. 34, 330–31.

124. "Otvet na opredelenie Sinoda ot 20–22 fevralia i na poluchenie mnoi po etomu sluchaiu pis'ma [A Reply to the Synod's Edict of 20–22 February and on Letters Received by Me on the Same Occasion]," Tolstoy, *Polnoe sobranie sochinenii,* vol. 34, 245–53, esp. 251–52, 253. I cite here the slightly amended translation of Robert Chandler, from *The Lion and the Honeycomb: The Religious Writings of Tolstoy,* ed. A.N. Wilson (London: Collins, 1987), 129–30.

125. Notice this thought in Heidegger's "The History of Beyng" (1939–1940): The "habitual lived experiencing," writes Heidegger, confuses victory with defeat, essence with existence, the "time-play-space" within which "history receives its future" and is "ascending" thanks to sacrificial descent, in which "death is a process through which Beyng appropriates being into itself." Martin Heidegger, *The History of Beyng*, trans. William McNeill and Jeffrey Powell (Bloomington, IN: Indiana University Press, 2015), 180. See also multiple examples in *On Hegel's Philosophy of Right* and *Ponderings* that consider whatever deserves to be discarded when it is limiting the conditions of "Race—Community (Socialism)—Leadershp—People's Dasein" (esp. no. 229 in *On Hegel's Philosophy of Right*, 184). See Herbert Marcuse's letter to Heidegger of August 28, 1947: "You are today still identified with the Nazi regime. [. . .] A philosopher can go astray politically, but then he ought to expose his mistakes. But he cannot go astray regarding a regime that has killed millions of

Jews merely because they were Jews." And Rudolf Bultmann's reminiscence: "I came back again to what he [had] said to me on the telephone: 'Now you must,' I said to him, 'like Augustine write retractions [retractiones] . . . in the final analysis for the truth of your thought.' Heidegger's face became a stony mask. He left without saying anything further." Both quotes are from Victor Farías, *Heidegger and Nazism*, ed. Joseph Margolis and Tom Rockmore (Philadelphia: Temple University Press, 1989), 282–83.

126. On Heidegger's graph of being and beings, and of deconcealment, see *Vom Wesen der Wahrheit*, a course delivered at Freiburg 1932. In Martin Heidegger, *The Essence of Truth: On Plato's Cave Allegory and Theaetetus,* trans. Ted Sadler (New York: Continuum, 2002), 228. And see David Farrell Krell's analysis in Martin Heidegger, *Nietzsche: Volumes Three and Four,* ed. David Farrell Krell, trans. Joan Stambaugh, David Farrell Krell, and Frank A. Capuzzi (New York: HarperOne, 1991), 289. On one type of Tolstoy's many graphs, see Medzhibovskaya, *Tolstoy and the Religious Culture,* 346–47.

127. Tolstoy, *Polnoe sobranie sochinenii,* vol. 35, 183. "Chto takoe religiia i v chem sushchnost' ee" ([1901–1902]; ibid., 157–98).

128. Ibid., 183.

129. Tolstoy, *Polnoe sobranie sochinenii,* vol. 54, 232. From March 24, 1902, "Three fashionable philosophies in my memory: Hegel, Darwin and now Nietzsche. The first justifies all that exists, the second equates man with an animal, justifies struggle, that is, the evil in men. The third is proving that whatever is resisting evil in the nature of man is a result of false education, a mistake. I don't know where to go with this any further"; ibid., 272.

130. By "conversational philosophy," Rorty means the "Nietzsche-Heidegger-Derrida" tradition of post-Nietzschean thought as opposed to the "Quine-Putnam-Davidson" tradition of analytic thought. See Richard Rorty, *The Rorty Reader,* eds. Christopher J. Voparil and Richard J. Bernstein (Malden, MA: Blackwell-Wiley, 2010) xvii and 142. Rorty dwells on the conversationalist aspect of Heidegger's thought and writing in the essay, "Heidegger, Kundera, and Dickens" (307–20). See also a mention that Nietzsche and Heidegger are a bad idea to specialize in since the one working on these thinkers becomes unsuitable for a professional position in a typical philosophy department (512).

131. Karl Löwith, *Martin Heidegger: European Nihilism,* ed. Richard Wolin, trans. Gary Steiner (New York: Columbia University Press, 1995), 83.

132. Ibid., 196, 197.

133. Tolstoy, *Polnoe sobranie sochinenii,* vol. 38, 395–411.

134. Georg Lukács, *The Historical Novel,* trans. Hannah Mitchell and Stanley Mitchell (Lincoln and London: University of Nebraska Press, 1962), 109, 333.

135. Georg Lukács, "Martin Heidegger," in *Lukács Reader,* ed. Arpad Kadarkay (Oxford, UK, and Cambridge, MA: Blackwell, 1995), 266, 281.

136. Hannah Arendt, "Heidegger the Fox," in Arendt, *Essays in Understanding 1930–1954. Formation, Exile, and Totalitarianism,* ed. Jerome Kolm (New York: Schocken Books, 2005), 361–62.

137. Ibid., 362.

138. Hannah Arendt, "History and Immortality," *Partisan Review* 24, no. 1 (1957): 30–33.

139. Isaiah Berlin, "The Hedgehog and the Fox," in Berlin, *Russian Thinkers,* ed. Aileen Kelly (London: Penguin, 1979), 81.

140. Emmanuel Levinas, *Existence and Existents,* trans. Alphonso Lingis (Dordrecht, Boston, and London: Kluwer Academic Publishers, 1988), 95.

141. See "Substitution," in Emmanuel Levinas, *The Levinas Reader,* ed. Sean Hand (Oxford, UK, and Cambridge, MA: Blackwell, 1989/1996), 118.

142. Levinas's summary of the plot is not entirely accurate, but his sense of Tolstoy's meaning is.

143. V. V. Bibikhin, *Dnevniki Tolstogo,* ed. O. E. Lebedeva (St. Petersburg: Ivan Limbakh, 2012), 379.

144. Ibid., 378–79.

145. "We are talking about the taking by conquest and on being taken hostage, or, in the old philosophical idiom we are speaking about a 'concept'" in Bibikhin, *Mir: Kurs prochitannyi na flosofskom fakultete MGU vesnoi 1989 goda* (St. Petersburg: Nauka, 2007), 428.

146. The edition is the already cited Heidegger, *German Existentialism,* which is based on Guido Schneeberger's *Nachlese zu Heidegger: Dokumente zu seinem Leben und Denken,* ed. Guido Schneeberger (Bern: Buchdruckerei AG, 1962).

## Chapter 4

# Heidegger in Crimea

## *Excerpt*

### Alexander Kluge

While our highly mobile troops were still taking the Isthmus of Perekop, which forms the entryway to Crimea, the 4th division of the Army High Command decided that university teachers would follow up behind the 11th army. Departing from the airbases at Freiburg and Marburg we fly via Berlin, Kraków, and Odessa to Simferopol. It all happens with a bold sense of access. It has only been three days since the motorcycle infantrymen captured the city, fortified it and tracked the enemy into the mountains, and today WE UNIVERSITY TEACHERS arrive and are brought from the airfield to our quarters. Rooms constructed of wood. I rush to the Commandant's office. We receive Wehrmacht uniforms (without regalia). A civilian officer, responsible for the takeover of the electric plants, chased after a boy, was not recognized as a German, and was stabbed to death by the inhabitants of the house in which his transgression occurred. That must now be avenged as a "deterrent," i.e., a reoccurrence must be prevented.

An "abstract" and "technical" kind of "reason" is at work.[1]

The army has surrounded Sevastopol. The Colonel-General concentrates all fighting forces on this spot and has otherwise stripped the peninsula of troops. (One can't actually see this, but only learns of it through hearsay.) There is a single railroad that serves the army (of 220,000 men), and this week only a single train travels on this iron thread, the five others are broken down. The supply line is insecure. Nervousness—except, that is, in the Colonel-General and his immediate entourage, all of whom, to draw a comparison, play the part of the dying Seneca, feigning "unshakable calm." Food is mediocre. The Colonel-General is summoned.

### 2.

### Vocabulary of Troop Management

The creation of a focal-point: for a fighting squad this means the same thing as gravity for bodies in physics.

Elegance: It was lost the moment in which the army-command and its subordinates had only the lack of provisions to manage. Rapidity now only as idea, decisiveness as an outward attitude that has nothing to decide and which maintains an impossible balance. It was a winning, but already lost, army. The Soviet leadership was planning a landing in Eupatoria. It was advent season. There was a "right time" for nothing.

Haste: Hurrying, to come running is activity. Haste (the word cannot even be *written*) means that an arbitrary or feeble activity has been granted the illusion of urgency. An army-unit was moved from Simferopol to the front. The officers shouted: "With haste!"

Technological provisions: If it is unrealistic to forget death, whose clock, THE HEARTBEAT, can be felt each and every moment, then *defiance of death* is the wrong expression for *courage*. The latter is the ability to decide between what I do in accordance with myself and what I can in no way bring into accordance with myself. It will therefore in no way suffice to steamroll, as it were, a foreign region with troops, technology, and vehicles; on the contrary, the land must be "turned," that is, penetrated and "plowed up," by my ABILITY TO DECIDE. However, the 11th German army hardly had philosophers at its command.

### 3.

### Heidegger in Crimea

What few people know: in the zeal of the autumn of 1941, the Supreme High Command of the German Army formulated a plan that immediately after the seizure of Crimea, a group of university professors (archaeologists, researchers of Gothic civilization, settlement experts, philosophers) would fly to the frontline. They were to secure and explore the remains of the Greek settlement there, and seek traces of the Ostrogothic empire. Among the members of the commission was Martin Heidegger. On December 4th, 1941, on the airfield at Simferopol, the group was unloaded from the JU 52 and immediately transported into sequestered quarters.

## What Is Thinking?

"To be able to question means: to be able to wait, even an entire life." Questions emerge, so to speak, on their own. *Legein* = to gather, which means therefore reading and, at the same time, thinking. Under the pressure of death, however, not everyone collects, not everyone reads. The few who educate themselves to be thinkers (in cool lecture halls as scholars, philosophers, lecturers) are organized as guides or shepherds, as leaders of thinking, as THOSE WHO SEDUCE THE YOUNG TOWARD A LOVE OF THINKING. This professionalization distorts the image of thinking.

In addition to their gasmasks, assault rifles, and emergency packs, the soldiers now carry miniaturized editions of philosophical writings through the expanses of Russia. They have been advised to warm themselves with these "written collections" just as they would at a campfire on the evening following a battle. In the evening they are too tired for it. Thus, thinking has shriveled down to the POINT where it is possible to remember that, at one time, there existed the arts of distinguishing and questioning. Thinking exists, in this way, in a lonely position. Is it the disclosure of secrets ("originary questions") through the enlightened? Heraclitus does not think so.

Instead, these are tumultuous times. In them, the current of events concentrates itself. It seems as though the world spirit has set itself in motion. In such a time, questions pop up in such an excessively oblique way that they organize themselves in everyone's head as THE ABILITY TO QUESTION. A true philosopher hopes for one of these moments through the course of his life; he can renounce contact with too much praxis if he is touched directly at least *once* by such a "gravitational maelstrom of history."

## 4.

Our task is (a) to explore and preserve the Ostrogothic artifacts, (b) to preserve and conserve the Greek ruins, and (c) to be a presence of German research and instruction near the frontlines, thereby enacting the PORTRAYAL OF SELF-CONFIDENCE. Directly behind the front, indeed in the very middle of it, the calm, natural activity of research and intellectual effort. We are to hold lectures.

Breakfast with the Squad leader Ohlendorf, who resides with his staff in the area around army headquarters. Everything a dimension of time and motif. One must gather the WILL; it tends to dissipate in wide expanses, lying for the most part far behind in the preceding campaign, i.e., in Greece, in France, anywhere but here. It takes time to re-gather one's willpower. Technically the troops stand before Sevastopol, but volitionally, says Ohlendorf, they still have not arrived anywhere. This is the problem endemic to National Socialist leadership: how to bridge the time factor. I answer: through magic? Ohlendorf laughs. At stake is the transport of the horizons. The way one transports opera scenery to a different city theater and then assembles it? No: rather, in the vast expanse of "inner images." They are carried along, says Ohlendorf, by soldiers and officers. Only as a result of these images will Sevastopol fall. The fall of the fortress is preceded by the idea that it will fall. Indeed, the army also needs a reason to be here in the first place. For no one wants to stay here. Ohlendorf confirms it: the majority in the army would rather be at the siege of Leningrad. And the march to India?

The engagement with the remaining resistance on the wintery Crimea is seen as a forced layover. If only it were summer, the beaches open, and no war! In this respect, if I grasp Ohlendorf's concern correctly, the imposing army in its essential power is invisible. A dangerous situation. We plan to meet again.

## 5.

We all must follow the funeral train, by which the civilian who was arrested for indecent conquest is carried to his grave. An entire battalion, sorely needed elsewhere, is relieved from duty to form a military band. . . . We who belong to the military staff are entirely present in our uniforms. It is to be shown that even one lone injury to the gigantic German body carries with it mourning, deployment, and punishment.

A causality not present in the essence of the event is organizationally "established." That is incorrect. I am not inclined to mourn a man unknown to me. Concerning the others, I also see nothing but a superficial performance, a certain haste, the kind that is connected to actions that I make impatiently, and against my will.

The musicians play three marches and one funeral composition, followed by the speech of the regiment's pastor. What did the civilian intend to do with the boy, after he had lured, bribed, or overpowered him? A fleeting desire. He would have had to kill him in order to silence him definitively. It was not a young hustler, but the son of a registrar, a former Bolshevik functionary, who is now assisting the German occupation as interpreter. Not a word is spoken about this during the ceremony, but there is gossip in the short breaks in the program.

The troops and mourners are then brought to one of the squares of Simferopol. An execution has been prepared here. Twelve people in exchange for the civilian who was killed. The victims, who had been gathered together, were restless, they moved about. It was not possible to keep them still, for the guards, in order to have a field of fire, had to move away: a massacre, for the marksmen did not hit their target, they simply shot into the restless mass. A few of them ran in the direction of the spectators (who had been required, since this was meant to be an example). Bullets in the back, the hostages fell, wounded. Officers had to go to the wounded and make them still with shots to the head.

The use of the military for the purposes of "deterrence" does not work, and I would like to add: it is illusive.

Party Comrade Ohlendorf, with whom I walked to the quarters, was of the same opinion. He was not here as a mourner, but rather as a *professional witness*. He has to examine the problem of reprisals thoroughly, prepare a sort of guideline, but he comes to the conclusion that these executions at the hands of the army will remain amateur, no matter what objections are raised on paper. It would be logical, he says, to have a replacement by the security detail that is subordinate to Party Comrade Ohlendorf here, an elite unit of schooled policemen of the highest rank.

One must dispense with the variable representations of a causal chain ("a German that has been shot causes twelve native deaths"), indeed, one must dispense with a rational justification entirely, says Ohlendorf. The sequence of reasons is endless. I quote: "FINITE is the wrath of the gods." Indeed, the era must approach us as a storm of wrath, and

TERROR creates a new one out of it. But it does not do so in small, logical steps. What a misuse of the word *logos*, I interject. Yes, only as a totality can one mold the era into another: TIME LEAPS, OR DOES NOT MOVE AT ALL. In the subjective realm of the island's inhabitants—that is, in the unmediated—change and overpowering are occurring. Such a power shift acts like gravity on one's own occupying forces, that is, if I understood Ohlendorf correctly.

## 6.

In a motorcycle sidecar toward the south of the island. The Temple of Diana, existing as remains. Presumably the place where Iphigenia appeared. This installation stood very naturally and "modern" beneath a hill, hidden from the sea. The natives could thereby initially trick ships: an empty beach, possibly rich in loot. The ambush by the natives from out of the valley and over the hill to the shore happened very quickly. Seizure of the ships and the leading of the captives into the sacrifice.

There was nothing to arrange. The temple was in no danger. I prevented the propaganda company from filming and taking photographs. As the tourist-trap of the future, this temple is too valuable.

I dismissed the little motorcycle troop to Simferopol and walked out over the mountains. There are presumed to be resistance fighters here. Around midnight I come back to the quarters, having passed through a good chunk of the island on foot. It is cold. Stars are visible.

"The paths of freedom. Justice as the function of a power with expansive vision, which looks beyond the perspectives of good and evil, and thus has the broader horizons of ADVANTAGE."[2] "Justice as storehouse, excessive, devastating way of thinking, beyond all values; highest representation of life itself."[3] "The essence of power is lordship over each degree of power attained."[4]

Such things cannot be discussed in relation to this particular army. It has penetrative power, i.e., a certain degree of power (if a Soviet landfall on the east coast of Crimea doesn't occur, this army will, for example, take over Sevastopol sooner or later), but it is not master of the attained degree of power. And if it had secured power, it would not know what it wants with it (the Reich as a whole would also not know). No one that I asked wants to stay in Crimea. Move here after the war, perhaps? Every bearer of the knight's cross gets a knight's estate in Crimea? Rather not. It is so far from all of the regions that interest me.

But there are nice hills here, wine cultivation, it is a new country. The plan is to resettle South Tyroleans here (following the promises of the Führer to the Duce they must leave their estates, but in exchange they will receive homesteads in Crimea). To become Ostrogoths? Would it be better to conquer Leningrad? To seek a resolution in the cold of the North? So asks Ia of the 22nd division. Does anyone want to go there? No, but it brings the end of the war on the eastern front closer. . . .

It is impossible to fill this campaign, that is, this conquered land, with life, for no one wants to cultivate this land. That is evidenced by a certain acceleration. One entirely different from motorization. Motorization fills the expanse with echoes and industriousness, thereby shrinking the expanse. But this acceleration empties the expanse, destroys willpower, enlarges the expanse.

To oppose this, Party Comrade Ohlendorf has motorized his little team (commissioners, police consultants, a sort of officer's legion). They wish to save the Reich. To change it beforehand, in the middle of the war. He is not concerned with conquering; within the fate of this unlucky war (Ohlendorf's expression) there only exists—for the denial of fate is useless—the chance, through the exertion of all powers, that a reeducation of the German people will be achieved.[5] Using all means of the will, mortification, terrorization, and fortification. But not by way of discussions and promises. I believe him, I believe this to be his will, and also that a few of his subordinates see themselves reflected in his will. "To the mortals they deliver the trace of gods escaped into the darkness of the world's night."[6]

## 7.

Artistic landscape, cold. Abruptly, the sea. It lies icy and grey. Battleships draw near, the image of an intimate connection with an inner space.[7] I begin to make the island my own. *I*, alone, wish to remain here. Just as I wanted to cast off life in Marburg. As image: the ships are burning. If a people relinquishes its former life, "were it to decide to entirely abandon an island," then gathered in this will lay all the power of past and future. This would be a "moment." Advance troops wandering into a new life, the form of a new era. This is what is actually happening in our times. I see the (very expertly and professionally produced) execution performed by the 2nd Company of Ohlendorf's Unit. As an invited guest. One sees a small table, a clerk. An orderly queue of men has stepped up. Calm. No waiting or loitering troops; rather, active members of the execution unit situated in position; to what task precisely they are appointed, however, no one here knows. The men in the queues see workers rushing back and forth. From time to time, groups of 12 to 16 of these men are loaded onto trucks and carted off. This is the execution. I hear that the execution itself takes place privately in a ravine some 13 kilometers away. Then this does not act as a deterrent, I say. Oh yes, it consists of the fact that word gets around. That which is invisible has an effect, says Police Superintendent Wernicke, who, since he himself delegates, exudes calm. It will be effective for weeks, he says, the effect begins after the end of the measure that has been taken.[8] Observe, Herr Professor, the calmness in the queue. Do you see any gawkers? Those are the right working conditions. We restrict the number of casualties to only what is necessary. I approach the queue. New people are being led up to it. I am among the few who do not work here. The role of a spectator at an event whose essential element is invisible is intolerable without that spectator having a function.

We find ourselves in a square with one-story buildings, trees in a quadrangle. Confusion arises because an army vehicle convoy is pushing its way through Ohlendorf's installation. A dispute between Wernicke and a Sergeant Major who directs the convoy. The queue of men must be opened, the table cleared away, so that the convoy, which cannot turn around here, may pass through. I feel something touch my hand. I grasp to find a hand in my grip, a small, dark-eyed woman has laid a child's hand in mine, and I have gripped it. The woman has disappeared into the queue; disoriented, I firmly hold onto the child, a minor. It is an embarrassing situation. I am not inclined to break into the queue. It would be peculiar. However, from where I'm standing I do not see the woman who has brought this child to me. The child holds my hand tightly. I cannot communicate with this unfamiliar human being. I give signs.

It was one of my basic positions that I would in no way ever bring myself into conflict with my own behavior, no matter the situation in which I were to find myself. "No one is wiser than his destiny." I had grasped the hand as it was laid into mine. I had allowed myself to be surprised or duped, Heidegger later says to war-councilor Dr. Wolzogen. "Nothing happens without a reason." I felt that what I held in my hand had been entrusted to me. The queue of men had advanced in the course of the morning. It had been reduced owing to the removals.

I assumed that the dark-eyed woman (a Greek?) had been taken off in the meantime. It was welcome to me (in the unpleasant, idle situation of my role as witness, with the entire content of my Dasein waiting for lunch in embarrassed loitering) to be surprised by something that was alive in my hand, and at the same time it would have been embarrassing for me to hand the child over to a guard or return it to the queue. Through a delayed impulse (after more than three quarters of an hour of inactivity it does not seem fitting to speak of an impulse, nevertheless there exists this instantaneous being-shaken-back-and-forth by a sudden shift in one's disposition, which not only surprises one, but seems to act without first asking the self or an administrative authority, and while one is in the process of noticing this, IT AMBUSHES US). I asked Ohlendorf, as he was hurrying past, whether I could keep the child. How did you get the girl? I reported. Wernicke officially gave the child over to me, i.e., he confirmed that it could remain with me. It is a time of abrupt decisions owing to the expanse of the country. *"Holding* originally means *guarding."*

## 8.

With the help of a Private from the neighboring sanitation company, the child is washed thoroughly. It has its own room next to mine in the quarters. It is protected by guards as am I, as is the staff. It finds itself now on the side of the conquerors. Theoretically, a German uniform should be tailored for it.

You cannot take the child onto the Reich's territory, says Police Superintendent Wernicke—it is of Jewish descent. I answer: Who in the Reich knows that? You cannot travel around with a foundling. As soon as you arrive in the Reich's territory, that is, as soon as you have left the front, you must be able to explain the status of the child. Is it adopted? Were you at the front with your own child? Is it a spoil of war? A young prisoner of war?

We are not in the Trojan war here. You are not Ajax the Younger. I say little in response. Wernicke's musings grow friendlier. At the very least one can speak about the unusual nature of the case.

That is the mark of the new era, which manifests itself in this war as "frontline experience": that a transformation of values and customs comes to the fore. It is also true that the homeland does not participate in this new law of the times. . .

I won't go back, I say to Wernicke. You wish to pitch your philosophical tent here? I waver. On the long foot march to the coast I have examined whether or not I wish to break with my former life and not return back home, choosing instead to accompany the armies around the globe. On this train I am allowed to bring along the "living plunder." I know that I, when I look into myself, am immune to pity. I do not wish to protect this human being—I want to possess it.

The boy jumps into the river after the girl, and in the *Elective Affinities* this remains the only happy destiny. What differentiates my desires from the catching of a lost dog?

Happy days. In the cold, I find a tablet in the temple of Artemis. I take it. Secured in cardboard, it lies in my quarters, which has evolved into a storeroom for spoils.

### Reality/Illusion

Days in Crimea. In many respects: "illusive." Thus marches Heidegger, following the old habits of his homeland, across the territory of the resistance into the Jaila mountains. He says that he had wanted to view the sea, and on his way to it, greeted it by its Greek appellation. However, he never penetrated the mountains all the way to the coast. Nevertheless, he is now prepared to evaluate his findings. Following such an effort, he no longer feels separate from this land. The liaison officer to the staff of scholars calls this attitude unrealistic, "estranged from reality," for there had been an eighty-percent chance that the scholar would have been shot by resistance fighters, who in groups of about 20 men have settled into caves in the Jaila mountains. In the late evening of the same day, during a round of red-wine drinking by the staff of the 11th army, the conversations flow "without thought."

### Discovery of a Heraclitean-Tablet

The attempt to make discoveries through archeological digs proved itself to be flawed. It was better to ask the enemy intelligence officers for advice. The advice amounted to a list of local museums and headquarters of collective farms. There were actually findings to be made there. That which is to be found is, so to say, already gathered. What matters is to follow THE TRACKS OF THE EARLIER TREASURE HUNT.

## No place

In no place can Heidegger keep his loot, the child entrusted to him, by his side. He is now absolutely certain that she is a young Greek girl. Upon urgent, wishful thinking, she will reveal herself to be a descendent of Iphigenia. No place. What does that signify?

It indicates, says Heidegger, that a place is not a point in space and time, but rather a process comparable to a tube or a tunnel or the convex of an hourglass. This narrowest of spots signifies: I am leaving that which is possible for me and I am coming up against (an invisible or visible) wall. This WALL constitutes the place. The narrowest spot was located between the front and *Heimat.* By which one can see that Germany is still *roped off*, that the military front keeps the war *away* from the Reich's territory; Germany does not yet find itself at war, as will soon be the case. Only at the edges, where the troops are stationed (they also mostly wait, only a few see fighting), a thin layer of EMERGENCY prevails. The state of emergency is the PLACE OF THE IMPOSSIBLE.

Heidegger recognized that he could not travel home with the child to the Reich's territory, could not take it to Todtnau (perhaps to hide it there? But where?). The inability wounded him.

He met with Ohlendorf.

–If one wants something wholeheartedly, then he will have to do it. Otherwise he will want nothing.
–There you are correct, Comrade Heidegger. That is the whole sense of the National Socialist revolution. However, that has nothing to do with the question which you, dear Heidegger, hold so close to your heart. You pose the question incorrectly.
–I had not posed it as a question.
–No; but I hear a question in what you say.

Ohlendorf wanted to explain two things to the comrade: the assumptions being made—namely, that this girl is in mortal danger and that she is Greek—have *not been proven*. The latter is merely wishful thinking, perhaps of little duration, and not sustainable over and against the opposition posed by reality (for example, the questions of a citizen's registry office, a customs official, a detective beyond Ohlendorf's sphere of influence). After every step taken, one should ask oneself: am I risking my life for this? Do I desire that this particular scene, in whose center I stand as actor, recur eternally? If it did, would I still want it?

   That is formulated in too severe a fashion, answered the scholar. He had noticed that Ohlendorf was paraphrasing words that he, Heidegger, had said during preliminary discussions. He therefore inferred that he presides over authority. He says, with seeming obedience, I must not only ask "do I risk my life"—I must also ask: what happens if I do not vouch for anything that concerns me? If I do not risk my life for anything? What is a blind follower [*Mitläufer*]? A person dies a little each minute. If risk no longer exists for a person, then why should they continue to live?

   Let us forget illusion, Ohlendorf answers. Pardon me if I do not tell you what you wish to hear. I speak from experience. I assume that this child is Jewish. I trust that it otherwise would not have been rounded up. We don't make too many mistakes. If we did make one, it will become evident when the child grows up. The child will be integrated into the BDM.[9] I will take into account the fact that a Jewish child may not look Jewish. However, it is still not the case that under your protection a Greek descendent of Iphigenia will grow up. How would you provide the proof of ancestry? You must, dear Heidegger, be able to say: even if she is a Jew, I will still commit my very existence on her behalf (i.e., not only my life, but also my rank and standing). Do you wish to say this? You have something personal in mind; you are acting on a personal feeling. And under the conditions OF THE STATE OF EMERGENCY, that is an impossibility.

   Heidegger answers: Then the state of emergency is not something real. At the same moment he saw the end of his influence. As sure as he was that Ohlendorf would cover for him "in case of an emergency," he was equally as unsure about his own influence on a customs official or ticket inspector while returning to the Reich's territory.

   Heidegger wandered on foot. He had given the child over to the care of Private Freitag. It loitered about in the kitchen. It would be well-provided for, and would become a well-fed woman. The child had no apparent Slavic features, but rather a lean, ambitious body. One Heidegger would classify as *Greek*.[10]

## 9.

The child coughs. In Simferopol there is no cough medicine. I procure some honey. I administer it with hot water.

The child has a fever. A strange, singular case pertaining to the Reich's defense: the defense of a child with illegal status. I speak to Military Court Counsellor Dr. Wolzogen.

*[Me:]* Is an adoption possible?
*Dr. Wolzogen:* That is a somewhat unusual question.
*Me:* In this war there is much that is unusual.
*Dr. Wolzogen:* Professor, where did you obtain the child? I cannot disclose all of the facts without exposing Ohlendorf.

Again I walk a significant distance into the mountains. Decision: to erect a center for the new way of thinking on this classical island. To that end I would have to return to the *Heimat* at least once more, in order to arrange matters. The CRIMEAN-ACADEMY OF THE GERMAN REICH. Under Greek rule this island was a garden, and it can become so once again. In accordance with the standards of horticulture and the art of governance. Guided by thinking, what would be at stake is the development of model landscapes, "living districts." One would have to repeat this in the Urals, in conquered Siberia, in order to appropriate the vast settlement expanses of this particular East. This would be the goal that would retroactively provide our troops with the willpower, which they need already now (on credit), in order to complete their military actions.[11] Only the gods can suspend the dislocation of time that thus far separates this willpower of the future from our now.

Late in the evening it turns out that the child is not suffering from a cold, but rather from a particular sort of local scabies, unknown even to head staff doctor Dr. Majus. The little body smells terribly. I pay the Private 5 Marks to bathe the child, whom I have named after Hercules's daughter, Phryge, in a sulfur solution. The child is feverish and does not understand me. I speak Greek, German, the language of my mountains, rather good Latin, not a word of Russian or of whatever may be the language of the child. It does not speak Yiddish. From where does the execution board have its certainty that this is a Jewish child?

The child sleeps. With a candle and my texts, I have sat myself down next to the bed and watch over its sleep. As superfluous and intimate as waiting troops . . .

A new era does not primarily need vineyards, it needs greenhouses, the capturing of the sun, coast, winds, a tightening up of the fighting forces, space flight; the appropriation by the human of earth, the horizons, the oceans, the cosmos (through which the human becomes an

objectified-human, that is, that which the human possesses ends up possessing the human and changing it). The objectified human (conquered by its own plunder) will fundamentally change the term "course of life."
"Indeed, our life is limited/we see and count the number of our years/but the years of a people, did a mortal eye ever see?"
"Earth protrudes out of, and through the world."

## 10.

During this time, Party Comrade Ohlendorf was not enveloped by the aura of a war criminal,[12] but rather a mix of soldierly charisma and the whiff of a scholar.

The 1919 settlement program of the corps of volunteers in the Baltic: farmyards, a militia according to the Swiss model. A repeat of the industrial revolution in the spirit of "craftsmanship" and "camaraderie," so to say, machinery as field, electronics as planting, chemistry as spirituality. Because that on which the human expends work also expends work back on the human, it is called: The National Socialist German WORKER'S PARTY.

After the revolution, a worker is no longer that which corresponds to the historical image of the worker. This continual revolution spans 6,000 years. The earliest coming to force of the first majorities among the national comrades (that is, *true* German unification!): 1952. Up to that point the Reich is destructible, later it is not. Me: Why the digression into the depths of the Russian realm? Must power over the planet first be achieved? He also does not know.

Only this much: It concerns the last attempt by the Middle-European human, the Alemannic Celt, to seize power over earth and cosmos. To that end, reason, shackles, the past, historicism, all must be shaken off. The executions here are only trial runs, says Ohlendorf, not yet a case of emergency.

"Time and space are the framework for a calculative, controlling ordering of the world, 'as nature and history;' this . . . measuring of the world is accomplished by the modern human in a way whose metaphysical hallmark is modern machine technology. It remains metaphysically undecided whether and how this will toward planetary ordering sets a boundary for itself. If through a look at this process, which has gripped all people and nations of the planet, it momentarily appears as though the modern human is becoming a mere planetary adventurer, another and almost opposite phenomenon immediately comes to the fore. Expansive movements stand in relation to settlement and resettlement. As a counter-movement, settlement is a movement toward attachment to *one* place."

## 11.

The plunge into a new, foreign life (life = having responsibility, care), that is, caring for the unfamiliar living creature in my quarters—this plunge is a massive, heavy object. All that is connected to it is ballast. Private Freitag and I were able to lower the fever through the use of leg compresses. It is absurd to think that I could sexually assault this stinking skin, made filthy by rashes and pus, absurd to think that I would want to mold a pagan for myself, like Gustav Adolf—yet that is precisely the allegation of Prof. Dr. Hirtz, who in our delegation behaves like a praeses. He threatens to file a complaint with the University Union, as well as with my faculty in Freiburg. The underlying issue: One can't just take people with one here on the front.

The assistant to the Colonel-General asks me to come see him. Dr. Hirtz had spoken to him. The Colonel-General has enough worries, and does not need any additional ones. Could I make a suggestion? I decline to make a statement.

At night I look at my "test case." The creature tosses itself to and fro among the sheets. My connection to Private Freitag, who helps me bathe the child, whom I have asked to come in often and without knocking, akin to a manservant, who can attest to my belongingness to the plundered girl, is more intimate in the care devoted to this mass of misfortune. It is affection for myself that allows me to continue on with what has begun. In this quadrant of the heavens, the weather is determined by a Siberian high, that is, from the East, during December. Against the groundswell there is an advance of clouds that come from the South, that is, from the Black Sea, bringing snow showers. Someone used to the constant westerly current of home is made uneasy by this fluctuation.

We can only finish this war if we settle here. If we burn the bridges, unmoor the ships of fate and advance here as far as we can work the land. As a soldier I would not be allowed to take along a young girl, says Colonel von Feldkirch.

## 12.

### The Retreat of the Scholar

Four Hindenburg lights form a lit square. On a wooden block, the fragment, "with a powerful, dark sound."

"Immortal mortals
Mortal immortals
Living the death of the others
And the life of the others, died." Is this supposed to look like this?

Gods and humans are one (they are different from one another, but penetrate one another). The abyss of opposition (or the impossible) divides them, but also connects them. And the godly-human lives in the gods, that is, human death lives also in them. The way the gods' indestructible life dies in the human.

They (humans) have become lesser since the ADVENT OF THE STATE OF EMERGENCY, that is, August 1914: in contradiction to all appearances, starting around 1928, that they would now become greater, that a new era was rising up for them. It did not arise. Nothing to hope for. And they lost their bearings in foreign lands.

The word *opposite* does not appear in any of Heraclitus's texts. The fragment carved into an iron plate, a fairly heavy object, is wrapped up in packing paper and then also stowed in a leather case. Heidegger himself brought this case to the airfield in Simferopel and stored it in a wooden locker. He thereby hopes to transport the case back to the *Heimat.*

He returns to the quarters. Phryge is not to be found in the custody of Private Freitag. Heidegger makes enquiries. "Guardian angels" (Police Superintendent Wernicke?) have carried off his guest, his charge; via a convoy the child had been brought to a kitchen unit in the North of the peninsula, it is said. Is that a safe place? No one seems to pay any mind to the will of the philosopher. Could the scholar secure the impossible? Could he interfere?

Here in Simferopel, the NIGHTS, in imitation of the far away *Heimat,* are decorated with lights and Advent-like structures of the

Western European type. "And they pray to this image of the gods; like someone who chatters with houses; for he does not intuit what gods and heroes are." The philosopher feels dispossessed. He has nothing at hand except his little suitcase. If only he had used a rucksack. No Phryge, and the fragment tucked away in a wooden locker. He carries nothing with him except a piece of thought, for which there is little practical demand. In 1942 he begins the lectures on Heraclitus.

### 13.

Confusion. A change in the weather. From now on the wind comes from Odessa. Soviet troops have landed on the eastern coast. The 22nd motorized division has flinched, movement in the military staffs. Wherever I appear, I am chased away. The staff officers push for the removal of us scholars. The time of palpable war, of luxuriating outings in enemy territory is now over. One day before the beginning of the attack, the storming of the stronghold at Sevastopol is delayed. Troops are ordered to march to the east coast.

The freedom of someone high ranking reaches only as far as his good relationships.

Beyond that begins the impossible.

### 14.

Withdrawal from time makes the circumstances less realistic. Amongst the group of scholars in Crimea the sense of time flowed away (like through the leak of a sinking ship), away through the Advent-like feeling that drove toward Christmas Eve. On December 24th, 1941, all ordinaries except Heidegger (the heathen) wanted to be with their families until at least 6 pm. The military brass found itself with another set of priorities. They oriented themselves toward the fact that Soviet troops had landed in the east of Crimea. They wanted to counter this with quick actions. No longer masters of time, the military staff behaved as though at the end of the year (and prior to that through the Christmas celebration), time were to vanish. Insight is not enough to allow oneself to pull away from this undertow. Until he had been forcefully driven to the airport of Simferopel, admonished by adjutants and colleagues, Heidegger did NOT WANT TO CAPITULATE.

## 15.

The windows of the Junker 52 are almost square. Through them the low-lying peninsula of Crimea appears. A Soviet fighter is hunting us, it is said. The pilot undertakes evasive maneuvers.

We fly back via Odessa, Kraków, Berlin. Switch planes there, then via Mannheim to Freiburg. From out of the gigantic we dive down into the small.[13]

"The human will not even experience that which has been withheld, as long as it hangs about in the simple denial of the era."

Translated by Julia Goesser Assaiante
and S. Montgomery Ewegen

## NOTES

Editor's note: This excerpt comes from Alexander Kluge, *Chronik der Gefühle*, vol. 1 (Berlin: Surkamp, 2004), 417–32. It appears here in English for the first time. Formatting was retained from the original.

1. "Thinking first begins when we realize that, for hundreds of years, glorified reason has been the stubborn adversary of thinking."

2. (*Will to Power*, XIV, 158).

3. (*Will to Power*, XIII, 98).

4. (*Will to Power*, 1887/88, 675).

5. "No era allows itself to be eradicated by the dictum of negation. Negation only throws the one negating off track." Since June 30, 1934, Party Comrade Ohlendorf's endeavor has been made in vain.

6. An absurd idea, that the gods were tame or friendly. The moment it occurs to them to lust after a new sort of life-form, they shatter humans with great indifference. The gods are innovative.

7. The interior between water and industry, both hostile to human beings.

8. Simultaneity is needed as little as a rational or causal connection.

9. The League of German Girls, a National Socialist youth organization.

10. *Greek*: That is an idea some three hundred years old. *Mignon* wanders about with a group of Gypsies. Wilhelm Meister buys her freedom. It is revealed that she is a descendant of a count, but proof of that is only found after her death.

11. "To will is, after all, something like wanting-to-become-stronger, wanting-to-grow: and wanting the *means for that*."

Key term: *wanting-to-grow*. This not only in a subjective way, for the human, but it also means plants—that is, willing by objects, because the objective and subjective relate to one another like gravitational fields.

12. Ohlendorf, head of the eleventh division of the Reich security central office. Publisher of the *Secret Reich Issues*, a confidential opinion survey in the Reich. He is given command over Einsatzgruppe 1D, which follows the Eleventh Army. The goal of granting this command was "that O. should get his hands bloody." During the Einsatzgruppen trial in Nuremberg, O. belonged to those who declined a cover-up or denial of the murders committed by the Einsatzgruppen.

13. "The fundamental process of modernity is the conquering of the world as image." "It displaces future humans into that in-between, in which the human belongs to being (*Sein*), yet remains a stranger within that-which-is (*dem Seienden*)."

*Part II*

# PHILOSOPHICAL TRACES

## Chapter 5

# Patočka and Heidegger in the 1930s and 1940s

## *History, Finitude, and Socrates*

### Josef Moural

Once there was a fairly widespread opinion that the early Jan Patočka was a follower of Husserl and that the influence of Heidegger came only later and in two waves: in the 1940s reception of Heidegger's *Being and Time* and the related texts, and in the 1960s or 1970s reception of Heidegger's later philosophy. However, several scholars noticed (not the least the author of this chapter) that there are, in fact, remarkable traces of Heideggerian influence in Patočka's work already since 1934 (and that they possibly escape the attention of the majority of readers since they are most prominent not in the major works but rather in the relatively lesser-known papers). Still, there has been no study so far focusing on Patočka's reception and elaboration of Heideggerian themes in the 1930s and 1940s.[1]

In this chapter, I shall first provide a biographical introduction and make a few points about the relevant circumstances. Then, I shall analyze two of Patočka's shorter texts from 1934 and 1935 and discuss the traces of Heideggerian influence to be found in them. Next, I shall provide a brief survey of Heideggerian themes in other writings by Patočka from the 1930s and 1940s, and finally I shall focus on the existentialist interpretation of Socrates in Patočka's university lectures from 1946.

\*\*\*

Jan Patočka (1907–1977) was a twenty-one-year-old visiting student when he heard Edmund Husserl lecturing in Paris in February 1929

117

and was greatly impressed by him. He adopted phenomenology as his main research interest, and in his PhD dissertation from 1931,[2] he became the first Czech to write intelligently and sympathetically about Husserl (then, mainly the Husserl of the *Ideas I*). With a fresh PhD, Patočka became a high school teacher (which was a standard career step for aspiring academics who needed next to submit a habilitation thesis in order to be acceptable as university lecturers) and applied for a Humboldt Stipend to spend a year at German universities.

In 1932–1933, he spent a semester in Berlin and a semester in Freiburg. We do not know why he went first to Berlin, but it is likely that the following aspects played a role: (1) Husserl was already retired, and Patočka was not sure that he would be willing to consult with him extensively; (2) in order to approach Husserl and make the best impression possible, he perhaps thought it worthwhile first to refresh and polish his (already very good) academic German; and (3) having spent a year in Paris and being a man of cultivated cultural interests, he must have been attracted to Berlin as one of the top cultural locations of the time. Anyway, Patočka met Jacob Klein[3] in Berlin, the two became friends, and Klein pushed hard to persuade Patočka that Heidegger was an even better reason to go to Freiburg than Husserl.[4]

In an interview conducted by Josef Zumr in 1967,[5] Patočka described his Freiburg semester as follows:

> Husserl, though already retired, accepted me with open arms. He warned me against attempts to combine his philosophy with that of Heidegger, and he even wished me not to attend Heidegger's lectures—which I nonetheless was obliged to do according to the conditions of the stipend, as I loyally pointed out. He gave me a lot of his attention and time and, most importantly, he asked his assistant Eugen Fink to systematically discuss with me basic problems of the introduction to phenomenology. Fink was an excellent teacher, perhaps even too brilliant: he used to start from a commonly accepted view, which he next refuted point by point and turned upside down—he was able to see and to analyze in a unique manner. Husserl then wanted me to summarize my talks with Fink, and in response he spoke himself and asked questions, mostly during our common walks. Privately, Fink was much interested in the differences between Husserl and Heidegger, and he lent me a variety of Heidegger's older lectures: he could criticize Heidegger masterfully from the standpoint of the current state of Husserl's phenomenology, but probably also Husserl from the point of view of Heidegger, which he put into practice only later.

I attended Heidegger's lecture on Hegel and his seminar on the concept of science: but he canceled many classes and was rectoring and rallying instead—this was his worst year. Yet I was attending diligently the seminar of his assistant Werner Brock on Aristotle's biological writings.[6]

We see that Patočka comes back from Germany with a mixed bag of influences: On the one hand, he starts a close relationship with Husserl and his assistants (and Husserl clearly forms a very high opinion of his young fellow-countryman[7]), but he does not get anywhere close to Heidegger—and most likely did not wish it either, given the repulsive circumstances. On the other hand, while he was being intensively trained in Husserlian phenomenology, the two closest discussion partners he had (Klein and Fink) both recognized the importance of Heidegger and provided him with a number of exquisite insights into the content and style of Heidegger's philosophy, as well as with a number of unpublished records of Heidegger's teaching (from which the diligent Patočka, of course, took excerpts).[8] On top of that, while Patočka apparently was fascinated by the widespread pro-Nazi enthusiasm he was observing, in no way can such fascination be understood as his taking sides with the Nazis. Patočka says quite clearly: "I saw the risen masses, carried by a fresh sentiment of hope, yet turned somehow dreadfully hostile to everything we lived for."[9] And he also notices about Brock (who, being Jewish, was to leave his position at the end of the semester): "He concluded the seminar work with immense sobriety, and then the entire audience asked him to provide one more extra class—I saw for the first time from a close distance how to react with integrity and spiritual superiority to ideological persecution."[10]

Back in Prague, Patočka's main task clearly is to submit the habilitation thesis and to get a university job. The book *Přirozený svět jako filosofický problém* (*The Life-World as a Philosophical Problem*) is printed in 1936[11] and accepted (after some adversities) in 1937, and Patočka becomes affiliated with the philosophy department at Charles University (he must return to high school teaching in 1939, when the Nazis close down all Czech universities). However, he certainly did not focus solely on writing the habilitation thesis in between 1933 and 1936: He became a secretary in the main Czech philosophical journal *Česká mysl*, he published papers and reviews, he was the cofounder of the Prague Philosophical Circle, and he co-organized Husserl's lecture trip to Prague in 1935 (the lectures were subsequently extended into

*The Crisis* book) and the important measures to preserve Husserl's manuscripts.[12]

Philosophically, Patočka is clearly full of Heideggerian inspiration in 1933 and 1934, as we shall see in the next section discussing two of his main papers from that time. However, subsequently he puts his Heidegger-oriented ambitions on a back burner and focuses on Husserl. There seem to be at least the following four factors playing a role in this reorientation:

1. The renewed communication with Husserl and the feeling of obligation to proceed along Husserlian lines. (Several of the listeners of Husserl's last public lectures, in November 1935 in Prague, felt that this was a testament of a sort, and for Patočka the feeling was reinforced when Husserl gave him his own lectern—that he got from Masaryk in the 1870s—as a present, making him "the heir to a great tradition."[13])
2. Husserl's previous research assistant, Ludwig Landgrebe, arrives in Prague in 1934 and becomes Patočka's closest discussion partner—but Landgrebe was not a witness to Heidegger's "star" years in Marburg and was less appreciative of Heidegger, anyway.
3. Around 1934, probably in connection with the invitation to the Prague philosophical congress (its main topic was "Philosophy as a Guide to Life"), Husserl's philosophical activity gets remarkably reinvigorated and the new *Crisis* project becomes rather exciting to those few who happen to learn about it.
4. After Germany's rearmament and an escalation of internal atrocities, it becomes far clearer that Nazism is a very serious threat, which should be enough to discourage anyone from publicly taking sides with its supporters.

In March 1939, Germany crushed what had remained of Czechoslovakia's independence after the Munich Agreement (of August 1938), and in November 1939 all Czech universities were closed down. Patočka returned to high school teaching (and, toward the end of the war, he got involved in the "total deployment" manual work). Husserl was dead, Landgrebe left for Louvain with the manuscripts, and the Circle dissolved. It was possible to publish, but not on explicitly Husserlian topics. Patočka, following Husserl's program from the *Crisis* of rethinking the history of European thought, finds a relatively safe haven in the area of the history of ideas (which will be his main profile again in the ten years after Stalin's death but before serious liberalization, i.e., 1954–1964), but he also drafts a few phenomenological manuscripts (with some discussion and development of Heideggerian ideas), and in the later years of the war he focuses on preparing the courses on the history of philosophy that he delivers between 1945 and 1949. He publishes a few papers between those years as well, but on the whole he seems to adopt the attitude of his teachers, Husserl and Heidegger, to focus on and to consider one's main output the lecture courses, new for each semester.

\*\*\*

Next, we should look at the two Heideggerian papers published between 1934 and 1935: "Několik poznámek k pojmům dějin a dějepisu [A few remarks concerning the concepts of history and of historiography]"[14] and "Několik poznámek o pojmu světových dějin [A few remarks on the concept of world history]."[15] They partially overlap, both starting from the question of status, topic, and method of historiography and proceeding toward historicity as a mode of being and history as a storehouse of life-projects for appropriation. The first was published in a nonprofessional journal and consequently is somewhat richer in illustration, more personal, and less sober (and more explicitly Heideggerian)—but they are both quite peculiar texts: at once informal and densely packed with intuition and argument (most often only sketched or suggested), at once highly ambitious and studiously modest, and at once a virtuoso show-off piece (or what a beginner takes for one) and a personal statement.

What made Patočka choose history and historiography as his topic? First, he was a gifted and diligent young man who had just returned to a somewhat backward province from the philosophical Olympus, where he had engaged in discussions with gods and demigods. "When I returned to Czechoslovakia, I was with all that [i.e., with the projects and problems brought back from Freiburg] nearly completely isolated; nobody understood what I was concerned with, not even the closest friends from the same generation, often more gifted than I," says Patočka in retrospect.[16] The fact that, in his Czech writings, he often addressed topics outside of philosophy may have to do not only with the breadth of his interests, but also with a feeling that if he wants to communicate with people of distinction, he needs to mix with historians or literary theorists rather than with philosophers (admittedly, the years from 1934 to 1938 were an exception in this respect, due to Landgrebe's staying in Prague, but again the point remains valid with regard to Patočka's writing in Czech).[17]

And second, Josef Pekař, one of the most prominent Czech historians of his generation,[18] mentioned Husserl and quoted Heidegger in his inaugural lecture on the occasion of his becoming the rector of Charles University in December 1931,[19] and the subsequent polemics involved a number of Czech intellectuals,[20] among them T. G. Masaryk, then the eighty-two-year-old Czechoslovak president (but originally, up to age sixty-five, a philosophy professor and Husserl's close friend from their youth) who took part through a pseudonymous twelve-page paper published in the leading professional philosophy journal.[21] The discussion certainly attracted Patočka's attention in 1932 (he even reviewed one of the texts critical to Pekař),[22] and when he returned from Germany with fresh expert knowledge of Husserl and Heidegger, he could easily have felt obliged to join and to deal with the philosophical—and especially with the Heideggerian—portion of the problem.

Let us now have a closer look at the texts, and let me choose the later of the papers as the point of departure. Patočka begins with a discussion of what he calls *theory of history*, by which he apparently means the self-understanding of the profession regarding subject matter and methodology.[23] Patočka claims that any *intellectualistic* approach to history is hopeless (where intellectualism is an attempt to keep the cognizing intellect out of the picture and to focus purely on the object—to imagine that we can just describe, analyze, and explain the data and that our intellectual activity is detached, neutral, and transparent).[24] For an intellectualist, "history is the human past understood as a series of events involving human objects." In the profession, this approach is represented by "naive historical positivism: all 'events' lay on principally the same ground and history is the system of continuous causal lines which are to be mentally reconstructed in order that the aim, historical knowledge, is achieved."[25]

According to Patočka, the Neo-Kantians (namely Rickert) already showed that not only was such a theory untenable but also that in fact no working historian could have ever followed it—in order to see it, it is enough to realize that, while the past is immense, the historians necessarily have to *choose their topic*. Nonetheless, despite having been refuted, such a naive view of history still remains commonplace—which has to do with the prevailing modern naturalism. When Patočka points to the crisis of naturalistic anthropology, he speaks quite like Husserl (it leads to skeptical relativism, intellectualist indifferentism, noncommittal aestheticism, etc.); but when it comes to proposing a solution, Patočka says that the key mistake of naturalism is that "it sticks to the same basic type of being, it remains in the same ontological sphere. One of the results of this attitude is . . . misunderstanding history."[26]

Thus, in order to learn what history is, one needs first to fix one's ontology (and to abandon the ruling but mistaken "objective presence" monism). On the way there, Patočka speaks for a while about "creative energy" in history, making use of some Bergsonian imagery perhaps in hope that it would facilitate understanding his ideas.[27] Next, Patočka distinguishes between superficial and deep history. Superficial history is the history of everything that can be objectified and stated, of the facts and data. Deep history is the history of individual and group *life-forms* that get expressed in the events but are not really to be found in them.[28] In other words, deep history is the history of the world understood as *the environment of human action*.[29] More precisely, the world in this sense "is the system of potentialities open to a human being at the moment: of potentialities in which one lives and to which one continuously relates in one's acting."[30]

Now since "the world is what governs our understanding of entities,"[31] it is clear that superficial history depends on the deep one and that even historians who wish to do merely the superficial history need to rely on their understanding of the relevant life-forms in making sense of their data[32] (only, if they disregard deep history, they would rely on naive, uncritically accepted conceptions of life-forms, often to their disadvantage). Thus, the aim of historiography could not be merely reconstruction of historical facts in their interrelations, but above all gaining access to historical facts on the basis of the relevant life-forms, of the historical worlds as systems of open potentialities. The actual historians, remarks Patočka, tend to master such a task intuitively, without being aware of its principal significance and philosophical relevance.[33]

And if we return to the issue of philosophical anthropology (announced in the criticism of naturalistic anthropology above), we see that the question "What is history?" is closely related to the question "What is human being?" and to the mode of being of us humans. We notice that the selection of historical material (required by Rickert) tends to be based on our non-indifference toward what we understand as *our past*—without it, all of the past would be for us as indifferent as the proverbial snows of the past years (and the study of the past events would be an idle theoretical curiosity). The main reasons of our non-indifference are:

1. Our actual life-form, our actual world as a system of open potentialities is the result of historical development. And in order to understand our actual world, we should understand that development.
2. The people of the past who contributed to shaping our actual world were, like us, bearers of the struggle characterized by limited freedom, and we cannot but feel compassion with them.
3. Not only the life-form determining what we can do, but also the life-projects determining what we aim to do within such limits very largely stem from the past, and we shape our own lives along the patterns inherited from our forerunners.

Let us look more closely at what Patočka says about these three (admittedly interrelated) points. With regard to the first, Patočka quotes Humboldt: The purpose of studying history is to "wake up and enliven our sense for the actual."[34] Patočka's description of the life-world (as we may name the world as the environment of human action) is rather sketchy and impressionistic, like that of Husserl and of Heidegger—which is to be expected, given that there was no philosophical theory of institutions[35] available at that time. He says things like "the basic characteristic of historicity is the co-determination of human action by the past,"[36] for the *formantia* of individual and social life are very largely accepted from the past through tradition. But it is not quite clear whether he means by the *formantia* only the individual and group life-projects (which is the topic Patočka emphasizes) or the institutional environment of action as well.

With regard to the second, Patočka says the "the world of history is our practical world, the world of our (conscious) interests."[37] That is, the agents of historical events were agents in the same sense (structurally) as we are, and their concerns, preferences, and skills (while not compatible with the "objective presence" ontology) are a very important component of historical explanation. Now the possible concerns, preferences, and skills are themselves (very largely) products of the previous historical development; they are not natural and ahistorical.[38]

But human creativity can bring something new into the already existing configuration, and the novelty can be appropriated and become a part of the stock configuration for the times to come. In the Heideggerian language used by Patočka, human freedom is a limited one, for our life is not just world-creation in the projected future, "but also thrownness amidst of things." It is *thrown freedom*, "and that means: all the potentialities of freedom grow up on the basis of what the past locates us into, they are co-determined by what has been. Thus, the past challenges our freedom to come to life in one's own question."[39]

And, turning to the third point, history is a repository of past life-projects, and they are the only stuff from which our own life-project can be built (and freely rebuilt, modified, etc.). "History is the way in which our freedom, grasping its resolution, . . . erects its models and objects of esteem."[40] To understand history means to re-create the sense/meaning of the thrown projects of the past, "to repeat the essential, original potentialities uncovered in past thrownly free resolutions."[41] History is needed in order that human freedom can understand itself in its thrownness, in its being conditioned by the situation, and can "overcome unfreedom by accepting the thrownness in criticizing lifeless traditions and suffocating untruths."[42] That is why history is unseparable from esteem and love, hatred and repulsion, and ultimately it is, according to Patočka, "a series of freely thrown resolutions."[43]

Such is the main line of exposition in the two papers, brought to a more explicitly Heideggerian territory in the earlier one. We notice that both terminology and content are very largely Heideggerian, with occasional loans from Bergson[44] and from Husserl. Modes of being, world as a system of open potentialities, historicity, project and thrownness, resolution, repetition: Of course, Patočka uses the corresponding Czech expressions, but the reference to Heidegger is very clear.

On top of that, Patočka adds a few clearly Heideggerian extras: At the very beginning of the earlier paper Patočka says that it would be futile to try to learn about G-history through historiography[45]—another direct loan from Heidegger.[46] In the middle of the paper, Patočka inserts two long paragraphs where he attempts—for the first time in his career—to mediate between Husserl and Heidegger: Heidegger's argument that *reflection* is not a viable method is strong and persuasive, but it demolishes the psychological kind of reflection, not necessarily the Husserlian (and it is not clear, according to Patočka, how we should proceed if we completely dismiss reflection).[47] Here, Patočka mentions Heidegger toward the end of the passage—after ascribing his objections first to "philosophers, influential today and marked by philosophical radicality"[48] and next to "the above-mentioned philosophers."[49] It is not clear why he avoids naming names and references (which will remain a longstanding habit in Patočka). After all, he is not consistent: He ends up mentioning Heidegger twice (the second occasion is the very last line of the earlier paper, where Patočka says simply that the historian "must, in Heidegger's words, want, quarrel and esteem"[50]).

***

Next, let us look at Patočka's other discussions of Heidegger in the 1930s and 1940s. I mentioned above that before 1932 Patočka did not know Heidegger very well and that after 1934 he largely put Heidegger aside, probably as a result of renewed connection with Husserl and of the attractiveness of the new Husserlian conceptions of Life-World and historicity (and perhaps also for political reasons). The two papers discussed in the previous section are thus exceptional in Patočka's early published output. However, there are a number of scattered remarks about Heidegger in the remaining published pieces, some of them interesting, and there are passages dealing somewhat extensively with Heidegger in manuscript notes written probably in the early 1940s.

The little that Patočka says about Heidegger before 1932 is not very interesting either concerning Patočka or concerning Heidegger, but it may be of interest with regard to the overall pattern of the early reception of Heidegger: In his 1931 dissertation, Patočka refers to Heidegger's lecture "What Is Metaphysics?" ("why is there something rather than nothing?")[51] and includes *Kant und das Problem der Metaphysik* in the list of literature[52] (without quoting it in the text). Besides, he briefly summarizes Gurvitch's unfavorable view of Heidegger in his 1931 review of *Les tendances actuelles de la philosophie allemande*.[53]

During 1932, Patočka reads extensively and at some point clearly becomes involved with *Being and Time*. Thus, he says that Heidegger "sharply modifies the concept of phenomenological method (he conceives it as 'hermeneutics of existence')" in an encyclopedia entry, "Phenomenology."[54] In his 1932 review of Hans Reiner's *Phänomenologie und menschliche Existenz*, Patočka mentions again the "hermeneutics of human existence" and a somewhat surprising list of Hans three "areas of human experience (Vorhandenes, Zuhandenes, Wertvolles)."[55] And the

1932 review of Paul Menzer's *Deutsche Metaphysik der Gegenwart* documents Patočka's growing acquaintance with Heidegger, as he criticizes Menzer for relying only on "What Is Metaphysics?" and portions of *Kant und das Problem der Metaphysik*, and not on the "main work" (and, otherwise, for misunderstanding Heidegger thoroughly).[56]

Thus, it is likely that when Patočka approached Klein and Fink in 1932 and 1933, he possessed serious knowledge of Heidegger's published work. His understanding of Heidegger must have improved very much thanks to discussions with Klein and Fink, to attending Heidegger's classes, and to reading student notes from Heidegger's earlier teaching (and in the previous section, we saw young Patočka making use of his improved knowledge and understanding in focusing on historicity). In the rest of this section, I shall point to a few passages that show further aspects of Patočka's ripening knowledge of Heidegger from 1934 to 1949.

In a survey paper, "Metaphysics in the Twentieth Century" (1934), Patočka gives Heidegger an intelligent summary of some thirty lines that includes the standard view of *Dasein*, project and thrownness, finitude, coping, world, authenticity, care, temporality, and resolution.[57] In his 1934 review of the Société Thomiste volume *La phénoménologie*, Patočka remarks that Heidegger's attitude toward Husserlian *reduction* is not an absolute rejection, contrary to what many people say.[58] In his 1938 review of Erwin Straus's *Vom Sinn der Sinne*, Patočka notices how attractive Heidegger's phenomenology is for recent psychiatrists Binswanger and von Gebsattel, as well as Straus.[59]

The most interesting (from our point of view) of Patočka's early reviews is his 1942 review of O. F. Bollnow's *Das Wesen der Stimmungen*. Bollnow complains that Heidegger one-sidedly emphasizes anxiety and neglects such elevated moods in which "the burden of life, far from being hidden, comes into play negatively in its complete disappearance. These are not states of mere forgetting, but rather the peak life moments of which we are not ashamed but which we rather desire, and which are thus different both from Heidegger's resolution . . . and from the level of inauthenticity."[60] Patočka reports that Bollnow supports his conception by interpretation of altered states of consciousness (on mescalin) of Proust and of Nietzsche.[61] Overall, Bollnow sticks to Heidegger's view that moods both unlock the world and generate potentialities for one's life; he just insists that swinging between the elevated and the anxious pole is required in order that a strong character can be built up. Patočka mentions disapprovingly H. Mörchen's polemic reply to Bollnow (that Heidegger's conception is a perfect unity that cannot be supplemented) and characterizes Heidegger's position as "forced heroism."[62]

In Patočka's 1936 habilitation thesis,[63] Heidegger's presence is set on low. He is mentioned or quoted five times, but mostly as a scholar whose work is relevant but can be left aside. The most affirmative are two short passages (three to five lines) where Patočka appreciates Heidegger's conception of the world[64] and his explanation of the vulgar concept of time[65]—without going into any details. Elsewhere, for example, in a short passage about moods, Patočka does not mention Heidegger and avoids a specifically Heideggerian approach.[66] As we know now, Patočka expected difficulties in the habilitation procedure (and he was right),[67] so it may be the case that, in addition to the incentives mentioned above, he thought it wise to minimize the Heideggerian connection on this special occasion also in order not to provoke the conservative senior faculty staff.

Patočka's short 1947 essay "Doubts concerning Existentialism"[68] is mainly about Sartre, but Heidegger serves as a term of comparison. Patočka interprets existentialism as a puzzling hybrid of sober transcendentalism seeking for an outworldly condition of all worldly appearance, on the one hand, and of passionate self-proclamation of human being as a finite unreflective intraworldly creature, on the other. This seems to be true, according to Patočka, of Kierkegaard, Jaspers, Heidegger, and Sartre.[69] He says that the position of those existentialists who "do not attempt to philosophize systematically and are satisfied with a protest against the philosophy that strives for objectivity without passion and without self-exposition" is easier than the position of those who (like Heidegger and Sartre) "wish to find in the concept of existence the key to the great traditional philosophical questions."[70] The difficulty consists in unifying the two components, apparently so incompatible, and this leads, according to Patočka, to "the complete absence of psychology in Heidegger, complete absence of inwardness characterized by recognition and reflection."[71]

Besides the published texts, we have a collection of Patočka's manuscript notes, written probably between 1940 and 1945. Here, Heidegger is again as strongly present as Husserl. Basically, Patočka likes Heidegger as a phenomenologist expanding and modifying the Husserlian conception. He appreciates here again Heidegger's elaboration of practical intentionality in the concept of project,[72] the concept of the world as a horizon of projected action,[73] and respect for human finitude reflected in the concept of thrownness. Besides, Patočka finds it generally attractive to expand the Husserlian conception toward moods[74] and toward the drama of responsible finite freedom. But he increasingly realizes that the particular steps of Heidegger's in pursuit of his "existential" agenda (1) are arbitrary and one-sided, and (2) prevent even a minimally rich description of limited freedom, the phenomena of human deliberation, choice, struggle, and learning from one's mistakes through retrospective evaluation, often in the light of other people's criticism and/or approval.

Anxiety, boredom, and death are important (and Heidegger's analyses are often brilliant), but they may not be as central and as mighty both in philosophical theory and in human life as it is actually lived.[75] And Patočka grows more and more impatient with Heidegger's views of resolution and of the forced and lonely heroism. Ultimately, Patočka is going to consider Heidegger as successful more in opening vistas and in sketching research programs, than in actually fulfilling them.[76] Slowly and tentatively, Patočka was building his own ways of responding to Heideggerian challenges: He paid more attention than Heidegger did to phenomena like embodiment, intersubjectivity, elevated moods, or historical change, and developed his own version of philosophical heroism.

\*\*\*

The last section of this chapter is a little bit more daring than the previous ones. Here, I would like to interpret Patočka's remarkable lecture course on *Socrates* (delivered in 1946) along "existentialist" lines and to trace Heideggerian motifs in it. We shall see that Heidegger's name is absent here—but that Patočka's thought has already adopted (and modified) some of Heidegger's ways of doing philosophy.

The written version of the course consists of six chapters. In the first chapter, Patočka provides a preliminary orientation to the hermeneutic situation, a survey of existing conceptions, and a plan of the course. In the second chapter, Patočka discusses Attic tragedy and the sophistic movement as two important preconditions of Socrates' philosophy. The third chapter is a survey of what is known about Socrates's life. In the remaining three chapters, Patočka discusses various aspects of Socrates's philosophy.

In the first chapter, Patočka applies a complex strategy. He flatly states at the very beginning of the course that the historical Socrates escapes the techniques of H-history (which he represents as united with classical philology for this historical epoch), and he sets out the standard arguments leading to this conclusion: Naive adherence to Plato as the source was criticized in the Enlightenment, and for a while, Xenophon was considered far more reliable given the lack of his own philosophical agenda; however, Xenophon was not on the spot for most of the time and must have used other sources whose reliability we cannot check (and, of course, we do not have a single word of Socrates's own writing). Thus, the methods of critical analysis conclude that Socrates could have been a myth—except for the fact that someone whom Plato called Socrates was of tremendous influence on the historical Plato and that, from the greatness of Plato, we can indirectly estimate the greatness of his beloved master (which is enough to rule out the shallow "clever man pretending he is not" picture in Xenophon).

This part of the procedure reminds one of phenomenological *epochē*: The students who enrolled in the course no doubt had heard and/or read a lot about Socrates and expected to learn even more, and much more precisely, from the expert (remember that most students were sophomore or younger in the autumn 1946, as there were no Czech university students between 1939 and 1945), and Patočka's first exposition goes straight against such expectation: The H-history experts could say very little—perhaps nothing—about Socrates. Fortunately, there is G-history coming to our rescue: Insofar as we are adepts of philosophy (a tradition reliably originating in Socrates plus Plato), our best chances to learn about Socrates lay not in the past but in our own future. In our own being questioned and refuted we experience structurally (eidetically) the same as what Plato and his contemporaries experienced from Socrates, and the events of our own philosophical training are events of re-creating, re-enowning philosophy in its archetypical experience.

In Patočka's words, what is important to learn concerning Socrates is "what Socrates cares for: something we can hear only if we do not study him as an object, as a remarkable curiosity, but when we enter into a discussion with him, when we experience being changed and refuted in our certainties and our presumed knowledge."[77] Consequently, the plan of the course is: After learning (in chapters 2 and 3) as much as the H-history (the classics) can provide, "we need above all to watch attentively Socrates as the awakener, as the one who calls people to look into their own eyes, who challenges them not only to have courage to live, but to know who (s)he is who lives in them; as the relentless exposer who performs not in play but out of worry that we might miss the substance of our lives—the substance that Socrates calls *psychē*."[78]

There is so much of Heidegger in this passage that one could wonder why he did not write something similar himself. First, given Heidegger's calling for *existential concreteness*,[79] it is odd that he says so little about the everydayness of being a philosopher. Second, it is clear that anyone's *project* of becoming or continuing to be a philosopher grows out of one's *thrownness* into the facticity of European intellectual history, with its founding event of the beginning of philosophy in Socrates and Plato. *Resoluteness* is thus a *repeat* of archetypal potentiality. Third, the case of Socrates illustrates beautifully how H-history is secondary to *G-history*. Fourth, the resolution to be like Socrates is quite straightforwardly *being-unto-death* (and accepting it). Fifth, Socrates challenges people to grasp their *authenticity*, to become who they really are (and to do so through examining the inauthentic, wherever-collected, false certainties about how *one is supposed* to lead one's life). Sixth, the core characteristic of Socrates's activity is *epimeleia*, as Plato's Socrates puts it in the *Apology* and elsewhere[80]—and that is *Sorge*, "care" (or *starost* in Czech).

In connection with Attic tragedy, Patočka draws a very existentialist picture of our finite freedom: (1) We cannot refrain from acting (temporality), but (2) most often we act with only limited information (finitude), which opens possibilities of doing things we would rather not do if we knew, and (3) even if our factual information was as complete as one could wish, we still might find ourselves entangled in a complex and opaque network of conflicting loyalties (thrownness) that make it impossible even for the best person to do the right thing (as there is no one available, given the conflicting legitimate demands on us). Socrates took his main question, "How to live a good life?" indirectly from the tragic authors: "The tragic hero is an embodied question, asked from the depths of human perplexity."[81]

It is tempting to dwell further on this fascinating lecture course, but that should be a topic of a separate study. Here, what I wanted to show was how much Patočka absorbed certain important topics and techniques from Heidegger as early as the 1940s and how he used them freely in his own philosophical work. And, before closing the chapter, let me remark that Patočka's own resolution to remain faithful to the Socratic project ultimately led him into a struggle in which he showed a remarkable heroism of his own, not only in writing but in action, and—quite like Socrates—somehow made his untimely death a victory for philosophy.[82]

## NOTES

1. But see Karel Novotný, "Dějinnost a svoboda: Heidegger a Patočkova raná filosofie dějin," *Reflexe* 14 (1995): 2.1–2.36 on Jan Patočka, "Několik poznámek k pojmům dějin a dějepisu," *Řád* 2 (1934): 148–56; also printed as Jan Patočka, *Péče o duši I,* vol. 1, *Sebrané spisy Jana Patočky* (Prague: Oikoymenh, 1996), 35–45.

2. Jan Patočka, "Pojem evidence a jeho význam pro noetiku [The Concept of Evidence and its Significance in Epistemology]," (PhD dissertation, Charles University, 1931). Printed in Jan Patočka, *Fenomenologické spisy I,* vol. 6, *Sebrané spisy Jana Patočky* (Prague: Oikoymenh, 2008), 13–125. Some of Patočka's texts are available in translations. Where an English translation exists, I refer to it; otherwise, translations are mine. Concerning translations of the texts from which I quote into other languages, the reader can consult the online bibliography on the web page of the Jan Patočka Archives in Prague that provides for each entry an updated survey of existing translations (http://ajp. cuni.cz/index.php/Bibliografie).

3. Jacob Klein (1899–1978), a philosopher and classical scholar of Latvian-Jewish origin who studied in Marburg, Germany, was among the post-docs closely observing the rising philosophical star of Martin Heidegger (with Gadamer, Löwith, and especially his lifelong friend Leo Strauss). Beginning in 1937, he taught at St. John's College in Annapolis, Maryland.

4. Jan Patočka, *Češi I,* vol. 12, *Sebrané spisy Jana Patočky* (Prague: Oikoymenh, 2006), 614. In fact, Patočka's original plan was to spend a semester in Berlin and a semester in Leipzig. He proposed to change the location of his second Humboldt semester when in Berlin (see Jan Patočka, *Fenomenologické spisy I,* vol. 6, 435) probably under the influence of Klein.

5. Josef Zumr and Jan Patočka, "O filosofovi a filosofech," *Filosofický časopis* 15 (1967): 585–98; printed also as Patočka, *Češi I,* 607–29. Another, largely overlapping memoir piece is Jan Patočka, "Erinnerungen an Husserl," in *Die Welt des Menschen—Die Welt der Philosophie: Festschrift für J. Patočka,* ed. Walter Biemel (The Hague: Nijhoff, 1976), vii-xix; translated into Czech as Patočka, *Češi I,* 630–41.

6. Zumr and Patočka, "O filosofovi a filosofech," 589; Patočka, *Češi I,* 614–15.

7. See, e.g., Husserl's letter to President Masaryk's secretary, Vasil K. Škrach, of December 4, 1934 (printed in original German in Patočka, *Fenomenologické spisy I,* 458–59).

8. For example, in a manuscript written in Czech probably in the 1940s, he quotes Heidegger (in German), without reference as nearly always, but now we can identify the quotation as coming from Heidegger's lectures in WS 1929/30, published for the first time in 1983, six years after Patočka's death (as volume 29/30 of the *Gesamtausgabe*). See Jan Patočka, *Fenomenologické spisy III/1*, vol. 8/1, *Sebrané spisy Jana Patočky* (Prague: Oikoymenh, 2014), 101. Other such quotations or paraphrases remain unidentified so far (see note 47 below).

9. Zumr and Patočka, "O filosofovi a filosofech," 589; Patočka, *Češi I*, 614.

10. Zumr and Patočka, "O filosofovi a filosofech," 589; Patočka, *Češi I*, 615. Patočka himself was to suffer his share of ideological persecution, and it seems he was influenced by Brock in shaping his own manners under similar circumstances.

11. Jan Patočka, *Přirozený svět jako filosofický problem* (Prague: Ústřední nakladatelství a knihkupectví učitelstva československého, 1936); also Patočka, *Fenomenologické spisy I*, 127–261.

12. On the Prague Circle, see Ludger Hagedorn and Hans Rainer Sepp, eds., *Jan Patočka: Texte—Dokumente—Bibliographie* (Freiburg and Munich: Karl Alber, 1999), 188–205. On Husserl's lectures in Prague, the Prague contribution to the preservation of Husserl's manuscripts and related correspondence, Hagedorn and Sepp, *Jan Patočka*, 206–51.

13. Patočka, *Češi I*, 637.

14. Originally Patočka, "Několik poznámek k pojmům dějin a dějepisu"; quoted from Jan Patočka, *Péče o duši I*, 35–45.

15. Originally Jan Patočka, "Několik poznámek o pojmu světových dějin," *Česká mysl* 31 (1935): 86–96; quoted from Patočka, *Péče o duši I*, 46–57.

16. Zumr and Patočka, "O filosofovi a filosofech," 590; Patočka, *Češi I*, 615.

17. The merits of the Prague Linguistic Circle are widely recognized. Czech historiography, while less well known internationally (largely because Czech historians published nearly exclusively in Czech in those days), was also very good at the time.

18. Josef Pekař (1870–1937) was a Czech historian at Charles University, a professor beginning in 1901, and rector from 1931 to 1932.

19. Josef Pekař, *O periodisaci českých dějin* (Prague: Historický klub, 1932), 7–8; also Miloš Havelka, ed., *Spor o smysl českých dějin 1895–1938* (Prague: Torst, 1995), 733.

20. The polemics did not deal with Husserlian and Heideggerian topics (or only very marginally), and it was the last round of a long debate in which Masaryk and Pekař had emerged as the main antagonists (a good anthology of the original texts is Havelka, *Spor o smysl českých dějin*).

21. Č. p., "O periodisaci českých dějin," *Česká mysl* 28 (1932): 131–42 (also Havelka, *Spor o smysl českých dějin*, 751–61). "Č. p." was a—not very concealing—pseudonym used by Masaryk when he wanted to enter a professional debate without being sheltered by the authority of his office.

22. Patočka, *Fenomenologické spisy I*, 475–76.

23. Like German, the Czech language has two very common words, "historie" and "dějiny," where English has only "history." Etymologically, "dějiny" is identical with "Geschichte" ("that what was happening"), and Patočka distinguishes between the two with a clear tendency but not entirely consistently: Historie is what remains of the past happenings (and what historiography attempts to describe), while Geschichte/dějiny is the real thing (which, at the moment when it is happening, still has all the future possibilities open, and the participants strive to influence it in this or that way). Where necessary, I shall mark the difference by using "G-history" for "Geschichte/dějiny" and "H-history" for "Historie/historie." As Heidegger puts it, H-history observes the past and G-history looks toward the future.

24. Patočka, *Péče o duši I*, 46.

25. Ibid., 47.

26. Ibid., 48.

27. Ibid., 48–50. By 1935, there were three Bergson books translated into Czech, and Patočka's friend Václav Černý was working on a fourth one. In general, France was the primary orientation point of interwar Czechoslovakia, culturally and diplomatically (and many more students would take French than English at school).

28. Ibid., 51.

29. Ibid., 52.

30. Ibid., 53.

31. Ibid.

32. Ibid., 52.

33. Ibid., 55.

34. Wilhelm von Humboldt, *Ausgewählte Schriften,* ed. Th. Kappstein (Berlin: Borngräber, 1917), 23; quoted in Patočka, *Péče o duši I*, 38.

35. On what kind of philosophy of institutions would be needed, see, e.g., Josef Moural, "Searle's Theory of Institutional Facts: A Program of Critical Revision," in *Speech Acts, Mind, and Social Reality: Discussions with John R. Searle,* ed. Günther Grewendorf and G. Meggle (Dordrecht: Kluwer, 2002), 271–86.

36. Patočka, *Péče o duši I*, 48.

37. Ibid., 49.

38. Ibid., 49–50.

39. Ibid., 43–44.

40. Ibid., 44.

41. Ibid.

42. Ibid.

43. Ibid., 44–45.

44. Novotný, "Dějinnost a svoboda: Heidegger a Patočkova raná filosofie dějin," pays attention to the Bergsonian line.

45. Patočka, *Péče o duši I*, 35.

46. Martin Heidegger, *Being and Time: A Translation of Sein und Zeit*, trans. Joan Stambaugh (New York: SUNY Press, 1996), 344; see also 358–59.

47. Patočka, *Péče o duši I*, 40–41. Somewhat later, Patočka notices that Sartre's *The Emotions*, while indebted to Heidegger, nonetheless is faithful to Husserl's method of reflective analysis (Patočka, *Fenomenologické spisy I*, 427).

48. Patočka, *Péče o duši I*, 40.

49. Ibid., 41.

50. Ibid., 45. The source of the quotation/paraphrase has not been identified so far (see note 8 above). Ivan Chvatík, the director of the Jan Patočka Archives and the chief editor of Patočka's *Collected Works*, confirmed this by e-mail on December 25, 2016 (my thanks to Ivan).

51. Patočka, *Fenomenologické spisy I*, 70.

52. Ibid., 122.

53. Ibid., 330.

54. Ibid., 332.

55. Ibid., 344.

56. Ibid., 347.

57. Ibid., 287–88.

58. Ibid., 359–60.

59. Ibid., 395.

60. Ibid., 400. It is tempting to connect these ideas with Patočka's late conception of the first movement of human existence (e.g., Jan Patočka, *Heretical Essays in the Philosophy of History*, trans. Erazim Kohák (La Salle, IL: The Open Court, 1996), 31–32).

61. Patočka, *Fenomenologické spisy I*, 401.

62. Ibid.

63. Originally Patočka, *Přirozený svět jako filosofický problem*; quoted from Patočka, *Fenomenologické spisy I*, 127–261.

64. Patočka, *Fenomenologické spisy I*, 200.

65. Ibid., 210.

66. Ibid., 197.

67. Ibid., 438–48.

68. Ibid., 322–26.

69. Ibid., 323.

70. Ibid., 324.

71. Ibid., 324.

72. Patočka, *Fenomenologické spisy III/1*, 71 and 184–85.

73. Ibid., 140–41.

74. Ibid., 200.

75. Ibid., 110 and 117.

76. Jan Patočka, *Fenomenologické spisy II*, vol. 7, *Sebrané spisy Jana Patočky* (Prague: Oikoymenh, 2009), 610.

77. Jan Patočka, *Sókratés: Přednášky z antické filosofie* (Prague: SPN, 1990), 27.

78. Ibid.

79. Heidegger, *Being and Time*, 156, 233, 396 ff.

80. Plato, *Apology of Socrates* 29 e1-3, 30 a7–b2 ff.

81. Patočka, *Sókratés*, 31.

82. My work on this paper was supported by an FF UJEP grant 2016: "16." The reader who wishes to learn more about Patočka's life and death can consult Erazim Kohák, "Jan Patočka: A Philosophical Biography," in *Jan Patočka: Philosophy and Selected Writings,* ed. Erazim Kohák (Chicago: University of Chicago Press, 1989), 3–135; or Josef Moural, "Jan Patočka: A Bystander Turned Dissident," in *Classics and Communism: Greek and Latin behind the Iron Curtain*, ed. G. Karsai, G. Klaniczay, D. Movrin, and E. Olechowska (Ljubljana, Budapest, and Warsaw: Znanstvena založba Filozofske fakultete/ Collegium Budapest/Artes Liberales, 2013), 107–28.

*Chapter 6*

# The Essence of Truth (*alētheia*) and the Western Tradition in the Thought of Heidegger and Patočka

Vladislav Suvák

The analysis of what truth means is one of the most important moments in Heidegger's thought. It plays an important role in understanding Heidegger's rethinking of the philosophical tradition, and (as the terms are often synonymous for him) the history of metaphysics or the history of Being.[1] Among Heidegger's writings, three deal directly with the problem of truth: *Sein und Zeit* (*Being and Time*, 1927),[2] *Platons Lehre von der Wahrheit* (*Plato's Doctrine of Truth*, 1942),[3] and *Vom Wesen der Wahrheit* (*On the Essence of Truth*, the lecture given in 1930, published in 1943).[4] These two later works revise the earlier concept of truth, but they do not deny the account given in *Being and Time*. Rather, they penetrate this early concept more deeply.[5]

In this chapter, I first try to sketch out Heidegger's path[6] concerning the question of truth and consider some possible criticism of it. Second, I focus our attention on Heidegger's rethinking of the metaphysical tradition which, according to Heidegger, has reached its end. In this context we will examine the thinking of Jan Patočka. I think Patočka is one of the most interesting, even if little-known and misunderstood readers of Heidegger's texts. My hope here is to show, first, how we can understand Heidegger's ideas better through the writings of Patočka and, second, that by considering Patočka's appropriation of Heidegger, which emphasizes the need to think with and even beyond Heidegger, we can avoid becoming mere 'Heideggerians.'

First, we must ask whether Heidegger is developing a 'theory of truth.' Theories of truth, such as the 'correspondence,' 'coherence,' or 'pragmatic,' can be taken as the theoretical attempts to formulate the criteria which one uses to determine the truth (or falsehood) of a proposition. In general, we can say that most traditional 'theories' have asked *under what conditions* something is true or false. Pragmatists, for example, would argue that something is true when it is practically useful. Of course, we could say from the pragmatic point of view that the theory of what is true also implies an answer to the question: What is the *nature* ('the essence') of the truth? It is possible to argue that truth not only occurs when there is practicableness or usefulness, but that usefulness is just the *meaning* of truth.[7]

Now Heidegger maintains that none of these theories (i.e., truth as correspondence, coherence, pragmatic, etc.) has clarified what truth itself *is*. Paragraph 44 of *Sein und Zeit* begins with words like *Untersuchung* (investigation) or *ursprüngliches Phänomen der Wahrheit* (primordial, original phenomenon of truth, etc.). This is no accident. Heidegger is seeking after the "original essence" of truth by way of a radical "de-construction" (*Abbau*)[8] of traditional metaphysical concepts (or theories) and, therefore, he does not want to formulate any alternative "new theory" or "criterion" of truth. He resists the traditional temptation and asks about the condition under which truth *manifests* itself to our knowledge. (Let's note that Heidegger is indeed speaking just about the *correspondence*, but his argumentation also applies to other modern theories.)

For Heidegger, the Western tradition has forgotten the sense of Being and also the sense of truth that belongs to the core-sense of Being. He believes that the very possibility of the question "What does it mean to be?" has been closed off by the tradition itself and, specifically, by its various accounts of "reality." Because the sense of Being has not been clarified, and the sense of truth depends on the sense of Being, the sense of truth has likewise not been clarified. Through his destructive retrieval, he wishes to disclose (re-find) an original experience of truth that has become lost. What does this mean?

Let us now start to speak about truth together with Heidegger, 'the last Aristotelian,' which is the title Hans-Georg Gadamer bestows on him. What does it mean to say that the original essence of truth was forgotten by the tradition itself? Furthermore, how is it possible to recover it when we are so far-removed from the Greeks? Indeed, how can we make this recovery without thinking of the Greek tradition 'traditionally' and hence missing its archaic *pathos*? Heidegger believes that even though we are entrenched in the tradition we can nonetheless look for its basis, as we have already indicated, by way of 'deconstruction' (*Destruktion der Ontologie = Abbau*). We need to examine our traditional understanding of truth and exhibit the no-longer-recognized conditions which make it possible, i.e., what it presupposes, and with which our traditional understanding of truth has lost contact.

Heidegger says that from the beginning *truth* is already connected with *Being*. In other words, truth was for the Greeks a feature of ontological inquiry. We can see this connection already in the oldest 'definition' of the term 'truth' attributed to Plato and Aristotle.[9] Truth never meant 'correspondence' (or 'representation') for them in the sense of the modern Cartesian idea concerning the relation between *subjectum* (a knower) and *objectum* (what is known by a knower). According to that view, the subject *determines* what truth is: if there is no proposition there is no truth, or at least there is no truth without presupposing a *subject* who is capable of making propositions. For the moderns, therefore, truth is guided by a regulative idea of self-certainty. Since Heidegger is trying to gain an insight into the nature of truth *as the Greeks understood it*, he emphasizes that we must not confuse truth with knowledge. For the Greeks *truth* was an ontological question; for the contemporary thinkers truth is an epistemological question. Truth is not primarily an epistemological question because the question of knowledge already presupposes a certain understanding of what truth *is*.

If we analyze and "deconstruct" the modern concept of truth as certainty, we see that it can be traced back to the definition of truth as correspondence first formalized by Aristotle that locates truth in *judgment* (*Aussage, Urteil*).[10] At the same time, though, we find a deep mistake. Heidegger contends that this supposed Aristotelian heritage is rooted in a misunderstanding of Aristotle. It rests not on Aristotle's account of truth but rather on Aquinas' (or Isaac Israel's) interpretation of Aristotle's account of truth as 'correspondence' (*Adequatio intellectus et rei*). Even Kant, Heidegger maintains, accepted the view that truth is a characteristic of judgment in which there is a correspondence between the *knower* and the *known*. Thus, already in St. Thomas' appropriation of Aristotle we can find the beginning of modern 'epistemological theory' (of truth) which misrepresents the thinking of the classical Greeks.

The Greeks did not believe that knowledge consists in a judgment of what is really true. Heidegger explains that this notion is alien to the Greek spiritual world. Thus, we must attempt to understand what Aristotle means when he claims that 'judgment is true' in a way that is faithful to his thinking. Truth for Aristotle above all means the disclosure of *Being to us by itself*. Only after Being has disclosed itself can it then possibly be presented in true judgment which refers to what is disclosed.

Heidegger's reading of Aristotle follows the critical post-Cartesian tradition ushered in by Franz Brentano and Edmund Husserl. According to Brentano, the sense of the truth has its source not in judgment but rather in Being. For Husserl as well the primary meaning of truth lies in the truth of the entity (*Seiendes*). Although Husserl's notion of epistemological certainty resembles that of Kant, Husserl is also critical of the Kantian epistemological position (cf. Aristotelian background in Husserlian concept of 'intentionality'). Truth must be understood as a type of self-manifestation or givenness. Still, truth does not mean givenness as such but rather the *possibility* of a superior mode of givenness. So self-givenness does not imply for Husserl any relation to transcendental being-in-itself (as Heidegger charged against Husserl). For Husserl, self-givenness or 'evidence' is something that is immanent within experience. Of course, Heidegger does not want to follow Husserl's desire to formulate any kind of 'transcendental subjectivity' in an effort to find a 'last island of certainty' (to use Patočka's phrase) of human knowledge. Heidegger's questioning of the traditional concept of truth, set in motion by Husserl's phenomenology,[11] thus proceeds by way of a strongly ontologizing interpretation of key texts of Aristotle (such as *De Interpretatione* I, *Metaphysics* Theta, and *Nicomachean Ethics* Zeta).

In order to gain a better understanding of Heidegger's position, we must consider how his concept of truth is articulated through his fundamental ontology of *Dasein*.[12] His treatment of truth found in *Being and Time*, follows immediately upon the existential analysis of Dasein, and so the essence of truth is investigated from the perspective of Dasein's Being. Heidegger's account of truth therefore emerges from an inquiry into what it means 'to be,' an inquiry that gets started with his radical question: How can we clarify the sense of Being independently of any dogmatic assumptions of what Being is? The introductory question of the work (*die Frage nach dem Sein*) is the question which can be investigated only by *human* being or what he calls Dasein. Unlike all other beings Dasein is occupied with its own existence and the sense of its own Being. Da-sein is literally the 'Da,' or place, where 'Sein' is disclosed. Heidegger says: "Understanding of Being is itself a definite characteristic of Dasein's Being. Dasein is ontically distinctive in that it is ontological."[13] This means that Dasein is not simply self-consciousness, but mainly and fundamentally is conscious of itself or conscious of itself as Being (-in-the-world). Being-in-the-world is a fundamental characteristic of Dasein and cooriginal with this openness to its own Being is an openness to other beings as well as the Being of other beings.

This dis-closedness of Being to Dasein is, according to Heidegger, what truth means in the most primordial sense. Truth in its original (*essential*) sense, therefore, refers not to an *object* but to *Dasein*. Only by an object's being *uncovered* can anyone then say that this object is true. Truth is an *Existential* of Dasein. This means, then, that truth as such does not exist independent of Dasein. There is truth only insofar as Dasein 'is' and only so long as Dasein 'is.'[14] For Dasein is 'in truth,' says Heidegger. It does not mean that Dasein has to be (always) in truth. Dasein can also be in un-truth (as an inauthentic mode of existence). Dasein can fail to uncover entities (including itself). Still, only because Dasein is already in the truth can Dasein fail to uncover entities.

This has led Heidegger to say that there is no truth without Dasein. There would be no truth because what makes truth possible is the world's disclosedness and being open to a world is a basic characteristic of Dasein. In other words, Dasein is only open to a world because in its essential constitution Dasein is 'worldly.' As Heidegger says, "only with Dasein's disclosedness is the most primordial phenomenon of truth attained."[15] Heidegger is not saying that Dasein *determines* what is the truth (as the 'subject' of modern epistemology does), but rather since Dasein is the site of disclosedness, truth can exist only as a mode of Dasein's Being. Therefore, it is not any new attempt to formulate a subjectivistic or relativistic theory of truth. All truths are 'relative' only *in* Dasein's *Being* (but not *to* Dasein)![16] The central idea here is that truth considered as disclosedness would not be possible without Dasein because then there would be no Dasein to do the uncovering of entities within-the-world. "For in such a case truth as disclosedness, uncovering, and uncoveredness, cannot be."[17] We might say that Dasein is the necessary though not the sufficient condition of truth. For Heidegger truth is something that *happens*, and so it is an *event of being* (*Ereignis*) which is only *revealed* to us. Therefore we cannot *see* truth; truth is just *shown* to us by itself. He says "What is demonstrated is not an agreement of knowledge with its object, still less an agreement between contents of consciousness among themselves. What is to be demonstrated is solely the Being-uncovered (*Entdeckt-sein*) of the entity itself—that entity in the how of its uncovering."[18]

Of course, we might ask: Is it possible to say that Heidegger's analysis of truth is 'true'? However, such a question is misplaced. The question itself assumes as absolute the correspondence theory of truth, or at least some understanding of truth in general. But Heidegger is inquiring into the sense of truth which allows this very question to be asked in the first place. He is not concerned with any particular true or false claims. His inquiry works, rather, at a formal level which seeks after the foundation of truth, i.e., the conditions which make possible anything like 'true' or 'false' judgment-claims. We must understand that Heidegger is not conducting an empirical inquiry. The question of Being and Truth is not one more fact about real things. Heidegger is asking about the *essence* of Being and Truth. Furthermore, he is not raising the Platonic question concerning the essence of the Being or Truth of any one particular thing; e.g. what is it (*ti estin*)?[19] Rather, he is concerned with clarifying the Being and Truth of anything whatsoever insofar as it is. We might say that Heidegger doubles the Platonic question: What is the essence of the Being and Truth of the Being and Truth of any such particular being? This doubling of the Platonic question is, at the same time, a deepening of it since the Platonic question already presupposes it. Or, as Heidegger explains in the *Contributions to Philosophy*, "The essence of truth grounds the necessity of the *why* and therewith of questioning."[20]

Heidegger's project is concerned with a single (Aristotelian) question: What is the Being of beings (*Was ist das Sein des Seienden?*). Heidegger believes that this search for the Being of beings first really began with Parmenides and Heraclitus, and then was continued by Plato and Aristotle. The original names given to the Being of beings by early thinkers included *phusis* and *aletheia*. *Phusis*, usually translated as 'nature' (*Natur*), does not signify 'natural' processes of becoming (*Werden*), but rather the event in which beings in general come to *presence*. The *presencing* (*Anwesen*) of an entity (*Seiende*) is the first level of existence which opens to us the way to understanding the *essence* (*Wesen*) of *Being* (*Sein*).[21] *Aletheia*, usually translated as 'truth' (*Wahrheit*), similarly refers to an *unconcealedness*. Heidegger calls attention to the etymology of the Greek word *a-letheia*. According to Heidegger, this term contains an alpha-privative, which the modern term 'truth' erases. For the early ancient thinkers (Heidegger often says that Parmenides and Heraclitus were the 'thinkers' rather than the 'philosophers') *Being* is that which enables the *disclosure* of beings. Following from our analyses above, this means that Being is truth in its original sense. The Essence of truth itself is *disclosure* (*Erschlossenheit*).[22] And so, *alētheia* is still '*unhiddenness*' (*Unverborgenheit*) in its primordial sense as given originally in early Greek thought.[23]

But these early (and primordial) thoughts of Heraclitus and Parmenides would soon undergo a transformation in Plato and Aristotle. This 'turning point,' Heidegger argues, marked the real beginning of Western metaphysics. With the rise of Socrates' polemic with Sophists, and mainly with the rise of Platonic dialectics, the focus on Being as unconcealment was lost.[24] Heidegger analyzes Plato's 'simile of the cave' given in Book VII of the *Republic*, and tries to show that a decline, which sets the stage for modern thinking, already takes place here. The process of degeneration began with the Platonic idea of truth as 'correctness of perception' (*orthotes*) which supplants the Presocratic notion of truth as 'disclosedness of being' (*aletheia*).[25] Heidegger's analysis, which reconstructs this transformation, centers on what he calls Plato's ambiguous attitude towards Being. When Being becomes an Idea situated in an eminent position, then truth, which should have been understood as the un-hiddenness of Being, becomes the correct perspective of a superior being. Truth becomes the correspondence between thought and the idea.[26] Correspondingly, the place of truth shifts from the original unhiddenness of Being to the correct statement of man.

In later works, especially in *On the Essence of Truth*, Heidegger underlines a 'hierarchy' of three levels of truth. We can roughly summarize this hierarchy, which Heidegger appropriates from the *Nicomachean Ethics*, as follows.

1. The lowest level of truth is *propositional* truth. Here truth is taken to be the correspondence (*adequatio*) or agreement between

a proposition, and thus the intellect, and a thing. Truth is *logos apophantikos*: The predicative assertion in its two forms of *kataphasis* and *apophasis* (affirmation and denial).

2. The next highest level of truth is the *ontic*. Propositional truth itself presupposes that beings show themselves to us. 'How something shows itself' is a more primordial characteristic of truth than the simple criterion of correspondence. In other words, the being-true of the assertion is a derivative mode of the primordial happening of truth on which it is grounded. This is also the first level of unconcealedness. Dasein first finds beings as unconcealed before the question of correspondence can emerge. Heidegger appropriates from Book 6 of Aristotle's *Nicomachean Ethics* the different ways beings can be uncovered by Dasein. The human *psuche* (Dasein) can be uncovering in the five ways being-in-truth: *techne*, *episteme*, *phronesis*, *sophia*, and *nous*.

3. The last level of truth is the *ontological*. This refers not to the unconcealedness of particular beings, but rather the Being of these beings. It refers to the event of openness itself which makes possible Da-sein's own openness to beings and the openness of beings themselves. Here Heidegger re-appropriates Aristotle's notion of *to on hos alethes* (Being as truth).

I think that one of the strongest criticisms raised against Heidegger's concept of truth as *a-lētheia* is the philological one first articulated by Heidegger's student, Paul Friedländer, which he develops in the context of his writings on Plato.[27] Friedländer's main objection concerns Heidegger's etymological analysis and, specifically, the alpha-privative Heidegger attributes to the Greek term *a-lētheia*. He argues that Heidegger's etymological interpretation has no foundation in Greek literature. Thus, he rejects Heidegger's translation of *alētheia* as *un-hiddenness*. The only place in Ancient Greek literature where *alētheia* was understood as *un-hiddenness* was in Hesiod's *Theogony*; it is not exclusively understood in this way.[28] Here it also means the 'correctness of perception' which Heidegger attributes to the period of the decline of Greek thought.[29] To bolster his argument, Friedländer also demonstrates that two other words which share the same semantic form as *alētheia*, namely *atrekeia* and *akribeia*, mean 'accuracy,' 'correctness,' or 'truth.' Thus, Heidegger's claim that *alētheia* is etymologically *a-lētheia* (an alpha-privative as the negation of *lēthē* = conceal) is at best questionable, and most probably misleading. He further shows that the term *aletheia* does not just have a univocal meaning as Heidegger contends. In addition to the ontological sense of this term we also find an existential and epistemological sense, and we find these other senses in Parmenides as well as Plato.[30] All of these points of criticism work together to undermine, Friedländer thinks, Heidegger's claim that Plato's simile of the cave constitutes a 'turning point' in the Greek idea of truth; or, in his own words, "The Greek concept of truth did not undergo the change from the unhiddenness of being to the correctness of perception."[31]

Friedländer's criticism that Heidegger unjustifiably reduces the original meaning of *aletheia* among the Greeks exclusively to unhiddenness is compelling. Yet, we must also point out that in his later writings Heidegger seems to acknowledge, most likely in response to Friedländer, that historically or etymologically it can be demonstrated that, among the Ancient Greeks (which *includes* Parmenides), the term *aletheia* was originally experienced as correctness of perception. In his 1964 lecture entitled 'The End of Philosophy,' Heidegger writes: "In the scope of this question we must acknowledge the fact that *aletheia*, unconcealment in the sense of the opening of presence, was originally only experienced as *orthotes*, as the correctness of representations and statements. But then the assertion about the essential transformation of truth, that is, from unconcealment to correctness, is also untenable."[32] Still, even though Heidegger concedes the fact that the Greeks understood *aletheia* as correctness, he nevertheless insists that this fact does not entirely undercut his position.[33] This *historical* fact does not imply that *aletheia* as correctness is ontologically prior to unconcealment. It only means that man has historically thought of what he has encountered in the open before thinking about the open itself.[34] The concept of opening represents for Heidegger the most fundamental pre-ontological phenomenon. Unconcealment is opening or clearing while truth in all its forms is an event that takes place within the clearing. Without the opening there would be no free space for the event of truth to take place.[35]

Of course, this Heideggerian apology assumes a non-traditional meaning of 'history,' one which, we might say, is even 'ahistorical' from the point of view of descriptive history. But Heidegger does not wish to interpret 'historical facts.' Rather, he is trying to re-think the tradition from the contemporary position. His position concerning the understanding of history is, therefore, 'hermeneutical.' This means that he is less concerned with actual 'historical events,' and more concerned with the event of our interpretation of history. We can see how this understanding of history applies to his rethinking of the Nietzschean metaphor that the whole of the history of metaphysics is but the history of Platonism.[36] It does not mean that Plato was the greatest philosopher and we are simply the followers of his past legacy. It means, instead, that our questions and our thinking are still Platonic, and so we continue to see the history of philosophy as Platonists. This Platonic 'past' is our 'present.' In recognizing ourselves as Platonists, we must though at the same time move beyond Plato and clarify the basis of Plato's questioning. We must, in other words, understand Plato better than he understood himself.

Now we leave Heidegger, though not the questions Heidegger raises, and focus our attention on Jan Patočka. Patočka, a Czech philosopher and one of Husserl's last students, attempts to reconcile his teacher's concept of *Lebenswelt* with Heidegger's Fundamental Ontology. Incidentally, Patočka was one of the first thinkers, i.e., before Merleau-Ponty and other phenomenologists, to develop further Husserl's concept of the *Lebenswelt* with consummate skill.[37] Patočka attempts to reread Heidegger's ontology into Husserl's account of the Western tradition which finds itself in a profound crisis.

Patočka, like Heidegger, rejects Husserl's concept of transcendental subjectivity, specifically by explicating the many paradoxes which emerge from it.[38] Moreover, we can say that his examination of the concept of truth is very similar to Heidegger's. However, his interpretation of the Western tradition is far more historically "accurate" than Heidegger's. A result of this difference is that he formulates some new ideas even though they correspond to the same problems. This does not mean, of course, that Patočka is an historian or an historicist in the tradition of Zeller, Windelband, Burnet, and the like. Instead, this means merely that Patočka analyzes the historical texts in a way that is more consistent with the actual historical unfolding of events and so does not, like Heidegger, interpret history "ontologically."

Among Patočka's writings we can find two that deal directly, or at least focus more than his other works upon, the problem of truth: *Negative Platonism*, which is an unfinished manuscript written in the middle of the 1950s,[39] as well as the series of lectures entitled *Plato and Europe* given in the beginning of the 1970s.[40] In both texts, Patočka starts his account by arguing that the entire history of metaphysics centers around the problem of truth, and that most of the problems which apparently do not concern the problem of truth are, in fact, deeply connected to it.[41] He tries to find what is common in the idea of truth in Western metaphysics and, like Heidegger, returns to the Presocratics as the pre-founders of that tradition who understand truth as *uncoveredness* and shows how there is a movement towards an understanding of truth as correspondence.[42] However, in this context he maintains that we must interpret Socrates' role in our tradition differently from Heidegger.[43]

For Patočka Socrates belongs to the Presocratics rather than to the 'metaphysical' tradition that originates with Plato and Aristotle. In so doing, he places a special emphasis on how *praxis* is both thought and unthought in this later metaphysical thinking. The tradition of the Presocratics, which includes Socrates, does not, according to Patočka, separate the problem of *noein* from the problem of *praxein*. This archaic tradition reveals that speaking (*logos*) cannot be separated from acting (*ergon*). Whether Socrates is a literary myth or an historical person (Patočka personally continues to favor the second possibility), it seems certain that in Plato's representation of Socrates we find a special 'active, anthropologically oriented version of proto-knowledge' (lets say, of Pre-Platonics). Plato is the creator of metaphysics with his concept of *idea*.[44] But the real entrance into metaphysics was achieved through the formulation of logic in Aristotle. Plato still remains rooted in the pre-metaphysical soil of the Presocratics and seeks to capture this in the figure of Socrates. Patočka writes that "Thanks to his (Plato's) towering philosophical and literary genius, he managed to create a figure whose symbolic *signum* vastly exceeds every historical reality, a figure, that with every reason, became a symbol of philosophy as such. Only a contracted, lifeless interpretation in the tradition of Aristotelean logic (and that means metaphysics) could present this figure as a prototype of a deadening intellectualism that transforms vital questions into ones of logical consistency and into an art of correct definitions."[45] This account reminds us also of Heidegger's analysis of *logos apophantikos*. But Patočka accentuates the role of *praxis* in these old polemics, which Heidegger overlooks. When he interprets the ancient concept of *bios theoretikos*, he emphasizes the noun *bios* (as a human condition) rather than the adjective *theoretikos* (as a divine knowledge) in this couple.

Yet, the Socrates of both early Plato and Patočka is not merely a moral thinker, 'striving for a harmony of a human interior.' Socrates is not a *moralist*. Socrates is rather a *philosopher* and therefore possesses a knowledge of a special kind. His knowledge is characterized as the knowing of unknowing or learned ignorance. His knowledge assumes the form of a question. Socrates is a great *questioner*. Only as a great questioner is he the grand participant in dialectical discussions whom Plato describes. So he is not bounded to anything finite in heaven or on earth: "Socrates sovereignty is based on an absolute *freedom*, he is constantly freeing himself of all the bonds of nature, of tradition, of others' schemata as well as of his own, of all physical and spiritual possessions."[46] With the help of his trivial schema—a *dia-logos* which constantly gravitates towards the question *ti estin*, what is it?—Socrates unveils one of the fundamental contradictions of being human. On the one hand, the human being has a relation to the whole which is expressed in the question *ti estin*, i.e., 'What is this in itself?' (*to pragma auto* in later Plato). On the other hand, the human being is unable to express this relation to the whole given its finitude. Socrates represents this 'in-between,' says Patočka, because "he formulates his new truth—since the problem of truth is at stake—only indirectly, in the form of question, in the form of a skeptical analysis, of a negation of all finite assertions."[47] In contrast, the tradition following Socrates, while it originates from the same questioning, nonetheless attempts to advance a positive answer to the Socratic (or 'Pre-Socratic') question.[48]

Now, we can see that Patočka's concept of *negative Platonism* is both a *criticism* of the philosophical tradition which redirects the response to Socratic questioning as well as an *attempt* to interpret this metaphysical tradition differently from the way in which the tradition, i.e., our tradition, understands itself. Thus, the meaning of negative Platonism is expressed by Patočka as follows. The philosophy of negative Platonism is *pure* because it knows only the One—and that One it does not communicate directly as an objective knowledge at hand in the world, something to which we can always point, to which we can always refer. But it is, however, always rich because it preserves for humans one of their essential possibilities: philosophy purified of metaphysical (positive) claims. Patočka claims that "It preserves for humans the possibility of trusting in a truth that is not relative and mundane, even though it cannot be formulated positively, in terms of contents."[49]

Patočka responds to Heidegger's question concerning the essence of truth by showing that perhaps *uncoveredness* alone is not the essence of truth, but also *praxis* belongs to its essence.[50] The essence of truth must not derive only from the structure of Being but also take into account the Socratic problem of human *acting*. Thus, Patočka's analysis of truth calls attention to something Heidegger's own analysis does not and, therefore, supplements Heidegger's account. For a thinker like Heidegger any problem is 'essentially' ontological, and so any other problems, i.e., epistemological, ethical etc., are secondary.[51]

Patočka also interprets the contemporary interpretation of truth as correspondence from a different perspective. Modern voluntarist thinkers such as Nietzsche and Kierkegaard take as their starting point a critical stance toward the concept of truth as the logical structure of correspondence. Through this critical engagement they demonstrate how certain paradoxes arise from it. The theory of truth as correspondence maintains that the truth must be separated from untruth. However, according to the voluntarists, this theory of truth cannot be absolutized, because there are cases in which we cannot think the true without implying the untrue. Illusions of the imagination that are purely perspectival serve as a counterexample.[52] The imagination does not conform to this logical structure of correspondence, but rather is rooted in our own *voluntas*, and this kind of criticism implies, for Patočka, that a theory of truth must take into account *praxis*. Therefore, *praxis* must be integrated into a *criterion* of truth. The problem of modern theories of truth as correspondence is that they neglect the role of human freedom. Contrary to the original meaning of truth as *uncoveredness*, the theory of truth as correspondence makes truth merely a thing amongst other things.[53] So understood, the problem of truth as such is lost as a problem for Patočka. "Since the truth in its basic nature is not an adequation of intellect and thing, but rather an inadequation of freedom, truth must be understood as a motion which does not terminate as a static accomplishment. Fixing Truth into truths is always merely an approximation which serves a regional task or function, and we must leave this approximation when it no longer serves this function."[54] Thus, truth as freedom assures us that objectivity is never final or never achieves completion for us.

In his later writings, Patočka elaborates on this relation between truth as uncoveredness and freedom. He connects the problem of truth with the problem of *responsibility*. He locates the basis of this relation in the Socratic words *tēs psuchēs epimeleia* (the care of the soul).[55] Patočka interprets the words of Socrates found in Plato's *Apology* as: The desire to achieve oneness or internal harmony with thyself.[56] This desire for belonging to the whole, to the totality of the 'world order', defines the human condition and the tradition has sought after this 'total order' from its early beginning and continues on this path today. The care of the soul describes the situation in which we already find ourselves.[57] For Patočka this care of the soul is grounded ontologically in our human *freedom* (*hē psuchē*), and the *care of freedom* (*tēs psuchēs epimeleia*) is thus its ontological expression.[58] Our understanding of the human being, which is based on Plato's account of the soul, furnishes us with the most primordial sense of truth: as living in the truth. So Greek ontology is not merely a speculative position towards a superior reality. It is, rather, the life-structure of the human being itself.[59]

Finally, we can say together with Patočka that the authentic basis of the contemporary European tradition is expressed first by Plato and then repeated later by phenomenology. Phenomenology tries to show that the soul is not a *res cogitans*, but rather *existence*.[60] In other words, their own definition of philosophy, still valid today, reaffirms what Socrates and Plato first expressed: *philosophy is an existence of the human being in the truth*.[61] Of course, Patočka's interpretation of Plato deviates from that of the tradition. Yet, his negative (re-interpreting) of Plato, i.e., his 'Negative Platonism,' helps us to understand better both contemporary Europe and ourselves.

## NOTES

We thank the author and the Institute for Human Sciences in Vienna for granting permission to reprint this article, first published in 2000, in *Thinking Fundamentals, IWM Junior Visiting Fellows Conferences*, Vol. 9 (Vienna 2000).

1. Cf. Martin Heidegger, "Das Ende der Philosophie und die Aufgabe des Denkens," in *Zur Sache des Denkens* (Tübingen: Max Niemeyer, 1976), 61.
2. Martin Heidegger, *Sein und Zeit*, GA 2 (Frankfurt am Main: Vittorio Klostermann, 1977).
3. Martin Heidegger, *Platons Lehre von der Wahrheit. Mit einem Brief über den "Humanismus"* (Bern: Francke Verlag, 1954).
4. Martin Heidegger, "Vom Wesen der Wahrheit," in *Wegmarken*, ed. Vittorio Klostermann (Frankfurt am Main: Vittorio Klostermann, 1978), 175–99.
5. Walter Biemel in his excellent introduction to the philosophical biography of Heidegger has connected the idea of truth (*aletheia*) as the central

concept (or as the metaphor) with all of the other basic concepts discussed in Heidegger's corpus. Cf. Walter Biemel, *Martin Heidegger* (Rembek bei Hamburg: Rowohlt Verlag, 1998).

6. With this German term *Wege* ("paths"), Heidegger distinguishes his own position from the modern tradition of 'methodical' or 'systematical' knowledge, and he also tries to return to the 'primordial' Greek status of *epistēmē*. With this term he does not mean judgments as answers which help us to understand ourselves better, but rather questions without definite statements. But it is possible also to say the reverse: 'the question is the path to the answers.' Cf. the introduction to Heidegger's lecture *Was ist das: Die Philosophie?* (Neske: Pfullingen, 1956). We see here what Heidegger means by this statement above.

7. To be more precise we must say that there is nothing like a unified 'pragmatic theory of truth.' It is possible to distinguish minimally the 'consensus theory' of C. S. Peirce from the 'instrumentalist theory' associated with W. James and J. Dewey (and also from neo-pragmatic theories of truths, etc.). But we can demonstrate our concept of the 'pragmatic theory of truth,' and recall that William James, for example, identifies truth with beliefs that are *useful* over the long run and all things considered. Cf. *Pragmatism* (Cambridge, MA: Harvard University Press, 1975), 106: "'The true,' to put it very briefly, is only the expedient in the way of our thinking, just as 'the right' is only the expedient in the way of our behaving. Expedient in almost any fashion; and expedient in the long run and on the whole of course; for what meets expediently all the experience in sight will not necessarily meet all farther experiences equally satisfactorily."

8. We should translate the German phrase *kritischer Abbau* into English as 'critical dismantle' or 'de-construction.' Heidegger says that the old ontology must be built up new again from the ground. We have to find again the 'basic experience' of Greek philosophy from which the tradition has 'fallen away' (*Verfallen der Philosophie*). See *Die Grundprobleme der Phänomenologie*, GA 24 (Frankfurt am Main: Vittorio Klostermann, 1975), 31–32.

9. Heidegger starts his account of the tradition concerning the question of truth with Aristotle's writings. Cf. Aristotle, *Metaphysics*. 1025b 3, 1026a 31, 1060b 32, 1064b 15, etc. 'First' (theoretical) philosophy is *epistēmē tēs alētheias* (knowledge of the truth), and knowledge of *on hē on* (being as being), etc.

10. Cf. Thomas Aquinas, *Questiones Disputationes de Veritate*, 1.1: *Veritas adequatio intellectus et rei est*. We could translate it as follows: truth is the correspondence of the mind with the thing.

11. Cf. the sixth of Husserl's *Logische Untersuchungen* for distinction between propositional and intuitional truth.

12. Cf. Heidegger, *Sein und Zeit*, 10. "Being which we ourselves in each case are and which includes inquiry among the possibilities of its Being, we

formulate terminologically as *Dasein*." This means that Dasein is not a '*subjectum*' or '*homo sapiens*' etc. Concerning the ontological difference of Dasein, Heidegger distinguishes between beings, entities (*Seienden*), and the Being (*Sein*) of entities—i.e., between empirically existing things (as actuality) and their essence (as potentiality). This accords with the Aristotelian idea of the meanings of *ousia*. So for Heidegger Dasein is that kind of existence that is always involved in an understanding of its Being. Dasein is therefore not Being. As Heidegger indicates Dasein is rather 'there being' (he often hyphenates the word *Da-Sein* = there-being), the openness to Being characteristic of human existence. (Dasein is no longer 'an existence' which belongs to all things, i.e., natural or cultural, as it was in the old German philosophy which had translated the Latin *existentia* into German by the word Dasein.)

13. Martin Heidegger, *Being and Time,* trans. J. Macquarrie and E. Robinson (New York: Harper and Row, 1962), 32.

14. Ibid., 269.

15. Ibid., 261.

16. Cf. Heidegger, *Being and Time*, 270, for the argument against the 'subjectivism of Dasein.'

17. Ibid., 269.

18. Ibid., 260–61. "Thus truth has by no means the structure of an agreement between knowing and the object in a sense of a likening of one entity (the subject) to another (to object)."

19. Cf. The introductory passage of the lecture *Was ist das: Die Philosophie?* for the interpretation of the Greek words *ti* and *estin*.

20. Martin Heidegger, *Beiträge zur Philosophie (Vom Ereignis)*, GA 65 (Frankfurt am Main: Vittorio Klostermann), 353.

21. Heidegger also translates/interprets the fragment 123 (Diels-Krranz) of Heraclitus (*phusis kruptesthai filei*) as follows: "being (*phusis*) loves (a) self-concealing." Heidegger's own interpretation of this is that "being essentially comes to be as *phusis*, as self-revealing, as what is of itself overt, but to this there belongs a self-concealing." Cf. Martin Heidegger, *The Principle of Reason*, trans. Reginald Lilly (Bloomington: Indiana University Press, 1991), 64–65.

22. Cf Heiddegger, *Sein und Zeit*, §§ 28, 29, 31, 34, 40, 44, 68, for analysis of *Erschlossenheit* and its connection with Dasein.

23. In the beginning of chapter 44 of *Being and Time*, 263ff., Heidegger centers the word *alētheia* around the other Greek terms such as *logos* (the common being of all things), *apophansis* (to show forth), *apophainesthai* (unhiddenness of things), *phainomena* (bringing to light), etc.

24. CF. Heidegger, *Zur Sache*, 74ff.

25. Cf. Heidegger, *Platons Lehre*, 41ff.

26. For the 'first discussion' of the problem in the history of metaphysics see 'the third man argument' as a possible criticism of Plato's positive concept of 'the Ideas' in Aristotle, *Metaphysics*, A 9, 990b 17; Z 13, 1039a 2; M 4, 1079a 13. What is very interesting is that Heidegger disregards these early polemics concerning this same problem.

27. Paul Friedländer, *Plato: An Introduction*, trans. H. Meyerhoff (New York: Harper, 1964). Original title: *Platon: Seinswahrheit und Lebenswirklichkeit*, vol. 1 (Berlin: W. de Gruyter, 1964).

28. Hesiod, *Theogony* 233.

29. Friedländer, *Plato*, 223.

30. Friedländer deals with Parmenides' doctrine of the One: "The three aspects of the Greek concept of *alētheia* are here indissolubly united in one knot." See *Plato*, 224.

31. Ibid., 229.

32. Heidegger, *Zur Sache*, 78.

33. Cf. Heidegger's note (Heidegger, *Zur Sache*, 77) for the validity of the translation of the word *alētheia* in *Sein und Zeit*.

34. Cf. also Heidegger's response to the criticism of Friedländer in the lecture called "Hegel und die Griechen," in *Wegmarken* (Frankfurt am Main: V. Klostermann, 1978), 437–38.

35. Heidegger, *Zur Sache*, 77.

36. Ibid., 63.

37. Jan Patočka, *Die natürliche Welt als philosophisches Problem*, trans. E. Melville and R. Melville, ed. K. Nellen and J. Němec (Stuttgart: Klett-Gotta, 1990), 23–179. Original title: *Přirozený svět jako filosofický problém*.

38. Cf. Jan Patočka, "Der Subjektivismus der Husserlischen und die Möglichkeit einer *asubjektiven* Phänomenologie," in *Philosophische Perspektiven*, Jahrbuch, vol. 2, ed. R. Berlinger and E. Fink (Frankfurt am Main: Vittorio Klostermann, 1970), 317–34. Also see Jan Patočka, "Der Subjektivismus der Husserlischen und die Forderung einer asubjektiven Phänomenologie," in *Sborník prací filosofické fakulty brněnské university*, nos. 14–15 (Brno: Brno University Press, 1971), 11–26.

39. Cf. also *Problém pravdy z hlediska negativního platonismu* [*The Problem of Truth from the Perspective of Negative Platonism*, uncompleted manuscript from the middle of 50], in *Péče o duši*, vol. 1, ed. I. Chvatik and P. Kouba (Praha: Oikoymenh, 1996), 447–80.

40. This lecture course was translated into French by E. Abrams, in *Platon et l'Europe* (Lagrasse: Verdier, 1983), 9–236. These lectures were important in the development of his later and famous work entitled *Heretical Essays in the Philosophy of History*, trans. Erazim Kohák (Chicago: Open Court, 1996).

41. Jan Patočka, "Negativní platonismus," in *Péče o duši*, vol. 1, 306–7, 447.

42. The Czech term 'odhalenost' could possibly be translated into English as 'bareness,' which is very similar to Heidegger's '*Entdecktheit*.' But it is formulated without the negative prefix as it is rendered in English as *un*-coveredness. Cf. Patočka, "Negativní platonismus," 307, 447ff.

43. I would like to thank my colleague Alexander Di Pippo who has kindly reminded me that Heidegger has also interpreted Socrates as 'the purest thinker of the West.' Cf. Martin Heidegger, "What Calls for Thinking?" in *Martin Heidegger: Basic Writings*, ed. David Farrell Krell (London: Routledge, 1994), 382. Of course, this might lead us to believe that Heidegger's Socrates stays on the border between metaphysics and pre-metaphysical thinking, and so he belongs rather to the Pre-Platonic tradition. But I think, as we see above, that Heidegger's view of Socrates differs in crucial respects from Patočka's because Heidegger focuses on Socrates in the context of a discussion of thinking and he neglects the issue of acting which is the focus of Patočka's account. Cf. Martin Heidegger, *Was heisst Denken?* (Tübingen: Max Niemeyer, 1971), 52, 56, 112. Here Heidegger connects the origin of thinking as the possibility of radical questioning with the development of the triad: Socrates, Plato, Aristotle. But the question of acting in the triad is neglected in Heidegger's account; instead he emphasizes Socrates' question of *ti estin* (cf. also *Was ist das: Die Philosophie?* 16). I think that this problem of *praxis* is not only very interesting, but whose consequences are also very important to work out in the context of contemporary philosophical questions.

44. Patočka, "Negativní platonismus," 309ff.

45. Ibid., 308.

46. Ibid.

47. Ibid., 309.

48. Plato and Democritus are considered by Patočka to be the founders of two different metaphysical positions concerning the nature of reality: the *immanent* (Democritus) and *transcendent* (Plato). Cf. Jan Patočka, "Démokrit a Platón jako zakladatelé metafyziky [Democritus and Plato as the founders of metaphysics]," in *Péče o duši*, vol 4, ed. I. Chvatík and P. Rezek (Praha: Archivni soubor, 1979), 285–99. Also see the French translation by E. Abrams, in *Platon et l'Europe* (Lagrasse: Verdier, 1983), 265–80.

49. Patočka, "Negativní platonismus," 335–36.

50. Ibid., 450.

51. Cf. Heidegger's "*Brief über den 'Humanismus,'*" in *Wegmarken* (Frankfurt am Main: Vittorio Klostermann, 1978), 311–12, 357ff. Heidegger analyses here the *theoria/praxis* problem whose approach is very similar to Aristotle's for whom *theoria* must surpass *praxis* (357–58): "But now in what relation does the thinking of being (*Denken des Seins*) stand to theoretical and practical behavior? It exceeds all contemplation because it cares for the light (*Licht*) in which a seeing, as *theoria*, can first live and move. Thinking attends to the

clearing (*Lichtung*) of being in that it puts its saying of being into language as the home of ek-sistence. Thus thinking is a deed (*so ist das Denken ein Tun*). But a deed that also surpasses (*übertrifft*) all *praxis*. Thinking towers above action (*Handeln*) and production, not through the grandeur of its achievement and not as a consequence of its effect, but through the humbleness of its inconsequential accomplishment. For thinking in its saying merely brings the unspoken word of being to language."

52. Patočka, "Negativní platonismus," 451.

53. Ibid., 452.

54. Ibid., 459.

55. Jan Patočka, "Platon a Evropa," in *Péče o duši*, vol. 4, 230.

56. Ibid.

57. Ibid., 9.

58. Ibid., 20–21.

59. Ibid., 43.

60. This is the main idea of Patočka's article "Vom Ursprung und Sinn des Unsterblichkeitsgedankens bei Platon," in *Denken und Umdenken: Zu Werk und Wirkung von Werner Heisenberg* (München and Zürich: Piper, 1977), 102–15.

61. Patočka, "Platon a Evropa," in *Péče o duši*, vol. 4, 217.

*Chapter 7*

# Apocalypse of a Polish Soul

## *On Krzysztof Michalski's Heideggerianism*

Andrzej Serafin

Krzysztof Michalski (1948–2013) was a Heideggerian philosopher who radicalized Heidegger just as Heidegger radicalized his own predecessors. Patočka's disciple, Gadamer's colleague, he was the first person in Poland to publish a book on Heidegger (1978), preceded by an anthology of his writings (1977) edited under the auspices of Heidegger himself. The theme of Michalski's thinking was time, or, to be precise, human finitude in its temporal aspect. This makes him a Heideggerian thinker par excellence. He was not an orthodox Heideggerian, though. It is questionable whether Heideggerian orthodoxy is possible at all. Michalski's description of Heidegger is the best description of himself as well: He was able to translate philosophy into questions that we all ask, or rather, he made us pose them again. In this chapter I will, therefore, present an outline of his thought—not only his interpretation of Heidegger—in order to show how he became the foremost Heideggerian thinker in Poland, how he developed his interpretation of Heidegger, and how he transformed it in further thinking of his own.

I could now simply enumerate the philosophers that Michalski commented upon (from Descartes and Spinoza to Schmitt and Agamben) but that would not reveal the core of his thought. Where he looked for the answer is of secondary importance. What is important is his question. And whatever, or rather whomever, he wrote about, he always posed the same question, the question of the relation of the divine to the human. Needless to say, this was also Heidegger's "single question."[1]

The way Michalski handles this question—which I would like to illustrate with a brief passage from his most important essay—shows both
his relation to Heidegger and his own hermeneutical stance, revealed in
all of his interpretations:

> Nietzsche and Heidegger do not refer to divine intervention. What rips the
> human being in every moment of his life out of perdition in his current
> situation, out of perdition in this "world," is not some "otherworldly,"
> "transcendent" being. [. . .] The world as we know it is not our home not
> because we are irrevocably alien to it, nor because our home is waiting
> for us somewhere else, beyond "this world." It is not "God," an other-
> worldly being that introduces eternity into our time, putting us in every
> moment of our life before a choice between eternal salvation and eternal
> damnation. "God" and "world," "eternity" and "time" are, according to
> Nietzsche and Heidegger, concepts artificially separating that which can-
> not be separated. "World" cannot be understood without its apocalyptic
> dimension. Time cannot be understood without eternity inscribed into it.[2]

This passage shows how Michalski continues the Nietzschean/
Heideggerian line of thinking. He also looks for the overman in man,
for *Sein* in *Dasein*, for "infinity in the palm of your hand, and eternity
in an hour" (Blake). It also clearly demonstrates the difference, for
Michalski openly uses such seemingly obsolete concepts as "God" and
"Man," although he tries to attach new meanings to them, which is a
characteristic trait of his hermeneutical strategy. The above-mentioned
radicalization of Heidegger (and Nietzsche) boils down to reading them
as religious thinkers against their explicitly stated intentions. According to Michalski, Nietzsche was not antireligious (as he liked to think
of himself), and Heidegger was not an exponent of the emptiness of
traditional concepts that lost their religious content without notice. Just
the opposite. What Nietzsche was struggling to achieve was the revelation of the divinity hidden behind forms devoid of meaning (therefore
in essence he was a religious thinker, which is also how Heidegger had
perceived both him and Hölderlin). Heidegger, in turn, by showing the
emptiness of traditional concepts, revealed the fact that they are ultimately pointing toward nothingness.[3] But it is precisely this nothingness
that ultimately points toward the ungraspable divine. Having understood this, Michalski concludes, we can again use traditional concepts
as metaphors of that which is beyond any human understanding.

What does this lead him to? Ultimately to a Heideggerian (and Nietzschean) reading of the Gospel, visible in his last two books and in the final interviews, examining the ontological implications of the possible realization of apocalypse, not only its transcendental conditions of possibility (e.g., a suitable concept of time), but also the influence of this mere possibility (which amounts to the possibility of death) upon human life. In other words, a contemplation of the possibility of death (Michalski returned to this Socratic-Heideggerian argument at the end of his life) enables us to realize the "Kingdom of God on Earth" (he holds to the same line as Taubes, whom he knew well). This view is supported by phenomenological analyses of temporality, corporality, and the Nietzschean concepts of overman and eternal return that in Michalski's view coincide with the Evangelical call for rebirth. "Eternal life is no other life," Michalski uses Nietzsche to understand Christ, "It's the very life you are living."[4]

Michalski can therefore be described as a Christian nihilist. He tries to reconcile Nietzschean nihilism with the teaching of the Gospel. Heidegger gives him support. But, as he claims after Nietzsche, nihilism is not a desired point of arrival, but a necessary point of departure towards truth.[5] In order to overcome nihilism, one must first realize it (again a Socratic-Heideggerian interpretation of Nietzsche, treating the knowledge of nothingness as the initial step in self-knowledge). How did this view develop? The last book that Michalski published before his death, a collection of essays entitled *Understanding Transience*,[6] traces his evolution since the transcendental beginnings in the early seventies. Already the first essays (on Kant's preface to the *Critique of Pure Reason*; on the limits of transcendental philosophy; on Schelling's philosophical silence) bear a strong Heideggerian mark. As their motto they should contain the opening sentence of Gadamer's *Being Spirit God*: "Anyone who has been touched by Martin Heidegger's thinking can no longer read [. . .] these three words that lie at the foundation of metaphysics in the same way that they have been read within the metaphysical tradition." In his early essays Michalski shows how Schelling's encounter with the unspeakable (darkness beyond reason) resulted in his long and early silence. The limits of reason point to something other than reason; reason itself is bounded, and hence historical. This also applies to the concept of truth. All this leads Michalski to the core problem of temporality, the binding thread of his entire thought:

The question of the historicity of reason [. . .] assumes a different form: whether understanding something implies finding the unity of that which one aims to understand. Can we discover meaning in the manifoldness of the experienced world only if in every fragment we are able recognize a part of a whole? Or perhaps every act of understanding implies the discovery of the boundaries of reason—i.e. the presence of something foreign in our experience, something impossible to assimilate, a possibility that cannot be fulfilled with hitherto known expectations? It is a problem that has bothered me since the early years of my studies. I have, therefore, written a book on the historicity of truth in Heidegger, on a (productive) tension between logic and time in Husserl, and finally on eternity that constitutes the nerve of time, that does not let it stand still, that makes it pass by, calling Nietzsche to witness.[7]

This statement clearly shows how Michalski perceived his own development, how he was led to Heidegger by a fundamental question that did not cease even when he switched his interest to Gadamer (late seventies), Husserl[8] (1977–1988), political theology (the aftermath of martial law in Poland and the events of 1989 in the entire Eastern Bloc), Nietzsche (1992–2007) and, ultimately, Christ (1999–2012). What he was constantly after was this ungraspable otherness (the condition of possibility of thisness), whether in time (conceptually conceived as eternity), in politics (the state of exception), or simply in life. Just like eternity is, for Michalski, the horizon and the innermost core of time in its every moment (its "sting," to use one of his metaphors), so is revolution to a regime, and so is death to life, as that which undermines the status quo, as the constant possibility of something completely different.

Michalski refers to this ultimate otherness with the traditional name: "God." As for Heidegger, God for Michalski is present through the "absence of his hidden fullness."[9] Nevertheless, this hidden fullness can be symbolically, metaphorically signified. Heidegger's entire philosophical endeavor can be perceived as an attempt to express the unspeakable.[10] If transience itself is a sign of the intransient, then everything transient, everything perishable, including our bodies, our physical presence, becomes a metaphor. "Alles Vergängliche ist nur ein Gleichnis," Michalski concludes after Goethe. The human is the ultimate metaphor, finite, imperfect human being, suffering, loving, and dying. "Who put me here? Whose order and will allotted this space and this time to me?" was his favorite Pascal quote. Why this "pain that cannot be separated from erotic ecstasy, the pain of merging and splitting, the pain of leaving this world, the pain of entering it anew"? "The more thou burnest the sweeter thou art."[11] Michalski's sensuous metaphors show a tendency toward *Brautmystik*, which the young Heidegger was also fond of. Michalski in his final Christian-Nietzschean period is a continuator of this tendency, so clearly shown in the last two chapters of his *Flame of Eternity* (on eternal love and insatiate desire of further moments). Death, in Michalski's analysis, appears as the final lover, the absolute face of God. But, as an absolute ending, it is not mere negation, lack of being. It is something absolutely different. As absolutely different, it is the same, eternally returning anew: the burning flame of eternity. *To auto*, the self-differentiating sameness, is the *lēthē* in *alētheia*; philosophy is tautology, as Heidegger concluded in his final seminar.[12]

Only by facing the nothingness of eternity and a resulting revaluation and vindication of life can we discover the eternal kingdom on earth in its eternal recurrence. Michalski ends up where he started; in Christian personalism (he was close to catholic personalists like Tischner and Wojtyła, to the personalist circles of "Znak" in Poland), but due to his Heideggerian detour he is able to see Nietzsche's Zarathustra as a fulfillment of the Christian ideal. He tries to achieve the Gadamerian aim of *Horizontverschmelzung*, uniting Christ with Zarathustra (or Dionysos). Or, to state it differently, achieving a Christ that is not only worldly, cosmic, but incarnate, human: as the possibility hidden in everyone. This also seems to be the basic conviction behind Heidegger's fundamental gesture, his destruction of metaphysics: to reveal something hidden in humankind that the tradition occludes. Tearing off the metaphysical veil reveals, in Heidegger's analysis, the world (or *physis*) in its movement, but also humankind as the scene of manifestation. Heidegger assumes that in order to get access to being, hidden behind the metaphysical tradition, behind the traditional concept of humankind, one has to see humans devoid of their humanity. Only getting rid of classical anthropological concepts can enable us to reveal our forgotten essence.[13] Only when reduced to Dasein (Heidegger's translation of *psychē*[14]) can one disclose one's hidden identity: Sein.

Michalski's attitude toward the tradition and its concepts, toward language in general, is different. This difference is not only terminological, though, for it entirely changes the resulting anthropology; it changes humankind itself. As Heidegger clearly demonstrated, language is not only an external instrument of description, since this description, or model, is a project of life, a project of world, which influences this world, my world. A change of the model is a change of the modeled world. This principle, discovered already by modern sciences (Galileo), was further exploited by Kant, as Michalski shows,[15] and Heidegger has only drawn the ultimate ontological and anthropological conclusions. Heidegger's project of Dasein and its assumption that only metaphysical and anthropological purification can reveal human essence, has far-reaching existential and political consequences. Heidegger criticizes metaphysics for being uprooted, detached from life, but his own decision to give up traditional metaphysics and fundamental concepts like God and humankind, is no less alienating. His experimental language is a speech of someone who returned to the cave after an ecstatic vision of Sein.

Michalski has learned the lesson of Heidegger's critique of metaphysical alienation. If the aim of his project was the renewal of humankind by entering the abyss (i.e., through the destruction of metaphysics),[16] then Michalski's revision is a step further, a return from this katabasis. Heidegger's radicalized concept of truth implies that Dasein itself is the place of manifestation (disclosure of lēthē, of the "hidden fullness"). The theological concept of hermeneutics is gradually opened by widening its scope from the Holy Writ, through *physis* (i.e., world, as in Schelling and theology of creation), to humankind. Alētheia is, therefore, a metaphor of the ontological status of the cave—that is, the world as the domain of phenomenal manifestation. Michalski draws the consequences of this radical project of *Dasein* by performing a retrieval of the traditional metaphysical metaphors, by showing their agreement with Heidegger's project, which amounts to the reconnection of the lost connection between metaphysics and physics. From such a perspective it is clearly seen how the entire Heideggerian project was guided by the aim to restitute classical theological concepts like *logos, physis, alētheia, zōē,* and *hodos* (cf. the metaphor of *Feldweg* and *Holzweg,* the errant way toward truth in Heidegger's analysis of the essence of aletheia). Michalski speaks directly about what Heidegger wanted to reveal indirectly through the device of metaphysical *epochē.* The consequence of this is his attempt to unite Heidegger, Nietzsche, and Christ.

This amounts to a difference in their attitude to language and tradition. Heidegger is distrustful. From the fact that each phenomenon by revealing something simultaneously covers it by this appearance, he concludes that one must reach beyond phenomena toward what they reveal. He applies this rule not only to phenomena but also to the metaphysical language which was supposed to reveal being but instead occludes it. This is the aletheic structure of being in the world. Michalski seems to make a step further. If we have already experienced what is beyond words, beyond phenomena, we can again perceive it through the phenomena, in the phenomena, and hence also in the tradition, in language, which can now serve as a metaphor. This radical concept of metaphor, stemming from Tischner and Ricoeur, is already suggested in Heidegger's late statement that his philosophy is a "phenomenology of the invisible."[17] Instead of rejecting the tradition, Michalski now aims to encompass it, by referring to the example of two seemingly most extreme poles: Nietzschean nihilism and Christian revelation. Michalski's ambition to vindicate traditional metaphysical language is a relief after a period of metaphysical fasting. This humble gesture shows that indeed, as Heidegger suggested in his interpretation of truth, everything, every phenomenon, points toward the unspoken, toward *lēthē*. But then, also every corporeal, personal presence. Not only abstract concepts. Each person in front of me.

Michalski is therefore deeply humanistic and personalistic in his Heideggerian-Nietzschean Christianity. Humankind is in the center of his thinking. It is no coincidence that the name of the institution that he established in 1982 in Vienna is *Institut für die Wissenschaften vom Menschen* [Institute for Human Sciences]. This institutional attempt to examine human nature scientifically is a major achievement of Michalski. The series of debates organized by the IWM in Castel Gandolfo (1983–1998) comprise an anthropological summa of our times (the participants invited by Michalski were, among others, Gadamer, Weizsäcker, Taylor, Lévinas, Ricoeur, Kołakowski, Kosseleck, Spaemann, Rosen, Gellner, Ebeling, Thom, and Schils). Michalski's attitude toward humankind is perhaps best reflected in his description of Tischner's "ability to concentrate on the individual person; the ability to approach each one personally; to meet the person."[18] This is also why Michalski's questions are ultimately the simplest questions each of us can pose: about the meaning of pain, the meaning of love, the meaning of life, the meaning of death. If philosophy detaches itself from human existence, it becomes uprooted and turns into inhuman, empty metaphysics.

To summarize, Michalski draws radical conclusions from Heidegger's statement that "Only one more God can save us. I see the only possible rescue in preparing a readiness for the coming of God in poetry and

thought, or for his absence in downfall."[19] This thought is a reminder
of the motto to Heidegger's *Nietzsche*: "two thousand years and no new
God." For Michalski this new God is the same old God, the last God,
Christ. This return of God to humankind amounts to a turn in our attitude toward humankind and world. This change is most clearly visible
in Michalski's attitude toward politics. Michalski's project of politics
is dialogical and pluralistic, to some extent Habermasian (it also stems
from Schelling). It can be perceived as an answer to the Heideggerian
experiment of the thirties (the lure of Syracuse), as an attempt to build a
model of politics and human relations that encompasses the manifoldness
of alētheia:

> The modern world in which we live is irreducibly diverse, incurably
> pluralistic—because the meaning it has for human life is given to it by
> humans themselves. Good and evil cannot be picked up anymore like
> flowers from a meadow. Nowadays good and evil are "values" devoid
> of meaning if they are not related to someone who establishes them, to
> a man (different than others), to a group of people (different from other
> groups). The "values" set by them are necessarily varied, incoherent,
> manifold. [. . .] Uncodified, unknown, ambivalent habits, preferences,
> and beliefs supply their contents, quietly giving them their particular,
> partisan character. We should not delude ourselves that conflict can be
> eliminated from the world. We should rather "equip ourselves with steady
> hearts, that can face even the fall of all hope. And do it immediately, for
> otherwise we will not achieve even that which is possible today" (Max
> Weber).[20]

Michalski's last writings were all devoted to the problems of the
secular and the sacred, the relation of time to eternity, the mysterious
connection of love and death. These cooriginal (as Heidegger would
have said) opposites are drawing near to each other, conditioning each
other and complementing: "Eternity is a physiological concept. For
body is the concept in which the fastening of our lives to time comes
forth. If eternity is to express itself in time, then our bodily presence
in the world must be its expression."[21] "Death is not opposite to life.
On the contrary: death, just like absolute love, defines life: [. . .] as a
possibility of new birth imminent for the human condition."[22] In his
late seminars Michalski concentrated on this aspect of life intimately
bound up with death. His final reading of Heidegger concentrated on the
apocalyptic, eschatological, kairotic moment of *parrhesia* in *The Phenomenology of Religious Life* (it will "come like a thief in the night,"

Michalski liked to emphasize) and the concept of death in *Sein und Zeit*. But one should not think that Michalski's Heideggerianism boils down to the abolishment of all opposites. His post-Heideggerian restitution of metaphysics leads him to something much more difficult: an attempt to establish the difference, the inconceivable difference between good and evil. His last published text, very brief, dense, is a meditation that leaves the reader in awe:

Whence evil? Whence good?

First and foremost: evil must be "done," somebody must do it. It isn't given, waiting in front of me, ready to be picked up. The difference between evil and good implies that there is someone who does evil, although he could do good; that there is someone who does good, although he could do evil. It assumes one's freedom, the freedom of choice. The piece of glass that wounded my finger, the mosquito that bit me, the sun that shines and heats me—they are neither evil, nor good.

But what does it mean: "to do good"? So many possible meanings—but one is, hopefully, certain: "to do good" is to help someone in real need, to help a widow, to help an orphan, to help regardless of myself, regardless of my own needs. To forget about myself and give someone else a hand.

But this is impossible, nearly impossible: so many hands reaching for help—how to forget among them, what I can do myself, what's good for me, how not to start counting them? These hands are waiting for me, when I wake up for the first time; they are a challenge for me to face. Whenever I try, it seems that I will not manage, that I will not cope. That it's impossible.

"Good" is therefore the answer to the call waiting for me at the threshold of my life, the call to help others regardless of myself—"evil" is the impotence to answer it. Good is to overcome evil; evil—to fail in this effort.

Isn't this a possible meaning of the story known to us from the Book of Genesis about this specific freedom that constitutes us, humans; about the freedom broken from the outset, corrupt by impotence, impotence to do good—the story about how inexplicable, how hard to comprehend, how impossible, how miraculous good is? The story of "original sin"?[23]

\*\*\*

In this second part of the chapter I would like to elaborate upon the influence of the recently deceased Krzysztof Maurin (1923–2017) upon Michalski, his interpretation of Heidegger, and his theory of time, the core of his thought. I first heard about Krzysztof Maurin from Krzysztof Michalski during one of his seminars at Warsaw University. Maurin was a mathematician and a philosopher, author of an acclaimed text-book on functional analysis,[24] and a specialist in Hilbert and Riemann. Michalski often told the story of Maurin's legendary mathematical seminar where he presented his PhD thesis ("Heidegger and Contemporary Philosophy," 1974) and first managed to understand Heidegger's thinking. All other departments of Warsaw University were purged due to the political events of March 1968 in Poland, and mathematics was the only one left untouched due to its intellectual neutrality. The intellectual elite of the philosophical department, Kołakowski, Pomian, and Baczko, Michalski's most important teachers, were forced into exile. Through Maurin, Michalski met the family of the physicists Carl Friedrich and his son Ernst Weizäcker, a meeting that led to the publication of two volumes of *Offene Systeme*, both devoted to the problem of time in science, or to the scientific understanding of the world as an open system that develops itself within time.[25] Another fruit of their collaboration was the article "Mathematik als Sprache der Physik" (1977)[26] in which Michalski and Maurin show how mathematics was initially rooted in physics and served as a symbolic representation of the processes described by physics and that its development was parallel to the development of physics. Mathematics has to be rooted in physics; it has to perform its essential function of symbolically expressing the processes of *physis*, or otherwise it will become uprooted, detached, and abstract. This claim is analogous to Heidegger's view of the relation of metaphysics to physics and his thesis that Aristotle's *Physics* is his most fundamental metaphysical treatise. It should be noted that in its most radical form this thesis on the relation of *physis* to physical sciences has taken the shape of the doctrine of Giambattista della Porta, whose *Academia Secretorum Naturae* gathered the natural scientists (*otiosi*, cf. Aristotle, *Metaphysics* A 981b 22) to whom nature has disclosed a hitherto unknown secret. Such an understanding of nature is in perfect accordance with Heidegger's view of *physis* as something vivid, sensitive, responsive, even divine, and his call to overcome our objectified attitude toward *physis*.[27] Michalski and Maurin were both involved in the papal seminars at Castel Gandolfo. Maurin presented three papers there (in 1980, 1986, and 1988), including his cornerstone essay on the "tradition" (i.e., the spiritual, theosophical tradition of *prisca theologia*). When I asked Maurin about Michalski after his death, he only uttered one sentence: "It is very sad when such a great love departs so early."

In order to show how Michalski's theory of time stems from Maurin, I need to present first the main premises of the latter's theology and theosophy. I would like to show thereby how theosophical thinking forms an undercurrent of Heidegger's phenomenology. This claim has already been made by such Heideggerian scholars as Henry Corbin and Daniel Dahlstrom. Corbin, the French translator of Heidegger's *What Is Metaphysics?* and a leading scholar of Iranian theosophy, whose writings Maurin studied and admired, pointed out striking similarities between Heidegger's understanding of alêtheia as *Lichtung* and the Iranian mystical doctrine of light, in particular Suhrawardi's *Philosophy of Illumination*.[28] Daniel Dahlstrom has shown the analogy between Heidegger's fundamental concepts and kabbalistic ideas like *tzimtzum* and *tikkun*.[29] Heidegger's admiration for the Christian theosophist Boehme and his acquaintance with Leopold Ziegler and Walter F. Otto prove that such an approach to Heidegger's philosophy is justified and might even be necessary to understand his thought fully. My aim is to elucidate some premises of Heidegger's thought without which one is unable to understand cryptic and hermetic utterances of the *Ereignis* period like *Die Herkunft der Gottheit*[30] or *S.-E.-H.*[31] or why he considered Jacob Boehme one of the foremost European thinkers. Ultimately I hope to explicate some features of Heidegger's theory of *kairos*, as well as Michalski's apocalyptic reading of the Heideggerian understanding of time, as presented in the second edition of his book on Heidegger.[32]

Maurin was well versed in the doctrines of Christian theosophy (especially Jacob Boehme) and Jewish kabbalah (which he learned from Friedrich Weinreb) but also Iranian theosophy and Platonism.[33] He was close to the Eranos circle of religious scholars like Corbin, Scholem, Eliade, and Jung, as well as syncretic theologians like Panikkar (to whom Heidegger dedicated his last poem *Sprache*[34]). He claimed that all those religious traditions were not only vehicles that transmit a theosophical doctrine (which forms the inner mystical core of every tradition) but also provide a symbolical means of accessing the divine. Mathematics in its original sense is also a theological science. The world is only apparently secular. A possibility of a turn is inherent in all people that allows them to turn the world inside-out and perceive it in its material, visible aspect as the manifestation of the immaterial, invisible. Maurin liked to quote the Islamic Hadith Qudsi to illustrate this: "I was a hidden treasure and I wanted to be discovered. Therefore I created the world as a mirror to reflect me." One can find similar statements in the mystical writings of all traditions. Another important claim is the reality of the domain of ideas (*kosmos noeseos*) and the possibility of its contemplation. Furthermore, Maurin identifies the kabbalistic *shekhina* with *sophia* (hence the name of *theosophy*), which is not mere wisdom, but rather the divine presence in the world, the divine dwelling, as described in Proverbs 8 or in Job 38–39. What's more, he identifies it with *physis*, especially in its Neoplatonic understanding.[35] But the most important part of Maurin's doctrine is his anthropology, or the concept of *anthrōpos* as the embodiment of the divine *logos*, as in the Johannine prologue. The dictum "God became man" denotes a transition of substance, the self-negation of the absolute and its embodiment in the world and in humankind as the summit of creation. Thereby the divine dwelling and presence is identical with human.

One can find traces of this doctrine in Michalski's concept of another human as the ultimate place to encounter God. Also, Heidegger's early "principal atheism"[36] of the twenties can be understood as the radical consequence of divine incarnation. Our only possible perspective is to accept the world in its facticity and thrownness, as it is given, within the limits of givenness: the perspective of Dasein. If Heidegger identifies the manifestation of the world with revelation, then he says nothing else than Schelling: that we are in possession of a revelation older that the written one, that is, nature (*physis*). Not only Heidegger's concept of aletheia stems from such a radical interpretation of the divine incarnation, but also his concept of originary time (*kairos*) and space (*khora*). Michalski's interpretation of Heidegger's concept of time and his kairotic reading of time in Husserl and Nietzsche stems from this theological intuition: that the world in its finitude and transitoriness is not only an image of eternity but its realization, incorporation, embodiment; that the condition of possibility of manifestation is the temporality and spatiality of the world (as Michalski would have said); time is the way in which eternity presents itself. To Maurin this is no mere play of concepts, but rather a matter of experience, a specific way of experiencing the world. He liked to exemplify this with a story by Anker Larsen:[37]

I was sitting in the garden, working. The weather was beautiful. The air was clear. Silence and stillness—around me and within me. Suddenly an infinite calmness started to come forth. Cleaner and deeper than the tenderness of a lover, than the clemency of a father towards a child. It was in me, but it came towards me, like the air comes to my lungs. I felt it first within me, then even stronger around me and above me. It expanded, spread further and further until it became omnipresent. I saw it; it became wisdom, omniscience, but also power and potency, omnipotence. It drew me into the eternal now. Only in this moment I met *reality*, for such is real life: some now that is, a now that happens. With no beginning and no end. I was sitting in a garden, but there was no place in the world in which I was not present. So what is this *now* that happens, takes place? It is a permanent creation with all its travails. I saw time and space as instruments or functions of this creation. They appear with it and with it they disappear. This blissful *now* that is, and this *now* that travails and takes place, are one and the same. To realize this truth is to experience the eternal and temporal essence of being, to fuse it together into one. The world is no maya, no delusion. The delusion is in us until we open our eyes to this *now*, in which eternity and temporality become one, every ordinary day becomes a feast, and life becomes a sacrament. The eternal sanctifies the temporal, the temporal realizes the eternal.

Michalski's constant philosophical effort is an attempt to conceptualize this originary experience of time. In one of his first publications, an essay on Heidegger's concept of time (1974), he wrote:[38]

"The river of time" is continuous and infinite. And constantly, ceaselessly present. With such an understanding of time not only "things in time" are present, existing, but also time itself is present, the "now" in itself. Time taken as such exists "besides" things, is empty.

This time in itself, or temporality, is a synonym for the traditional notion of eternity. Its relation to "things in time" is analogical to God's relation to the world in traditional theology. God is only a container "in which we are and live," a receptacle (*khora*), empty in itself. After a detailed analysis of the concept of time from the perspective of Dasein, Michalski draws the following conclusion:[39]

Such a concept of temporality is neither objective, nor subjective. *Dasein* is not a subject or one of its features, and neither is it an object, but rather it creates a "space" in which both subject and object become possible [. . .] an open space, in which that which is can only appear. [. . .] Such "now" is not something primarily empty, that only later accepts being, which thereby becomes contemporary to us. Just the opposite—"now" is always the result of the *manifestation* of some being, and is never empty. [. . .] "Now" is always somehow articulated. Time is therefore no longer a "river" of subsequent moments of "now," existing "besides" that which is. Time is no longer empty. Time is an order established by temporality, in which things appear in the world. It is always full and diversifies, because it originates from temporality, from presencing.

That which is hidden (temporality, "timeness," *Zeitlichkeit*), is the condition of possibility, or origin of that which is revealed, present in time. It must be hidden in order to allow for anything to appear:[40]

Temporality is always the manifestation of something, the time of something, and therefore it has the tendency to hide behind that which is manifested.

Nevertheless the metaphysical concept of time that objectifies it is a necessity that cannot be overcome once and for all, because "it results from the sole essence of self-concealing time."[41]

In his "Time, Consciousness and the River of Time" (1981; republished in *Logic and Time*, 1988) Michalski continues this line of reasoning; there is a constant theological undertone behind his analyses:[42]

It is precisely this self-creating, living time, and not the time fixed in the dead unities of Before and After, that Husserl refers to as "stream." That the stream "flows" means neither that it changes in fact ("There is nothing here that changes, and for that reason it also makes no sense to speak of something that endures") nor a succession of acts of consciousness. [. . .] The life of time, the pre-phenomenal, pre-objective time, the self-constituting time, rather than time already constituted—is the actual content of the metaphor of the river. [. . .] The stream of time is not in time, it "temporalizes" ("er zeitigt"), as Husserl puts it in later works; that means: thanks to it reality develops in a succession of time; thanks to it unities arise, are constituted, which we call objects; the fluid lava petrifies into identical objective forms. [. . .] "We lack names" to describe the flow of time; [. . .] all these explanations fail to make the river metaphor redundant. [. . .] The "flow of time" can only be described metaphorically;

living time can only be described in the perspective of time already fixed; fluidity can only be grasped in the perspective of already existing objective forms. Here, metaphor is an irremovable element of the description.

Already here Michalski comes to the conclusion that the description of time from the perspective of finite being-in-time is doomed to inadequacy. No logical discourse can overcome this obstacle. A different, metaphorical mode of speaking is necessary. Metaphors, Michalski notes, are:[43]

not merely a heuristic operation, nor [. . .] an attempt to illustrate a meaning that is otherwise available to us. The metaphors cannot be removed from [the] answer; the meaning of what is happening to the world, to us, cannot be told without them. "And the best metaphors [. . .] speak of time and becoming: they should be praised for and a justification of passing!" [. . .] We should not be surprised, therefore, that Nietzsche so frequently reaches for metaphors; it's not (only) because of the need to illustrate but is first of all a result of his belief that knowledge, inherently incomplete, cannot do without them. [. . .] His central metaphor is [. . .] the metaphor of the flame of eternity: in Nietzsche's eyes, this is an image of the link [. . .] between successive moments and the blink of an eye, which interrupts that succession; it is an image of this tension [. . .] which makes our concepts hurt—scorch—and break apart as they open us to the unknown.

Michalski falls back on apocalyptic imagery, bestowing it with existential and kairotic meaning:[44]

Apocalypse takes place in every moment. [. . .] Every moment has in itself the possibility of an end, a limit, a closure of the world as it is—and a new beginning, transcending the limits of the hitherto known, a possibility of a world radically new. [. . .] In every movement of mine, in every act of my life the world ends and begins anew. For every person in a different way—we can never know in advance how. [. . .] The time of apocalypse is the time in which I live now.

We are trying to hide this apocalyptic destructiveness of time by covering it with worldly activities:[45]

I am trying to fill the time so that its emptiness does not confront us with its apocalyptic dimension: with myself (alien to this world). [. . .] But no

one has time anymore, "the time is close," today is the doomsday, this is
the judgment day, in every moment a judgment takes place, determining
my damnation and redemption. [. . .] Apocalypse occurs in every moment,
or, in other words, eternity is present in time. [. . .] It reveals the fragility,
the transiency of every bond with that which surrounds us, of every habit,
every obviousness, every moment of happiness and peace. [. . .] The
"world" cannot be understood without its apocalyptic dimension, "time"
cannot be understood without eternity inscribed into it. [. . .] It is not some
otherworldly being, "God," that introduces eternity into time, facing us in
every moment of our lives with a choice between eternal condemnation
and eternal salvation. "God" and "world," "eternity" and "time" are [. . .]
two concepts artificially separating that which cannot be separated.

This leads Michalski to the consideration of death as the ultimate limit,
the totally unknown:[46]

The confrontation with death puts us in front of something unconceivable,
unthinkable. Our own annihilation. [. . .] Let us consider for a moment our
fear, the fear of nothingness. It is not a fear of something in particular: a
robbery, an influenza, or a bear. Nothingness is nothing like that, it is not
a possible "object" of fear. When I say that I fear death, I mean the end,
the dissolution, the annihilation of everything that I know and that I can
possibly imagine, of all my feelings, concepts, obligations, of everything
that I can describe as "something." The perspective of death puts this
"nothing" in front of our eyes: the limit of all possible knowledge, and
thereby the limit of the human within me, the human that I know [. . .]
the end of my world.

Such a meditation on death is not a pessimistic contemplation of nothingness, just the opposite:[47]

The power of death and love consists in their ability to break that which
is and release my life to new, inconceivable possibilities. Inconceivable
and therefore uncertain, unattainable with knowledge or even probability
calculus, but only with hope. It is a hope for the unknown, for that which
was hitherto hidden, a hope that does not undermine the reality of death
and its dread. [. . .] The fear of death is not a result of ignorance, it is not
stupidity. On the contrary, it is a result of abundant knowledge. [. . .] To
prepare for death is to get rid of all burdens, the fear of possible loss. It
is to fall in love with the absolutely new. [. . .] Death is a release towards
the radically new [. . .] and therefore it must be a step into the absolutely
unknown, into absolute renewal.

To treat every moment, every thing, every face, every event—even the ultimate event of death—as a metaphor of the invisible is to conceive the world and human life in its every single detail and aspect as the signature of that which is beyond words. Michalski liked to quote Goethe: "Alles Vergängliche ist nur ein Gleichnis; Das Unzulängliche, hier wird's Ereignis; Das Unbeschreibliche, hier ist's getan; Das Ewig-Weibliche zieht uns hinan." Heidegger's "phenomenology of the invisible" can be conceived as an attempt to understand the human Dasein as the place of manifestation, the scene of apocalypse.[48]

Let me conclude with a poem by the great Polish poet Adam Zagajewski:

Krzyś Michalski has died unexpectedly.
It was he, among my numerous acquaintances
who could pass for someone in part immortal.
Combative, towering over others. Phenomenally intelligent.
He did so many good things. When one thought of him
the word *success* emerged from the cave in which
normally it vegetates. Success, real success.
And not *requiem* and other moving relics.
I think he flew business class exclusively,
stayed at the best hotels.
He was friendly with the pope and presidents,
all while remaining a philosopher, that is
a man invisible, someone who listens with attention.
This combination is so hard, impossible.
Only what is impossible can be magnificent.
In a well-cut black suit, slim,
dressed like a traveler preparing
for a great expedition, unwilling to reveal
where to.[49]

## NOTES

1. Martin Heidegger, *Besinnung*, GA 66 (Frankfurt am Main: Vittorio Klostermann, 1997), 415: "die Eine Frage, ob der Gott vor uns auf der Flucht ist oder nicht."

2. Krzysztof Michalski, "Krótka historia apokalipsy i jej zeświecczenia," in Krzysztof Michalski, *Heidegger i filozofia współczesna* (Warsaw: Państwowy Instytut Wydawniczy, 1998), 282.

3. As in the Angelus Silesius couplet: "Die zarte Gottheit ist ein nichts und übernichts/Wer nichts in allem sieht, Mensch glaube, dieser sieht's."

4. Krzysztof Michalski, *The Flame of Eternity. An Interpretation of Nietzsche's Thought*, trans. Benjamin Paloff (Princeton, NJ, and Oxford: Princeton University Press, 2012), viii.

5. Cf. John 8:32 and Heidegger's comment on this verse in his series of lectures on "The Essence of Truth," in *Vorträge, Teil 1: 1915–1932*, GA 80.1 (Frankfurt am Main: Vittorio Klostermann, 2016), 327–428.

6. I.e., impermanence, Polish *przemijanie*, German *Vergänglichkeit*, the fact that something *vergeht*, "passes by."

7. Krzysztof Michalski, *Zrozumieć przemijanie* (Warsaw: Fundacja Augusta hr. Cieszkowskiego, 2011), 11–12.

8. His 1986 habilitation on Husserl is available in English translation: Krzysztof Michalski, *Logic and Time. An Essay on Husserl's Theory of Meaning*, trans. A. Czerniawski (Dordrecht, Boston, and London: Kluwer Academic Publishers, 1996).

9. Martin Heidegger, *Erläuterungen zu Hölderlins Dichtung*, GA 4 (Frankfurt am Main: Vittorio Klostermann, 2012), 170; Martin Heidegger, *Vorträge und Aufsätze (1936–1953)*, GA 7 (Frankfurt am Main: Vittorio Klostermann, 2000), 185.

10. "Das erste Gesagte ist das Ungesagte" in Martin Heidegger, *Zum Wesen der Sprache und Zur Frage nach der Kunst*, GA 74 (Frankfurt am Main: Vittorio Klostermann, 2010), 131; "Das Wahre ist das Ungesagte, das nur im Streng und gemäß Gesagten das Ungesagte bleibt, das es ist"; "die alētheia anfänglich noch nicht und noch nie gennant ist," in Martin Heidegger, *Heraklit*, GA 55 (Frankfurt am Main: Vittorio Klostermann, 1994), 180, 174. Cf. Martin Heidegger, *Wegmarken (1919–1961)*, GA 9 (Frankfurt am Main: Vittorio Klostermann, 2004), 203.

11. Michalski, *The Flame of Eternity*, 126.

12. Martin Heidegger, *Seminare (1951–1973)*, GA 15 (Frankfurt am Main: Vittorio Klostermann, 2005), 397–400, 405.

13. Martin Heidegger, *Ontologie. Hermeneutik der Faktizität*, GA 63 (Frankfurt am Main: Vittorio Klostermann, 1995), 21f.

14. Martin Heidegger, *Platon: Sophistes*, GA 19 (Frankfurt am Main: Vittorio Klostermann, 1992), 21; cf. Martin Heidegger, *Einführung in die phänomenologische Forschung*, GA 17 (Frankfurt am Main: Vittorio Klostermann, 2006), 6; Martin Heidegger, *Phänomenologische Interpretationen ausgewählter Abhandlungen des Aristoteles zu Ontologie und Logik*, GA 62 (Frankfurt am Main: Vittorio Klostermann, 2005), 376f; Martin Heidegger, *Vorträge, Teil 1: 1915–1932*, GA 80.1, 15f.

15. Krzysztof Michalski, "Próba interpretacji: Przedmowa do pierwszego wydania 'Krytyki czystego rozumu,'" in Michalski, *Zrozumieć przemijanie*, 23–41.

16. Martin Heidegger, *Holzwege (1935–1946)*, GA 5 (Frankfurt am Main: Vittorio Klostermann, 2003), 269f.

17. Heidegger, *Seminare*, GA 15, 399.

18. Video recording of Michalski remembering Tischner at http://www.archiwumjp2.pl.

19. Martin Heidegger, *Reden und andere Zeugnisse eines Lebensweges (1910–1976)*, GA 16 (Frankfurt am Main: Vittorio Klostermann, 2000), 671.

20. Krzysztof Michalski, "Polityka i wartości," in Michalski, *Zrozumieć przemijanie*, 457–58.

21. Michalski, *The Flame of Eternity*, vii (translation modified).

22. Krzysztof Michalski, *Eseje o Bogu i śmierci* (Warsaw: Kurhaus Publishing, 2014), 47.

23. Krzysztof Michalski, "Cud dobra," *Gazeta Wyborcza*, April 7–9, 2012, 27.

24. Krzysztof Maurin, *Analysis*, vols. I–III (Dordrecht and Warsaw: PWN-Reidel, 1980).

25. E. U. v. Weizsäcker, ed., *Offene Systeme I: Beiträge zur Zeitstruktur von Informationen, Entropie und Evolution* (Stuttgart: Klett, 1974); Krzysztof Maurin, Krzysztof Michalski, and Enno Rudolph, eds., *Offene Systeme II: Logik und Zeit* (Stuttgart: Klett-Cotta, 1981).

26. Krzysztof Maurin and Krzysztof Michalski, "Mathematik als Sprache der Physik," *Philosophia Naturalis* 16, no. 4 (1977): 363–82.

27. Andrzej Serafin, "Heidegger on Nature," *Kronos Philosophical Journal* 4 (2015): 171–75.

28. Martin Heidegger, "Qu'est-ce que la métaphysique?" trans. H. Corbin, *Bifur* 8 (1931): 1–27; Henry Corbin, "De Heidegger à Sohravardî and Post-Scriptum a un entretien philosophique," in *Cahier de l'Herne: Henry Corbin*, ed. Ch. Jambet (Paris: De l'Herne, 1981), 23–37, 38–56; Sylvain Camilleri and Daniel Proulx, "Martin Heidegger et Henry Corbin: Lettres et documents (1930–1941)," *Bulletin heideggérien* 4 (2014): 4–63.

29. Daniel Dahlstrom, "Heidegger, Scholem, and the Nothingness of Revolution," (lecture at the Colloque Heidegger et "les juifs," Paris, January 24, 2015).

30. Martin Heidegger, *Zum Ereignis-Denken*, GA 73.1 (Frankfurt am Main: Vittorio Klostermann 2013), 813f.

31. Ibid., 723f.

32. Michalski, "Krótka," 267–83.

33. I'm basing this brief presentation on an unpublished typescript of the 1988 Castel Gandolfo lecture where Maurin presented his most essential ideas. Some of them were also presented in German articles: "Geburt des integralen Bewußtseins," *Zeitschrift für Ganzheitsforschung* 3 (1983); "Logos-Symbol-Darstellung," *Zeitschrift für Ganzheitsforschung* 1 (1985); "Mystik–Mathematik–Magie," *Zeitschrift für Ganzheitsforschung* 4 (1986); "Mathematik als Leben von Ideen," *Reports on Mathematical Physics* 35, no. 2 (1995).

34. Martin Heidegger, *Aus der Erfahrung des Denkens (1910–1976)*, GA 13 (Frankfurt am Main: Vittorio Klostermann, 2002), 229; Martin Heidegger, *Gedachtes,* GA 81 (Frankfurt am Main: Vittorio Klostermann, 2007), 289.

35. Cf. Plotinus, *Ennead* III.8 and the Neoplatonic corollaries on time and space of Simplicius.

36. Heidegger, *Phänomenologische Interpretationen*, GA 62, 363.

37. This translation is based on Maurin's rendering of the Danish original, *For åben dør*, (Copenhagen: Gyldendal, 1926).

38. Krzysztof Michalski, "Heidegger: filozof i czas," *Teksty: teoria literatury, krytyka, interpretacja* 18, no. 6 (1974): 58.

39. Ibid., 67–68.

40. Ibid., 69.

41. Ibid.

42. Michalski, *Logic and Time,* 140–41.

43. Michalski, *The Flame of Eternity*, xi, 93.

44. Michalski, "Krótka," 270.

45. Ibid., 274, 280, 282.

46. Michalski, *The Flame of Eternity*, 81 (translation modified).

47. Krzysztof Michalski, "Śmierć Boga," *Gazeta Wyborcza,* June 15, 2000, 20; Michalski, *Eseje*, 46.

48. Andrzej Serafin, "Apocalypse and Truth: On Heidegger's Unknown God," *Kronos Philosophical Journal* 3 (2014): 124–33; Andrzej Serafin, "Heidegger's phenomenology of the invisible," *Argument: Biannual Philosophical Journal* 6, no. 2 (2016): 313–22.

49. Translated by Jeff Love and Andrzej Serafin.

## Chapter 8

# Heidegger

### *Krzysztof Michalski*

### Introduced by Ludger Hagedorn and Piotr Kubasiak

#### "READING HEIDEGGER IN COMMUNIST POLAND IN THE MID 1970s"

Below we publish, for the first time in English translation, an article that the young Polish philosopher Krzysztof Michalski wrote in 1975 for the monthly journal *Twórczość*.[1] The article was reprinted two years later as an introduction to a Polish collection of essays by Heidegger that Michalski edited.[2]

Besides these Polish publications, the author also made sure to prepare an English translation. It is not known whether this was done because Michalski envisaged a concrete publication or whether he simply wanted to have an English version of it on hand by way of precaution. In any case, it remained unpublished until today. The translation has been preserved as a typescript[3] and is part of Michalski's *Nachlass* at the Institute for Human Sciences (*Institut für die Wissenschaften vom Menschen*) in Vienna, which he had founded in 1982 and where he served as rector until his death in 2013.

The typescript bears the simple title "Heidegger" (as does the Polish original). It does not mention Michalski as the author, nor does it provide any information about the translation process. In particular, we do not know the year of the translation or the translator's name. From the character of the typescript, it seems clear that the translation must have been finished before the mid-1980s. Roughly speaking, we can therefore date it between 1975 and 1985. The standard of translation is very good, and the phrasing in English is excellent. People who knew Michalski well agree on the fact that his English by that time was not good enough to have possibly done the translation himself alone. It seems probable, however, that the author was closely involved in the translating process, particularly with regard to philosophical terminology and the specific Heideggerian vocabulary and neologisms.[4] The very few and carefully written notes in the margins testify to the fact that Michalski actively took care of improving the translation, but that he also seems to have had no major objections or points of disagreement with the final result presented here.

Evidently, the main ambition of the article is to provide the reader with an introduction to the thought of Martin Heidegger; hence also the unspecific title. But the achievements of the essay are, in fact, nevertheless considerable: While, at one level, this chapter will be a highly insightful reading for those not fully acquainted with Heidegger's philosophy, it, at another, advances a perspective guided by its own, independent research question: "Why is it that Heidegger's thought had—and still has—such fascinating force?"[5] In endeavoring to provide an answer, Michalski's reflections lean as well on Heidegger's erstwhile students, Hannah Arendt and Walter Biemel. The special fascination with Heidegger, he would hold, was—and is—that he teaches his students and readers to think. His philosophy is not just another trend or school, but rather a manner of learning to think for oneself, a "path" that is its own reward. In this sense, it can never be sufficient to characterize his thought as an overcoming of metaphysics and philosophical subjectivism, and rightly so! Following Michalski, Heidegger's philosophy should, above all, be understood as "an attempt to grasp our life-historical situation from scratch and to show to us the possibility of another life."[6]

In addition to his doctoral thesis (published in 1978 and reprinted in 1998),[7] Michalski edited the aforementioned collection of essays by Heidegger entitled *Budować Mieszkać Myśleć* (*Building, Dwelling, Thinking*). Notably, the selection of essays for this volume is not identical with the original 1954 edition *Vorträge und Aufsätze*.[8] Besides four essays from this German collection (including the eponymous "Bauen Wohnen Denken"), Michalski's edition also comprises other well-known studies by Heidegger, such as "What Is Metaphysics?" (1929), "What Are Poets For?" (1946), and *Letter on "Humanism"* (1947). As he writes in the introduction, the aim of his selection was to retrace Heidegger's *Denkweg* (his "path of thought") for the Polish reader, including the reinterpretation of his philosophy by Heidegger himself in the time after his *Kehre* (the "turn" of his thought). According to Michalski, the selection of essays for this volume was agreed upon consensually with Heidegger.[9]

The importance of Michalski's work for the reception of Heidegger in Poland must be understood in historical context. Prior to his works, only two notable studies on Heidegger were accessible to the Polish reader. The first was an article by Franciszek Sawicki entitled "Pojęcie i zagadnienie nicości u Heideggera" ("The Concept and Problem of Nothingness in Heidegger"). Published in 1955, the aim of this article was essentially to depict Heidegger's thought as an atheistic existentialism. The second major publication was the volume *Filozofia egzystencjalna* (*Philosophy of Existentialism*, 1965). It was edited by the two outstanding philosophers Leszek Kołakowski and Krzysztof Pomian and saw the first Polish translation of selected passages from Heidegger's *Sein und Zeit* (*Being and Time*).[10] Hence it was the volume conceived by Michalski that for the first time made a broader selection of studies by Heidegger available for Polish readers. Alongside the editor himself, there were four other well-known philosophers involved in the translation works: Krzysztof Pomian, Marek J. Siemek, Józef Tischner, and Krzysztof Wolicki.[11] It is noteworthy that major decisions concerning the translation of crucial terms were made consensually. As an appendix to the volume, Michalski also added a "dictionary" of Heideggerian terms. His edition thereby set a standard for the further translation of Heidegger into Polish, and even today it continues to serve as a kind of guideline.[12] It strongly influenced the reception of Heidegger in Poland, and we can rightly state that "his translation of Heidegger's neologisms, being basically an imposition of a certain interpretation, is by now well-rooted in Polish philosophical jargon."[13]

In 1974, Michalski finished his dissertation on "Heidegger i Filozofia Współczesna" ("Heidegger and Contemporary Philosophy") at the University of Warsaw.[14] His main advisor was Jan Legowicz.[15] After the 1968 political crisis in Poland, with its ensuing anti-Semitic campaign and the repression of dissidents, many intellectuals were forced to leave the country, among them the philosophers Leszek Kołakowski und Krzysztof Pomian, who were principal influences on Krzysztof Michalski.[16] Without an adequate advisor, Michalski tried to get into

contact with the Czech phenomenologist Jan Patočka, whom the Polish philosopher Irena Krońska had recommended to him. This was the
beginning of an intense philosophical correspondence between the two
and the initial impulse for a development that lead to the establishment
of a Patočka Archive at the Viennese *Institute for Human Sciences*
(IWM) a few years later. Michalski would therefore insist that Patočka
was the "true, though unofficial advisor" of his doctoral thesis.[17]

How much the authors envisage Heidegger's thought as a potentially liberating force against the political constraints of their day is a
highly remarkable aspect of this correspondence between Prague and
Warsaw in Communist times. In one of the letters, Patočka explicitly
highlights the "particular meaning of Heidegger's philosophy for our
East-European nations"[18] and bases this claim on the fact that it entails
"a certain philosophy of history"[19] that promises to offer an alternative
to the historical determinism of Marxist ideology. "This philosophy,"
Patočka continues in the same letter from 1974, "concerns the history
of being itself and therefore is about to supersede the one which is
prevailing today."[20] In his answer, Michalski does not directly react to
this sweeping assertion by Patočka, but there is almost too nice a coincidence and a funny echo of it to be found in his letter, when Michalski
reports on his dissertation defense, where he was attacked by one of
the referees for not acknowledging that "Heidegger's philosophy is a
deliberate and deliberately hidden polemic against Marxism."[21] Had
the critic known how close his remark came to the candidate's most
recent correspondence! What Patočka considers the "greatest and most
vibrant" side of Heidegger's philosophy—namely, its historical dimension that, as he says, "no one in the West has connected to"[22]—remains
an important impulse also for the later reflections of Michalski. It is
telling evidence that one of his best known and most widespread essays
is entitled "Iron Laws and Personal Responsibility,"[23] criticizing the
deterministic view of history and offering an alternative in existential
philosophy. Ten years later, in the 1998 foreword to the second edition
of his book on Heidegger, Michalski coins another remarkable phrase
that in some sense sums up much of his earlier correspondence with
Patočka: "Heidegger (. . .)—in my eyes, as in the eyes of my teacher
Jan Patočka—offers us an antidote to the 'Hegelian bite' (*ukąszenie
heglowskie*) which for so long transformed the lively faces of intellectuals into the bumptious mugs of secretaries."[24]

Michalski's correspondence with Patočka in this sense is not only the documentation of a philosophical friendship but, as Nicolas de Warren nicely holds, it testifies to "the development of a civil society founded on institutions of conversation" and shows how *civil society* for many Eastern European dissidents came to mean "an engagement with a *life in truth* at odds with the aesthetics of banality (. . .) and the bureaucratization of life."[25] Patočka's often quoted "solidarity of the shaken" in this sense finds its vivid expression in his epistolary discussions with Michalski. Not accidentally, Michalski also ends the article published below with a reference to Patočka that reflects his admiration and gratefulness for the professor from Prague whom he had, in fact, met only once.[26]

The importance of this chapter ought to be understood in light of the fact that for more than thirty years now, Michalski's article has served as an introduction to the philosophy of Martin Heidegger to Polish readers. Michalski insightfully depicts the development of Heidegger's philosophy and outlines important sources of his thought. Above all, however, he argues against the common prejudices against Heidegger's philosophy as mere psychologism, anthropologism, or atheistic existentialism.[27] Or in Michalski's own words: "I wanted to portray Heidegger's thought as a *problem*, neither adopting nor rejecting it."[28]

Yet the most striking feature of Michalski's article is, indeed, something else: More than anything else, it is a document of his own fascination with the philosophy of Martin Heidegger—the fascination of a young Polish scholar who, against all odds and political circumstances, sets out to explore a philosophy that does not help to master the world and promises nothing but persistent inquiry.

## HEIDEGGER

### Krzysztof Michalski[29]

It began a rather long time ago, more or less in 1919. A young lecturer, Martin Heidegger, at that time started his teaching career at the University of Freiburg in Baden. This was also the start of his fame, which immediately grew among students who came from all over Germany to Freiburg and then to Marburg, where Privatdozent Heidegger assumed his first chair in philosophy—and later also beyond the academic community and beyond Germany.

What drew crowds of students to the lectures of the young professor long before his books made his name famous throughout the world? What was the basis of the renown which soon made Heidegger the most famous philosopher of our century? His name later many a time disappeared from the field of interest of so-called "public opinion" only to reappear once again—raised up by the wave of fashion. Nonetheless, from the time of his first lectures in Freiburg the abyssal current of fascination thanks to which Heidegger's thought in a mysterious way describes the spiritual life of our century has not faded. Where is the source of this trend?

It is significant that at the beginning Heidegger's fame really had nothing to feed on: there was no theory, views which could be communicated to others or, once heard, to evaluate their profundity and importance. What did Heidegger teach? For the most part he analysed classical philosophical texts: mainly Plato and Aristotle. These analyses unquestionably contributed many new insights to research on Plato and others—but Heidegger's fame was not the same as Wilamowitz-Moellendorff. Those who attended Heidegger's lectures from all accounts went out of them moved, touched in mind and heart. What can one say about Plato to make such an impression?

I doubt whether any interpretation of Plato's theory, even the most innovative one, is capable of doing this. This was not what Heidegger had in mind. One of his students, today a well-known professor, Walter Biemel, recalls that at Heidegger's seminars students were forbidden to cite his own, earlier expressed opinions on the text under discussion. The goal was not to assimilate the "correct" interpretation, become persuaded concerning this or another substantive position. Something more was involved here—and this is what drew such throngs to Heidegger. Thinking was the aim.

"It was technically decisive that, for instance, Plato was not talked *about* and his theory of Ideas expounded; rather for an entire semester a single dialogue was pursued and subjected to question step by step, until the time-honored doctrine had disappeared to make room for a set of problems of immediate and urgent relevance."[30]—said Hannah Arendt in recalling Heidegger's seminars. Heidegger was able to translate Plato—as well as Aristotle and others—into questions which everybody asked himself, more precisely: he was able, as Socrates once did, to inspire every participant in the seminars to make this translation himself. He was able to teach people to think. And no one had been able to do this for a long time.

But what does "to think" mean? And how can a text written long ago help us in thinking about what concerns us today—what is immediate and vital?

Sometimes it is said: philosophy is the skill of asking questions. Its real contents are problems and not their solution. That is why the history of philosophy is the history of problems; it is an account of our stubborn circulation around the same questions. We are hardly—it is said—ever closer to the solutions: problems are not solved, they are not mathematical problems. The only progress possible in the history of philosophy is progress in the skill of asking questions: we know better and better which questions trouble us and nothing more.

So perhaps this is the answer: traditional philosophy comes to life when under its historical form we discover the same "eternal questions" that also torment us today.

Why should this be so interesting, though? Why should we become fascinated by Plato, since the gist of his theory boils down to the same questions which we also ask ourselves—and hence to questions which hardly do not concern *precisely* us? And besides—how do we know that these questions are the same? When asking about truth, did Plato really ask about the same thing as Descartes? Isn't this simply a myth from philosophy textbooks? Is it not an illusion—perpetuated by textbooks and the structure of universities—that philosophers respond only to a certain list of questions: epistemological, metaphysical, ontological, ethical?

In fact, it is an illusion; for there are no questions which can be understood independently from the context, from the situation in which they are raised. The question: "What is truth?" has a completely different sense in the mouth of Pilate and Descartes, Aristotle and Heidegger. To understand this sense each time one must consider the ways in which they are posed, the position, perspective in which they appear. The situation in which the questioner finds himself, the motives which lead him to ask about truth—and to any question at all, for every question is asked for some reason—modify the sense of the question. The same sounding question can be asked in despair and from boredom, it may concern life or amusement; and hence each time it is not the same. And do words, even when they sound identical, always mean the same thing? Is their real meaning not defined by the "work and days" of those who speak them?

Thus the "timeliness" of a philosopher cannot be measured by the number of timeless problems which can be found in his doctrine—for there are no such problems. The unique situation in which we live defines the meaning of what directly and vitally concerns us. A philosopher moves us when he helps us to better understand it—not by reducing it to some universal human situation and making our problems, problems in general. On the contrary—he moves us when he speaks directly to us, about the unique situation in which we find ourselves? How is this possible?

The philosopher in this is like a partner in any real conversation. Everyone can see that a discussion with someone who thinks differently teaches us new things about ourselves: in the encounter with other views our own come to the surface. The reason is that our self-knowledge never encompasses all of our knowledge; we are not fully aware of what we know. Many things we assume, take from others, accept as obvious—without knowing it. For just this reason sometimes the words of someone else "strike" us. They "strike" us—because already before this we knew something about what is being said, though we weren't aware of this. Now in the encounter with another point of view this previously hidden knowledge emerges as a problem.

The dialogue with tradition is just such a conversation. Under the pressure of tradition our biases change into questions—since they speak about the same thing, but in a different way. The philosophical tradition plays a special role here. For philosophy asks each time about our entire situation in the world; hence in confrontation with the philosophy of a different time our unique situation as a whole, our own perspective of seeing things as such, becomes a problem.

If we were to read Plato in such a way, finding in him not ostensible analogies and not eternal problems, but questions addressed to the foundations of our life, our own individual experience—the venerable doctrine indeed would give way to urgent and immediate problems.

The ability to read in this way, or rather: the ability to teach how to read in this way—this was what distinguished Heidegger from among other philosophers already at the beginning of the thirties. This also is a source of his renown at that time. Moreover—I believe that here lies the core of his thought as a whole: Heidegger does not seek new, unexplored realms, does not create new theories that explain more—but in dialogue with the philosophical tradition of the West he attempts to inquire into what we always knew and what secretly defines our present situation.

Precisely for this reason, in order to understand Heidegger's thought it is worth referring to accounts of his first lectures, to the times before the appearance of his first fully independent work—*Sein und Zeit* (1927).

For at the moment this book appeared the situation changed radically. Now the source of Heidegger's fame was not as elusive as before. No longer did people say that in Freiburg a professor lectures who "teaches you to think," but that he "teaches this and that." Heidegger in print expressed certain convictions; so people began to talk about "Heidegger's philosophy" along with "Jaspers' philosophy," "Scheler's philosophy," and others. Moreover—at the turn of the twenties this "philosophy of Heidegger's" became extremely popular in Germany. What were its main theses?

The sciences—Heidegger says in *Sein und Zeit*—investigate various areas of things, different regions of that which is. At the foundations of each of them always lies some design of what it refers to; the natural sciences always assume some answer to the question "What is nature?" history—"What is the past?" etc. Obviously, these are not answers accepted once and for all: it sometimes happens that they cease to be adequate—in place of the answer a question then appears, and in the sciences one speaks of a "crisis of foundations." These questions are the domain of ontology—its task is to consider various possibilities of ways of *being*.

Though for the sciences the leading thread are ontological questions, for ontology itself it is the question: *What does "to be" mean?* Hence this is a question for our fundamental knowledge—but despite this,

Heidegger writes, the history of European thought shows that it has been totally forgotten.

The problem of being is crucial for Heidegger not only in consideration of knowledge. It is also—or rather, above all—the basic question of our existence in general. For man can be in one way or another, can be himself or not be himself, always has some possibility of being before him which he consciously or unconsciously chooses. To be—in one way or another—is a vital matter for man. In short: man not only is, but he always assumes some attitude towards his existence.

Taking an attitude towards existence distinguishes man among other beings. Heidegger calls it *existence*. The question about being is then no longer an ordinary theoretical problem; it only radically formulates what concerns man in life. In Heidegger's opinion, precisely this, doubly important (for knowledge as well as for life in general) question is the first task for thought.

Choosing such or another possibility of being, man—not with reason but simply with his life, living in one way or another—already gives some answer to the question: "What does it mean 'to be'?" Most often, however, he is not aware of this. His attention is primarily directed towards what is around him; man occupies himself mainly with things and people with which he deals. He forgets about himself, about his specific subsistence: existence. That is why the history of Western thought is the history of forgetting about being.

This forgetfulness is never complete, however. For man is a mortal being; slumbering in him is not only anxiety about this or that, but about being pure and simple. Anxiety that strips him of any support whatsoever; when it seizes someone, the links with others, things which absorb attention on a daily basis cease to be important—man is left alone. Only one thing remains important: being. And then man is authentically himself.

A thinking which sets itself the task of renewing the long since forgotten problem of being should return then, Heidegger says, above all to where it really appears: towards authentic human existence. Hence man—but not man in general, rather every one of us, alone and thrown completely on his own resources—should be its subject.

This in brief is the main thread of *Sein und Zeit*. Let us now imagine the contemporary readers of these views: Germans of the Weimar Republic. The same picture is repeated in many accounts from that time: loss of belief in the previous hierarchy of values, in the ground justifying the existing manner of life, in the philosophies of life offered till then. The catastrophe of the war shook the foundations of the previous spiritual order. People lost faith in the supra-individual order and in traditional institutions: they felt alone, in despair, lost.

Academic philosophy was unable to show the ways out of this situation—the university chairs were mainly held by Neo-Kantians, Neo-Hegelians, etc., professional philosophers who "before their lectures left their lives in a corner, like a wet umbrella." They were able to talk about substance, but were unable to help in the drama which everyone was living through alone.

So it is hardly surprising that in this situation words appealing to man as a forlorn individual, not only to the intellect but to life itself, words describing the human condition here and now, in fear, in the face of death—touched hearts and minds. Even in style *Sein und Zeit* was unlike the works of academic *Professorenphilosophie*: the pathos with which it was written was more reminiscent of Kierkegaard, Pascal, Dostoevsky or Luther—than Kant or Husserl. It is also understandable that this pathos and appeal to individual life overshadowed the real intention of this book: revival of questions on being. Brilliant analyses of fear, death, human loneliness concealed the goal for which they had been undertaken. Hence in common opinion Heidegger, beside Jaspers, became the main representative of "existential philosophy."

This philosophy was a phenomenon, it was, as Golo Mann writes, "typical of the age and highly conscious of it, but not in the sense that it concerned itself with the latest products of history: the republic, democracy, the economy and society. This it did not do at all. If it referred to the state, civilization, society and economic matters at all it was only to demonstrate to the individual that in this, the public sphere, he could not find the meaning of life. [. . .] The individual who wanted to fulfill his life must do so together with other individuals, freely, on the strength of his own daring, in alliance with other individuals."[31]

The wave of interest in Heidegger as an existentialist soon receded in Germany, but rose again after World War II, this time in France. Sartre recognized Heidegger as his teacher. Heidegger's terms—"existence," "project," "authenticity," "fear"—occupied a central place in the vocabulary of the existentialists. This wave also reached Poland, though with a certain delay. Thus Heidegger was seen in Poland mainly through the prism of Sartre's existentialism; *Sein und Zeit* was regarded as a precursor of *L'être et le néant*. Popular ideas about Heidegger are based on Sartre's brief comments in the essay "Existentialism Is a Humanism" (1946), where he qualifies the philosopher from Freiburg as an "atheist existentialist."

Meanwhile, Heidegger's following works, starting from the thirties, indicate that the existentialist interpretation of his thought does not grasp the core of his philosophy. *Sein und Zeit* unquestionably gave it points of support—but they were scattered over its superficial layer. Like every philosophical work, *Sein und Zeit* was written in the *language* of its time and was influenced by its *mentality*; hence its "existential" pathos. What is most essential, though, is *what* was said with this pathos.

Two years after *Sein und Zeit*, Heidegger published three works in the same year: a book on Kant (*Kant und das Problem der Metaphysik*), the treatise *Vom Wesen des Grundes* (On the Essence of Justification), and the lecture *Was ist Metaphysik?* (What Is Metaphysics?). These are all regarded as "early" works of Heidegger's—in later works there is a characteristic shift of emphasis, allowing one to speak of a "turn" in Heidegger's views from more or less 1930.

This does not mean, however, that Heidegger simply changed his views with time, rejecting those which he professed earlier. I would rather say that Heidegger now perceived more clearly what he had said in *Sein und Zeit*—in spite of contemporary interpreters and even in spite of his own self-awareness.

Evidence for the turning-point in Heidegger's views are also the fates of some works from his early period: *Sein und Zeit*, for example, is only part of a larger whole, which did not appear in print, however. Heidegger planned (some say even wrote) a two-volume work—but only two parts (out of three) of the first volume appeared. A fragment of analyses of the second volume was published as an independent work on Kant (see above). The rest was never published. The history of the lecture *What Is Metaphysics?* is also instructive: Heidegger published its last edition in the volume *Wegmarken* in 1967—hence he did not regard the views expressed there as incorrect. Nonetheless, with time an introduction and an epilogue were added to the lecture which cast entirely new light on its contents. Finally, in 1930 Heidegger wrote the treatise *Vom Wesen der Wahrheit* (On the Essence of Truth)—but did not publish it then. It appeared for the first time thirteen years later, after it had been completely rewritten.

What is the real meaning of this turning point? How can one change one's views, while simultaneously retaining the validity of those professed earlier, what is more—just now discovering their real essence?

The history of European thought knows at least one answer to this question: it was provided by Hegel. It is he who attempted to show that no idea is simply false; that a point of view is possible which allows the discovery of truth even when it is hidden for the one who professes it. Moreover, it was Hegel who perceived that the way to truth is not indifferent for truth itself—"nor is the result—he writes in *The Phenomenology of Spirit*—the actual whole, but rather the result together with the process through which it came about."[32] The development of spirit comes to a place from which a view opens up on the meaning of everything we had done and thought up to that time—but this place is a fragment of the road we have traveled to get to it and is inconceivable in separation from it.

Is Heidegger's answer similar? I believe that consideration of a different question will help to answer this one: Why does the existentialist interpretation of Heidegger not give justice to his thought? In other words: what did the "turn" in Heidegger's thinking bring to the surface?

The intention of existentialist philosophy was to save the personal world from the reductionist endeavours of contemporary thought: to grasp subjective reality without the help of instruments foreign to it— hence without referring to "things," "psyche," or the sphere of public life. Thus the problem of the subject, more precisely—the problem of personal life, was the starting point for existential philosophy; it developed in opposition to the "metaphysics of essence": thought reducing subjective to non-subjective reality. Hence the standard motto of existentialists was "existence precedes essence."

Hence the area in which existentialism operated was the traditional subject matter of modern philosophy: the problem of subjectivity. Yet Heidegger's thought does not fit into this space. For he is not interested in the problem of the subject, but in the problem: how can something *be* a subject at all? He is concerned not with subjectivity, but with being—and the problem of being, as he states, has been forgotten in all of modern philosophy.

The same argument which does not allow one to qualify Heidegger as an existentialist also makes it impossible to call him a phenomenologist—at least in the sense in which it was understood by its founder:

Edmund Husserl. To be sure, during his university studies Heidegger was strongly influenced by Husserl—later (from 1916) he became his pupil and assistant and the influence naturally became even stronger. Husserl supposedly even used to say (before the appearance of *Sein und Zeit*) "phenomenology is me and Heidegger."[33] With the publication of *Sein und Zeit*—though in assumption it was an attempt at phenomenological analysis—basic differences between Heidegger and Husserl appeared, however. Their significance came to the surface only after some time, really after the "turn" of which I spoke earlier: as long as Heidegger was regarded as a "philosopher of existence," it seemed that he set philosophy as expression of lonely and desperate authentic existence against the program of "philosophy as an exact science" outlined by Husserl. Husserl himself so believed. But the crux of the matter was not hidden here. For like existentialism, Husserl's phenomenology moved along the tracks of modern philosophy. "Phenomenology—Husserl said—is, as it were, the secret longing of all modern philosophy."[34] For Husserl as well the basic problem of philosophy is subjectivity. According to him, phenomenological thought was supposed to show how the things with which we deal are formed in subjectivity recognized as the absolute foundation. Thus Husserl, like the existentialists, was also fascinated by the modern problem of subjectivity and forgot about inquiries into being—and this is what troubles Heidegger.

In short: the problem of subjectivity stands in the very center of modern philosophy. Existentialism and Husserl's phenomenology circle around this problem—that is why they belong to the philosophical horizon of modernity. Meanwhile, for Heidegger the essence of things lies elsewhere: not in subjectivity but in being itself, concerning which questions have long been forgotten.

To forget to ask means: not to be aware that what we speak or think is an answer. Hence Sartre, Husserl, and with them all modern philosophy also know in their own way what "to be" means, though they are not aware of this. In Heidegger's opinion, for them "to be" means "to be presented," to be given to some subjectivity (he writes about this in later works). Something "is" in so far as it is present for . . .—no matter whether it is a concrete human individual, man as a species, transcendental subject, absolute spirit, or phenomenologically reduced consciousness. Thus however the subject is understood—it turns out to be the basis that something is and how it is. And this is an absolute basis; subjectivity differs from the object in that it is turned towards itself, that it is present for itself—and hence that it is always its own foundation. For Sartre as well this definition of being is valid; he only reverses the traditional point of view, defining subjectivity as nothingness. But reversal alone is still not the solution. It belongs to the same problem field.

Thus according to Heidegger, the reason why the problem of subjectivity is the decisive question of modern philosophy is that "to be" here means the same as "to be presented"—though for modern philosophers this is an assumption and not a problem. Meanwhile, Heidegger attempts to question this assumption—hence to revive a forgotten question: "What does 'to be' mean?" thereby placing himself beyond the horizon of modern philosophy.

Therefore, the existential interpretation of Heidegger does not grasp the gist of the matter about which he was concerned. This was not a common error, however: *Sein und Zeit* is hardly an unambiguous work. And its subject is subjectivity: human life, lonely and essentially on its own resources, existence which is the sole foundation for understanding being: one's own, that of other things. To be sure, the main problem of *Sein und Zeit* is the meaning of the word "is," but the question is asked from the perspective of subjectivity, from the point of view of the subject. So one can say that in his first independent work Heidegger still spoke in the traditional language of modern philosophy: asking about being, he simultaneously asked about subjectivity, about the foundation...

At a certain moment, however, it turned out that this language does not fit what has to be expressed. For in what sense is existence for Heidegger the *basis* for understanding being in general? Does "basis" here mean *fundamentum inconcussum* as for Descartes or Husserl?

According to Heidegger, human existence is the basis, for it constitutes the meaning of its world. A hammer is a hammer, a tree is a tree, and the world as a whole is precisely such a world *on account of* particular human life, though on the other hand the concept of life or existence is identical with the concept of presence in the world which surrounds it—and hence for Heidegger the "debate on the existence of the world" is a "scandal in philosophy." However, the enactment which man makes by simply living does not lie in his power; man enters into it like a child unexpectedly "enters" speech, when it begins to talk. That is why we *encounter* the world, though it is never finished—the idea of a person who would begin everything from the absolute beginning is just as absurd as imagining the world without human presence in it.

In short, being itself, our own (i.e., enactment) as well as the world's, is not dependent on us; "before" we thought, did, willed anything—we already were and the world was. Man is not the creator. His power is finite, his possibilities limited—but this feebleness, finiteness, and limitation at the same time are his strength; for they signify previous union, independent of his will, with what is, thanks to which man is able to see and understand his world at all.

Thus subjective human existence is not the certain foundation on which the world rests, it is not the final reference system that would enable us to understand the being we encounter. Man—as a subject—is not a sufficient basis for the question: "What does 'to be' mean?" If we want to ask about being, we have to ask differently than modern philosophy does: not about subjectivity as the basis of everything.

Precisely this experience: the impotence of questions asked in the traditional way in the face of what is involved, in the face *of being*, prompted the "turn" in Heidegger's thought.

*Sein und Zeit* now appears in a new light. In accordance with the plan of the whole contained in the introduction, the preliminary analysis of human existence was to be followed by an analysis of the meaning of being itself. But this analysis was never published; it turned out that no longer could one ask in the same way as before. Hence the author's intention—to reveal the meaning of being—was not accomplished. This was not an ordinary failure, however. I would say rather that only this failure constitutes the meaning of the work as a whole. For the real meaning of *Sein und Zeit* is that modern philosophy as such becomes a problem; not such or another problem is stated or taken up here, but the very way of formulating problems, philosophizing itself—as it is understood in modern times—is questioned. This is the "result" of this book: modern philosophy as a problem.

In order to understand the problematicity of modern philosophy we have to return to its source. Heidegger claims that it goes all the way back to Greece. That is why Heidegger's reflection—unlike Husserl and the existentialists—is a continual conversation with ancient Greek thought.

Why does Heidegger search exactly in Greece for the beginnings of philosophy in the modern sense of the word? For it was the Greeks, in his opinion, who opened up the intellectual horizon in which modern philosophy moves. In Greek thought—most clearly in Plato—an experience which determined all later European philosophy in a decisive way was expressed for the first time: the experience of being as continual presence.

From that time the goal of thinking became to reach that *which is continually present*—and in this sense "truly is." This has been named in different ways: *archē*, God, principle, eternal laws of nature or iron laws of history—but each time the matter concerns a certain continually present reference system which enables us to understand the phanomena around us or at least to regard them as understandable. "To understand" something now means "to relate it to a certain foundation," "to grasp it as a case of some principle, some law." Thinking enters into the service of *truth*: it is supposed to correspond with what is present. The ideal of thought becomes absolute knowledge, knowledge in "full light"—even if this is only a goal towards which fragile humanity must infinitely strive. Knowledge is a gradually erected structure based on unshakable foundations: laws of nature or principles of thought.

According to Heidegger, modern philosophy is only a consistent development of the Greek experience. Starting from Descartes, European thought has gradually become aware that presence is complete and permanent only when it is presence for oneself, that is: for the subject. "In my view (. . .)—Hegel writes—everything turns on grasping and expressing the True (of philosophy—KM), not only as *Substance* (i.e. as the unshakable basis of what is—KM), but equally as *subject*."[35]

What are the consequences of this conviction? Man—as a subject—gains primary importance as the basis and universal center of reference. Only thanks to this reference can something become being. This reference is *representation*: a relation in which man becomes the subject, and being becomes the object.

Hence modern philosophy, Heidegger says, expresses the relation of man with being as representation. Representation (Vorstellung) means the same as placing something before oneself. Thus one can say that in representing, man—as subject—places what is in relation to himself. He makes it dependent on himself to a certain degree. He gains control over it. Only what has been so placed, controlled, hence what man can be certain of—only this truly is: truth is certainty of representation. So now the vital question becomes: how to do this? in what way ensure oneself something?—thus the leading problem of modern thought is the problem of method.

Consequently, thought also becomes harnessed to the mastery of being. It becomes calculation whose goal is to make being secure for man. It is supposed to present the world in such a way that it will be open to human expansion; so that man can exploit ever new fields of being for goals which he himself sets.

If the basis of what is lies in subjectivity, man, as the subject, becomes the master of being, and his relation to being—mastery of it.

We can see that more than merely academic questions are involved here. Not only modern philosophy. For the phenomena which take place around us turn out to be a consequence of its fundamental conviction: the progressive mastery of being by man, the exploitation of the world for goals imposed on it. In short: modern technological civilization.

When Heidegger talks about modern technological civilization, he does not have in mind technique in the common sense of this word, but a particular form of the world: a world upon which man imposes himself as a goal, a world which man attempts to make commandable. The essence of technique does not lie in technical progress—but in a relation of man and the world in which the world becomes material for arrangement in *consideration* of man, and man—the official of such an order. Thus for Heidegger the consequence of the essence of technique is both machine technology as well as contemporary science, as well as the contemporary attitude toward art, in accordance with which a work of art is supposed to be material of experience, and the totalitarian state. Hence we have to do with technological civilization—in the way Heidegger understands it—not only where technological progress is the most advanced.

The same conviction which is the center of modern philosophy—the conviction that man is the master of being—is also, in Heidegger's opinion, the essence of our times in general: an age determined by technique.

As we can see from what has been said previously, this is not an arbitrary conviction. It is not merely a certain idea that occurred to philosophers. Its source is not spontaneous human mind but certain experiences: the experience of being as a constant presence. This experience shapes in advance the space in which European humanity moves—also when with the help of machine technology it subdues the world surrounding it. Hence the lot that has fallen to us—Heidegger states—depends on how we experience being itself. In other words: the form taken by the being among which we live, and also the form which we ourselves assume are determined by the way something is present in general—and hence on the kind of its presence. What being is, is determined by the way something can be at all; hence by "what" being is.

Thus to understand the sense not only of modern philosophy but contemporary civilization as a whole, thought must turn towards the sphere in which this sense is determined: towards the sphere of being. This sphere escapes our attention, however; absorbed by being, which we strive to master, we forget about being which determines this aspiration. This forgetfulness—Heidegger says—is the lot of our culture as a whole: the experience of being as a constant presence opening up this culture flows precisely from this experience. For when in the face of the world with which we have to do the question is asked: What does it mean that this world "is," what is really affirmed by conceding existence to *this* tree, nation, event—what is involved is a more precise qualification of this "something," hence defining the presence of something. Hence "being" turns out to be identical with "presence" when we ask about the "being of something," that is, when we are concerned in essence with being, with what is. The experience of being as presence assumes, then, that being itself, being as such—not as the horizon, qualification, or basis of what is—remains forgotten.

Forgetting being as such is not merely an oversight which can be made up for the sake of truth. For "being" is not an object which one can simply have in mind. It is not an object at all, even more—one cannot say about it that "it is." Being—is. Asking about being, we ask about this "is." Hence being cannot be given directly—but only through the mediation of something, through the mediation of being. It is not obvious—rather, it lies hidden behind what is, behind what is present.

Our experience of being, as Heidegger describes it, is like roaming through a forest: when walking through the darkness of a dense section we suddenly enter a clearing—and the trees thin out, yielding to the play of light and shadows. Then we are absorbed by what we see, and pay no attention to the clearing itself.

Forgetfulness of being, then, stems from its very essence; from the fact that it is open space which hides, an evasive clearing.

Thinking about this clearing—according to Heidegger—is the real task of thought. For here, as we have seen, the meaning of our time is determined, leaving its mark on all our thoughts, words, deeds.

How can one conceive this clearing—despite the fact that by its nature it hides, eludes us, conceals itself in oblivion?

This question is always asked too late. For there is never a situation in which thinking would find itself in the face of being as in the face of some new task or problem. For we already were—in one way or another—before we thought anything. Thinking always moves already in a certain space—in a certain clearing, as Heidegger says—which is opened each time by the fact that we are in one way or another. In this sense being (the clearing) is the "element of thought" just as air is the element of birds.

Thus asking about being we ask about something which is not foreign to our thought, about something which has already somehow touched it, making it what it is.

In our answer, though, we cannot present being as we present something that is present: a thing or some state of things—because being is not only a presence, but is a presence which hides and eludes us. Thinking, when it is itself, when it is "in its element," cannot be "presentation . . . which supplies us what is present, in its presence, thereby placing it before us,"[36] hence placing it with respect to us, as it were. Thought cannot be merely *making present*: reaching some constant presence, ultimate frame of reference, the foundations.

Meanwhile, this is precisely the way in which we think. We forget about being—because forgetting by the nature of things belongs to the experience of being as such. The meaning of being, the sphere decisive for thought, eludes us. It eludes us to such an extent that we are not even aware of this: we pay no heed to it whatsoever.

What happens when we focus our attention on being as such? What does "to focus attention" mean in this case? We do not mean here turning away from one object, one thing and towards another. Being is neither a thing nor an object. It is given only indirectly, only through something that is—and hence only elusively, only in forgetfulness. To focus attention on being is like "remembering about forgetting."

So what will happen when we focus attention on being itself? It will not cease to elude us—but we shall be aware of this, we shall experience this. This means: our thinking will become a problem for us. For a problem arises where not everything can be grasped, where something remains in the darkness—for otherwise we would not ask but assert.

Hence thinking in the strict sense—as Heidegger understands it: thinking turned towards being itself—is only a change of attitude towards what and how we are already doing, speaking, thinking. It is a perspective in which thought becomes problematical—not this thought or another but thinking in general. We think—in the real sense of the word—when we do not forget the question: What does it mean to think? When does this question arise? What prompts us to turn towards the real field of thought? I believe that this is simply an encounter with someone who thinks differently. Not only on this matter or another—but differently in general. An encounter with thought determined by an experience of being different from our own. For Heidegger this is the encounter with Greek thought. To be sure, with the Greeks the experience of being as a constant presence was expressed for the first time (since Plato), but it was not the sole and dominant experience: for Heidegger Greek thought is a picture of the birth of thinking directed towards constant presence from thought of a different kind. From thinking for which being is *alētheia*, non-secretiveness, presence and non-presence at the same time. For this reason one can say that in Greece the experience of being as a constant presence appeared *for the first time.*

Hence the matter appears as follows: thinking already in advance, whether we know this or not, is determined in the sphere of being: depending on what "to be" means, we think as we do. We are usually not aware of this. Only when we encounter some other experience of being can our own come to the surface. Then our thinking in general becomes a problem for us. Hence the way in which we think *changes*—the subject of our thought is now something else, and we see its real field elsewhere.

This is the case with Heidegger's thought as well. It changes in the dialogue with the Greeks: its own assumptions become a problem for it. These assumptions also turn out to be assumptions of modern philosophy in general and with time of all European thought since Plato. Hence the "turn" which Heidegger experienced on the path of his thought brings to the surface—as a problem—European thought as a whole. And this is its only "result."

Furthermore—thought cannot have any other results. It lives only in questions—for its field is the incessantly escaping presence: being. There is no constant presence which thought could reach on which to later base the edifice of human knowledge. Being, that "clearing" each time shaping the meaning of the time in which we live, continually eludes thought—hence one must constantly ask about it anew.

Hence there cannot be—Heidegger asserts in opposition to Hegel—such a place from which a vision opens up on the meaning of everything we had done and thought to that moment. Thought always remains only "love of wisdom," it never becomes wisdom itself—in the form of absolute knowledge. Thought is a continually renewed effort of asking about the meaning of our times—continually anew, for being determining this meaning is not a constant presence deciding it once and for all.

The observation that human thought is fated to engage in constant inquiry is rather common. Very rarely is it stated that human knowledge has already attained a satisfactory state that makes further inquiry unnecessary. It is also doubted whether such a state will ever be attained. For most of us are convinced of the incurable finiteness of human reason—the tradition of European thought as well as everyday experience teach us this.

Philosophers—and not only they—have written for a long time about the "prison" in which the soul finds itself during life, which makes it impossible to see the complete truth, about passions which disturb our clear judgment of things, about the range of our cognition necessarily limited by the historical situation—and daily sufferings and the prospect of death do not allow us to forget about the limits of our possibilities.

In the European philosophical tradition this finiteness of the human mind was basically regarded—and for the most part is—as a negative factor, as an obstacle on the way to truth. Sometimes as an obstacle that can be overcome—when one assumes that the situation in which man finds himself here and now is not the ultimate situation. The negation of this assumption—common to the Christian thinkers, Plato, Hegel— leads to the belief that complete truth is unattainable for human thought.

For Heidegger the innate finiteness of human thought is not only a negative circumstance. For at the base of such a traditional point of view lies the opposition between thought and what it wishes to attain—between finite reflection and its infinite object, between thought immersed in time and constant presence which requires a timeless look. Heidegger, though, negates the correctness of this opposition—for in his opinion the aim of thinking, the meaning of being as such, is not a constant presence which we can grasp by virtue of our being at the mercy of time and suffering. This meaning is presence and non-presence at the same time—just as time is never fully given, but is constantly open to the future.

Being—I believe it can be put this way—appears only in an infinite process: through the history of human thoughts, words, deeds it appears infinitely as the space in which they move.

Thus the finiteness of human thought means its emergence in history which does not depend on it. But it is this—according to Heidegger—that enables man to understand anything at all: for participation in history is participation in *being*—in a pre-established union with what is independently of human thought. Signs of human finiteness—death, suffering, a view limited by the historical situation—are not obstacles to understanding but open it up. As long as human finiteness is understood only negatively, "the mystery of pain remains veiled. Love has not been learned."[37] No timeless look is necessary to really understand something—it is rather "the mortals who reach sooner into the abyss"[38] of what there is to understand.

The meaning toward which thought strives is not only its goal, an object to be grasped—but also something in which the mind, knowing it or not, participates, something which only through it is expressed. Thought can be only "on the way" to this meaning: only through incessant inquiry.

Thus there is no such thing as Heidegger's philosophy; a set of views which elsewhere and at some other time could be accepted or rejected. There is only the way of a thinker who tries to become aware of what every one of us really thinks and does—and sees a problem in this. Precisely here, in my opinion, lies the hidden source of fascination with Heidegger's reflection: reflection which shows that all our experience—'our' means people of contemporary technological civilization—is an *answer* to a question which is not visible to us in our everyday world. In other words: Heidegger includes us—such as we are today, with space travel, modern art, the atomic bomb—in the unfinished dialogue which began in Greece, a dialogue in which everything, all our knowledge about the world, becomes a problem, in "the dialogue which we are"—and that is why he fascinates so many people.

"When thinking attempts to pursue something that has claimed its attention, it may happen that on the way it undergoes a change. It is advisable, therefore, in what follows to pay attention to the path of thought rather than to its content"—says Heidegger in the introduction to one of his lectures.[39] I believe these words could be the motto of all of his work.

Heidegger teaches one to think. This is a lot, but at the same time it is little. Plato in *Theaetetus* cites an anecdote about Thales, of whom it was once said that while gazing at the sky, he fell into a well and was ridiculed by a servant girl who was a witness to this. In this way, however—Plato writes—one could make a mockery of all philosophers.[40] For philosophy—says Heidegger in reference to this place in *Theaetetus*—is in fact a kind of thought which serves no purpose and which for this reason is ridiculed by servants. Philosophy—thought as Heidegger understands it—serves neither theory nor practice; it does not help to master the world or to discover unchangeable laws which govern this world. Philosophy gives no support, no leading thread. It promises nothing—says Jan Patočka about Heidegger's thought[41]—it offers no dogma, it teaches only to inquire and to be persistent in this inquiring.

# NOTES

1. Krzysztof Michalski, "Heidegger," *Twórczość* 8 (1975): 361.

2. Martin Heidegger, *Budować Mieszkać Myśleć. Eseje wybrane* [*Building, Dwelling, Thinking: Selected Essays*], ed. Krzysztof Michalski, trans. Kr. Pomian, J. Tischner et al. (Warsaw: Czytelnik, 1977), 335.

3. It has the signature VI.26 and consists of twenty-seven properly type-written pages with almost no typing mistakes and very few Tipp-Ex corrections. Some of the pages show handwritten notes in the margins. Carefully written with a pencil by the author's hand, these notes typically suggest small amendments, such as replacing the word "fountain" by "source," etc. In all cases where it seemed advisable, these suggestions have been tacitly integrated into the text published above.

4. As a translator of Heidegger into Polish, Michalski was certainly familiar with the specific problems of translating his works.

5. This is how Michalski himself characterized his crucial inspiration in a one-page German summary of this article, written in 1975–1976 (*Nachlass* of Krzysztof Michalski, signature VI.9; trans. Ludger Hagedorn and Piotr Kubasiak).

6. Ibid.

7. Krzysztof Michalski, *Heidegger i filozofia współczesna* [*Heidegger and Contemporary Philosophy*] (Warsaw: Państwowy Instytut Wydawniczy, 1978); new edition (Warsaw: Państwowy Instytut Wydawniczy, 1998).

8. Martin Heidegger, *Vorträge und Aufsätze* (Pfullingen: Neske, 1954).

9. Cf. Krzysztof Michalski, "Editorial Note," in *Budować*, 25.

10. Regarding the history of Heidegger's reception in Poland, see Janusz Mizera, "Uwagi o recepcji i przekładzie tekstów Martina Heideggera w Polsce

[Remarks on the Reception and Translation of texts by Martin Heidegger]," *Argument: Biannual Philosophical Journal* 3 (2013): 245.

11. Michalski had originally asked Leszek Kołakowski to contribute to the translations of Heidegger in that collection. Kołakowski—by then living in exile in Oxford—agreed, maybe he had even translated something already, yet the publisher in the end refused to allow the publication if he contributed. Michalski had to write to Kołakowski—regretfully, explaining the situation—and "uninvite" him.
We very much thank Marci Shore (Yale) for first mentioning this to us. The letter by Michalski is part of Kołakowski's *Nachlass* in the Polish National Library (dated June 5, 1972; inv. no. Karta 7, BN: 13583). A special thanks also to Mrs. Maria Gamdzyk-Kluźniak from the *Archiwum Leszka Kołakowskiego w Bibliotece Narodowej* in Warsaw, who takes care of Kołakowski's literary estate and was very helpful in sharing her knowledge about this correspondence with us.

12. Mizera, "Uwagi o recepcji i przekładzie tekstów Martina Heideggera w Polsce," 245, 251.

13. Krystyna Górniak-Kocikowska, "Poland," in *Encyclopedia of Phenomenology*, ed. Lester Embree et al. (Dordrecht: Springer, 1997), 539.

14. Cf.: "Curriculum Vitae (Deutsch) Krzysztof Michalski," accessed January 13, 2017, http://www.iwm.at/wp-content/uploads/michalski-cv-dt.pdf.

15. As stated in an interview with Piotr Graczyk and Piotr Nowak, in Krzysztof Michalski, *Zrozumieć przemijanie* [*Understanding Time*] (Warsaw: Kronos, 2011), 17.

16. *Nachlass* of Krzysztof Michalski, document entitled "Lebenslauf" (without signature; trans. Ludger Hagedorn and Piotr Kubasiak), 1.

17. Ibid.

18. Cf. Patočka's letter to Michalski from June 16, 1974: "Letters Between Krzysztof Michalski and Jan Patočka (1973–1976)," in *New Yearbook for Phenomenology and Phenomenological Philosophy*, vol. 14, ed. Ludger Hagedorn and James Dodd (London and New York: Routledge, 2015), 241.

19. Ibid., 242.

20. Ibid.

21. Ibid., 243. The evaluation where this statement is made is also part of Michalski's *Nachlass* at the Institute for Human Sciences—IWM (signature VI. 3; page 4).

22. Ibid., 242.

23. Krzysztof Michalski, "Iron Laws and Personal Responsibility," trans. E. Kohák, *Cross Currents. A Yearbook of Central European Culture* 7 (1988): 129–35.

24. Krzysztof Michalski, *Heidegger i filozofia współczesna* [*Heidegger and Contemporary Philosophy*], second edition, trans. Ludger Hagedorn and Piotr Kubasiak (Warsaw: Państwowy Instytut Wydawniczy, 1998), 12.

25. Nicolas de Warren, "Introduction," in *New Yearbook*, 221.
26. Cf. Michalski's letter to Patočka from May 31, 1974, in *New Yearbook*, 241.
27. Cf. Mizera, "Uwagi," 245–46.
28. *Nachlass* of Krzysztof Michalski (signature VI.2; trans. Ludger Hagedorn and Piotr Kubasiak).
29. Krzysztof Michalski (1948–2013) was a Polish philosopher. For many years, he taught philosophy in Warsaw and Boston. He was founder and rector of the Institute for Human Sciences in Vienna. His most important books are *Heidegger and Contemporary Philosophy*; *Logic and Time. An Essay on Husserl's Theory of Meaning*; *Understanding Time. Selected Essays*; *The Flame of Eternity*; and *Essays about God and Death*. The core of his academic interest was the problem of time. His books deal with Heidegger's historicity of truth, Husserl's tension between logic and time, and Nietzsche's concept of eternity.
30. [Hannah Arendt, "Martin Heidegger at Eighty," in *Heidegger and Modern Philosophy: Critical Essays*, ed. Michael Murray (New Haven, CT, and London: Yale University Press, 1978), 295.] All notes in square brackets added by editors Hagedorn and Kubasiak.
31. [Golo Mann, *The History of Germany since 1789*, trans. Marian Jackson (New York and Washington: Praeger Publishers, 1968), 374.]
32. [G. W. F. Hegel, *Phenomenology of Spirit*, trans. A. V. Miller (Oxford: Oxford University Press, 1977), 2.]
33. [According to legend, Husserl in the early 1920s said: "Phenomenology, that is Heidegger and me." Cf. Herbert Spiegelberg, *The Phenomenological Movement. A Historical Introduction* (The Hague: Springer, 1965), 352. There are a number of variations of this saying that seems to have been mentioned the first time by Spiegelberg.]
34. [Edmund Husserl, *Ideas: General Introduction to Pure Phenomenology*, trans W. R. Boyce-Gibson (London: Allen and Unwin, 1931), sec. 62: "It is therefore not surprising that phenomenology is as it were the secret longing of the whole philosophy of modern times."]
35. [Hegel, *Phenomenology of Spirit*, 9f.]
36. [From the 1952 article "Was heißt Denken?" that has not been translated into English (different from the eponymous lecture series). The full quote in German reads: "Demgemäß ist das Denken jene Präsentation des Präsenten, die uns das Anwesende in seiner Anwesenheit zu-stellt und es damit vor uns stellt, damit wir vor dem Anwesenden stehen und innerhalb seiner dieses Stehen ausstehen können." Martin Heidegger, "Was heißt Denken?" in *Vorträge und Aufsätze*, GA 7 (Frankfurt am Main: Vittorio Klostermann, 1952), 141.]
37. [Martin Heidegger, "What Are Poets For?" in *Poetry, Language, Thought*, trans. Albert Hofstadter (New York: Harper Perennial Classics, 2001), 94.]

38. [Ibid., 90; Heidegger is quoting Hölderlin's hymn "Mnemosyne."]

39. [Martin Heidegger, *Identity and Difference*, trans. Joan Stambaugh (New York: Harper and Row, 1969), 23.]

40. ["On all these occasions, you see, the philosopher is the object of general derision"; see Plato, *Theaetetus*, trans. M. J. Levett, rev. Myles Burnyeat, in Plato, *Complete Works*, ed. John M. Cooper (Indianapolis, IN, and Cambridge: Hackett Publishing Company, 1997), 194.]

41. [The meaning of Heidegger's philosophy was discussed intensely in Michalski's correspondence with Patočka; cf. "Letters Between Krzysztof Michalski and Jan Patočka," 223–69.]

## Chapter 9

# The Ecology of Property

## *On What Is Heidegger's and Bibikhin's Own*

### Michael Marder

Upon hearing the word "property," immediate associations with the bedrock of the economic sphere flood the mind. In the bipolar universe of value, neither use nor exchange have any sense in the absence of something to be used or exchanged, the notion of ownership supplying a secure substratum for all economic operations. With Marx, we specify, however, that such a foundation belongs fundamentally not to economics *per se* but to *political* economy, where both property and the subject of legitimate appropriation are the foci of struggle: private or public, individual or communal. Marx intuits, to paraphrase Heidegger's well-worn dictum concerning technology, that the essence of economy is nothing economic. We should add that, deeper than political contention, the abyssal foundation of its foundation is ecological.

Before property and the right to possess it are legally enshrined and sealed, the first word must resound, articulating the claim to ownership (think of John Locke's or Jean-Jacques Rousseau's theories of appropriation) and, in a performative gesture, the very being of the owner. That first articulating word, that *logos* establishing economy's law, may be "mine," "ours," or a still more basic semantic unit in the statements "This is mine," "That is ours": "this" or "that," cutting off and individuating a piece of the world into a manageable possession, let alone "is," the copula, at once relating me or us to and separating me or us from "that" which is appropriated (and to or from myself/ourselves). To sum up, the proprietors are articulated by their

own articulation of the claim to property, put together or drawn apart
by what they wish to draw toward themselves.

The muting of *logos* and the dismissal of the ecological orientation
it underwrites in the most aggressive acts of seizing, parceling out, and
fencing in portions of the world as property are expressions of the forgetting of being, the two-way abandon that sees the humans, who con-
sign being to oblivion, themselves consigned to ontological oblivion.
Violent silence, a silence not pregnant with the word, rules the day (or
the night) here. What Marx designated as "primitive accumulation" is
a far cry from the civil and civilizing affair that Locke had depicted;
rather than articulation, including of the proprietors and their property,
pure economy freed from the constraints of *logos* effects multiple levels
of disarticulation (Rousseau's and Marx's "alienation") safeguarded by
an arbitrary and violent *nomos*-law. In this way, economism militates
against ontology.

If we are to believe both Plato and Heidegger, there is no more important role reserved for the philosopher than to recover if not the material
word itself then the other, fruitful silence and to un-forget being in the
midst of its profound amnesia. In their eyes, that is the true philosophical task and the "definition" of truth—*alētheia*—as such. By contrast
to the ancient conception of *oikonomia*, elaborated among other places
in the writings of Xenophon and Aristotle, according to which the pro-
prietor was supposed to preserve and indeed augment the ontological
domain by taking care of the goods, the modern institution of economy
unglues property from the ends it might serve and, with nihilistic indifference, hands it over to the work of destruction, be it environmental,
social, or of another kind. The task of the philosopher becomes more
complicated yet: The un-forgetting of being must engage in a painstak-
ing analysis of economism and its corollary modes of appropriation that
endanger planetary existence.

***

In an effort to salvage the ecology of property in the era of rampant
economism, Russian philosopher Vladimir Bibikhin heeds the call
issued at the dawn and dusk of metaphysics. Heidegger, he relates in a
lecture course *Sobstvennost': filosofia* svoego (*Property: The Philosophy of* What Is One's Own), "insists on standing on guard by being, for
being [*stoianii nastorozhe pri bytii dlia bytia*]."[1] Asking rhetorically

if what is guarded is the property of the other or one's own, Bibikhin responds: "It is the property that is close, albeit on the hither side of what is one's own and what is other [*pri blizkoi sobstvennosti, no po siu storonu svoego i chuzhogo*]."[2] The ecology of property could not be closer to us than this proximity beyond the ultimately economic opposition between the self and *its* other, the proximity that cannot be gauged through the categories of physical spatiality or the measurements supplied by metaphysics.

In the same series of lectures Bibikhin concentrates on the underside of the appropriative drive, namely the unconscious receptivity of the appropriator-to-be, intensely interested in, absorbed, and captivated by the world and by the prospect of its capture. "People are captivated by capture [*liudi zakhvacheny zakhvatom*]," he says, highlighting "the captivating might of capture [*zakhvatyvaiushchaia moshch' zakhvata*]."[3] Rather than a thing (*a* being, in the substantive) to be transformed into property, the act of appropriation itself is what we are addicted to; irrespective of its intended content, the formal actualization of this act is the goal, to the extent that it replaces the lost verbal sense of being. We are taken hold of by the unlimited desire to take hold of everything.

Granted, the world does not vanish entirely from the panorama of the appropriative view. Bibikhin knows this full well, and he identifies in the world "the captivating goal of every capture [*mir kak zakhvatyvaiushchaia tsel' vsiakogo zakhvata*]."[4] Aiming at an object, consciousness (i.e., voracious intentionality) invariably overshoots the mark and sets its sights on the entire world. Yet the act of appropriation is unable to appropriate itself, since it cannot master its beginning in a fascination that, before any decision, entrusts it with its mission. The "captivating might of capture" is both powerless and exceeds all power exercised in capturing something or someone. It fascinates, and so is uncontrollable, ungraspable. Under philosophical guardianship, proximity on the hither side of economy negatively interrelating what is one's own and the other's refers to the untamable beginning that had already begun before we became aware of it: above (or below) all, the proximity of a life I call "my own." It is this beginning before or without beginning that delineates the ecology of property, that is to say, the overarching context wherein the economic text is rooted and, at the same time, a factor in this text's uprooting, invalidating its mainstay in the sense of property as a set of discrete individual objects receptive to the will of the master-subject.

That Bibikhin's course spanned the years 1993 and 1994 is highly significant. The period immediately following the collapse of the Soviet Union was one of a rapid and unregulated privatization, leading to the astronomic enrichment of the few, the worsening of socioeconomic inequalities, and a dramatic rise in murders-for-hire as a way of resolving property disputes. Against this bleak background, the philosopher implores his audience (which consists of the present and future Russian intellectual elite and, hence, of those who have already made a decision to quit without ever entering the race after obscene wealth, something that puts the effectiveness of his intervention in question) to stop and think not only about the meaning of property but also, in the first place, about the event of appropriation that appropriates the appropriators to itself and thereby expropriates them *in advance of* the appropriative act. Be the desired property philosophical understanding or be it a previously government-owned company, "the goal, the whole, the world [of which these potential properties are a part] eludes every cunning skill and cannot be captured by any ruse or stratagem [*tsel', tseloe, mir ostaëtsia ni dlia kakoi lovkosti neulovimym, nikakoi khitrost'io ne skhvachennym*]."[5] The limits of appropriation are its "own" enabling factors: (1) the unwilled and unchosen spark of interest, prompting us, in Hegelian terms, to confine our will to a determinate thing (with this, the will itself becomes objectively determined), and (2) the horizon of the totality, whence the appropriated chunk is snatched. For Bibikhin, the name for this horizon is *the world*. Heidegger in *Being and Time* is more specific than that: it is not the world as a conjunction of interrelated things but worldhood (*Weltlichkeit*) as *Dasein*'s ontologico-existential *apriori*.[6]

Bibikhin perspicuously identifies the process of post-Soviet privatization with "the capture of the world [*zakhvat mira*]."[7] It is as though not this or that piece of property is targeted by the insatiable drive toward appropriation but the entire world, not to mention the world's worldhood, that is converted into capture's unarticulated goal. Of course, in keeping with Bibikhin's earlier statements in the *Property* course, the fulfillment of this dream is actually impossible. All the world might be a stage for capture, but it cannot be, itself, captured. More than an isolated historical occurrence, the *ab initio* frustrated striving toward world-capture is the crux of the human condition, which is why Bibikhin is in a position to conclude that "on a steep turn, at a breaking point, Russia has clearly demonstrated the essence of a human being's customary relation to the world [*na krutom povorote, na razlome, Rossiia otchëtlivo pokazala sut' vsegdashnikh otnoshenii cheloveka s mirom*]."[8] The "customary" relation he invokes is that of the always-already-appropriated appropriators, who are, nevertheless, blind to their captivation by and reception into the world they futilely endeavor to lay hold of as a whole. Their repressed passivity is a remnant of the ecological infrastructure for property, which requires an ontological, and not only a physical, space (the *oikos* of both economy and ecology) wherein it could be accepted.

At the same time, in Heidegger's thought, the ownmost, that which is most proper to Dasein, is its finitude, never to be appropriated. In *Being and Time*, after all, "death is Dasein's *ownmost* possibility [*der Tod ist eigenste Möglichkeit des Daseins*]."[9] Whatever we do, we are articulated and disarticulated by this possibility complementing the ecology of property with finite time, or with being *as* finite time, instead of the material possessions prioritized in the economic construal of property. We are, in other words, ultimately privatized by death. Although Bibikhin does not go so far, a question that surfaces in the context of the 1990s Russia is whether, in the heat of privatization, captivation by capture was so extreme and so all-absorbing that it had to be undersigned with the appropriators' deaths, carried out by contract killers. Is dying a literal way, in which "we mysteriously depart, go deeper into *what is our own*, drown in it [*my zagadochnym obrazom ukhodim, uglubliamsia v svoë, tonem v nëm*]"?[10] There is always a risk in radical individuation (for instance, in the course of frantic privatization—or in death that seems everywhere to shadow it) that the individuated would be lost precisely in the midst of the individuating element, dissolve into anonymity within that which is most proper. Now, the Russian "case" is a singular-universal realization of this possibility.

Privatization, Bibikhin shows in the footsteps of Heidegger, is imperceptibly underway insofar as we relate to the world by refusing to relate to it *as world* and reduce it to a bunch of objects taken together. To privatize is to separate, to set apart, to cast away: The Russian "private property [*chastnaia sobstvennost'*]" speaks of a part [*o chasti*]," while the Latin-derived "*private, privatization* emanates from the same word (*privus, privo*) as our *away* [*proch'*] or *special guard* [*oprichnik*]."[11] Grasping the world chunk by chunk, through appropriable objects "chopped off . . . from the common [*otrublennye . . . ot obshchiny*],"[12]

I cannot reconstruct the whole from its privatized parts. The capture of the world and its flight from me are mutually reinforcing phenomena: The more private properties or parts cut from the whole I amass, the further away the world (which is ineluctably common or shared) is from me. The event of privatization distances me from being in the measure that I bring beings close to myself; the price for the crystal-clear legal, epistemic, and other correlations between an individual subject and the objects under its control is the expulsion of both from the world and from the purview of *logos*—it, too, necessarily shared with the other even in a monologue.

In this event, the economy of property muscles out its ecology, but we should not labor under the illusion that we are faced with a simple choice between two modalities of appropriation. Without the ecology, we are not only reduced to mute violence devoid of *logos* but are also left ontologically homeless, without the world, as good as dead albeit still biologically alive. The horrors of the Russian privatization merely exacerbate the overall tendency to world-destruction and the obviation of *logos* inherent in the economic or economicist attitude. Bibikhin's point, with which Heidegger would undoubtedly concur, is that "we"—East and West, global North and South—are all the Russia of the 1990s, to a greater or lesser degree.

***

Perhaps somewhat more relevant to the second half of this century's second decade, the retreating ecology of property leaves in its wake the two options that have come to dominate electoral politics worldwide: technocratic liberalism and fascism. On the underside of the appropriative drive, we might remember, the ecology of property articulates our capture of the world with captivation by it. In the economicist universe of liberalism, and in line with "calculative thinking," the dogma is that the passivity of captivation is an anachronistic relic of our irrational past. What is demanded from thinking is the activity of "grip [*Zugriff*], grasp [*Griff*], and concept [*Begriff*]," understood "on the basis of grasping."[13] Bibikhin's *zakhvat* sends the Russian reader back to the German *Zugriff*, mindful of the fact that this word "in the history of the Russian language not by chance points toward *cunning* [*khitrost'*], *theft* [*khishchenie*], *ravishment* [*voskhishchenie*]."[14] A trace of passivity survives in this semantic kinship, intimating that one's capture of the world happens as a consequence of having been already cunningly captured, stolen away, ravished by it. As for the concept, Bibikhin reiterates Heidegger's insight: "*Begriff* is from *greifen*—to capture. Understanding is capturing. Conception comes from *capio*, I capture; probably, it is the same word as our "to grab" or "to swipe," *khapat'*."[15] Here, the activity of activity is paramount; I grab, grasp, clasp, appropriate things within the economic matrix of property. My ravishment, my being stolen away (especially from myself), recedes from this thoroughly economic move.

The ideal of pure conceptuality is one of a grasp that precludes being grasped. That is the logic of global manipulability and calculability, politically expressed first in possessive liberalism and later on in technocracy. Sooner or later, the repressed, nonetheless, returns: Fascism betokens the fascination, captivation, and ravishment of being-grasped without grasping. After the ecology of property that articulated the active and passive voices of *grasp, Griff, khvat,* or *capere* is defeated, nothing can prevent a totally irrational, illogical, *logos*-free fascination from setting the existential and political moods. Fascism is a direct consequence of conceptual excess, to which it overreacts by delivering humans to a totality wherein they will be appropriated. It cannot be straightforwardly repudiated, least of all by appealing to the modern and technocratic paradigm of dispassionate rationality—its hidden source, as Theodor Adorno and Max Horkheimer have shown. Instead of insisting, once again, on active capture that further represses the *pathos* of the proper, we need to work through both conceptual excess and its still darker obverse side.

So when Heidegger stresses ontological captivation in noting that "the human being exists as captivated by 'being' [*als genommen vom 'Sein'*],"[16] or when Bibikhin writes that the forest, roughly synonymous with matter, "captivates [*zakhvatyvaet*] and leads us out of metric space,"[17] they do not veer toward fascism, but, rather, restore the ecology of property, foreclosed by economism, liberalism, technocracy, and calculative rationality. Heidegger, for one, situates fanaticism on the side of "the will to willing [*der Wille zum Willen*]," bent on pure activity, on "activism [*Aktivismus*]."[18] There is no space for ecology in the active will to appropriation and self-appropriation, because there is no more space for *logos* in the sense of a gathering *gatheredness* and, as a result, no space for that which makes space or gives room, granting every *oikos* its receptive mark. The real fanaticism is passing being-grasped (by being) for fanatical irrationality, one that is out of control, unmasterable, dangerous.

Let us take the example of ecstasy, the I standing outside or beside itself. Far from Dionysian abandon, in *Being and Time* the "ecstatic" constitution of Dasein signifies its finite temporality and noncoincidence with itself prior to the moment of death. Even the rational virtue of self-control presupposes this noncoincidence of the self with itself, a difference to be subsequently brought in line and continually reined in through the correct use of reason. What is most proper to the I is its essential impropriety, also known as existence; reflecting on Heidegger's *Beiträge*, Bibikhin confirms that, for the German thinker, "the thought about *what is one's own* conducts outside the *I* [*mysl' o svoëm vyvodit iz ia*]."[19] A tacit and subversive reference to Max Stirner's *Der Einzige und sein Eigenthum*, this pithy statement ties, in a single knot of the double bind, thought, existence, and ownness. Allied to the essential impropriety of existence, the thought of ownness set to the rhythm of finitude guides the I beyond the sphere that is its own. Fascist ecstasy, conversely, is self-abandon oblivious to the three threads Heidegger and Bibikhin weave together. It is a pale reflection of the movement we have been following here, the reflection lingering as a reaction to the overwhelming active grasp that has muted the experience of being grasped.

We are thus duped by the demand to make a choice between two false alternatives: the indifferent grasp of beings on the one hand and the ecstatic surrender to them (especially, to a group or to its leader) on the other. With the gathering gatheredness of *logos* shattered into polar opposites and with captivation and capture taken to be incompatible, the quest for freedom hits a dead end. This dead end is an end of history quite distinct from that which Francis Fukuyama prematurely celebrated after the collapse of the Soviet Union and the establishment of a global liberal hegemony. If history (*Geschichte*) is defined as our capacity "to be constitutively exposed to beings out of belongingness to being [*die schaffende Ausgesetztheit in das Seiende aus der Zugehörigkeit zum Sein*],"[20] then the refusal of exposure to, or captivation by, beings coupled with the nonbelonging to being cuts history short. Just as an ecologico-phenomenological attitude subtends an economico-political approach to "property," so ontological propriation into the history of being undergirds our fascination with and our very grasp of beings.

Analogous to the proper that remains fundamentally improper and unappropriable, history sways in the doubling of each event announcing and erasing itself, the event of ecology grounding and destabilizing that of economy. This, too, is a deconstructive double bind, the work of *différance* that translates, after its own fashion, Heidegger's onticoontological difference. In sharp contrast to history's sway stands the one-dimensionality of liberal technocracy and fascism that irrevocably, if also inarticulately, decide on gathering *or* gatheredness, capture *or* captivation. (The history of being is inconceivable without such forgetting of being, without forgetting our admittedly immemorial ontological exposure, the impropriety of the proper. Which means that, by and large, ontological history proceeds by way of ending, its "process" twisting into the ends, two of them now looming before us as the only destiny.)

Neither liberal-technocratic nor fascist mutations of the proper, of what is one's own, have anything to do with freedom, which, for Heidegger as well as for Bibikhin, is an ontological (and, we might add, an ecological) affair. Under the heading "properness," *Die Eigentlichheit*, the former remarks: "As appropriated into the truth of beyng, humans are now themselves [*Ereignet in die Wahrheit des Seyns ist der Mensch jetzt der Mensch selbst*]."[21] This follows his affirmation that "humans come to themselves, come into their own [*kommt zu sich, in sein Eigenes*], because they must now be themselves out of the arrogation into the event."[22] Freedom is being ontologically appropriated by being and, in this way coming into one's own (which never belongs only to one, nor truly belongs to anyone), becoming an articulated articulator, an ecologist of the proper, eager to sway between the different edges of the event. Bibikhin concurs, in his own way: "Freedom is, prior to all else, captivation by what is one's own [*svoboda est' prezhde vsego zakhvachennost' svoim*]."[23] To equate freedom with autonomy is to indulge in a liberal daydream, while to negate it and embrace its opposite (heteronomy, submission to the other) is to fall into the snares of fascism. Freedom is not a matter of -nomy, of *nomos* that economizes on it, submitting it to a law, whether of the self or of the other. The ecology of freedom is dwelling in, being articulated by, and articulating the proper—that is, the finite—"truth of beyng."

\*\*\*

Within the economy of liberalism and fascism, the possibilities of thinking are all but eliminated, and the efforts to revive them are mercilessly stemmed out, as the ongoing treatment of Heidegger by the denizens of liberal ideology demonstrates. Besides the apparatus for thought, inexistent in the latter and supplanted by calculation in the former, what is missing is, as I have already pointed out, the space where such an activity could take place. Between the Scylla of calculative rationality and the Charybdis of sheer thoughtlessness, between the concept and its total rejection, Heidegger senses the need to free up some breathing room for thinking to flourish. His preferred designation for this undertaking in *Beiträge* is "inceptual thinking [*das anfängliche Denken*]." "Concept," he writes there, "is here originally the '*in-con-cept*,' and this is first and always related to the accompanying co-concept of the turn in the event [*Begriff ist hier ursprüglich* 'Inbegriff', *und dieser zuerst und immer bezogen auf den mitgehenden Zusammengriff der Kehre im Ereignis*]."[24] Grasping-with, co-concept (*Zusammengriff*) sends us a memento of the articulating articulatedness inherent to *logos*; in-grasping, in-con-cept (*Inbegriff*) bespeaks the receptiveness of the dwelling, of *oikos* that admits everything and everyone into itself. Combined, they amount to an ecology of thought, the overarching frame of inceptual thinking. Inside and out, in and with, such thinking is the most proper and the most improper, immune to sharing and utterly common. It runs on the track of relationality, understood ontologically as the coincidence of separation and attachment, a disarticulated articulation preceding differentiation into passive and active postures, rather than an amorphous mesh of things typically connoted by "relation" and, even more so, by "ecology." "The turn in the event" is this twisting of the proper into the improper in the relational in-between of the absolutely singular and the generic.

Bibikhin is alive to the ecological configuration of thinking in Heidegger, who inspires him to write, in a quasitranscendental vein, that to think is "to free up the place where something new could happen [*osvobodit' mesto, gde moglo by proizoiti novoe*]."[25] At one pole of the event, that place is already freed by death, by the absolutely singular "property" that is both my ownmost and completely other. At the other pole, being itself makes room as that which is common to all that is "in" being and yet is unique to each and not locatable among beings. "*What is one's own* and *what is one's own* are fissured here to the point of polarity, intimating that we are approaching the real and, hence, risky things [*svoë i svoë raskalyvaiutsia zdes' do poliarnosti, pokazyvaia, chto my priblizhaemsia k nastoiashchim i, stalo byt', riskovannym veshcham*]."²⁶ That is, precisely, the twist or the turn of the event Heidegger has spotted: the proper slipping into the improper and back again within the spasmodic movement of thought, whose twists neither preexist nor are preexisted by the room that opens up for it.

In the ecology of thinking, freedom no longer contradicts captivation, because the task of thought is not the capture of the world but dwelling with and in the world, all the while articulating and being articulated by this difference between "with" and "in." It hints, in fact, at a relation to the world prior to the branching of *capt-* into "capture" and "captivation," transcribed later on into activity and passivity. The ecology of thinking stretches toward the *oikos* before its modifications by *logos* and *nomos*, an ecology that is inclusive of itself and of its other, which is why the economy of thought can rely upon, while at the same time abnegating, ecological articulations. In its ecological modality, thought whispers—Bibikhin concurs with Derrida's reading of Heidegger—its *yes* to the world antecedent to the formal enunciation of affirmation or negation. Such "concurrence with the world" (or else, a peaceful concurrence: *soglasie s mirom*) is "the affair proper to thought [*sobstvennoe delo mysli*]."²⁷ Hence, the core property of thought is to divest itself of its claim to the proper vis-à-vis the world, to which it delivers itself. Inceptual thinking does not sit in judgment of actuality, does not impose its laws (*nomoi*) onto *what is*; it does its own job and minds its own business (*sobstvennoe delo*), which is, however, not limited in scope but is concerned with and interested in everything insofar as it is: a world affair, or else an affair with the world, of the world.

The opposite dimension of inceptual thought, namely its preoccupation with death, similarly unfolds below capture and captivation, as well as activity and passivity. Supplementing and bringing to naught Dasein's properly improper dispersion—my dispersed interest in the world—being-toward-death is a concentration on the improperly proper, on a singularity that can never be mastered or appropriated. "Death is to be thought inceptually, i.e. out of the event and with respect to Da-sein [*Der Tod ist anfänglich und d. h. aus dem Ereignis da-seinshaft zu denken*]," Heidegger announces in *The Event*.²⁸ To translate: The end is to be thought from the beginning, without being conceived, co-grasped, or exchanged with the other. Aneconomically *and* anecologically? As Heidegger specifies, "in inceptual thinking, beginning is thought 'intransitively'; not to begin (tackle, take hold of, undertake) something but *to be taken hold of* by something [*an etwas angreifen*] (*in-cipere*)."[29] So, the inception, experientially felt in Dasein's exposure to the thought of death, is inclined toward captivation ("to be taken hold of by something"), though this time that by which one is captivated is the future of one's own worldlessness, one's own absolute expropriation. Whereas "agreement with the world" provided the articulations for *logos* comprising the ecology of thinking, the inceptual consideration of death disarticulates the I, abstracting what is proper to it from the world. Relationality is an articulated disarticulation or a disarticulated articulation, the concurrence of "with" and "in" investing ecology with meaning.

Bibikhin undersigns Heidegger's appeal to inceptual thinking: "It is not we who should order thought; we should be rather ordered by thought, to the extent that it gives a word to the world [*Ne my dolzhny rasporiazhat'sia mysl'iu, skoree my dolzhny byt' v ee rasporiazhenii, naskol'ko ona daët slovo miru*]."[30] Here, as well, the contours of the ecology of thought come through. The word of the world itself is a pre- or nonhuman instantiation of *logos*, which thought can only welcome, lending itself to use as a dwelling, or, better still, as a resonance chamber for a discourse that does not begin with or in it. Between "us" and the world, thought articulates us with the world and with ourselves, orders us in keeping with the word that is not originally ours.

Nothing could be further than this ordering independent of *nomos* and its conventional arrangements from economy, where thought serves as an instrument in the management of the world converted into our property. Thought, to be sure, remains in the intermediate position—itself degraded and reduced to pure means—but the arrow of appropriation now moves in the other direction, putting us in charge of being that is "utterly weightless [*schlechthin Gewichtslose*]," "empty of weight [*Gewichtsleere*]," evacuated due to the "unconditionality of power."[31] Being without weight is certainly not without mass, which is an ontic quality, the property of beings. Rather, it is deprived of the weight of the word, of the world's own *logos*. The moment we order thought with unconditional authority and make being unbearably light, the word of the world is silenced, the dwelling wherein it could have resonated shut.

Echoing Heidegger in *The Language of Philosophy* (*Iazyk filosofii*), where the weight of being is transferred to thought and word, Bibikhin writes: "A philosophical thought weighs exactly the same as a philosophical word. . . . What kind of an ecology should we expect of the human, who creates dirt upon the first contact with things? The first touch of this kind—thought and word [*Kakoi ekologii zhdat' ot cheloveka, delaiushchego griaz' pri pervom prikosnovenii k veshcham? Pervoe takoe prikosnovenie—mysl' i slovo*]."[32] Just as the weight of being has nothing to do with mass, so the "dirt" generated upon contact with things is not physical, but metaphysical. In fact, from the perspective of existence with all its visceral messiness, metaphysics *in toto* is such dirt either imputing to things that which is not in them or subtracting from them that which is their own. To anticipate a Derridian critique, the ecology of thought would not idolize things as untouchable, guided by an aspiration to cleanliness (Derrida often plays with the French *propre*, which unites the senses of "own" and "clean.") It would only respect and remark the articulations of the things themselves—the mystery proper to them, "the elusiveness of that which captivates [*neulovimost' zakhvatyvaiushchego*]"[33]—obeying the phenomenological injunction and realizing that the first touch, the first contact, is never first.

Should it succeed, the ecology of thought and word would grow indistinguishable from that of thing and world until, finally, the possessive form of its genitive would dispossess the thinker, expropriate the proper name attached to a body of thought, and hand it back to the world. In Bibikhin's eyes, Heidegger has achieved just that: "The affair that captivated Heidegger was not at all Heidegger's personal affair. . . . There is, strictly speaking, no such thing as 'the Heidegger affair.' In its place is the affair of the world [*dela Khaideggera v strogom smysle net. Na ego meste delo mira*]."[34] Let us bracket what the French refer to as *l'affaire Heidegger*, to which Bibikhin is undoubtedly alluding with the locution *delo Khaideggera*. At the level of thought, a dis- or expropriation of the proper is the moment of releasement, or *Gelassenheit*, inconceivable on the terms of the concept and its economy. Bibikhin's Heidegger has lived up to the precepts of the ecology of the proper and has given his life and thought to it without giving up on anything—not in the form of self-abnegation or some other form of a regrettable sacrifice but in the manner of a primordial *yes* that locates the word of the world in the place of the word of a thinker.

Although it appears that at stake in the quarrel of economy and ecology over thought are two diametrically opposed (because symmetrically inverted) images of appropriation, this is a pure misconception attributable to the undiminished power of the concept in thinking the proper. Whenever we order thought, we obfuscate our being-ordered by thought; whenever we capture, we downplay our captivation by the captured; whenever "the allegation that the human being 'has' language [*daß der Mensch die Sprache 'hat'*]" is made, those who make it are generally "unaware that this 'having' of language derives from the fact that the word of beyng 'has' the human being [*daß das Wort des Seyns den Menschen 'hat'*]."[35] The weighty word of the world, the *logos* in the ecology of thinking, is the language that appropriates the human and, once we are or have become its own objects or targets, withdraws, its withdrawal enabling us to claim the capacity to speak and to order our surroundings as our essential properties. Economic and ecological attitudes are not equal partners in the making of the human; to live well it is not enough to establish just a little more balance between our activity and receptiveness to the environment. *Logos* is so generous as to open the door even to its own closure, to consent—silently, or in words we either do not hear or do not know how to interpret—to its expropriation. It prompts us to think the same and the other at the same time, nonsynthetically, nondialectically. The economy of thinking is an ecology expropriated in the full confidence of appropriating the world and oneself.

\*\*\*

Ever a translator, Bibikhin specializes in making his own what is of the other and, conversely, in making other what is his own. More than a translator's duty, this is the task of thinking as such. Translating Heidegger is trickier still, to the extent that his translators must render their own that of which the author has expropriated himself, turned over to the world. It is pointless to ask what is proper to Heidegger and what to Bibikhin in the thinking of the proper or of anything else, for that matter. Received by the Russian, the German stands for the event of thought as such, for how to think properly, that is, by ceding one's proper name and the identity of one's thinking to the world. This event is an antipode to that of privatization. The question is how to achieve the sort of poverty, the sort of total expropriation "necessary for ontological wealth,"[36] which may permit us to think again or perhaps for the first time. And, if we are to believe Bibikhin, the germ of an answer lies hidden in Heidegger's little-known text "Poverty," *Die Armut.*

One remarkable feature of the short essay on poverty is that, despite circling around Hölderlin's dictum on the spiritual need to "become poor in order to become rich," Heidegger singles out Eastern Orthodox spirituality, and particularly the figure of Holy Sophia central to Russian mysticism, as the embodiment of spirit's efficaciousness.[37] At odds with the Western idea of spirit as subject, substance, or both, this figuration approximates Heidegger's ontological reading of spirit; after all, in the Orthodox tradition, Holy Sophia is the hypostasis of divine *logos*, which delves below the economy of spiritual subject and substance. A little heretically, then, Sophia might be said to be ecological.

As we know, the ineluctable correlative of the subject is an object, and ontic wealth is made up precisely of objects multiplied in our environs. In his interpretation of Hölderlin, Heidegger is satisfied with nothing less than a paradigm shift in the meaning of our "surroundings" vacated of objects. We must, he thinks, become ontically poor to become ontologically rich: to transition from the economy of beings to the ecology of being. That is what the figuration of spirit in Sophia, or in *logos*, presages. "The human," Heidegger writes, "abides in a relation to that which surrounds him. . . . What surrounds us normally, what individually stands over against us (= the objects), we also call a being that is. . . . [But] the exalted relation wherein the human abides is the relation of beyng to the human, namely so that beyng itself is this relation that draws to itself the ownmost of the human as the ownmost that abides in this relation and preserves and inhabits this relation by abiding within it."[38] In the circular ecological frame, the human abode (*oikos*) is the relation (an articulation, *logos*) to being that, in turn, is the relation that captivates the human drawn into it. The ownmost, the most proper to the human is this other-than-human ecology, in and with which we abide. It has nothing to do with the objective surroundings, upon which the economist attitude preys and in which the obverse of intentionality (our being targeted, captivated, drawn in) is diluted to fascination with the unlimited possibility of acquiring more material possessions.

In *Being and Time*, impending mortality was the event that accomplished the work of vacating the world of objects and confronting Dasein with worldhood. Death impoverished ontic reality to impart ontological richness to the one to whom it singularly "belonged." But its workings, indeed its energy, exaggerated the element of disarticulation and, on its own terms, incapacitated *logos* itself. Death leaves no room for the word, for speech, for an address. Quite simply, there can be no ecology of death, even if it beckons with a complete expropriation most proper to Dasein. For this reason, Heidegger consults the poetic word, itself secretly resonating with theosophic mysticism, in an effort to reconcile ontic poverty with the wealth of ontological (or ecological) dwelling.

In order for thought *qua* thought to achieve ontic poverty, it must rid itself of the customary vocabulary, within which conceptual terms play the role of objects surrounding the thinker. According to Bibikhin, Nietzsche and Heidegger manage to do just that, untying themselves with ease from the philosophical lexicon. "And, in both [Nietzsche and Heidegger], this untethering to the lexicon has for its obverse the unprecedented attention to the word."[39] The vocabulary of philosophy is a collection of weightless words generating metaphysical dirt, light on being and fit to double as coins in the economy of thought. It needs to be aired, ontically impoverished so as to make our thinking ontologically rich. The same is true for our unresolved relation to Heidegger who, as we have observed, stands for the event of thought, as far as Bibikhin is concerned: We, who are still too accustomed to conceptual cogitation, are not yet poor enough to receive him—not to appropriate, but, precisely, to receive in the liberated place prepared for the event of thought. Until this can happen, Heidegger, in the words of Bibikhin, is "yet to come in the same way in which Plato is still yet to come [*Khaidegger poka eshche predstoit, kak Platon do sikh por eshche predstoit*]."[40] And what is more proper to Bibikhin himself, what is more his "own," than a series of sketches portraying Heidegger's to-come without representing it, without making it present, or predigesting it for the conceptual apparatus of understanding?

## NOTES

1. Vladimir Bibikhin, *Sobstvennost': filosofiia* Svoego [*Property: The Philosophy of* What Is One's Own] (St. Petersburg: Nauka, 2012), 334. All translations of this and other Bibikhin's texts from the original Russian are mine.

2. Ibid.

3. Ibid., 22–23.

4. Vladimir Bibikhin, *Drugoe nachalo* [*The Other Beginning*] (St. Petersburg: Nauka, 2003), 372.

5. Bibikhin, *Sobstvennost'*, 27.

6. Martin Heidegger, *Being and Time*, trans. John Macquarrie and Edward Robinson (San Francisco: Harper and Row, 1962), 65.

7. Bibikhin, *Sobstvennost'*, 373.

8. Ibid., 374.

9. Heidegger, *Being and Time*, 263.

10. Bibikhin, *Sobstvennost'*, 101.

11. Ibid., 97.

12. Ibid., 98.

13. Martin Heidegger, *The Event*, trans. Richard Rojcewicz (Bloomington and Indianapolis: Indiana University Press, 2013), 33.

14. Bibikhin, *Sobstvennost'*, 44.

15. Ibid., 46.

16. Heidegger, *The Event*, 56.

17. Vladimir Bibikhin, *Les* (*hylé*) [*The Forest*] (St. Petersburg: Nauka, 2011), 58.

18. Heidegger, *The Event*, 98.

19. Bibikhin, *Sobstvennost'*, 240.

20. Martin Heidegger, *Contributions to Philosophy (From Enowning)*, trans. Parvis Emad and Kenneth Maly (Bloomington and Indianapolis: Indiana University Press, 1999), 10.

21. Heidegger, *The Event*, 133.

22. Ibid.

23. Bibikhin, *Drugoe nachalo*, 372.

24. Heidegger, *Contributions to Philosophy*, 45.

25. Bibikhin, *Sobstvennost'*, 138.

26. Ibid., 148.

27. Vladimir Bibikhin, "Delo Khaideggera" ("The Affair of Heidegger"), introduction to the Russian translation of Martin Heidegger, *Being and Time* (Moscow: Respublika Publishing, 2003), 10.

28. Heidegger, *The Event*, 165.

29. Ibid., 154.

30. Bibikhin, "Delo Khaideggera," 12.

31. Heidegger, *The Event*, 94.

32. Vladimir Bibikhin, *Iazyk filosofii* [*The Language of Philosophy*] (Moscow: Yazyki Slavianskoi Kul'tury, 2002), 7.

33. Bibikhin, *Drugoe nachalo*, 374.

34. Bibikhin, "Delo Khaideggera," 12.

35. Heidegger, *The Event*, 137.

36. Bibikhin, *Sobstvennost'*, 149.

37. Martin Heidegger, "Poverty," in *Heidegger, Translation and the Task of Thinking: Essays in Honor of Parvis Emad*, trans. Thomas Kalary and Frank Schalow (Dordrecht, London, and New York: Springer, 2011), 4–5.

38. Heidegger, "Poverty," 6, translation modified.

39. Bibikhin, *Sobstvennost'*, 39.

40. Ibid., 59.

*Part III*

# POLITICAL CONTEXTS

## Chapter 10

# Heidegger in Communist Czechoslovakia

## Daniel Kroupa

If I were to characterize briefly Czech thought in general, I would say that (admitting that such an attempt must be precarious) ever since its origins in the Middle Ages it has tended toward practical philosophy. Thomas Štítný strove to reform morality, John Huss was a reformer before the Reformation, Peter Chelčický the father of pacifism, and John Amos Comenius designed the grand-scale project of the *Improvement of All Things Human* through education.[1] Similarly, in the nineteenth century, the followers of Bernard Bolzano supported the "rebirth" of the Czech nation as well as political reforms of the Habsburg monarchy. Tomáš G. Masaryk, who studied with Franz Brentano, worked mainly in practical philosophy and later became the president of Czechoslovakia, a republic founded largely thanks to his efforts. Accordingly, it should be no surprise that the thought of Martin Heidegger, itself grounded in the highly theoretical discipline of ontology, had an impact in the practical realm in Czechoslovakia.

A certain exception in this respect is Jan Patočka, whose thought took the path from the late Husserl's concept of the Life-World toward phenomenology of the bodily movement of human existence influenced by Heidegger's ontology of openness. But even Patočka, as an old man, entered public life as one of the three original spokespersons of Charter 77, whose aim was to see that communist Czechoslovakia fulfill its international obligations in the area of human rights. At that moment, he felt obliged to cross the boundaries of practical philosophy and to formulate, shortly before his death, a succinct philosophical justification of his activities.[2] Regarding Heidegger's thought, Patočka was certainly the one who most strongly contributed to its reception in Czechoslovakia. But he was not the only one.

As early as 1939, Ladislav Rieger devoted a chapter of his book *Idea filosofie* to Heidegger.[3] There, he critically analyzed the main ideas of *Being and Time* and especially of Heidegger's interpretation of Kant. He reproaches Heidegger for departing from a by and large correct interpretation "into his own metaphysics" when he finds nothingness hidden in Kant's concept of an object.[4] Further, Heidegger emphasizes the finitude of reason which weakens the importance of transcendental logic. Besides, as Rieger points out, "through his existential pre-understanding of resoluteness, Heidegger was close to understanding the structure of the moral self, of moral existence."[5] Such were Rieger's reservations. He took Heidegger for a follower of Husserl's phenomenology who attempted to provide it with a more fundamental dimension.

During the short, less than three-year period of relative freedom after the end of World War II, Czechoslovakia experienced a wave of interest in existentialism. Responding to that interest, there appeared an issue of the quarterly *Listy* devoted to the topic. It contained a translation of Heidegger's lecture "What Is Metaphysics?"[6] together with papers by Ladislav Rieger, Václav Navrátil, and Jan Patočka, and translations of Kafka's and Sartre's fiction. In his introductory paper, Rieger ascribes to Heidegger an inspiration in Christian religion from which he adopts his concepts by way of secularization—but in spite of his nihilist standpoint, the religious problem remains unsettled in Heidegger.[7] In a sense, it remained unsettled in Rieger's own thought, too, as he was by that time already inclining toward the Marxist-Leninist worldview that was becoming the prescribed ideology of communist Czechoslovakia. By saying it was "prescribed" I mean that it was the only acceptable doctrine everywhere, not just in the academy. The professors who would not subscribe to it were forced to leave the universities at the beginning of the 1950s and their publication opportunities were severely restricted until the mid-1960s. Admittedly, Rieger could not foresee all this, which allowed him to bravely assert that "socialism, too, has its existential idea, existential philosophy, its 'human' face." By saying that, he anticipated the development within Czech Marxism that took place around the mid-1960s and became the inspiration of Czech reform communism.

One of those who was forced to leave the university in 1950 was Jan Patočka. However, between 1945 and 1949 there had gathered a circle of his students, many of whom later became his friends, who attempted to elaborate further the philosophical themes of their teacher. Jaroslav Kohout, Radim Palouš, Josef Zumr, and others belonged to groups that would meet with Patočka in private in the 1950s. In 1957, Patočka was hired by the Philosophical Institute of the Czechoslovak Academy of Sciences to work in the publishing department.

In the new workplace, Patočka got in touch with gifted young Marxist philosophers who, in the time after Khrushchev's condemnation of the "personality cult" and of Stalinism, were seeking ways to enliven the languishing dogmatic Marxist-Leninist ideology. A characteristic feature of this movement was the turn to studying the young Marx and topics like human being, praxis, and alienation, which allowed them to find points of correspondence with phenomenology and existentialism.[8] By this time, they were suspected of revisionism.[9] Prominent among them were especially Karel Kosík, Ivan Dubský, and Robert Kalivoda, and later (at Charles University) also Karel Michňák, Jiří Pešek, and Ladislav Major. Against ideological dogmatism in favor of party unity, they emphasized the dynamic character and the richness of reality. Zumr played an important role by organizing a reading group that met from 1958 to 1960, included Kosík, and read Heidegger's texts under the guidance of Patočka.[10] Kosík probably was the one who benefited most from talks and readings with Patočka, as the insight into Heidegger's thought opened for him new vistas especially in the areas ignored by the orthodox ideology. Due to his original approach, Kosík became an informal leader of the reform Marxism that was providing ideological scaffolding for the opposition movement within the Communist Party of Czechoslovakia, the movement that later, under the leadership of Alexander Dubček, attempted to carry through the so-called socialism with a human face, democratic socialism, or simply the Prague Spring in 1968. By that time, Kosík himself entered the political playground and became a member of the Central Committee of the Czechoslovak Communist Party.

Kosík's book *Dialectics of the Concrete*, published in 1963, probably remains the most significant product of Czech Marxist philosophy, and it deservedly received considerable appreciation at home and abroad. Its central idea, elaborated in four chapters, is formulated concisely at the end of the book. "Dialectics is after the 'thing itself.' But the 'thing itself' is no ordinary thing; actually it is not a thing at all. The thing itself that philosophy deals with is man and his place in the universe or, in different words: it is the totality of the world uncovered in history by man, and man existing in the totality of the world."[11] This seemingly innocent formulation was, at the time, the gauntlet thrown down to dogmatic Stalinist Marxist-Leninist orthodoxy at least by making the human being its central topic. For Kosík, the human being is not a mere intersection of external economic relations, but rather a being transforming the world it inhabits by its activity, and thus a historical being. Hence, praxis becomes the central topic. "To the things themselves" is the main slogan of Husserl's phenomenology, and Kosík's use of the term here means a requirement that Marxism should be open to dialogue with contemporary philosophical schools. By speaking of a "man existing in the totality of the world," Kosík refers to Heidegger's analyses. But how was it possible for Kosík to dare to borrow concepts from the German existentialist? What serves as a justification is a further unspecified claim "that the terminology of existentialism is frequently an idealist–romantic, i.e. concealing and dramatizing, transcription of revolutionary–materialist concepts," which "permits a fruitful dialogue between Marxism and existentialism."[12]

Let us have a closer look at how Kosík appropriates the concepts of existential philosophy. In his chapter 1, where he elaborates on the idea of "concrete totality" (as opposed to the concept of "pseudoconcreteness") as the proper topic of dialectical cognition, he makes use of Karl Marx's *Grundrisse*. The concrete totality is the unity of the base and the superstructure, which however remains abstract "when it is not demonstrated that man is the *real historical subject*, and that in the process of social production and reproduction he forms both the base and the superstructure, that he forms social reality as a totality of social relations, institutions and ideas, . . . realizing hereby the infinite process of 'humanizing man.'"[13] But real humans live under real conditions, within certain pre-given economic relations by which they are formed. The primary way by which economics exists for a human in *everydayness*[14] is *care*, which not only holds sway over the human being, but which the human being is. "Care is the world in the subject," says Kosík; "in his subjectivity, man as care is outside himself, aiming at something else, transcending his subjectivity."[15] Kosík criticizes Heidegger for not distinguishing sufficiently between *procuring* (*besorgen*) and *work*: "Procuring is praxis in its *phenomenally alienated form* which does not point to the *genesis* of the human world . . . but rather expresses the praxis of everyday manipulation, with man employed in a system of *ready-made* 'things.'"[16] Further, he reproaches him for not having "recognized praxis as man's primary determination which implies authentic temporality. Care and the temporality of care are *derived* and *reified* forms of *praxis*."[17] It is worth mentioning that Jan Patočka found this Marxist conception unsatisfactory too, at least for its reducing praxis to production.

Besides, Kosík's understanding of *inauthenticity* merely in the sense of dynamic stereotypes without which life is impossible is problematic, too. A transition from inauthenticity toward authenticity is understood by Kosík as a historical process. "The pseudoconcrete of the alienated everyday world is destroyed through *estrangement*, through *existential modification*, and through *revolutionary transformation*."[18] The term "existential modification" refers to "the *drama of an individual in the world*,"[19] that of his liberation from an inauthentic mode of existence. But such liberation depends on a revolutionary change in external conditions.

After criticizing the metaphysics of everydayness, Kosík proceeds to the criticism of the metaphysics of science and reason and to the metaphysics of culture. Against positivism and scientific rationalism, he champions dialectical reason; against the idea of an autonomous existence of a work of art, he emphasizes its interaction with the historical development of humankind—that is, its totalization. In his view, human reality is both a production of the new and a reproduction of the old. "Totalization is the process of production and reproduction, of reviving and rejuvenating."[20] In Kosík's presentation of the temporality and timelessness of the work of art, we can find a modification of Heidegger's thought once again: "To exist means to be in time. Being in time is not movement in an external continuum, but temporality."[21] And it depends precisely on this temporality, whether the work has or will have something to say to its time.

In the chapter "Philosophy and Economics," one of the topics is "to abolish philosophy," which should happen, according to Kosík's interpretation of Marx, on the one hand, by its being brought to actuality (becoming a dialectic theory of society), and, on the other, by its falling apart and surviving as a residual science (a formal or dialectical logic).[22] Marx's *Capital* is such a critical theory of capital, and only such philosophical analysis (transcending the boundaries of economics) makes it possible to grasp the essence of economic concepts. By doing that, it also uncovers the internal relationships between economic categories and social being. It also uncovers the sociohistorical forms of objectification of the human being, the concrete historical level of subject-object relationships, and the unity of "ontological and existential determinations."[23] Kosík's philosophy of labor requires that labor be understood not merely from a narrowly economic or sociological viewpoint, but rather as "a *happening* which permeates man's *entire* being and constitutes his specificity."[24] In labor, human beings relate to objectivity, they humanize objects and by objectification or realization of meanings they create a human world. From this point of view, the tool is a "reasonable mediation" between human being and the object.[25] That is why Scheler and Heidegger's disdain for tools and technology is mistaken. Besides, their view of human mortality is also idealistically distorted, for "man knows his mortality only because he organizes time, on the basis of labor as objective doing and as the process of forming socio-human reality."[26]

Also in the final chapter of Kosík's book, dealing with the relationship between praxis and concrete totality, we can find passages reminiscent of Husserl's and Heidegger's thought, for example, about the determination of the task of philosophy as questioning and about the end of philosophy—that is, in the conception of praxis and the historical agency of human beings as the actualization of philosophy. Praxis is, according to Kosík, "the determination of human being as the process of *forming* reality . . . it is active and self-producing in history, i.e. it is a constantly renewing, practically constituted unity of man and world, matter and spirit, subject and object, products and productivity."[27] Related to nature, it is the realization of human freedom, and it is also a process in which the being of reality opens for humans and becomes understandable and knowable. History is made by people; it is a human product, and humans realize themselves in history. People are born into given conditions, but they transcend them, transform and by their activity ascribe meaning to them. "Reality is not a system of my meanings nor is it transformed in accordance with the meanings my project gives it. It is in his action that man inscribes meanings into the world and forms a structure of meanings in it."[28] Kosík finishes the book with a criticism of philosophical anthropology and by emphasizing the fact that human beings transcend their determinations and their subjectivity in recognizing the things as they are, by which reality in its totality gets reproduced in their being. The issue of dialectics, as quoted already at the beginning, is thus "the totality of the world uncovered in history by man, and man existing in the totality of the world."[29]

Kosík's *Dialectics of the Concrete* was met in Czechoslovak Marxist philosophy with a uniquely strong response. The importance of the book was emphasized even by its opponents, for example, Jan Fojtík (later the ideological secretary of the CP in the bleak times of "normalization" following the Soviet military occupation), who reproached Kosík for underestimating "the role of the revolutionary party" and the development of sciences during the scientific-technological revolution.[30] Among the supporters, Zumr prevailed with an opinion appreciating the novelty of Kosík's approach and the fact that his "philosophy of human being is a negation of the mechanistic and antihumanist conception of Marxism that had been commonplace during the Stalinist era."[31] In his review in the *Literární noviny* (which was soon to become the main platform of the pro-reform communists) Zumr unwittingly formulates the reformatory potential of the book: "The Promethean conception of human being, found in the young Marx and . . . permeating all of Marx's work, makes it possible to oppose to the mechanistic reduction of human being to a product of objectified conditions and an object of bureaucratic manipulation a conception of human being that provides real foundations for a real Marxist humanism."[32] The reader should notice the characteristic ambiguity between the possible reading of such statements as criticizing the conditions of capitalism, on the one hand, but possibly also (and much more relevantly for the readers of the weekly) criticizing the present centrally planned, bureaucratized and dysfunctional communist regime, on the other hand.

Kosík became not only the leading figure of reform Marxism, but also a part of the wider reform movement within the Communist Party, which included the group of economists around Ota Šik proposing a reform of the centrally planned economy toward market mechanisms as well as writers, filmmakers, and other figures from the area of culture who strove for the easing of censorship. At first, the movement was confronted with the strong opposition of party apparatchiks whose power once was nearly unlimited and who were afraid that easing of censorship and weakening of the repressive apparatus would lead to the exposing of their crimes committed during the Stalinist era and consequently to their losing their positions. But by electing the previously unknown and seemingly colorless Alexander Dubček as the leader of the CP, the balance of power was shifted and the pro-reform communists could start to realize their program. Censorship began to collapse and the noticeable breath of free spirit in the media woke up the hitherto apathetic population. Out of the hope that they would regain basic human rights (such as freedom of expression, free travel, small- and middle-scale enterprise, etc.), people provided the reformists with massive support.

It remains an open question how far the pro-reform communists were ready to go in their democratization struggle. Within the Soviet bloc it was out of the question to consider an independent Czechoslovak foreign policy, and this limit on the reforms was never challenged (out of fear of possible military intervention). The interior reforms also had a limit in section 4 of the constitution, declaring the leading role of the Communist Party, which seemed to prevent introduction of political pluralism and free elections. Kosík's programmatic paper "Our Present Crisis," from May 1968, remains abstract and provides no answer to the specific questions of the limits on reform. But the final sentence of the discussion of the crisis of socialism shows clear traces of a Heideggerian inspiration: "But the minimal steps by which we renounce political crimes could not hide or put off the urgency of the *basic questions* which we did not even touch so far and without which socialism as a *revolutionary* alternative for people in the 20th century is inconceivable: the questions (posited anew) as to *who* is the human being and what is truth, what is being and what is time, what is the essence of technology and of science, what is the purpose of revolution."[33] However, at that moment, philosophical ideas sounded too abstract, though they had previously helped to set the reform movement in motion because they covered the truly urgent questions, such as those formulated by Ivan Sviták, Kosík's former colleague expelled from the CP and fired from the Academy of Sciences as a "revisionist." In his lecture on April 18, 1968, in the freshly founded Club of Engaged Non-Partisans, he said: "Do the six million non-partisan citizens of this state have the same rights as the members of the Communist Party, or are they merely allowed to have some more liberty, provided that it does not threaten the privileges of party members? Are we to expect democratic, free and secret elections, or just the old game with new players? Are we to live in a sovereign European state with a polycentric political system or in a non-sovereign state-like structure whose leaders fear above all the tank divisions of their allies?"[34]

Indeed, on August 21, 1968, Soviet tank divisions brought to an end the Czechoslovak attempt at "democratic socialism," or "socialism with a human face," called the Prague Spring, and the subsequent "normalization" involved once again a wave of purges, also in the academy, and changed many former communists into nonpartisans and second-class citizens. They could not be employed in their professional fields; often the only jobs they could find would be manual labor. And even if they would be willing to continue research in their free time, no periodical and no publisher would accept their work. Thus, they experienced firsthand and in a milder way the situation of non-Marxist philosophers who were victims of the purges of 1949 and 1950. The remaining options for publication (admittedly somewhat risky) were *samizdat* or the West. Dozens of Marxist philosophers were victims of such measures.[35]

Let us look now at those philosophers for whom studying Heidegger's philosophy contributed to their abandoning Marxism. The most prominent among them is Kosík's colleague from the Philosophical Institute (ČSAV) Ivan Dubský.[36] Originally, Dubský's field was labor and alienation considered from the Marxist point of view, but subsequently his approach became more independent, influenced especially by studying existential philosophy. In the mid-1960s, Dubský studied alienation in connection with the work of Franz Kafka and Albert Camus, and he became increasingly inclined to find the source of alienation in the uprootedness of the modern human being. He writes on home and homelessness, on Heidegger, on technology and being, and on the philosophy of time in Augustine, Hegel, Nietzsche, Bergson, and modern fiction.[37] He also devoted a number of studies to the philosophy of Jan Patočka. In the 1970s, he signed Charter 77 and became a dissident.

As a young miner and a communist, Karel Michňák excelled in the shock-worker movement, was sent to study Marxism-Leninism, and up to 1967, as an associate professor at Charles University, had remained faithful to this creed. But then, influenced by studying Patočka, Heidegger, and Gadamer, he abandoned Marxism. In March 1968, he addressed the student body with the following statement: "I am guilty—as a member of the CP I am responsible for the crimes of the 1950s, as a member of the CP I became an associate professor while others, more gifted and more suitable for the position, ended up in jail as a result of their moral stance, could not finish their studies or could not enroll in them at all."[38] He canceled his membership in the party and he held lecture courses and seminars on Heideggerian topics.[39] The last one was a seminar on history and historicity where he argued that the alleged knowledge of the laws of social development contributed to the emergence of totalitarian movements and regimes. At the beginning of the "normalization," he was fired from the university and made his living as a worker. His wife, Irena Michňáková (née Šnebergová), another of Kosík's, Dubský's, and Zumr's colleagues from ČSAV, significantly contributed to the Czech reception of Heidegger, especially as a translator[40] (and she, too, was among those who had to leave the profession between 1970 and 1990).[41]

In the 1950s, non-Marxist philosophy was studied in reading and discussion groups that met in private. In the 1960s, with the successive easing of restrictions, it would slowly show up in public. The respect for Heidegger's thought was manifest in the increasing number of both papers devoted to Heidegger's work[42] and translations.[43] Also the Heidegger-inspired theology of, for example, Rudolf Bultmann and Karl Rahner was of significance, as it spread the recognition of Heidegger in Christian circles and among the younger philosophers belonging to them. Among the protestants, the leading figure was Ladislav Hejdánek, whose philosophy of objectlessness was partly inspired by Heidegger (as well as by Emanuel Rádl, a Czech philosopher of the interwar period). Among the Catholics, where the reforms of the Second Vatican Council encouraged intellectual curiosity, the central figure was Jiří Němec, an erudite psychologist and philosopher and tireless translator, also of Heidegger. It is quite likely that Němec was the first to tell the playwright Václav Havel about Heidegger.[44]

In 1968 conditions became liberal enough to make possible Jan Patočka's return to Charles University as a professor, and a group of his students took form at his lectures and seminars. Many of them would remain philosophically active even after the purges in the academy during the "normalization" era, in private seminars and reading groups, or in the so-called gray zone.[45] In one of the private groups were recorded lectures that, transcribed by the participants, became Jan Patočka's book *Plato and Europe*.[46] In another group, Ivan Chvatík, Jiří Němec, Pavel Kouba, and Miroslav Petříček translated Heidegger's *Being and Time*.[47] One of the most prominent venues of the 1980s was the Monday group of Ladislav Hejdánek, with dozens of foreign philosophers lecturing there. The Tuesday class of Daniel Kroupa, started in 1979, focused on phenomenology (Husserl, Heidegger, Patočka) and was the most successful in terms of educating several of the leading figures of

Czech and Slovak philosophy of the post-1989 era. In the 1970s, the reading group "Kecanda," including Jan Sokol, Jiří Němec, Zdeněk Neubauer, Tomáš Halík, Dan Drápal, and others, shifted from Max Scheler to a slow and systematic reading of Nietzsche's *Zarathustra*, taking into account also Heidegger's interpretation. Occasionally, Jan Patočka would join the group with a lecture. There were also regular lectures (not only philosophical) in the flat of Václav and Ivan Havel, and similar activities took place also out of Prague, especially in Brno.

Let us have a closer look at one such group called "Kampademie," for it is going to have a special relevance for our story. It evolved from the cooperation of Ladislav Hejdánek, Martin Palouš, and Daniel Kroupa in translating Heidegger's *Die Sprache* in 1973, from the attempted translation of Aristotle's book XII of *Metaphysics* by Kroupa and Zdeněk Neubauer, and from a group study of Plato's unwritten doctrines. Its elected scholarch was Radim Palouš, Patočka's student from 1945 to 1948 who later became the first rector of Charles University in the post-1989 era. His field was philosophy of education, and he opposed any violent or technicist formation of the educated. He was inspired by Heidegger's conception of "letting-be" (*Seinlassen*), and in education he emphasized the need for creating an environment in which the educated person—with the help of the educator—can become him- or herself.

Other participants of Kampademie were, besides the author of this paper:

Zdeněk Neubauer, whose original field was microbiology[48] and who passionately opposed objectivist conceptions in the philosophy of science and based his own conception on Heidegger's views of the technological foundation of science.

Martin Palouš, who also was educated as a scientist but later focused mainly on political philosophy, inspired especially by the work of Hannah Arendt and Eric Voegelin.

Tomáš Halík, a priest with a philosophical, sociological, and psychological background, who adopted a number of Heidegger's thoughts in his attempts at a new theological approach to interfaith dialogue (for which he was awarded the 2014 Templeton Prize).

Pavel Bratinka, educated in nuclear physics, who introduced to Czech thought the works of Eric Voegelin and Friedrich Hayek.

Ivan M. Havel, educated in computer science, who had broad interdisciplinary interests and applied the philosophy he knew from

Kampademie in his own work. Before 1989 he was also the editor and organizer of the *samizdat* series "Expedice." After 1989, he was the founding director of the Center for Theoretical Study (affiliated first with Charles University and later jointly with the Czech Academy of Sciences).[49]

Dozens of foreign visiting lecturers gave talks in the Kampademie in the 1980s; among them were Charles Taylor and, repeatedly, Paul Ricoeur. Most of the Kampademie participants were active signatories of Charter 77; consequently, they were spied on, persecuted, and occasionally arrested by the secret police.

Václav Havel, the playwright, dissident, and later president, got in touch with Kampademie during his longest term in prison (1979–1982), first through correspondence with his brother Ivan. He needed some food for thought (having enough time for reflection there) and the members of Kampademie, especially Radim Palouš and Zdeněk Neubauer, wrote him letters of philosophical content that were sent as letters signed by Havel's wife, Olga, and inspired Havel's philosophical replies (unfortunately, even the correspondence with the closest family was subject to censorship and occasionally seized). Václav Havel's letters are well-known as *Letters to Olga*, and they show remarkably how he was influenced by Heideggerian ideas despite not having any access to his texts except for two shorter pieces, "The Country Path" and "Language," written down (in translations) as letters by Ivan.[50] Besides Heidegger, other philosophers were prominent topics in this long-distance conversation, especially Jan Patočka and Emmanuel Levinas. Of course, as the author of the intellectual portrait of Václav Havel, Martin C. Putna, remarks: "Such connections can be misleading, for they were academic philosophers . . . and Havel in comparison with them merely an informed layperson who makes instrumental use of their concepts and techniques for his own 'practical,' i.e. ethical and political purposes."[51] And Havel himself, with a flair for self-irony, says about his philosophical attempts: "And here I am certainly influenced by the fragments of contemporary philosophy chance has cast my way over the years, though in no way bound by them (in any case, that would be technically impossible: how can one be bound by something one doesn't properly know?)."[52]

One of the most interesting philosophical topics discussed by Havel (and connected with Heideggerian influence) is the crisis of identity understood as the situation of humans who, by "conquering" the world, at the same time lose it. As if a cow in the dairy farm was not an animal any more, but rather a machine with its "inputs" and "outputs," its plan of milk production, and its operator. What causes this situation is, according to Havel, "a crisis in our experience of the absolute horizon,"[53] which leads to loss of "sensitivity toward the integrity of Being, the mutual coherence between existences, their diversity and independence; the secret meaningfulness of the phenomena of this world vanishes (they are neither secret, nor meaningful any more)."[54] The result of that is another crisis, this time concerning human responsibility "to and for this world," which makes the identity based on this relationship disappear, and the human being loses its place in the world. Hence the crowd-mentality of consumerism, loss of home, and the fragmentation of life into anonymous functions, which leads to the total helplessness of humans vis-à-vis macrostructures and manipulation. One gets used to it; one identifies with it successively and thus yields to being robbed of historical life: One "gives up trying to understand the world and his responsibility for it. This blurs the human 'I' and makes it uncertain: the locus of that connection between what was or should be and what is has been shifted once and for all outside itself and outside the sphere of man's proper concerns, which of course destroys any connection between what he is in a given moment and what he is at any other time."[55] The world created by modern humans seems to be an image of their own state, gotten out of hand, powered by anonymous and particular forces that drive humans down into yet more desperate alienation, yet deeper depersonalization, and ultimately into "apathetic contentment" with such a state.[56] Are humans really helpless in the face of that? If they will identify with their role as a little screw in giant gears, devoid of their human identity, then yes. But it is also true that each of us "irrespective of the state of the world—has the basic potential," as an autonomous human being, to take up responsibility and to act.[57] Havel finishes this letter by saying: "To the objection that it makes no sense, my response is quite simple: It does!"[58]

The initial condition of humanity is "separation," reflects Havel. "With the advent of humanity, however, something intrinsically new has appeared, something that ultimately is not referable to anything else, something that is but is no longer spontaneously in 'Being in general'; something that is, but somehow 'otherwise,' that stands against everything, even against itself. Beings pose Being as a question, themselves being in question, being out of Being, facing themselves."[59] Humans as beings "fallen out of Being";[60] an alienated being thrown into the world. We bear in mind that, according to Heidegger, the "thrownness" of *Dasein* into its *da* is a constitutive characteristic of *Dasein* "which is veiled in its whence and whither, but in itself all the more openly disclosed."[61] Havel speaks of two kinds of thrownness: into the strangeness of the world and into the origin within the integrity of Being. "Thus is man—thrown to the world—alienated from Being, but precisely because of this he is seared by longing for its integrity (which he understands as meaningfulness), by a desire to merge with it and thus to transcend himself totally. As such, however, he is also alienated from the world in which he finds himself, a world that captivates and imprisons him. He is an alien in the world because he is still somehow bound up in Being, and he is alienated from Being because he has been thrown into the world."[62] The second kind of thrownness, the present absence of the universality of Being, first and foremost covered by entities and mundane interests, builds up from within the presubjective, preconscious, and prerational phase our connectedness with other beings and originates our responsibility for the whole and for others. Thus, that responsibility is not rationally justified in any way, for it precedes all justifications. In the other's being exposed and vulnerable, not only are we reminded of our own being exposed and vulnerable, but, due to our longing for the integrity of Being, we hear in it something like the "voice of Being" awaking our non-indifference.[63] Thrownness into the relatedness to the lost integrity of Being and into responsibility for Being is paradoxical in a triple sense: (1) It is more original than "me," which gets constituted on its stage, but as an experience it already presupposes "me"; (2) the conscious and reflecting "I" exists and simultaneously knows that it exists, and thus it presupposes a more or less developed consciousness of thrownness; (3) the "I" is longing for the integrity of being, but it is itself constituted by the unsurpassable "separation" from the universality of Being.

And yet the longing for a reconciliatory merging with Being can reach a kind of fulfillment, namely in the experiences of meaningfulness.[64] These experiences can vary from an intense feeling to an unfocused noticing of an absence of "something," but it is due to them that the "I" becomes itself in its uniqueness. Paradoxically, this way the "I" uncovers that "the most mature identification [with Being] is most powerfully revealed as quasi-identification. Joy has an undertone of horror, tranquillity of anxiety, good fortune a touch of the fatally tragic."[65] In other words, a full identification, fulfillment of meaning, perfect happiness is the death of the "I." As in Patočka, in Havel's view the human being is exposed to the problematicity of meaning that is not ready-made but rather in an unceasing search found and again problematized.

The "I" thrown into the world and oriented toward Being expresses its will to be, to understand what it means to be in the world, and to becoming at home in it. It cannot escape its Dasein, but "to focus one's attention exclusively on Dasein as such and thus mistake the means for an end means inevitably to reject the fullness of Being."[66] Dasein draws human beings to the world of things, superficiality, and self-care; it takes them away from the relationship with Being toward what Havel calls "succumbing to Dasein." The "I" succumbs to non-I and "in renouncing the transcendental dimensions of his 'I,' man renounces his paradoxical constitution, disrupts that fundamental tension from which his very existence, subjectivity and ultimately his identity all stem, dissolves himself in aims and matters that he himself has defined and created, and finally loses himself in them entirely. He becomes a mechanism, a function, a frantic consumer, a thing manipulated by its own manipulations."[67] This is also the trajectory of our contemporary civilization built on the development of science and technology with its tendency to conquer nature and humanity; the humanity enslaved by consumerist needs is fragmented into individual functions, and it loses responsibility and human identity.[68]

On the other hand, orientation toward Being, leading to investigating the meaning and not the utility of entities, transcends the horizon of entities in general and the horizon of the world, because it questions the world and itself: One "seeks with his entire being, and in that quest, his being is entirely transformed, as the world is entirely transformed in it as well. . . . As an existential experience, this quest cannot be answered, not in any specific way. The only possible response to it is another experience—the experience of meaningfulness as a joyful encounter with the unity between the voice of Being within us and the voice of Being in the world."[69] The ways of hearing that voice in conscience Havel illustrates with remarkable analyses of specific cases: the free-ride of a passenger who takes no risk; and his own failure in 1977, when he submitted a letter asking to be set free after being arrested for more than four months in too conciliatory language that the regime used to (actually more in Havel's own eyes than in anybody's else) defame him.

Here Havel gets very close to the area of religious experience, but he does not step across the boundary between philosophical investigation and mystical experience, for he keeps questioning. He does not adopt any clear standpoint with regard to the question about who speaks in the voice of conscience or the voice of Being, he just considers various characterizations that can but need not be understood religiously.[70] Basically, conscience is a call of moral authority or of an eternal law, and the voice of Being speaks of a universal integrity, the last aspiration, the fullness of meaning. Admittedly, according to Havel, "the Being of the universe, at moments when we encounter it on this level, suddenly assumes a personal face and turns it, as it were, towards us."[71] Havel actively takes into account that such personal characteristics can result from a play of our "anthropomorphic imagination," but he leaves open other interpretations as well. He just resists an unequivocal religious classification and emphasizes that "the 'voice of Being' does not come 'from elsewhere' (i.e. from some transcendent heaven) but only and exclusively 'from here': it is 'the unuttered in the language of the world' that Heidegger writes about on his 'Country Path.'"[72] More important than the question of whose the voice is and where it comes from is what it calls us to: to responsibility for the world, for nature, for the others, and for oneself. Havel does not prevent anybody from taking the orientation toward Being as a faith, for it is a faith in life and morality and it is accompanied by wonder, humility, and respect for mystery.[73] That is why the "experience of Being" that he attempts to analyze in the letters is not a philosophical assertion that can be accepted or rejected without appropriately modifying one's fully concrete life commitments. On the contrary, it provides a life orientation and a path—admittedly not a path that one can carelessly walk, but rather "one that I must redefine at every step, wherein each misstep or wrong turn, though caused only by one's neglecting one's bearings in the terrain, remains an ineradicable part of it, one that requires vast and complex effort to set right."[74] What is at stake on this path is a struggle for one's identity and integrity, and a single misstep in a momentary loss of vigilance can thwart all the effort—or it can, in a true endeavor for setting the matter right, lead to personal maturation. It is, as Havel puts it, a confrontation "between the primordial radicalism of the unbridled intentions of the 'pre-I' and the deliberation and stability of their self-aware projections into the world of our earthly 'existential praxis.'"[75]

In words that recall Heidegger's forgetfulness of Being, Havel characterized our epoch as the age of a "general turning away from Being, founded on a grand upsurge of science and technology" and carried by an "automatism," by the crisis of human identity accompanied by a loss of responsibility. That results in social systems alienating themselves, abandoning their original moral ideals in order to serve particular interests and degenerating into a mere "self-service" of power: "One consequence of this alienating process is the enormous conflict between words and deeds so prevalent today: everyone talks about freedom, democracy, humanity, justice, human rights, universal equality and happiness, about peace and saving the world from nuclear apocalypse, and protecting the environment and life in general—and at the same time, everyone—more or less, consciously or unconsciously, in one way or another—serves those values and ideals only to the extent necessary to serve himself, i.e. his 'worldly' interests—personal interests, group interests, power interests, property interests, state or great-power interests."[76] The abyss between words and deeds will not be bridged and mutual trust among people, nations, and states will not be revitalized "until something radical—I would even say revolutionary—changes in the very structure and 'soul' of today's humanity."[77] The reorientation toward Being is not to be preached but carried, and hence one should begin with oneself. And who begins, finds that he or she is neither the only one nor the first nor the most important one. Here it appears difficult to separate Havel's thinking from his personal engagement in the struggle for respecting the international human rights agreements in communist Czechoslovakia.

After Havel's return from prison, his philosophical interests were expressed not only by his joining the company of Kampademie and organizing its annual symposia at his country house in Hrádeček, but especially by his developing certain philosophical themes, first elaborated in prison, in his essays and plays.[78] Gradually, his interest turned toward political philosophy, forming and confirming his conviction that human rights were universally valid, his democratism, his conception of politics based on morality and his emphasis on responsibility, especially with regard to the natural conditions of our life. The Velvet Revolution, whose *spiritus movens* Václav Havel was, was marked by the slogan (later much derided) "truth and love must prevail over lies and hatred." At that moment, the practical consequence of the slogan was that the Communist regime must not be defeated by violence. Most of Havel's

philosophical friends were active and close to him in the Coordination
Center of the Civic Forum, the hegemon of the post-November situation in the Czech Republic (then still a part of united Czechoslovakia),[79]
and some of them remained in politics after the first free elections in
summer 1990 and contributed to shaping the renewed democracy of
Czechoslovakia and later of the Czech Republic.[80]

It is quite a paradox with regard to the reception of Heidegger's
philosophy in Czechoslovakia that, despite his clearly not being a supporter of liberal democracy, his thought significantly contributed both
to the attempt at democratizing the Communist regime in 1968 and to
the renewal of democracy in 1989. Georg Wilhelm Friedrich Hegel
showed in his *Aesthetics* that the impact of a work of art transcends
the intentions of its author. It seems that the same is true of a work of
philosophy.[81]

Translated by Josef Moural

## NOTES

1. Only portions of the large project were published in the seventeenth century. The full edition of the extant texts is Johann Amos Comenius, *De rerum
humanarum emendatione consultatio catholica*, ed. Jaromír Červenka et al.
(Prague: Academia, 1966).

2. Patočka's short *samizdat* essay "Co můžeme očekávat od Charty 77?"
was translated into English as Jan Patočka, "What Can We Expect of Charter
77?" in *Charter 77 and Human Rights in Czechoslovakia*, ed. H. Gordon Skill-
ing (London: Allen and Unwin, 1981), and again as Jan Patočka, "What We
Can and Cannot Expect from Charter 77," in *Jan Patočka: Philosophy and
Selected Writings*, ed. Erazim Kohák (Chicago: University of Chicago Press,
1989), 343–47.

3. Ladislav Rieger, *Idea filosofie I: Cesta k primátu idee* (Prague: Filoso-
fická fakulta University Karlovy, 1939), 297–305.

4. Ibid., 303.

5. Ibid., 305.

6. Martin Heidegger, "Co je metafyzika," trans. Bedřich Baumann and
Jindřich Chalupecký, *Listy* 1 (1947): 377–86.

7. Ladislav Rieger, "O významu filosofie existenciální," *Listy* 1 (1947):
327–36.

8. A similar interest was pursued also by Yugoslav philosophers gathered
around the journal *Praxis*.

9. See Michal Kopeček, *Hledání ztraceného smyslu revoluce: zrod a počátek marxistického revizionismu ve střední Evropě 1953–1960* (Prague: Argo, 2009), 302. The case of "revisionism" among philosophers was dealt with by the leadership of the Czechoslovak CP in *Zpráva o současné situaci ve filosofii*, published by the Central Committee of the Czechoslovak CP in March 1959. The measures adopted were to fire a few individuals and to reprimand and temporarily transfer to factories others—but the punishment obviously did not discourage the reformers.

10. Jan Patočka proposed to Zumr and Kosík to read together Heidegger's texts. First they read (in German) *On the Essence of Truth*, then other writings. The reading group met from 1958 to 1960 in Patočka's room at his home in Hošťálkova Street. This note is based on an interview with Josef Zumr, February 8, 2016.

11. Karel Kosík, *Dialectics of the Concrete: A Study on Problems of Man and World*, trans. Karel Kovanda and James Schmidt (Dordrecht: D. Riedel Publishing Company, 1976), 152–53 (originally Karel Kosík, *Dialektika konkrétního: studie o problematice člověka a světa*, [Prague: Nakladatelství Československé Akademie věd, 1963], 173).

12. Ibid., 87 note 9/58. (Page numbers after the slash, in this and the following notes, refer to the Czech original.)

13. Ibid., 30/41.

14. Everydayness has been a hot topic in Czechoslovakia since 1956, especially in poetry (but also in film, theatre, etc.). In 1956, a group of young poets and writers gathered around the journal *Květen* (founded 1955, canceled 1959) and proclaimed their focus on the "everyday" (implicitly opposing the pathos of poetry glorifying the Communist regime). In 1966, a large part of the original team founded another journal, *Orientace* (canceled in 1969), where some Heidegger translations were published.

15. Kosík, *Dialectics*, 38 (*Dialektika*, 48).

16. Ibid. 39/49. Kosík's talk of "manipulation," while referring to capitalism here, could be understood also as a criticism of the hypertrophied and fossilized apparatus of Stalinist communism.

17. Ibid., 86 note 4/52.

18. Ibid., 48/60.

19. Ibid., 49/61.

20. Ibid., 85/103.

21. Ibid., 81/98.

22. Ibid., 101/115.

23. Ibid., 114/131.

24. Ibid., 119/137.

25. Ibid., 123/142.

26. Ibid.

27. Ibid., 137/154.

28. Ibid. 147/167.

29. Ibid., 152–53/173.

30. Jan Fojtík, "Filosofie aktivity—aktivita filosofie," *Kulturní tvorba* 3, no. 28 (1965): 4–5.

31. Josef Zumr, "Marxismus jako filosofie člověka," *Literární noviny* 12, no. 30 (1963): 5.

32. Ibid.

33. Karel Kosík, "Naše nynější krize," *Literární listy* 1, no. 12 (1968): 3.

34. Ivan Sviták, "Vaše nynější krize," *Student* 4 (1968): 30.

35. Famously, over one thousand pages of Kosík's drafts and notes for his two projected books were seized by the police on April 28, 1975, and never returned (in spite of protests from Jean-Paul Sartre, Jürgen Habermas, Ernst Bloch, Norberto Bobbio, and many others)—with the result that Kosík abandoned the projects (and any more ambitious philosophical work) for good.

36. This paragraph is based on an interview with Ivan Dubský conducted on October 31, 2016.

37. See especially Ivan Dubský, "Über Hegels und Heideggers Begriff der Zeit," *Hegel Jahrbuch* 1 (1961): 73–84; Ivan Dubský, "Heidegger o technice a bytí," *Dějiny a současnost* 7, no. 2 (1965): 10–12; and Ivan Dubský, "Domov a bezdomoví," *Filosofický časopis* 14 (1966): 181–97.

38. "Karel Michňák," https://www.phil.muni.cz/fil/scf/komplet/michnk.html (retrieved on December 11, 2016).

39. See Karel Michňák, "Heidegger a osudy 'boha metafyziky,'" *Filosofický časopis* 15 (1967): 686–702; Karel Michňák, "Ke kritice humanismu a antropologismu," *Acta Universitatis Carolinae: Philosophica et historica*, no. 1 (1968): 57–82.

40. Martin Heidegger, "Zrozeni uměleckeho dila," trans. Irena Michňáková. (Orientace 3, no. 5 [1968]: 53–62; no. 6 [1968], 75–83; 4, no. 1 [1969], 84–94).

41. Michňáková edited a *samizdat* Festschrift for Kosík in 1975, which included her translation of Heidegger's "Was ist das—die Philosophie?"

42. Besides already mentioned papers see Ladislav Major, "Heidegger a Hegel," *Filosofický časopis* 12 (1964): 539–46; Jan Bodnár, "Heideggerova nová iniciatíva vo filozofii," in *Existencializmus a fenomenológia*, ed. Jan Patočka et al. (Bratislava: Obzor, 1967), 213–41; Arthur Geuss, "M. Heidegger a umělecké dílo," *Filosofický časopis* 15 (1967): 676–85.

43. Further published translations (besides those mentioned in notes 3 and 6) were Martin Heidegger, "Hölderlin a podstata básnictví," trans. Věra Linhartová and Jan Patočka, *Tvář* 2, no. 1 (1965): 18–23; Heidegger, "Co je člověk," trans. Jiří Němec, *Tvář* 2, no. 6 (1965): 28–29; Heidegger, "Výbor z díla Sein und Zeit," trans. Stanislav Vítek, in *Antologie*

*existencialismu I* (Prague: Vysoká škola politická ÚV KSČ, 1967), 25–135; Heidegger; "Polni cesta," trans. Arthur Geuss, *Orientace* 3, no. 4 (1968): 87–88. Heidegger, "Věk obrazu světa," trans. Jaromír Loužil, *Orientace* 4, no. 5 (1969): 59–64; no. 6, 49–51; Heidegger, *O bytostném určení pravdy,* trans. Jiří Němec et al. (Prague: Vyšehrad, 1970). Of course, all these texts were made inaccessible (in libraries and elsewhere) in 1970.

44. According to Václav Havel's brother Ivan, in an interview on November 3, 2016.

45. The *gray zone* was an area between the public pro-regime activities, on the one hand, and private dissent/the underground, on the other; in the gray zone, a legally existing institution would temporarily shelter activities incompatible with official ideology. For example, the medical association organized a discussion group on the psychiatry of Medard Boss where the participants would also study Heidegger's philosophy. The Czechoslovak Society for Science and Technology organized lectures on cybernetics where some of the lectures would deal with modern phenomenology; similarly, the great Czech mathematician Petr Vopěnka would invite dissent philosophers as lecturers to a series of public talks on the philosophy of mathematics.

46. Jan Patočka, *Plato and Europe,* trans. Petr Lom (Stanford, CA: Stanford University Press, 2002); originally circulated in *samizdat,* 1979.

47. Martin Heidegger, *Being and Time,* trans. Joan Stambaugh (New York: SUNY, 1996); originally circulated in *samizdat* installments, up to thirty-five pages long, starting in 1983 and containing seventeen installments by November 1989.

48. Beginning in the 1970s, he focused rather on his second, philosophical vocation, as he was prevented from continuing to cooperate with Western microbiology, as he had in the 1960s.

49. Further (and only temporary or occasional) participants of Kampademie included the theatrologist Helena Weberová, the priest Zdeněk Kratochvíl, and the mathematician Václav Benda.

50. Recently, the letters to prison by Ivan Havel and the coauthors were published in Czech as Ivan M. Havel, *Dopisy od Olgy* (Prague: Knihovna Václava Havla, 2010). The Heidegger texts are in letters 57 and 87–89; Heidegger is also discussed explicitly in letter 61 (and indirectly in further letters written by R. Palouš and Z. Neubauer).

51. Martin C. Putna, *Václav Havel* (Prague: Knihovna Václava Havla, 2011), 11–12.

52. Václav Havel, *Letters to Olga: June 1979–September 1982,* trans. Paul Wilson (New York: Henry Holt and Company, 1989), 358 (letter no. 140).

53. Ibid., 293 (letter no. 118).

54. Ibid., 294 (letter no. 118).

55. Ibid., 294–295 (letter no. 118).

56. Ibid., 295 (letter no. 118).

57. Ibid.

58. Ibid., 296 (letter no. 118).

59. Ibid., 319 (letter no. 129; the last sentence is missing in the book translation).

60. Ibid.

61. Heidegger, *Being and Time*, 127.

62. Havel, *Letters to Olga*, 320–21 (letter no. 129).

63. Ibid., 324 (letter no. 130).

64. Ibid., 332–33 (letter no. 133).

65. Ibid., 333 (letter no. 133).

66. Ibid., 338 (letter no. 135).

67. Ibid., 338–39 (letter no. 135).

68. Ibid., 365 (letter no. 142).

69. Ibid., 341 (letter no. 136).

70. Havel's attitude toward religion remains a topic of discussion; see Putna, *Václav Havel*, 285.

71. Havel, *Letters to Olga*, 346 (letter no. 137).

72. Ibid., 354 (letter no. 139). The book translation here mistakenly renders Havel's reference as *Holzwege*, while Havel's real reference is the lecture "Der Feldweg" (Czech "Polní cesta")—sent to him in prison, as we know, by his brother Ivan in one of his letters (see note 50 above and the related text).

73. Ibid., 360–61 (letter no. 141).

74. Ibid., 355 (letter no. 139).

75. Ibid., 362 (letter no. 141).

76. Ibid., 367 (letter no. 142).

77. Ibid., 369 (letter no. 142).

78. See especially the plays *Temptation* (Václav Havel, *Selected Plays: 1984–87* [London: Faber and Faber, 1994], 61–135) and *Redevelopment* (Havel, *Selected* Plays, 137–207) and the essays "Stories and Totalitarianism" (Václav Havel, *Open Letters: Selected Writings 1965–1990,* ed. Paul Wilson [New York: Vintage Books, 1991], 328–50) and "A Word about Words" (Havel, *Open Letters*, 377–89).

79. Radim Palouš chaired the daily plenary meetings of the top Civic Forum committee. Ivan M. Havel served in the broader collective leadership of the Civic Forum up to the summer of 1990. Martin Palouš was nominated as the leader of the Civic Forum (before that, he was a part of a four-person collective leadership body) and his loss to Václav Klaus at the Hostivař Congress on October 13, 1990, was one of the decisive turns in post-1989 Czech history. Daniel Kroupa participated in the committee that drafted the Civic Forum program, and Pavel Bratinka worked in the foreign relations office.

80. Martin Palouš became a deputy minister of foreign affairs and an ambassador to the United States and the United Nations Organization. Pavel Bratinka founded a political party, served as a parliamentary representative and as

a government minister, and finally turned to entrepreneurship. Daniel Kroupa served as a representative in all legislative bodies of the state he successively belonged to: in the National Assembly of the former Czechoslovakia, in the lower and in the upper chamber of the Czech parliament and the European parliament, and for a while as a party leader.

81. I would like to thank my student Rudolf Kardoš and my colleague (and former student) Josef Moural for help in assembling materials used in this chapter.

## Chapter 11

# The Post-Soviet Heidegger

## Jeff Love

Given his political orientation and obvious rejection of Marx, it cannot surprise anyone that Martin Heidegger's thought did not find a particularly welcoming audience in the Soviet Union. As with many other Western authors, Heidegger's writings were not readily available in any language, and the risks of holding copies of his works or propagating his thought were such that it made little sense to engage with Heidegger in public or even in the private sphere. While phenomenology did make some furtive headway in the Soviet Union both immediately after the revolution and after Stalin's death in 1953, Heidegger's work did not find a reception in the Soviet Union in any way comparable to his reception in much of the rest of the world. Indeed, Heidegger's writings did not become available in Russian until the late 1980s, with the translation of *Being and Time* published first in 1997. One is thus faced with a remarkably different history of Heidegger reception in Russia. This history is in part so distinctive because Heidegger became accessible to Russian readers roughly at the same time as other philosophers, notably Derrida and Foucault, who were deeply influenced by his work yet oriented to the political left as fundamentally progressive thinkers.[1] It is also distinctive in part, however, by virtue of the alacrity with which Heidegger's thinking was taken up as a possible bastion of Russian religious and cultural renewal. These two differing directions have a lot to do with Heidegger's entry into the Russian philosophical scene—on the one hand as father of radically questioning currents in modern philosophy as to the nature and purpose of philosophy itself and, on the other, as providing the basis for new initiatives in a theological tradition very distinct from that of the West. Yet, they both evince a surprising underlying unity of purpose: developing a distinctively Russian identity—a distinctively Russian way forward—amid the ruins of the Soviet Union.

In this sense, the reception of Heidegger's thought in Russia has coalesced around a venerable political and intellectual divide in Russian thought between those who have sought to turn Russia into a modern state based more or less explicitly on a properly Russified liberal-democratic model, and those who have aligned themselves with a long nationalist and postcolonial tradition that seeks to liberate Russia from the West along with the pieties of Western politics. While it would be overstating the case to identify this distinction as merely an extension of that most famous nineteenth-century distinction between Westernizers and Slavophiles, it would be equally remiss of me not to view Heidegger's reception as a sort of "lightning rod" illuminating broad lines of argument concerning Russian identity that may be traced back into the nineteenth century and, indeed even further, to antagonisms arising from the traumatic opening of Russia to the West under Peter the Great.

From this perspective, Heidegger's entry into the post-Soviet philosophical scene is doubly fascinating: It accompanies the revival of arguments that had never really lain dormant while acting at the same time as a powerful inducement to renew those arguments and adapt them to the difficult circumstances attending the collapse of the Soviet Union. In the following, I want to address Heidegger's influence in the post-Soviet context first by giving a brief account of the antagonism between Westernizers and Slavophiles merely to orient my subsequent discussion of two significant and influential figures in the post-Soviet philosophical landscape, Vladimir Veniaminovich Bibikhin (1938–2004) and Alexander Gal'evich Dugin (1962–). The former is a major Russian philosopher, translator of *Being and Time* into Russian and creator of a distinctive approach to philosophy that has not yet received the attention it deserves in the West. The latter is a controversial political theorist and ardent Russian nationalist who seeks to root his increasingly bellicose political stance in Heidegger's thought, especially the texts of the 1930s. Both of these figures draw on the rich Russian intellectual and literary heritage to create a Heidegger that belongs to that tradition and serves as a spur to recovery of its distinctive merits, which are so often unfairly maligned or neglected in the West.

***

The struggle between Westernizers and Slavophiles holds a venerable position in the intellectual history of the nineteenth century in Russia. The basic principle of distinction between the two tendencies is fairly obvious.[2] The Westernizers sought to bring Russia out of its ostensible backwardness by continuing to adapt European ideas and institutions to Russian realities, whereas the Slavophiles insisted on finding a distinctively Russian course, one that neither devalued nor dismissed the complex history of Russia. At issue of course was the status of the fundamental revolutionary event in modern Russian history prior to the Soviet revolution of 1917 itself: the opening of Russia to the West imposed on the country with immense speed and severity by Peter the Great. This event is remarkable insofar as it is an example of a very rare phenomenon indeed: an act of colonization of one culture by another conducted not from without but from within.[3] Peter the Great's reforms would in effect create two different countries, a separation reflected most dramatically by differences in class and language. For the upper classes chose in the wake of the Petrine reforms to speak and write in French, a circumstance comically depicted in Lev Tolstoy's *War and Peace* in which some aristocrats are unable to describe even the simplest activities in comprehensible Russian. The upper classes constructed in this way the most intimate and estranging of walls in a relation to the other classes that bears more than passing resemblance to that between colonizers and their colonized.

Both the Westernizers and the Slavophiles sought a way out of the self-imposed colonization of the Russian mind. The similarities between the various parties likely surpassed the differences. Indeed, one may argue that the primary intention of both groups was to eradicate the chasm or distance created by the Petrine reforms—they both sought to bring about a process of healing and reunification that eliminated the various aspects of the wall constructed between the classes. If the means of bringing about healing and reunification were different, that difference had more to do with an estimation of tactics on the way to healing and reunification rather than with the final goal itself. Yet, the estimation of tactics reveals two radically different notions of reintegration,

one devoted to an essentially egalitarian political revolution on the
Western model, the other to a rejection of the West in favor of an egalitarian organic community rooted in distinctively Russian traditions of
community (*sobornost'*) and "integral knowing" (*tsel'noe znanie*).[4]

The revolution of 1917 settled the issue by deciding dramatically in
favor of a Western model that featured as a centerpiece the putative
elimination of class distinctions. Russia thus took the position of the
political vanguard in the West while attempting to achieve a distinctively Russian goal. Nonetheless, the revolution of 1917, the liquidation
of the peasantry, and the industrialization that took place in its wake
transformed the country and, by suppressing the Orthodox Church,
made a decisive turn away from the central cultural orientation of the
Slavophiles. At the same time, Russia's special status was affirmed
frequently as well, the peculiar contradiction between communist universality and Russian self-assertion taking shape more clearly with the
isolation of the Soviet Union and, subsequently, within the prolonged
conflict of the Cold War. The abject collapse of the Soviet Union and
its formal dissolution in 1991 brought to a disastrous close the second
profound movement in the Westernization of Russia. But this disaster
did not lead to a definitive defeat of the Westernizing forces; rather, the
fraught Russian attempts to create a parliamentary democracy in the
1990s contributed to exacerbate a crisis of national identity that has not
yet been mastered.[5] Indeed, Russia once again finds itself in the difficult
position of attempting to define itself according to its own venerable
cultural tradition while participating in a world dominated by the victor in the Cold War and perhaps the final modern representative of the
Western tradition: the United States.

The complicated reception of Heidegger in Russia took place in this
atmosphere of collapse and continues unabated today as Russia seeks to
become a bulwark against what is frequently perceived as the arbitrary
exercise of power in the world by the United States. It is perhaps unsurprising then that Heidegger would become important in these circumstances since Heidegger faced a strikingly similar set of questions in the
1930s, the decade of his most sustained and radical political activity. It
is also unsurprising that the major figures responsible for introducing
Heidegger into Russia were preoccupied with issues of identity. They
saw in Heidegger a crucial turning point in Western thought in which
its inherent imperialism was finally unmasked and could be adapted to
the circumstances of post-Soviet Russia by encouraging the creation of

a new Russian identity freed of the disasters of the West, political, environmental, and social. This new sense of identity could show the way in Russia as well as in other countries seeking to construct a new world order not in thrall to the hegemonic ambitions of the United States.

\*\*\*

The most aggressive and notorious disciple of Heidegger in Russia today has to be Alexander Dugin. If it were absolutely necessary to apply a traditional label to Dugin, I would be inclined to include him in the Slavophile tradition, if for no other reason than his adamant rejection of the West, and especially of the United States, as well as his cultivation of the Orthodox Church. Dugin first appeared on the Russian political scene in the early 1990s as a conservative figure aligned with the more extreme nationalist currents in the turbulent Russian political life of that time period, which included the dissolution of the Soviet Union, the disastrous coup of August 1991, and the construction of a new government under Boris Yeltsin.[6] Thanks to his versatility and constant stream of publications, Dugin became increasingly inevitable in the bourgeoning Russian right, assuming the role of one of the Russian right's most fecund and comprehensive theorists next to Lev Gumilev and Alexander Panarin. Dugin is a major figure in Russian Eurasianism, an important "ideology of empire" that conceives of Russia as an arbiter between the West and East that also may show the way to a new synthesis of West and East or to new possibilities of cultural integration and interaction that move beyond the clichés of West and East. While it is fair to refer to Eurasianism as an "ideology of empire," it is not only that but, in the hands of Dugin, the expression of a new identity for Russia and, perhaps, a new kind of cultural identity *tout court*. Dugin has gained increasing notoriety over the last several years. He founded an Institute for Conservative Studies at Moscow State University but was forced to resign from that position, after the invasion of the Crimea in 2014, due to his violent statements against Ukrainians. More recently he has gained attention in the United States because of his outspoken opposition to the United States as well as his association with Americans having connections to the extreme or alternative right, including several people who support movements advocating white power, like Richard Spencer.

Dugin is perhaps best known for his 1997 book, *The Fourth Political Theory*, which provides a comprehensive account of the dominating ideologies of the twentieth century and their decay into a senescent and supposedly triumphant liberalism.[7] Dugin opposes his fourth political theory to the liberal consensus as a politics of resistance to the "real domination of capital," globalization, and universal human rights, all of which Dugin refers to as the conditions of "post-modernity." Dugin seems to draw on several different kinds of resistance to the liberal (or, better, neoliberal) order with the intent of preserving traditions and alternative ways of thinking that the modern consensus tends to seek to overcome. Indeed, one of Dugin's more striking characteristics is that he takes over the resistance to many features of the modern consensus expressed by the left and adapts them to serve what appears to be a traditionalist and conservative attitude; in this respect, the fourth political theory seems to combine the most notable features of resistance to modern liberalism from the left and right while accentuating the emphasis on national identity in a multipolar world.

The concept of multipolarity is an interesting case in point. Dugin advocates multipolarity as a doctrine that promises freedom from the hegemonic rule of liberalism (he even mentions Francis Fukuyama's thesis about the end of history with the triumph of the liberal order) by encouraging different cultural unities to resist hegemonic liberalism. Such a doctrine seems quite appealing insofar as it encourages otherwise endangered identities to express themselves—one can even align the notion of multipolarity with postcolonialism to the degree that both seek freedom from overweening imperial power. Yet, the irony of this position should not be lost on us. For multipolarity also encourages nationalism and a kind of relativism according to which no culture can be wrong in and of itself but only in relation to another culture whose precepts it does not need to accept because there can be no binding grounds for such acceptance. Hence, what appears initially as an attractive emancipatory doctrine that justifies self-determination also eradicates at the same time any limits to self-determination (while, of course, not justifying the imposition of one culture upon another). In the final account, no doctrine, not even the doctrine of the multipolar world can insist on being accepted. Dugin's speech contradicts itself insofar as there is no reason for anyone to accept the multipolar world—the arguments attempt to "incline but not necessitate."

Although evidence for Dugin's interest in Heidegger is not easy to find in his earlier writings, it has come increasingly to the fore in the twenty-first century with the publication of two separate monographs and then, finally, an immense nine-hundred-page work that includes the two monographs with two new ones. The title of the collection gives one a good idea of its contents: *Martin Heidegger: The Last God*.[8] This title refers of course to the notion of the "last god" (*der letzte Gott*) that Heidegger introduces early on in his important manuscript, *The Contributions to Philosophy*, completed in 1938 and not published until 1989. While the tremendous increase in focus on Heidegger is itself worth investigating, Dugin's interpretation of Heidegger provides ample evidence of why he finds Heidegger so attractive. Dugin focuses on two central narratives that are intimately linked: (1) the narrative of the end of Western metaphysics as nihilism; and (2) the transition to the other beginning. These narratives fit together nicely if we accept that the one is the necessary condition of the other—in other words, that the end of metaphysics is the condition of possibility of there being another beginning.

Dugin's strategy, cunning and provocative, is to draw on Heidegger as the last great representative of the Western philosophical tradition in order to overcome that tradition, indeed, to show that it must be overcome and has been overcome, at least in principle, from within, by Heidegger himself, the "last god." For Dugin, Heidegger is the prophet of the end of the West, the thinker who most persuasively shows the way out of the hegemony of Western culture and who is most important for those forces in the rest of the world seeking to escape the domination of the West. If Heidegger is the prophet, Dugin now takes the position of loyal disciple, and he develops what I might call a postcolonial Heidegger of the right, a most unusual postcolonialism to be sure since postcolonial thought is pervasively associated with a progressive, left-leaning politics. To adapt essentially postcolonial arguments to a conservative and traditionalist politics is yet another provocation and example of how Dugin skillfully adapts arguments associated with a left politics of emancipation to a very different notion of emancipation.

This very different notion of emancipation includes, as I have noted, two principal Heideggerian narratives. I should like to linger on how Dugin views both these narratives within the Russian context as one integral narrative in which the moment of the final destruction

of the foundations of Western thought is at once the transition to the
other beginning vouchsafed to Russia as an invitation to liberate itself
completely from the Western tradition that has dominated it since the
Petrine reforms.

Dugin explains the revolutionary importance of Heidegger's thought
within relatively simple terms. On the one hand, Heidegger's comprehensive reading of the Western philosophical tradition is for Dugin the
only way for Russia to confront the influence of the most powerful form
of Western philosophical thought to have shaped Russia, that of G. W.
F. Hegel and, of course, the apostate Hegelian, Karl Marx. On the other
hand, Heidegger's reading of that tradition as ending in nihilism offers
the best possibility not only for confronting but also for overcoming the
impact of Hegel and Marx in Russia. Dugin reflects Heidegger's own
position insofar as he seeks to free Russia from the shackles of Bolshevism and Marxism in order to revive a national vitality and cultural
health that had been almost eradicated by Bolshevism.

Dugin's own reading of Heidegger is oriented to justifying this
account. He discerns three different ontological levels in Heidegger's
thinking, the first two of which emerge most straightforwardly in *Being
and Time* (1927) while the third remains for the extensive investigations into Being that occupy most of Heidegger's work in the 1930s.
Dugin assures us that each of these levels features a different kind of
relation (*Bezug*) to Being itself.[9] The first relation is the most obvious.
It is our everyday relation to things and it remains on what Dugin refers
to as the ontic level. When we refer to cups and rocks and stars in our
everyday discourse, we are merely pointing to each as a kind of being
without ever thinking about what that kind of being is or about what
our relation to that being is outside of contexts of utility that we may
not even recognize. The moment we begin to consider these other questions, of kind and relation, we move to a different level of investigation
in which we examine the ways in which that being is made available
or disclosed to us—how what we take for "given" is in fact given.
The second ontological level thus does not merely consider things in
their quotidian or more or less average roles; rather, it considers how
those things came about as such—their conditions of possibility. The
investigation that begins on what Dugin refers to as the second level
is concerned with what allows for things to be as they are, and it ends
up with a definition of the Being of beings that reveals what all beings
must have to be as they are.

If these first two levels are concerned with establishing the defining normative principles of objects and persons, then the third is concerned with a wholly different ontological task—the origin of ontology itself or fundamental ontology. Dugin's claim here is that the first two levels examine the principal aspects of ontology understood as a product of a third level that they necessarily conceal from us. Is this origin beyond ontology or viciously compromised such that it cannot be said to be an ontology simply because it is at the origin of ontologies? Or has Dugin something else in mind? He begins at first with a fairly orthodox reading of this, the "third" level. It is the level of what Heidegger calls in the 1930s *Seyn*, and it is an attempt to describe being as something other than an object or thing or specific identity. As Heidegger himself writes in one of the *Black Notebooks*, the challenge of thinking being is to think something that is not a thing, not a being, not an "it" (*die* Gegenstandslosigkeit *der Philosophie*).[10] Hence to think being as an origin is also problematic to the extent the origin has an identity as origin. To think on the third level is to think free of any restrictions or conditions on thinking—it is a thinking that refuses to coalesce into dogmas or principles, even in regard to its own conditions, such as language and logic.

Dugin holds that the Western tradition from the very beginning works to avoid the third level or suggests that there is no such level. The dogmatic advance of a certain notion of what being is—and thus beings as well—comes to its end when it finally becomes accepted by all or universal. This full and final acceptance of one basic normative order brings philosophy and history to an end in one fell swoop, in a possibly utopian order that brooks no opposition or alternatives. Dugin's interpretation of Heidegger effectively equates the egalitarian and universalist tendencies of Western thought with nihilism, the impulse to create an endless and final empire in which all questions have been resolved and the only free act has to be the result of error or madness (the will to persist in error). In this sense, Dugin's interpretation falls in line with critiques of radical enlightenment and Hegel stretching back to the nineteenth century and forward to the remarkable group of French thinkers who became prominent in the later 1960s, and who, under the influence of Nietzsche and Heidegger, opposed a certain notion of Hegel's thought as tyrannous, suffocating. As I noted above in regard to postcolonialism, Dugin again takes an attitude largely associated with thinkers on the left and turns it toward his much more conservative way of thinking.

What does Dugin seek in the end? If Dugin considers Heidegger a liberating thinker who offers the best arguments for a Russian generation seeking to free itself from the baleful influence of the West, what does Dugin seek to advocate in place of Western influence? What exactly does Heidegger's destruction of the West allow Dugin to achieve in Russia?

Dugin seeks to transform one of Heidegger's basic innovations, the notion of *Dasein*, to the Russian context. He does so by developing his notion of a distinctively Russian Dasein within another important "mytheme" created by Heidegger—that of *das Geviert* or the fourfold. While the notion of the fourfold is often associated with Heidegger's postwar thinking, Dugin places it squarely with Heidegger's thought of the 1930s. He refers to both the Hölderlin lectures from the winter of 1934–1935 and the *Contributions* to indicate that the fourfold was already very much on Heidegger's mind in the 1930s. Dugin grants the fourfold a crucial role as the basic structure Heidegger identifies with the other beginning. For Dugin the other beginning begins with the fourfold.

Dugin proceeds to read the fourfold as granting to Russia an extraordinary role in the other beginning. He has only to cite Heidegger himself in this respect. Volume 69 of the GA is his principal text, and Dugin draws on two important statements by Heidegger. The first: "The History of the future of the earth is contained in the essence of Russianness (*Russentum*), which has not yet been freed to itself. The history of the world is the task set to the Germans for consideration (*Besinnung*)."[11] The second: "Russia—that we do not conquer and exterminate it technically-culturally but rather free it to its essence and open it to the breadth of its suffering as to the essentiality of an essential salvation of the earth."[12] Dugin proceeds to create a narrative of the Russian other beginning whereby Russia becomes the site of the creation of a new attitude to being, the fecund earth that allows for salvation from the metaphysical illusions of the West. Russian Dasein (ironically Russianized by Dugin as *Dasain* (*дазайн*))[13] becomes the bearer of a distinctively Russian way of being that not only shall liberate Russia itself but also can be a beacon of salvation to the rest of the world. If one hears in this claim something of Dostoevsky's famous claim that the world shall be freed by a star from the East, that is no coincidence. For Dugin renews, albeit in his complicated manner, the notion that Russia not only has the task of freeing itself from the shackles of the decadent West but also provides an example to the rest of the world in doing so as well. It is indeed difficult not to hear echoes of Dostoevsky in Dugin's salvation narrative. The same sense that the West has run its course that one finds in Dostoevsky's *The Brothers Karamazov* is repeated and renewed in Dugin along with the attempt to find new narratives no longer beholden to the verities of the West.[14]

\*\*\*

Vladimir Bibikhin is of another cast of mind entirely, and this difference is shown perhaps most dramatically by Bibikhin's interest in Tolstoy as against or instead of Dostoevsky. While Dugin draws on Dostoevsky's narrative of virtually messianic national exaltation, Bibikhin seeks a new kind of identity for Russia in Dostoevsky's great rival and counterweight whose expression of Russian identity could be equally strident though not as clearly—and certainly not as violently— nationalistic. One of Bibikhin's last courses was devoted to Tolstoy's diaries, and it is a remarkable document, not only in regard to its exposition of Bibikhin's thought, but as to the way Bibikhin winds Heideggerian insights into the complicated structure of Tolstoy's diaries. Before I discuss that course, however, I want to give a brief overview of Bibikhin's philosophical career.

Bibikhin taught philosophy for many years at Moscow State University and possessed a considerable following among students who eagerly awaited his unusual lecture courses. But before that Bibikhin already had a considerable reputation as a translator of difficult philosophical, religious, and literary texts from many modern languages including French, German, and Italian as well as ancient languages— Greek, Latin, and Sanskrit. As I have already noted, Bibikhin first translated Heidegger's *Being and Time* into Russian. Not surprisingly one of Bibikhin's primary concerns was language, and his thinking is itself a sustained attempt to develop a distinctive Russian philosophic idiom emancipated from its Western models. This concern to create a distinctive Russian philosophic idiom stretches to Bibikhin's focus on basic themes, such as matter, energy, and property, that have been treated extensively in Western thought but receive rather different treatment in Bibikhin's hands.

Bibikhin's philosophical corpus is of considerable size, and it is a
shame that nothing except for an important excerpt from *Les (hyle)*—
*The Wood(s)*—has yet been published in English.[15] These lectures are
unusual both in their approach and penchant for linguistic experimentation. By unusual I refer to the lectures' frequently nonlinear style and
lack of singular approach to their subject matter. Bibikhin is not about
explication or the orderly development of a given subject matter, as if
that subject matter were already clear, decided, and in need only of a
capable elucidation. Rather the lectures engage in an active process of
working through the material at hand—they are much closer to what
one may describe as an active instantiation or happening of thought as it
reacts to and with its subject matter. Bibikhin's approach—if it may be
called that—is thoroughly Heideggerian in this respect. One has only to
recall a striking paragraph from Heidegger's *Contributions*, a text that
also defies linear approaches or contests approaches as such, the apparent addiction to method that seems to afflict "proper" investigations of
important questions and blinds us to important aspects of them:

> In philosophical knowledge, on the contrary, the first step initiates a
> transformation of the person who understands, and this not in the moral-
> "existential" sense, but rather in relation to her Da-sein. That is: the rela-
> tion to being, and always prior to that, the relation to the truth of being,
> are transformed in the mode of a displacement (*Verrückung*) into Da-sein
> itself. Since in philosophical knowledge everything is in each case dis-
> placed at once—the being of humans into standing in the truth, the truth
> itself, and thereby the relation to beyng—an immediate representation
> of something objectively present is never possible, and on that account
> philosophical thinking will always seem strange.[16]

Here is the description, one might say, of an approach that defies
approaches insofar as the people who understand change in relation to
what they understand—the relation is thus one of mutual transformation, and there seems to be no given pattern for this mutual transformation. To the contrary, the transformation is one that must not be
beholden to already existing patterns or models since those models map
out the steps of the transformation into a narrative that may be repeated.
Repetition of this kind, however—if not all repetition—simply avoids
the possibility of the active transformation that Heidegger seems to
have in mind.

Bibikhin's detailed account of the transformational relation should help clarify the point. This account acts as the backbone of his often elusive lectures on Tolstoy. I say "elusive" because the central principle of organization of the lectures is by no means obvious—nor should it be if we take seriously Bibikhin's concern to create lectures that are to a high degree untrammeled or "free" explorations of various lines of thought. Bibikhin's chosen texts are Tolstoy's diaries and, particularly, his later diaries. Bibikhin openly states in the first lecture that Tolstoy's philosophical richness has been largely ignored in favor of Dostoevsky as the truly thinking Russian writer. Bibikhin thus seeks to bring out several aspects of that richness that appear in the diaries—these may be collected together as describing Tolstoy's consistent challenge to models of thinking or narrative itself. While this characteristic of Tolstoy's has been discussed in connection with the novels, Bibikhin's choice of the diaries is innovative, to say the least. Bibikhin grounds his choice of the diaries precisely on their openness to experimentation, on their variance from any generic expectations, which reaches more deeply to a central expression of variance that evinces no principle of variance.

Variance that expresses no principle of variance is perhaps another way of expressing the openness to transformation and to following a thread of discussion rather freely with a minimum of preconception, if indeed that is possible. For the unavoidable question here, with regard to Heidegger's *Contributions*, is whether one can really engage in a mode of thinking that has not always already been rooted or presupposed in what had initially been established. Put more bluntly, can one think and explore thoughtfully a given subject matter in ways that have not already been set out through the initial identification of that subject matter, either explicitly or implicitly? By "implicitly" I refer to the notion that initial identification or grounding prescribes all subsequent possibilities of understanding such that what appears to be new is rather only the making explicit of what had already lain implicit in the founding. From this point of view, all thinking about a given subject matter that discovers new aspects to that subject matter is only the unfolding of what was always already there. The new, understood in a more radical sense as a kind of invention, is simply impossible. Discovery is never open-ended; only creation is. And the basis for this distinction is the claim that the founding determines all, that, in essence, all learning is merely making explicit a framework "hidden" in the subject matter and not a creation or revelation of different aspects of the subject matter that come about because of an extraordinary encounter with it.

Bibikhin's response to this distinction is not immediately clear; it has to come from the whole of the lecture itself. In this respect, Bibikhin reflects Tolstoy's splendidly irreverent description of his great novel, *War and Peace*:

> What is *War and Peace*? It is not a novel, even less is it an epic poem, and still less an historical chronicle. *War and Peace* is what the author wished and was able to express in the form in which it is expressed. Such an announcement of disregard of conventional form in an artistic production might seem presumptuous were it premeditated, and were there no precedents for it. But the history of Russian literature since the time of Pushkin not merely affords many examples of such deviation from European forms, but does not offer a single example of the contrary. From Gogol's *Dead Souls* to Dostoevsky's *House of the Dead* in the recent period of Russian literature there is not a single artistic prose work, rising at all above mediocrity, which quite fits into the form of a novel, epic, or story.[17]

Tolstoy's description makes two central points: (1) that his great "novel" is not really a novel following any pre-given form; and (2) that this disregard for pre-given forms is distinctively Russian.

Bibikhin implicitly upholds these two points in his account of Tolstoy's diaries, though Bibikhin deploys a different terminology. The epigraph to the lectures provided by Bibikhin's widow, Olga Lebedeva, may give a hint of what Bibikhin is after in them: "All people are sealed up, and this is terrible [*Vse liudi zakuporeny, i eto uzhasno*]."[18] The implication is that people are decided, that they assimilate modes of thought and action seamlessly from whatever tradition is theirs and thereby seal themselves up from interacting with their surroundings in any way other than as decreed by that tradition. They are sealed up and thus ensure that the kind of dynamic interaction described by Heidegger or the distinctively Russian insouciance described by Tolstoy may be safely and permanently avoided. To use another terminology from Heidegger, people effectively become *Bestand* within the context of their given tradition—there is no freedom, no need to take or risk a decision since every decision has been taken already—these people are finished products even as they begin or they are products on the way to a final unfolding of the "system" in which they find themselves, the kind of progress from a given beginning to its final end that Heidegger otherwise identifies with nihilism.

Bibikhin's lecture offers a radical contrast as, indeed, do Tolstoy's diaries. For, if anything may be said about the diaries, it is that they bear witness to an incredibly restless life, one that never concedes to tradition, that cannot but question everything it encounters, and always from what seems to be a differing vantage point. Tolstoy's diaries are implacably differential in this respect—they refuse to accede to any dogma. As such, they are a striking reflection of the kind of differential relation Heidegger describes in the *Contributions*. Within Bibikhin's terms the diaries show a life that is not sealed up, that is constantly controverting the position of the observer and the observed.

Bibikhin puts it thus: "Love for Tolstoy, that is removing the position of the observer [*Liubov' u Tolstogo eto sniatie smotritel'stva*]."[19] Bibikhin's claim is striking since it inserts into the framework provided essentially by Heidegger a conception of love that likely appears initially to have no place in Heidegger's thought (unless we claim that care or *Sorge* is love in the Tolstoyan sense).[20] More radically, perhaps, Bibikhin insists that love for Tolstoy means a relation to people and things that is not conceptual but resides in direct interaction with one's environment or world. Yet, we should be careful here because Bibikhin is not so much proposing a pre- or nonconceptual relation to one's environment or world but rather one that does not relate to that environment or world in a traditionally conceptual way—that is, as measuring and shaping according to a "conceptual scheme" that regulates all relations with one's environment or world as if from above or from the point of view of a final picture that includes in some (necessarily) vague way all other potential pictures.

Bibikhin's account of Tolstoy seems to be after fostering a relation to one's environment or world that dissolves traditional boundaries among people and things, subjects and objects, concepts and the objects to which they refer. This dissolution of boundaries as a kind of love is a striking facet of Bibikhin's argument—love is the courage, it seems, to let one risk oneself by immersing oneself in one's environment or world. Love is letting go of the final picture as having decisive import for how one relates to any situation or circumstance in which one finds oneself. Following Tolstoy, Bibikhin's commitment is to rejecting the position above all positions in favor of the only ever relative or changing position that must be the result of abandoning what we may call an absolute position. If that absolute position is missing, the consequence has to be that no one position can be found that governs or ascertains the relation of all other positions. It is to move from one notion of letting beings be, a partially divine one, to another quite different notion of letting beings be within the confines of our multiple, seemingly unending, relations to them.

This argument also seems to contain an allusion to Heidegger's notion of "letting beings be" (*Seinlassen*). The argument may even challenge a conventional reading of the notion of letting beings be understood as letting beings take their course by relinquishing our interest in them, by becoming free of interest—"The freedom to the opening of the open lets each being be the being it is."[21] This heady freedom is precisely a relinquishment of our interest in beings, in using and exploiting them for our material survival. Bibikhin takes a different course that offers, at the same time, another interpretation of Heidegger. The love Bibikhin discusses in his lectures on Tolstoy lets beings be not by relinquishing our interest in them but by relinquishing our *separation* from them as ostensibly disinterested observers. Love emerges from relinquishing the position of observer or disinterested spectator that might emerge from one reading of Heidegger's notion of freedom to another freedom that results from affirming our interest in beings.

In this respect, Bibikhin's account of Tolstoyan love seems to accord far better with the description of *Rausch* Heidegger offers in the first Nietzsche lecture.[22] While Bibikhin avoids the largely overdetermined vocabulary of Apollonian and Dionysian in his lecture—and with good reason given their immense influence in Russian culture—he ends up developing an account of love that seems to set forth an account of our relation to our environment that bears considerable resemblance to the Nietzschean distinction. The position of the observer or spectator is Apollonian whereas the position of the ardent lover is essentially Dionysian.

If we accept these layered allusions to Heidegger and Nietzsche, we arrive at an account of Tolstoyan experimentation and openness to difference as an unsettled negotiation between the position of observers that seeks to give a final and complete form to whatever they encounter and that position—which is really no position at all—of persons amid things, uncertain of their identity and likely incapable of becoming certain of them. Now it is quite obvious that the latter case poses a challenge to description or elucidation because the immersion into things dissolves boundaries of all kinds—the best one can do, it may seem, is to attempt to provide an account of an experience that in its polyvalency must defeat any one account. This challenge may be met by insisting on boundaries and, by doing so, enabling us to ignore the potential problem arising from their constitution from a complex of relations to our environment or world that cannot be reduced to any one account. Or the challenge may be met by what Bibikhin refers to as Tolstoyan love, this love being nothing more or less than a commitment not to close oneself off from others or the world. We might say that Tolstoyan love recalls more accurately not *Sorge* but *Entschlossenheit*, or what Heidegger refers to in the 1930s as *Verhaltenheit*; namely, the refusal to heed the temptation to closure. Yet Tolstoyan love emerges in a distinctly Russian framework of love for the whole and for others as well. One of Bibikhin's astute moves is to place a notion of love that is not obviously Greek at the center of Tolstoy's thinking and to assure us that this notion of love is Russian or comes from a Russian capacity to interact with beings that has not been erased by years of devotion to the status of the observer or master over the world.

For Bibikhin, love is this stubborn refusal to close oneself off from the world. And this is evidently what Bibikhin finds so compelling about Tolstoy's diaries. For these diaries are in this sense diaries of love that put in question the need for final narratives, for closing oneself off in a chosen or decided way of being that requires no diary, since everyday life cannot tolerate any changes or events. Everyday life becomes routine. But, as Bibikhin shows, everyday life for Tolstoy is not and cannot be everyday in the sense of being reduced to some repeated model. Hence, the diaries. They are a "record" of continuous displacement and estrangement from the everyday. Far from being the minute biography of the everyday life of the writer, the "genius" Lev Tolstoy, the diaries constitute a series of explorations that put in question the identity of the investigator as well as what he is investigating. As Tolstoy put it in another book he intended for daily usage:

Underfoot frozen, hard earth, large trees all around, bleak sky overhead, absorbed in thought I feel my body—and at the same time I know, I feel with all my being, that the trees and the sky and my body and my thoughts—that this is all chance—merely the products of my five senses, my imagination, the world constructed by me, that all of this is such as it is merely because I make up such, and not another, part of the world, that such is my being closed off from the world. I know, that I must die—and all this will not disappear for me but change in appearance just like one has changes of scene in the theater: out of the bushes, rocks, castles, towers and the like. Death produces in me such a transformation, if only I am not completely destroyed, but transform into some other being, differently separated from the world. Now, I consider myself, my body with its senses, to be myself, while something completely different emerges in me. And then the whole world, remaining the same for all who live in it, becomes for me a different one. Indeed the world is such, and not another merely because I consider myself as such and not another being differently closed off from the world. And there may be an infinite quantity of beings closed off from the world and the same goes for the ways of being closed off.[23]

This sense of transformation and estrangement without pause or end, other than in death, pervades Tolstoy's diaries and gives them their peculiar power as irregular explorations of routine. Bibikhin imagines through Tolstoy a radical displacement of the everyday and, along with it, of the many ways in which we hold ourselves apart from others and our environment or world.

At one point in the lectures, Bibikhin clarifies what is ultimately at stake in them:

> Our goal is not a portrait. But it is also not an attempt at an empathetic reading, living in Tolstoy's world. We consider the man a prophecy, directed to us now and containing in itself the very mystery in which it is most necessary for us to participate for our salvation today.[24]

Bibikhin could hardly be clearer, and he brings out the salvific import of Tolstoy (and not Dostoevsky) for contemporary Russia. Though it is facile to engage in the elaboration of political allegories based on Bibikhin's course—something in the nature of salvation through a rediscovery of the world—the very Russian world—lost before one's nose or hidden in plain view by the final collapse of seventy years of domination by ideals of control and domination from which Tolstoy seems to demand the most extreme liberation—these allegories are relevant to Bibikhin's reading of Tolstoy. Bibikhin assures us that they must be, and they are salvific in exactly the sense I have suggested because they are a letting go of the need to free oneself of the world by shutting oneself off from it in favor of a radically renewed relation to that world and the others one finds within it. Bibikhin's reading of Tolstoy in effect finds the origins for some of Heidegger's more distinctive ideas in the diary of one of Russia's greatest writers. By locating Heidegger in Tolstoy and further locating in Tolstoy the potential for a truly salvific Russian future, Bibikhin frees Russia from the influence of the West by incorporating into one of the greatest pillars of Russian culture a point of view as to the way forward for Russia that both accepts some of the most powerful aspects of Heidegger's criticism of modernity while interweaving them with Tolstoy's own—according to Bibikhin—most powerful philosophical experiment. Bibikhin presents what amounts to a distinctively new (and Russian) way of creating the everyday, a Russian everyday, an everyday that may provide the essential ground for a renovation of Russian life from its simplest components.

\*\*\*

If I began by situating the reception of Heidegger in Russia within the debates about Russian identity that took place in the nineteenth century among intellectuals, theologians, and philosophers, I end by situating that reception within a tradition shaped decisively not by intellectuals, theologians, and philosophers but by two immensely influential writers. Why do I take such an approach—if, indeed, it is an approach? One reason should be obvious and draws on a venerable cliché about Russian culture: that Russian writers pose the great questions with more force and urgency than any Russian thinkers ever did. But this cliché, like so many others that have been imposed on Russian culture, cannot be defended unless one accepts the fact that Dostoevsky and Tolstoy have had so much greater influence in the West than any Russian thinkers. There are even those who assert that Russian thought is a meager thing, that Russian philosophy cannot pretend to hold up to its Western counterpart—Russia has no Kant, no Hegel, no Schopenhauer, no Nietzsche, no Husserl, no Heidegger, no Wittgenstein.

This general derision of Russian thought shows itself in the reception of Heidegger as well, even though that reception exploits Heidegger for the purposes of asserting a Russian philosophical tradition with its own complicated roots and new possibilities—a tradition that, at least in the case of Dugin, can now begin to shine in conspicuous contrast with a Western tradition that has become largely moribund, having admitted its own abject failure or exhaustion with the last wave of Western philosophy, dependent in its way either on an Austrian, Wittgenstein, or on Heidegger himself. Perhaps the most daring possibility opened up by Russian philosophy as Dugin and Bibikhin attempt to develop it, is to bypass the impasse of Western philosophy, stuck between analytic and continental schools.

In this respect, both Dugin and Bibikhin, despite their enormous differences, seem to be in accord with the judgment of Alain Badiou, himself one of the last representatives of the French generation of 1968 that produced Deleuze, Derrida, and Foucault. Badiou claims that Heidegger is the last philosopher whose importance is uncontested.[25] Badiou's statement is of course exaggerated; Heidegger is very much contested, indeed, now more than ever with the publication of his *Black Notebooks*. Nonetheless, it is interesting that the Russian reception of Heidegger treats the end of the Western philosophical tradition not with nostalgia but with evident delight in that the end of Western philosophy opens up possibilities for thinking in different ways that seem foreclosed to Western thinkers far too entrenched in their own tradition to see clearly outside of it—a defense, of course, for Russians in the face of Western incomprehension or derision.

In this sense, the Russian reception simply follows Heidegger himself, whose essay on nihilism seems to have had such a powerful impact within Russia. For Heidegger emphasizes the liberating effect of attempting to overcome the nihilism of the West:

> The coulisses of the world theater may for some time remain the old ones, the game that is being played is already different. That the goals held hitherto are disappearing and the values losing their value is no longer experienced as simply an extermination and lamented as a loss and deficiency, but rather greeted as liberation, and recognized as a final victory and a *completion* (*Vollendung*).[26]

Heidegger's Russian reception declares and explores this heady liberation. There is no lament, no sense of loss, but rather an eagerness to find a new way forward. In this respect, Dugin's interpretation of Heidegger seems to run the risk of falling into the trap of a traditional nationalism and a covert politics of empire that Heidegger puts under critique in his nihilism essay with obvious, though inexplicit, reference to the burgeoning German imperialism of 1940. Bibikhin, to the contrary, offers what appears to be a much more radical liberation from the Western tradition insofar as he attacks in a central way its apparent emphasis on the control and conquest of nature and others. Bibikhin hews much more closely to Heidegger's critique of domination by unfolding in his Tolstoy lectures—which are in this respect a cynosure of Bibikhin's work as a whole—not only a critique of the need to control but also a fecund reinterpretation of the notion of self-interest that anchors the need to control.

The reinterpretation of self-interest is one of Bibikhin's most intriguing moves. Rather than resorting to the more traditional understanding of self-interest that revolves around the twin poles of self-abnegation or self-affirmation, Bibikhin fashions a notion of self-interest that rejects the choice of self-abnegation or affirmation in favor of a flexible identity that effectively discards the overwhelming fear of death by accepting our status as a being among beings or, better, as a being whose status as a being among beings does not congeal into a pattern of self-abnegation or self-affirmation. One may discern an echo of Heidegger's notion of the "between" in this attempt to overcoming the dichotomies of self-abnegation and self-affirmation. Yet, Bibikhin's association of this different notion of identity with love is an attempt to transform that notion as well from tyrannical erōs or kenotic love to a notion of love as a seeking out, a questioning, a courage to let oneself explore and move into the world.

This fundamental change in attitude to the world can be an extraordinarily fecund source of resistance to that pursuit of technological hegemony that dominates us now more than ever. If Bibikhin rejects the language and symbols of Russia's messianic mission, he does offer a potent retort to the unthinking will to extermination, to the elimination of all relations to the world that do not enhance our power over it. This power whose fragility, if not absurdity, Heidegger recognized with exceptional force, Bibikhin, as one of Heidegger's astute readers, attempts to counter in a comprehensive philosophy that ought to receive more attention than it has. For Bibikhin's philosophical investigations are a plea to rethink our lives and our relation to others and our environment at a time when the darkness Heidegger himself saw coming seems upon us as perhaps never before.

## NOTES

1. The translation of *Being and Time* by Vladimir Bibikhin first appeared only in 1997. But Heidegger's presence in Russia was considerable throughout the 1990s. For an account of Heidegger's earlier influence in Russia, see Maryse Dennes, *Husserl-Heidegger: Influence de leur oeuvre en Russie* (Paris: L'Harmattan, 1997).

2. This traditional distinction is of course reductive and insufficiently supple to convey the complicated positions of many of the thinkers it covers. Nonetheless, it is useful as a means of differentiating degrees of adherence to, and rejection of, ideas perceived largely as Western. For a basic overview, see Andrzej Walicki, *A History of Russian Thought,* trans. Hilda Andrews-Rusiecka (Stanford, CA: Stanford University Press, 1979), 71–182.

3. Rome is of course a fascinating example. Recall Horace's famous statement: *Graeca capta ferum victorem cepit*, in Epistles 2.1.156. Rome shows no comparable internal imposition of Greek culture. Yet the colonization of the Roman mind, if we may call it that, shows fleeting similarity to the Russian case insofar as the class divisions in imperial Roman society were marked by use of a prestige language—Greek—that the lower classes could not understand in most of the empire.

4. See Boris Jakim and Robert Bird, trans., *On Spiritual Unity: A Slavophile Reader* (Hudson, NY: Lindisfarne Books, 1998), 7–25.

5. Alyssa DeBlasio provides an excellent overview of the debates concerning the definition of Russian philosophy in the 1990s. See Alyssa DeBlasio, *The End of Russian Philosophy Tradition and Transition at the Turn of the 21st Century* (New York: Palgrave MacMillan, 2014), 15–39.

6. See Marlène Laruelle's excellent chapter on Dugin in her book *Russian Eurasianism: An Ideology of Empire* (Baltimore, MD: Johns Hopkins University Press, 2008), 107–44.

7. Alexander Dugin, *The Fourth Political Theory*, trans. Mark Selboda and Michael Millerman (London: Arktos, 2012).

8. Aleksandr G. Dugin, *Martin Khaidegger: Poslednii Bog* (Moscow: Akademicheskii Proekt, 2014).

9. Alexander Dugin, *Martin Heidegger: The Philosophy of Another Beginning*, trans. Nina Kouprianova (Arlington, VA: Radix Publishers, 2014), 53–64.

10. Martin Heidegger, *Überlegungen VII-XI (Schwarze Hefte 1938–1939)*, GA 95 (Frankfurt am Main: Vittorio Klostermann, 2014), 68.

11. Martin Heidegger, *Die Geschichte des Seyns*, GA 69 (Frankfurt am Main: Vittorio Klostermann, 1998), 108.

12. Ibid., 119.

13. Dugin, *Poslednii Bog*, 349.

14. I am alluding here to Ivan Karamazov's famed description of the West as a "graveyard":

I want to go to Europe, Alyosha, I'll go straight from here. Of course I know that I will only be going to a graveyard, but to the most, the most precious graveyard, that's the thing! The precious dead lie there, each stone over them speaks of such ardent past life, of such passionate faith in their deeds, their truth, their struggle and their science, that I—this I know beforehand—will fall to the ground and kiss those stones and weep over them—being wholeheartedly convinced, at the same time, that it has all long been a graveyard and nothing more. And I will not weep from despair, but simply because I will be happy in my shed tears.

F. M. Dostoevsky, *The Brothers Karamazov*, trans. Richard Pevear and Larissa Volokhonsky (New York: Farrar, Straus and Giroux, 2002), 230.

15. A Russian edition of Bibikhin's work is underway, with three volumes having appeared so far.

16. Martin Heidegger, *Contributions to Philosophy (of the Event)*, trans. Richard Rojcewicz and Daniela Vallega-Neu (Bloomington: Indiana University Press, 2012), 13; translation modified.

17. Tolstoy, *War and Peace*, trans. Aylmer Maude and Louise Maude (Oxford: Oxford University Press, 2010), 1309.

18. Vladimir V. Bibikhin, *Dnevniki L'va Tolstogo* (St. Petersburg: Ivan Limbakh, 2012), 5.

19. Ibid., 51.

20. In the *Contributions to Philosophy*, Heidegger interprets Sorge in a way that resembles what Bibikhin means by love in Tolstoy. See Heidegger, *Contributions to Philosophy*, 29–30.

21. Heidegger, "Vom Wesen der Wahrheit," in *Wegmarken* (Frankfurt am Main: Vittorio Klostermann, 1976), 188. My translation.

22. Martin Heidegger, "Der Wille zur Macht als Kunst," in *Nietzsche I* (Pfullingen: Neske Verlag, 1961), 109–26.

23. L. N. Tolstoy, *Polnoe sobranie sochinenii*, vol. 41 (Moscow: 1928–1958), 354–55. The original text comes from Tolstoy's *Krug chteniia* (*Circle of Reading*). The Russian reads: Под ногами морозная, твердая земля, кругом огромные деревья, над головой пасмурное небо, тело свое чувствую, занят мыслями—а между тем знаю, чувствую всем существом, что и крепкая, морозная земля, и деревья, и небо, и мое тело, и мои мысли—случайно, что всё это—только произведение моих пяти чувств, мое представление, мир, построенный мною, что всё это таково только потому, что я составляю такую, а не иную часть мира, что таково мое отделение от мира. Знаю, что

стоит мне умереть—и всё это для меня не исчезнет, но видоизменится, как бывают превращения в театрах: из кустов, камней сделаются дворцы, башни и т. п. Смерть произведет во мне такое превращение, если только я не совсем уничтожусь, а перейду в другое, иначе отделенное от мира, существо. Теперь, я себя, свое тело с своими чувствами считаю собою, тогда же совсем иначе выделится что-то в меня. И тогда весь мир, оставаясь таким же для тех, которые живут в нем, для меня станет другим. Ведь мир такой, а не иной только потому, что я считаю собой то, а не другое отделенное от мира существо. А отделенных от мира существ может быть бесчисленное количество, а также и способов отделения.

24. Bibikhin, *Dnevniki L'va Tolstogo*, 300. My translation.

25. Alain Badiou, *Being and Event*, trans. Oliver Feltham (London: Continuum, 2006), 1.

26. Heidegger, "Der europäische Nihilismus," in *Nietzsche II* (Pfullingen: Neske Verlag, 1961), 34; my translation.

*Chapter 12*

# Plural Anthropology—The Fundamental-Ontological Analysis of Peoples

## *Excerpt*

### Alexander Dugin

## ONTOLOGISCHE DIFFERENZ

To approach the anthropological problem in the perspective that interests us, we can recall Heidegger's main thought, with which *Being and Time*, his basic work, begins: the introduction of the *ontologische Differenz*. We take the word *Differenz* in its German spelling, to emphasize that we are not talking, for instance, of the later developments of analogous terms in Derrida—différEnce and différAnce (in the context of postmodern grammatological studies), but of return to the basic use of this concept by Heidegger. Thus, we propose to preserve the German pronunciation of the word *Differenz*.

This Latin term means "distinction," but it has a specific sense in Heidegger. What does Heidegger mean by *ontologische Differenz*? He means to raise the problem of how to relate Being and beings. In German, "das Seiende" is beings, "that which is" (from "Seiendes," the active participle) and "Sein," that which makes "Seiendes" existent, involved in Being.

Why in *ontologische Differenz* do we accent the word *ontologische*? The issue is that in this gap, in this distinction, lies the fundamental difference between phenomenological thought, which deals only with Seiendes, and speculative thought, where at issue is the secret search for that which is not given immediately in experience, i.e., Sein.

If we place Heidegger in the context of the philosophical tradition to which he belonged, i.e., in the context of Husserl's phenomenology, we understand that in this *ontologische Differenz* at issue is the basic idea, discovered by Brentano, Husserl's teacher, and his whole school, including Adolph Reinach, Alexius Meinong, etc., that there is a difference between the intentional-noetic level, which operates with the data of human (or non-human, animal) perception and the level of ontological argument. On the basis of this idea, Brentano tried to build his psychology and his logic, where he introduced the concept of an "existential quantifier."

According to Brentano, how we perceive surroundings immediately, on the level of consciousness, is *noesis* (in Husserl) or intentionality. There is another level above this one that permits us to conclude whether we perceive correctly or incorrectly. It is connected with the postulation of the objective reality of the thing, separate from our perception of it. This is the level that compares how we represent the thing to ourselves (*noema*) and how it is in itself, outside us. Thus, Aristotelian logic, with which training in scientific thought begins, is an extremely enigmatic thing, since it is based on an instantaneous leap, a transition from the phenomenal to the logical or speculative, to the assertion about whether the thing exists or not in itself, separately from our perception of it. This transition, entirely trivial in logic, is from an ontological perspective a colossal problem, which is placed at the center of phenomenological philosophy.

Heidegger's thought unfolds in the phenomenological mainstream. His work *Sein und Zeit* becomes fully comprehensible when we contextualize it, placing it in the general phenomenological context. This is precisely the source for what Heidegger called the *ontologische Differenz*, the distinction between beings and Being. At the same time, beings are that which is given to us immediately; to us and to animals, to all who can perceive and distinguish, since even rocks, for instance, distinguish temperature, and a flower or any other plant can perceive and distinguish many things. A sunflower, as we know, "follows" the sun; it is "heliotropic." Proclus had the idea that there also exist "selenotropic" plants, plants that "follow" the moon. If "heliotropes" are known, "selenotropes" exist only in Proclus's reference. (I am convinced that they do exist, just we seek them badly and without diligence.) Plants can *distinguish*; they have a certain degree of "phenomenal thought," if you like. Human phenomenal thought is nothing other than penetratingly distinguishing phenomenological perception as such (in German, *Wahrnehmung*). Man distinguishes *intensively*. But in this intensive distinguishing, even more intensive than among the animals, he still remains on the level of phenomenological thought: his intensive distinguishing occurs between one Seiendes and another, between a part of Seiendes (beings) and another part. But remaining in the framework of phenomenological perception or noetic thought, he, according to Husserl, operates only with noemata, i.e., with his perceptions of things, animated by attention, intentionality. Man becomes a ζῷον λόγον ἔχον, i.e., *a living being endowed with logos* (in Aristotle's definition), not when he distinguishes too keenly. Thus, an eagle distinguishes things with its eyes better than we do. There are animals, for instance dogs, that hear sounds we do not hear. And the apparatus of differentiated phenomenal perception in man is not the most developed, compared to animals.

Man differs from other well-distinguishing animals in something else; precisely in his capacity for the *ontologische Differenz*, for raising the question of the *Being* of beings, the location of which is unknown and which is not just another being (even the highest one), but that which makes beings. The disclosure of Being, its unconcealment, as Heidegger says, is the definition of truth among Greeks. "Alētheia" (ἀλήθεια), truth, is *unconcealment*. Seiendes is perceptions of the concealed. Aletheia, truth, is the disclosure of some additional dimension, which is possible only in a flash of Logos, the lightning that rules all, Heraclitus's κεραυνός. Thus, *how* the transition from the phenomenological to the speculative, from the consideration of beings to the postulation of something more general, more fundamental than beings, is carried out is, properly speaking, *the birth of man*.

Here we can recall that Gramsci regarded all people as *intellectuals*: only, some as full-fledged and others not. In classical Greek Aristotelian anthropology, the complete man is precisely the *philosopher*. What, then, you will say, about the rest? From the perspective of the Greco-Latin classics, which we follow one way or another, the rest are strictly speaking not fully human. From the position of the foundations of our culture, the real man is only the man capable of philosophy, i.e., the man who raises the question how Sein differs from Seiendes, who carries out the *ontologische Differenz*. At the same time, the answer to the question *how* to relate Being and beings can be different and complex.

For man as species, what is most important is whether this question is raised or not, and not what response is given to it.

Then, another history sets in, the history of philosophy, according to Heidegger: how concretely Greek philosophers conceived of Being. And now here, *how* the *ontologische Differenz* is carried out becomes fundamental. (I hope that we have established the previous stage, the distinction between beings and Being, correctly). Now, Heidegger complicates the problem in the following way: maybe the relation toward the *ontologische Differenz corresponds to the First Inception* in Greek philosophy, under whose shadow unfolds all philosophy, culture, Logos as such, theology, and the history of culture from the Greeks to our day, to Nietzsche and Heidegger. And there is *another* response to the question, another way of deciding the *ontologische Differenz;* Heidegger himself proposes it. What is this answer?

Man's first coming-to-be or disclosure of Logos consists in the assertion that man, observing beings, says that there is the totality of beings and at the same time something common to these beings, a koinon, in Greek. This koinon lies at the basis of Aristotle's concept of ousia (οὐσία), essence. There are beings, and there is essence. Beings are what we deal with phenomenologically, what we come into contact with. Essence is that which constitutes the Being of beings. Not only the essence of that being, but the essence of that which makes the being a being. That is "ousia" (οὐσία).

Heidegger introduces the following neologism: there is Seiendes as beings and Sein as Being, but also *Seiendheit.* This word is difficult to translate into Russian. We get something like "beingness." Heidegger semantically translates through *Seiendheit* Aristotle's ousia. οὐσία is the present participle of the Greek εἶναι, to be.

Heidegger says that one answer to how to carry out the *ontologische Differenz,* the distinction between beings and Being, is the notion of ousia, i.e., essence. The identification of *Sein und Seiendheit* is the First Inception of philosophy. Everything else follows from this principle. Being is *common* to all beings, i.e., their essence. Being, Sein, is equivalent to Seiendheit, the koinon or common in beings, ousia. Further, all theology and culture, according to Heidegger, are built around this, since this is Logos. This is a form of Logos, given even earlier by Heraclitus's decision about "listening not to me, but to the Logos," because Heraclitus himself could only distinguish between being and being, between one Seiendes and another "it is wise to agree that all is one" (οὐκ ἐμοῦ, ἀλλὰ τοῦ λόγου ἀκούσαντας ὁμολογεῖν σοφόν ἐστιν ἓν πάντα εἰδέναι). From this, Heidegger draws out the notion of the common, the "koinon," as a specific form of ontology, which later becomes the *destiny* of the West.

But Heidegger asserts that precisely *such* a resolution[1] of the question of the *ontologische Differenz* led to the gradual forgetting of Being or loss of Being and to the onset of the rule of Nietzsche's nihilism. From this there emerges the need to raise anew the ontological question, which should be formulated on the basis of trying to understand the *collapse* of the philosophy of the First Inception. That is, the *ontologische Differenz* must be carried out *differently*.

Next, Heidegger describes *how* to do that: with the help of Dasein and a throw toward the perception of Being, not by collecting beings and detecting what is common to all the variety of beings, but by a vertical throw of Dasein toward Being itself as nothing (Nichts). And then Heidegger introduces the concept of *another* Being, Seyn-Being (with a "y"), which indeed is a different experience of the perception of Being, carrying out the *ontologische Differenz* in the framework of not the First Inception of philosophy, which has been exhausted and leads to nihilism, but the second, New Inception of philosophy.

## ANTHROPOLOGISCHE DIFFERENZ

The *ontologische Differenz* in Heidegger's interpretation is of principal importance for the whole anthropological picture of the Fourth Political Theory, which strives to be existential and is thus built to a significant extent on the Heideggerian analytic of Dasein.

When we employ the concept *ontologische Differenz* in our seminar on the plural man, we are interested in the first place in *Differenz*. Why *Differenz*? Repeating the same logic, Eugen Fink, a bearer of phenomenological orthodoxy, Husserl's student, and Heidegger's friend, introduced the concept of *kosmologische Differenz*. Ontological in Heidegger; cosmological in Fink. What does that mean? Fink fully adopts the Heideggerian model of thought and applies it to the concept *world* (*Welt*), *cosmos*. He asserts that there is an *experience of the world*, which is unique and not inherent in *the things of the world*.

All the things of the world, all *innerweltliche Dinge*, can be formed into a whole in *two* ways. First of all, this can be done through collection. The things of the world, taken in general, appear as a sort of "thingness." But this aggregate of things of the world does not give us a notion of the world, because the world is something else.

The world is an experience realized in *another* way. Following Heidegger, Fink speaks of the *kosmologische Differenz*. Where in Heidegger there was Sein in relation to Seiendes, in Fink there is the world, Welt, in relation to innerweltliche Dinge, the aggregate of inner-worldly things. The experience of the world is as unique and ambiguous as in Heidegger. It can be in the framework of the First Inception, in which case we are dealing with the cosmos of the Greeks, or in the framework of the Second Inception, in which case we come to an entirely unique experience of the cosmos as a specific *finite game*. *Play as the Symbol of the World* is one of Fink's main works.[2] Without getting into the details, I want to say that in this way, *Differenz*, beginning with Heidegger and through Fink, acquires for us a *methodological* significance. We must remember all that Heidegger put into the *ontologische Differenz* and how Fink applied this methodology: two Inceptions, the distinction between the given and the general or the inner dimension, applied to Being (in Heidegger) and the cosmos (in Fink). We can continue that logic, that same path (μέθοδος) and apply Differenz to anthropology, which interests us here. For understanding the anthropological problematic, I propose to introduce the term *anthropologische Differenz*, methodologically grounded by Heidegger, the broader relevance of which Fink's works demonstrated.

And so, *anthropologische Differenz*. The approach will be exactly the same here as in the case of the *ontologische* and *kosmologische Differenz*. Man exists as an individual. This is a kind of unconditional given. However complexly we might philosophize, the individual man is what is given to us. It is us, "without contrivance," as simple, verifiable things, the individual entities who are in the crudest and most brutal sense. This is the individual man, the individual, analogous to Seiendes or innerweltliche Dinge. There exist people or humanity as the aggregate of individuals. We can generalize to everyone who has ever lived; the whole historical aggregate of individuals. We get: "people" and their full multitude: humanity. So we get humanity and the humanness intrinsic to this humanity as one answer to the *anthropologische Differenz*. Then there exists a common humanity (according to Heidegger, "ousia"; according to Fink, the aggregate of inner-worldly things), and precisely this is one response to the question of the *anthropologische Differenz*. Both humanity and its individuals exist. Humanity, in fact, still does not coincide with the aggregate of individuals, but with that common quality intrinsic to all these individuals.

This is one possible form of anthropology. Moreover, it is the broadest, most acceptable, well-known, and universal model of anthropological thought. Here there are also possibilities for differentiation, taxonomies, and the allocation of segments of humanity on a temporal and spatial scale. We can speak of the change of historical types and models and distinguish various segments in presently existing humanity. Here, there is a possibility for pluralism, but, following Heidegger and Fink, we can raise the question of the existence of a *Second Inception of anthropology*, a *New Inception*, in which it is proposed to execute the *anthropologische Differenz differently* than by appeal to the generally human. In this case, something unique emerges, the concept of a *Homo Novus* (new man), not identical to humanity; man who does not coincide with the general; a *second man*, who is a unique, finite, and not guaranteed punch, coming from where we do not expect it. This is the experience of humanity not as general but as *unique*; not as an aggregate, not as integrated, but rather as differentiating, not in the direction of the individual, but in the opposite direction; in the course of these differentiations, the individual is precisely overcome, not horizontally (through his integration with other individuals and through the elucidating analysis of what they have in common) but *by a path of overcoming the individual in a radically different direction*. Vertically, we can say; transversally in relation to the notion of humanity. Thus, we carry out an *anthropologische Differenz* that overcomes the individual, but *not* through the collective and general. There emerges a kind of *differentiated* human, who becomes man as such.

Here, we approach the idea, on one hand, of Julius Evola's *differentiated man* and, on the other, Corbin's *man of light*. I want to draw attention to the fact that Henry Corbin, the eminent French philosopher and scholar of Islamic thought who developed the theme of the man of light, was the first translator of Heidegger into French. From my perspective, Corbin is interesting not only as a researcher of Islamic traditions, but as the one who, following Heidegger, came right up to the problem of the *anthropologische Differenz*. Corbin's ideas, set out, for instance, in the book *Man and his Angel* and in the majority of his other works dedicated to the idea of "inner Islam," Suhrawardi, Ibn Arabi, etc., are in fact nothing other than a historico-cultural, theological, philosophical illustration of Corbin's main problem, *luminous anthropology*. This is the *anthropologische Differenz*, carried out in a different anthropological framework, alternative to the classical one. Here we are dealing with the *anthropology of the Other Inception* (or with an Other Inception of anthropology), where relations among humans change from horizontal-collective to individual-luminous. Thus arises the figure of the *man of light*, the Angel, the human eidos, the πατρικὸς νοῦς of the neo-Platonists, which is in a *different* position relative to man than humanity and the individual.

Classical anthropology is built up as follows: there is the individual, and there is humanity. There are also various intermediate groups, types, and societies. All sociology fits in here, all forms of historical sociology. The Corbin model of anthropology, the *new anthropology*, proposes a *radically different relation of the individual to the species*: not collective generalization, not integration, but the unique and finite experience of experiencing simultaneously all humanity in its integral dimension—unique, but, of course, not guaranteed. Here, for man to become man he must undergo the experience of being illuminated by the human as eidetic, as found in transversal geometry in relation to the individual. This *illumination by the human* as such, the Big Man, homo maximus, the man of light, occurs individually, but in a moment of the withdrawal of the individual. This experience is always unique; it is intended for single units because it is an experience of the utmost strain of all one's inner forces. And at the same time, plunging the human into the individual, it opens for him the essence of the universal in humanity. Thus, this path is analogous to carrying out the *ontologische Differenz* in the spirit of the anthropology of the New Inception, developed by Corbin. It was later taken up by those who followed after him; for instance, his students Christian Jambet and Pierre Lory, who continued the Islamic line of research, and, moreover, by such philosophers as the Frenchman Guy Lardreau and the Italian Massimo Cacciari. It was also taken up by those who recognized and figured out that Corbin's philosophy was broader than the context of his Islamic research, those who could notice the connection between Corbin the Heideggerian, student, and translator of Heidegger, and Corbin the specialist in Islamic philosophy—for instance, the Italian philosopher Glauco Giuliano.

## THE PROBLEM OF THE PLURALITY OF
## DASEIN: EXISTENTIELL OR EXISTENTIAL

Heidegger's definition of Dasein is an answer to the *anthropologische Differenz*. The introduction of Dasein is an introduction of an authority[3] that does not coincide with the individual, the collective, or humanity. Dasein is not an individual, but is also not all humanity. And, at the same time, Corbin translates Dasein into French as "*la réalité humaine*" ("human reality"), and this is paradoxical: the concept "*réalité*" means "thingness, reality, objectness," and "humaine" is "human subjectivity," so "*la réalité humaine*" is not such a simple term. This is a term *in which subject and object coincide*. That which Heidegger defines as Dasein is found *between* the subject and the object; it projects itself into the object and conceives of itself as a subject. The notion "*la réalité humaine*" is precisely a notion of "human reality," which precedes both the individual and the collective, or more accurately is found geometrically, topographically, *vertically* in relation to them.

Dasein can accordingly be taken as the unique experience of the revelation, of the flash of the human, the more so as Heidegger himself writes in one place that *Dasein is human being*. And since Heidegger thinks of Being (*Sein*) in both Da*sein* and in Mensch*sein* in the context of the ontology of the New Inception, Menschsein refers us to the *ontologische Differenz*. The entire problematic of Dasein fits precisely here.

In our discussion with Heidegger's student and later secretary Friedrich-Wilhelm von Herrmann in Freiburg in 2013, we raised the problematic of the plurality of Dasein. I gave him my book *Martin Heidegger: The Possibility of Russian Philosophy* and I tried, in a few words, in unconfident German, to set out the main thrust of how I honestly came to study Russian philosophy, proceeding from its roots, according to Heidegger's fundamental-ontology, starting from the trust that Dasein is a universal reality.[4] And through coming closer to Russian Dasein, to Russian Being, I came to the conclusion that a significant part of the Russian existentials does not coincide with the existentials described by Heidegger. That is, Russian Dasein at the level of its inner structure, Russian anthropology as such, proved significantly different from what Heidegger described. Not formally, not on a cultural level, but essentially. Von Herrmann became rather animated and said, that cannot be. So he understood what I was trying to say.[5]

Then he answered approximately as follows: The difference between the Dasein of a Russian, a German, a Japanese person, and so forth, reduces to the level of the *existentiell*. The existentiell is the structure of a cultural, sociological approach to Dasein. This does not occur on the level of the *existential*, which refers to Dasein's inwardly intrinsic form of existing. "Because," he continued, "death means the same thing for a Russian, a German, and a Japanese."

I objected, Herr von Herrmann, you are likely mistaken, because, studying death in different cultures, I came to the conclusion that death is culturally conditional. And Japanese death, Russian death, and German death certainly represent three fundamentally different phenomena. Only a Russian understands Russian death; it is possible that a Russian does not stand face-to-face with it, as a European death. Death is behind a Russian's back, and he acts in its name and in its authority.[6] A Japanese person is found in some more complex configuration in relation to death. Being-toward-death, the finitude of human Being, is conceived of radically differently depending on cultural context. This is precisely the topic of my book, *Martin Heidegger: The Possibility of Russian Philosophy*—in particular, the fact that even the most grammatical constructions of the Russian language reflect a different *existential*, precisely *existential* [i.e., not existentiell], that is, essential, and not only existentiell structure of Dasein. To this, von Herrmann responded, If you continue this research, it will be grand. Nobody is working on this problem. Heidegger was personally convinced of the universality of Dasein. And all our constructions reduce to the fact that distinctions among societies and peoples are found not on the level of Dasein, but on the level of an existentiell, cultural, sociological, if you will, approach to Dasein. If you will establish the principle of the plurality of Dasein and demonstrate the distinction on the level of Dasein's *existentials*, and not only on the existentiell level, that will be a very serious accomplishment.

## FUNDAMENTAL ANTHROPOLOGY

As for the universality of Dasein: of course, the Heideggerian *anthropologische Differenz* would be enough. Even if we believe von Hermann that there is a universal Dasein, while the attitude toward death and other things actually concerns not the essential relations of existential structures, but merely some environs of Dasein, this relative, existentiell pluralism is by itself enough and productive. But then we will say that Dasein has only one Selbst (Jungian or Heideggerian). Jung, by the way, following Adolf Bastion, was a supporter of the unity of Selbst; he saw the unity of the collective unconscious, for which he traveled to America to do psychoanalysis among the African Americans, who, as Jung established, see "Aryan dreams," Celtic crosses, swastikas, etc. The Jungian model of the unconscious is the unconscious not only of Indo-Europeans, but of all (at least, he himself thought so).

But there is another approach. I advance that thesis that *there exist a plurality of Daseins,* which are, in fact, a few fundamental, "fundamental-anthropological" zones. This is a very important term, *fundamental-anthropology.* Let us recall that Heidegger's *fundamental-ontology* is the attempt to construct an ontology without breaking away from the ontic, which is why he also calls it onto-ontology, i.e., to build a Logos that would not break itself away from phenomenology; to create a speculative philosophy that would constantly maintain a connection with its phenomenological basis, on which it would be constructed, and this is, in essence, one of the tasks of phenomenology as such. We now speak similarly of the construction of *fundamental-anthropology.*

At once, this fundamental-anthropology, which gets developed on the basis of reflections on the *anthropologische Differenz,* offers us two variants from which to choose: the universal form of fundamental-anthropology or the plural one. It is evident that any form of fundamental-anthropology, even the universal one, would be a highly important theme for reflection. But we would like to raise an even more difficult question in the context of this already difficult problematic: the question of the *plurality of Dasein,* of the fact that the Selbst of Dasein differs fundamentally, that *humanity is existentially differentiated* and that this distinction is connected not only with the organization of the basic, elucidative initiatory experience of encounter with the Angel, but lies even deeper. [At issue is] the plurality of Daseins; the plurality not of the arrangements of Dasein, but of Daseins themselves; not Dasein's existentiell aspects, but its existential structures.

## THE PROBLEM OF MONOTHEISM
## IN THE LATE HEIDEGGER

Here I would like to mention Heidegger himself, how he resolves [*reshaet,* "decides"] the problem of monotheism in the *Contributions to Philosophy.* In my opinion, Heidegger has a stunning idea about how to settle the question of the plurality of gods or the uniqueness of God. Heidegger says approximately the following: Look: we, bipedal mortals, of course, are pretentious, learned, impudent beings. Shouldn't we be more humble? We want to know what it is fundamentally impossible for us to know: whether there is one God or several gods. And we assert that God is one or that there are many gods, or we doubt both, with such impudence that we are stifled by our own idiocy. But we intrude thereby into an affair that is altogether not ours. It does not concern us at all. A person who talks on about this pompously simply heard it somewhere, but for him in his essence it is nonsense, "trolling," because it does not affect him and cannot affect him. The most that is given to man is *the experience of the Divine*, which is the last and highest horizon and which is possible if Dasein will exist authentically (eigentlich), i.e., in Er-Eignis. When Dasein awakens, when it will be illuminated, when it will be struck by a certain luminescent humanity, when the human [characteristic, i.e., adjectival form] will start to be apprehended in the radiance of death as final and concrete, and not in general, when it will come up against its own "perfected nature," as the Hermetics said, the Angel-Dedicator, the "Imam" in Shiism, then it (this is its maximum experience) will become the *lowest* step of Jacob's ascending ladder. But what is further on is already the following non-human stage. But while man is as man, the greatest of the serious things he can attain in the domain of theology is to receive the experience of the Divine.

Then, Heidegger concludes in the following tone: If we really esteemed the Divine, if we were to relate to it in the way it deserves, delicately, without burdening it with our pitiable projections, without entreating it with our prayers, which annoy it and scare it away, we would be more sensitive toward it. The experience of the divine is subtle. It demands the utmost delicacy. As soon as man crosses the line too brutally, as soon as he begins to speak of the Divine disrespectfully, as soon as he turns to God or the gods with his tiresome prayers (and a prayer is always a request), the gods simply flee from human impudence, they don't want to hear this, they sidestep this unpleasant being, as we sidestep some dirty beggar.

So how is the problem of monotheism/polytheism decided, according to Heidegger? People's respect to the gods is expressed in *man's letting the gods themselves decide the question how many there are, one or several.* This is not for humans to argue about. Heidegger rejects neither polytheism, nor monotheism; it is simply not at all our business.

Let the gods, when they gather for a *veche*, a *thing*, *themselves* take up this question, whether there is or is not among them a chief who created them. They will think this through and make their divine decision, *Entscheidung*. We should be satisfied with what is within the limits of our possibilities, in relation to the subtle sphere of the Divine as such.

This thought of Heidegger's promises radically new conditions for theology, a practical, operative, *respectful* theology.


## THE POLYTHEISM OF DASEIN

Now let's look at what concerns the projections of this principle onto Dasein. I think that here the same thing is fitting, and a similar method can be transferred onto our anthropological dimensions. The question is: How many Daseins are there, many or one? As soon as we make an a priori, obstinate, importunate decision in regards to this, we at once make the experience of Dasein *closed* for us, because we replace the problematic that *stands* before us with one that *does not stand* before us. But there is only one problematic before us: the experience of authentic existence, i.e., the experience of discovering Dasein.

Incidentally, in the given case, the very idea of the plurality of Dasein can also be false, because it is too hurried.

How did Heidegger solve the problem of truth and falsity? He correlated truth, *Unverborgenheit* (literally "unconcealment," as he interpreted the Greek ἀλήθεια), and *Verborgenheit* ("concealment," λήθη, oblivion, ψεῦδος, falsity). But concealment points toward openness, and openness conceals something. Like "re-volution," according to Guenon, it is simultaneously *both opening and concealment*. The heaven (coelum) covers the world and opens its [i.e., heaven's] one essence for it.

So in my opinion, as regards Dasein we can full well follow a *false* hypothesis, too. In this case it makes no difference whether we begin from falsity or truth. Nietzsche said wonderfully that false ideas have served mankind more than true ones, since they arouse the imagination, are more alive, and force us to awaken and to take part at least in that for the sake of which we appeared here, i.e., thinking. So, I propose to take the idea of the plurality of Dasein not as a final answer, but as an invitation for an awakened, concrete Dasein to a *thing*, a *veche*.

A dialogue of civilizations, a dialogue of cultures, can result from this. But this dialogue of cultures or *thing* of Daseins, this council of Angels, of Corbin's humans of light, must also decide whether each has its own inner, special Dasein or not. Thus, we set aside (but do not put away) the problem; we do not insist on the plurality of Dasein; we simply say: *so it seems*. Because in fact when we move to try to understand the existentials and try to make our experiment authentic, we do not come to a general, divine universal Dasein, but to *our* Angel (*noster Angelus*), which is simultaneously general and individual, but in a certain limited field, for instance like a tribe's totem, differing from the totem of another tribe, or like the Angels of peoples in monotheism. The monotheistic Judaic tradition counts seventy-two Angels, among which whom? Michael, "the angel of the Jews," is, naturally, the most important (for Jews themselves). Thus, the idea of an "Angel of peoples" is present even in the monotheistic tradition.

Who are the Angels of peoples? In our new fundamental-anthropology, they are the *existential Angels*; they are concrete, because their awakening requires the individual, who carries out the fundamental act of awakening Dasein, activating Dasein, to bring it to exist authentically. And at the same time each apprehends the universal, but *the concrete universal* that matches the culture, the anthropological fragment it represents. Then the awakened Angel of the people becomes the priest of the people, the national genius, the tsar. The metonymy of tsar and Angel is very interesting, since the prince of peoples is regarded as the Angel of peoples. This is fundamental: metonymically they represented the *whole* people, but in its elevated, rectified dimension. The people is not so much a collection of liftmen, traders, barmaids, and passengers resting on benches. . . . That boring aggregate, the private burdening of the people by the many, interests no one. What is interesting is only the authentic, intense, saturated *moment of the people*, which is embodied in the person who makes the decision, in the tsar, the prince of the people, the Angel, the creative genius, who poetizes and confirms, who personifies the people as people, who acts as its Selbst. That is the Angel of the people.

## Ἦθος ανθρώπῳ δαίμων

Here we can recall Heraclitus' expression ήθος ανθρώπῳ δαίμων. How do we interpret it? Ethos—ethics, morals [*moral'*], mores [*nravy*];

anthropos—man; daimon—in this case, god. But consider, what is ethos? Ethos is the morality [*nravstvennost'*] characteristic of a certain *place*. That is, morality is plural: in Megara, there is one custom; in Thebes, another; in Attica, a third. There are as many ethoi as there are localities, at least in Heraclitus (and after him, too). What does he mean? That a man from Megara takes the morality and culture of Megara as the absolute divine voice from within, not as a subjective element but as a certain basic given, a daimon, the *concreteness of a subjective god*, with whom man is in direct, immediate contact. It is Socrates' daimon, the *inner god*, who at a critical moment makes the individual do even what he doesn't want to do or does not understand why he must do it. Then ethics comes in, but collective ethics, the "ethos" of the city, the polis, the region.

Accordingly, we can say that Dasein has an ethnocultural basis, which we approach through the *ethnocultural tradition*. However, such "ethical ethnism" is found even deeper. Note that one of the most Russian poets, Sergei Esenin, to whom Yevgeny Vsevolodovich Golovin dedicated a separate project, writes these lines, known to Russians probably from kindergarten:

If the holy host would offer:
  "Leave your Rus, live in Edem!" [Lit.: Leave you Rus, live in heaven]
  I would say: "This way's the wrong way. [Lit.: I will say, I don't need heaven]
  Give me just my native land."[7]

What is this about? Fundamental-anthropology. It is about the fact that for Esenin, the experience of the divine, the experience of the sacred, the experience of the last and the authentic lies concretely *in the Russian context*. He doesn't need those Angels and that heaven that represent alien forms of the universal. He will converse only with the Russian cow, the Russian birch, Russian maple, Russian mud, the Russian grandmother, the Russian home. He will not converse with those in the sphere of abstraction. Everything sacred for him exists concretely here and now, *as Russian*. That does not mean that Yesenin denies the sanctity of the non-Russian. It simply hinders him; he does not need it. Yesenin tries to fence himself off from it: "Heaven, hell, sanctity, sin—this is not my problematic. My problematic is Russia. Everything that is here concerns me fundamentally. And that for me just is the question of authentic or inauthentic being."

We have a direct, strict, simultaneously individual and trans-individual fundamental-anthropological *experience of humanity as Russianness*, and of Russianness as humanity. And here it is extremely important that in such an approach we are not talking about rejecting the universality of Dasein, but of setting that question aside and delegating its decision to other authorities. For the poet, *the universal is the Russian*. The rest is not his affair.

## THE TOPOGRAPHY OF ANGELS

*The council of Angels* can be a definite project. One of Henry Corbin's followers, Glauco Giuliano, a contemporary Italian philosopher, wrote a book on Corbin and on Corbin's time.[8] He begins the book with quotes from my interviews and early writings, which were translated into Italian in the early 1990s. Then he says something interesting: what for Corbin is Persia and the Archangel of Persia is for Dugin Eurasia and Russia. In other words, there is a certain point of contact between West and East, where the eastern moves into the western, and vice versa, where a *great encounter* takes place. In the philosophy of Suhrawardi, which Corbin studied, the place of this great encounter is the Cafcuh mountain, at the peak of which stands the Archangel, the purple Angel: one of his wings is dark, the other is light. This is the *angel of humanity*, the Angel of return from the western wells of banishment into the country of the eastern Motherland. West and East are united in this Archangel: he is the center, the key to initiation. He is He Who Is, the pole of the fundamental, cultural, historical, and ontological dialogue between the anthropological West and the anthropological East. Giuliano emphasizes that in Ancient Iran it was embodied in a female Archangel—pre-Islamic—Ardwisur Anahid (avest. Arədvī Sūrā Anāhitā), the goddess of the waters of Persia and of Persia simultaneously. Giuliano writes approximately thus: "Look, the logic of the Russian Eurasianists reproduces the logic of Corbin and his sacred geography. In the very concept of 'Eurasia,' with its combination of Europe and Asia, West and East, Earth and Sky, we meet the figure of the purple Archangel." Further, Giuliano writes that there exists an *Angel of Eurasia*, who is the initiator of the angelic *veche*, the *thing*, the Council of existential Angels. Precisely this Council decides the problem of the oneness, the universality or Dasein or its diversity. Such a Council is not the answer to our question, but the problematization of the question, the raising of the question. The Angels of the East and the West fly together to the Angel of Eurasia. The Daseins of awakened cultures congregate here.

Of course, I cannot say that all these correspondences are accidental. In the period in which I was writing the Eurasian texts that were translated into Italian even in the late 1980s, I was studying Corbin very carefully. It is striking that those texts where the parallels between Eurasianism and Corbin were most explicit, in particular the essay "Russia—The Motherland of the Angel," were not translated into Italian. However, despite this Giuliano absolutely correctly completed these correspondences and interpreted them astutely.

What is the Angel of Eurasia? It is a certain topos (place—τόπος), the topos of the Angelic Council, of the dialogue of awakened Daseins. It is the center of humanity, the pole of a new anthropology, the anthropology of the New Beginning. It is very important that Giuliano considers the Angel *topographically*. He understands the Angel to be a *spatial entity*; for that reason, it is not a heavenly Angel, but an *Angel of the Earth*. It is a winged giant that is intimately connected to the earth, but it has a certain heavenly dimension: It is connected to the *heavenly Earth*.

Glauco Giuliano discusses a text by Suhrawardi about the Simurgh. Suhrawardi's history is this: Birds—symbols of the soul, of Angels, of spirit, of the awakened Daseins of peoples of the Earth—decided to set out on a journey to discover *who is the Simurgh*, king of the birds. In other words, their task was to clarify the nature of universal Dasein. They heard of the existence of a "bird of birds," that lives on the mountain of the world (Cafcuh), and decided to get there at all costs. Many of them died along the way, some turned back, and others fought with each other and lost their lives. Only thirty birds made it to their goal. They approached the peak of the world-mountain Cafcuh, stood around the Simurgh, and asked him in chorus: "Who are you?" And he responded, "Si-murgh," which in Persian means "thirty birds." That is, he said: "I am you, and you are I." This, as Giuliano writes, is the *Angelo dell'Eurasia,* the Angel of Eurasia. It is also the *place* where thirty birds ask themselves what they have in common. It is the *thing* of the gods, where they decide the problem of [their] oneness or multiplicity. It is a place, and it is a problem. It is the problem in which the Daseins of cultures congregate in one special, central point that should unite East and West, Heaven and Earth, the depths and the heights, South and North.

We identify this symbolic point with Eurasia, with Russia; apparently, the paradoxes of the Russian character and of Russian history are somehow connected with this *intersection of oppositions*. We identify this topos of Simurgh with the space of the *existentially awakened Rus'*, with the true Rus'-Eurasia, and not simply with statistical Russia, with its technical burden, collectives, consumers, individuals, and population, to which it is possible simply to *close the eyes*. As Plotinus said, all illumination begins with closed eyes; to open the eyes, one must close them; to see something, one must turn away from it; one must stop looking at that which clatters and sparkles around us. Then, in silence and inner existential boredom, in the absence of meaningless news and roaring events, it is possible to discover something actually important, something new and fundamental.

## PLURAL ANTHROPOLOGY AND ITS ENEMIES

Let's imagine that collective humanity is a wheel or circumference and man is a point on this circumference, which consists of an indefinitely large number of individuals. Belonging to the circumference, an individual can calmly say that *he is the circumference*, since he is found on it. In addition, he can say that *he is a part of the circumference*. Both approaches are accurate: the human as individual is a fragment of the circumference, and the human as human is the circumference itself. In a critical situation, the human regards himself not as an individual, but as a human being, that is, he recognizes his nature acutely. During catastrophes, wars, tragedies, and upheavals, people sometimes act humanly—rarely, but sometimes. And this belonging to the circumference can be grasped in a certain acute experience of humanity. And so, there is the individuality of the human and the experience of collectivity, of humanity. Between these two modes of understanding the nature of the human lies a line of distinction, which has a direct relation to the *anthropologische Differenz*. In one case, this *Differenz* is decided in favor of the *individual* (the formula: the essence of the human is in the individual), through the rejection of the actuality of nature; at the extreme, this can be defined nominalistically: "there is the human, but not humanity." Then we get liberal philosophy and liberal anthropology, where the individual is the measure of things. In the other case, the universality of humanity, the collective, the shared idea about the essence of the human takes precedence. The formula this time is: humanity is real, the individual is only its fragment. Here we have socialism or communism, social holism. There is a tension between these resolutions of the *anthropologische Differenz*: in the first, liberal, case, nominalism altogether denies the existence of essence, of humanity, i.e., it patently rejects *Differenz* (although denial, the decision not to recognize something, is already recognition and action, only negative). One group wants to preserve the wheel even in the necessity of sacrificing the individual as a point on the circumference. Another group denies that the wheel exists at all. The one who puts all reality into the individual, asserting that individuality is higher than humanity, breaks off ties with the human standing alongside him. Thereby, the wheel becomes rotten and stops being a wheel. This is the putrefaction, decline, and abomination of desolation. It is also the feet of the clay colossus in the dream of Nebuchadnezzar. Individualism is a form of breaking up the wheel, which leads to its dispersion and disappearance. There is nothing here among individuals. And if there is nothing among them, the wheel is wrecked and scatters, and the human as such no longer is; there remains only the pure individual, as a chimera, a simulacrum, and later as a dividual, a combinatorial code, a rhizome.

That is the last stage and consequence of the radical decision of the *anthropologische Differenz* in favor of the individual, right up to the refusal to acknowledge the possibility of its execution at all. The liberal ideology of "human rights" cannot but lead to the abolishment of all content in the concept of the human; it is a strictly dehumanizing ideology. In the postmodern era, the wheel finally (imperceptibly) splits into fragments. If we take that into account, it is clear why in the course of the development of the autonomous humanism of the old type precisely liberals, insisting on the primacy of the individual, are victorious. The socialists, humanists of an old model, try to object: "Man is a friend to man. Let's try to keep to at least the level of social dialogue; we'll secure society, if the community has been destroyed. Since there is no organic unity, we'll try to make artificially *ex pluribus unum*, 'from many, one.'" The liberal project is more radical: man is no one to man. One can only "put up with" another (*tolérer*, in French). Hence the imperative of tolerance as a strictly negative (in the substantial sense) trans-individual attitude: the most important thing is to give the other maximal freedom to be other, to be whoever he wants to be, indifferently and sovereignly, in no way affecting "oneself."

Here are two approaches to anthropology, which produce two anthropological matrices widespread today: the humanistic (socialistic, democratic) and the individualistic (liberal). In one case, humanity is equated
with the individual; in the other, it becomes an integral principle.

For the *new anthropology*, which we contemplate from the perspective of the Fourth Political Theory, both these conceptions of the human
are antitheses. The Fourth Political Theory sees that humanity is held
in the form of a circle not at all on account of the cohesion of its circumference, but *on account of the existence of a center,* because of the
existence of a nave and the spokes (axes) proceeding from it, which
unite individuals with the whole, with the pole located in the center, and
not with other individuals. The experience of the center is the experience of one point, not of all, and not of the whole wheel; the condensed,
implosive experience of the human explosion, when humanity is found
not in itself, and not in another, but in the flash of the break with self
and others, in the throw within, in a certain "gesture from," absolutely
unimaginable in the context of the routine rotation of the wheel and its
everyday conditions, in the vertical "gesture from," in the move to a
different axis, a different anthropological dimension. This radically new
version of anthropology is disclosed not through dialogue, but through a
*throw into the center*, to where the bird-Angels of Suhrawardi's parable
of the Simurgh flew.

## WHERE DO ANGELS FLY?

In order to describe the experience of plural anthropology more precisely, we can introduce the concept of local universality. If we will
be able to fully integrate the angelic, which predetermines us culturally and ethnically, if we will be able to experience the Angel, then
the problematic of collection, integration, and combination will be
removed. We will always be able to gather our Russian world, the German world, the Japanese world, and so on, according to the rules of the
Russian topos, the German topos, the Japanese and any other topos.
Even if we are talking about a little archaic tribe, this world, correctly
gathered, authentically awakened, the world in which the polar outburst
prevails and man exists authentically, will be a perfect, full-fledged, and
genuine universal, inasmuch as a step within, into the center, gives the
key to genuine universality and greatness. Raised to the angelic center,

the particular becomes whole. Even a single individual, if he enters the mode of authentic existence, can become a hologram of the entire people, as are the prince, genius, prophet, and high priest of the people and the shaman of the tribe. This center or pole is essentially the most important part of the people or tribe.

Anthropologists have observed that even in the smallest archaic society there are interregnums, "dark times" between rulers. This is a period when one shaman has died and another has not yet been initiated or born. Time without a shaman is a time of extreme danger. When there is no priest, king, holy ruler, or prophet, then the tribe, society, collective, or Empire is in a situation of complete defenselessness before all existential threats. The genius, poet, priest, or holy monarch embodies the people's sacrality, i.e., that which is most important in the people, the whole people. He is the personified spokesman of the inner angelic dimension, the center of the anthropological wheel. When this pole is lacking a civilization will disintegrate into dust, however massive it may be. Each minds his own business, but everything goes to pieces. That is how a gigantic political or ideological system based on a universal ideology can collapse momentarily. No artificial clamps can hold the rim of the wheel if the nave has been knocked out and the spokes removed. And at the same time, a small African, Australian, or Latin American tribe remains preserved over millennia, changing in nothing, always preserving its identity and fullness. So universality is not a quantitative, but a qualitative concept. A small collective can be universal, preserving its identity however long, while a huge imperial agglomerate can scatter in the winds in the blink of an eye. What is most important is not whether the collective is big or small, complex or simple. What is most important is its relation to authentic existence. Either people have a center (shaman, genius, prophet, holy ruler) or not. Because in certain circumstances, any manager, even the most "effective" one, can only ruin even the most stable system—if it is spiritually dead and its central place has been abandoned by the Angel. Everything human is supported by very delicate powers, by poet-visionaries, "philosophers with closed eyes," daydreamers.

Heidegger says that only a blind person can really see. So all prophets should be blind. It is impossible to think about something genuinely human while we are looking at what surrounds us. The pictures we contemplate are incompatible with thought. Only when all of that finally fades are we able to see not what we imagine but what really is. That is why Homer was blind, as were many prophets and seers, the creators of true visions.

Local universalism is a fully attainable, concrete, and at the same time unbelievably saturated goal. I think that the question of where the angels fly, that is, of how one local universalism correlates with another, how it resolves the problem of the Simurgh, how it moves in the direction of the Angel of Eurasia, is a very serious question, but it is not a question for us. It is a question for the Angels. So "where do the Angels fly" is a question mark, but a question mark that strictly tells us: "do not think to answer this question."

Translated by Michael Millerman

## NOTES

This chapter is excerpted from Alexander Dugin, *Martin Khaidegger. Poslednii Bog* (Moscow: *Akademicheskii Proiekt*, 2014). [Editor's note: I have corrected some minor errors in the Greek and German in the original text, as well as other minor errors that do not affect the sense.]

1. *Reshenie*, a word that can mean both "decision" and "resolution."

2. Eugen Fink, *Spiel als Weltsymbol* (Freiburg im Breisgau: Verlag Karl Alber, 2010).

3. *Instantsia*

4. Dugin, *Poslednii Bog*.

5. [Editor's note: Dugin summarizes a conversation he had with Friedrich-Wilhelm von Herrmann in Freiburg in January 2013. While Dugin puts this conversation in quotation marks, what he provides is largely a paraphrase of the conversation. I have taken the quotation marks out for that reason. There is a video recording of this conversation on YouTube: see ARCTUR, "Prof. Alexandre Dugin mit Prof. Friedrich-Wilhelm von Herrmann," January 31, 2013, https://www.youtube.com/watch?v=b93z2yPo4pA.]

6. *Polnomochie*.

7. Sergei Esenin. *Sobranie Sochinenii,* vol. 1 (Moscow: *Khudozhestvennaia Literatura*, 1966); S. Yesenin, "Goi you, Rus," trans. Lyudmila Purgina, http://www.poemhunter.com/poem/s-yesenin-goi-you-rus-translation-rus.

8. Glauco Giuliano, *Tempus Discretum. Henry Corbin all'Oriente dell'Occidente* (Travagliato and Brescia: Torre d'Ercole, 2012).

*Chapter 13*

# From *Being and Time* to the *Beiträge*

## Vladimir Bibikhin

The final essay, first published in the journal *Voprosy literatury* ["Literary Questions"] no. 4 (2005), was included as an appendix to the book *Early Heidegger* (Moscow: Saint Thomas Press, 2009).

1. When Hannah Arendt visited Heidegger in Freiburg after the war, she was disturbed that his house was filled with manuscripts, tens of thousands of pages lying around in only one copy, and Elfride Petry did nothing at all to assist in preserving them; she did not even concern herself with typing them up. Only a few such intimates knew that there were so many papers, however. Just a bit later began the legends. Another child of Heidegger who wrote a book on him, Karl Löwith, noted condemningly in the 1950s that Heidegger had reached an impasse because of his political mistake: Of all the lectures on Nietzsche, five or six lecture courses given before and during the war, only one remained, the little brochure, "Nietzsche's Phrase 'God is Dead.'"

But not long afterwards, in 1960, the large two-volume *Nietzsche*[1] appeared that is being readied for publication now in St. Petersburg. Right after Heidegger's death, lecture courses on Hölderlin and Nietzsche from before and during the war came out—this is a large corpus of work. In 1989 volume 65, from Division III, "Unpublished Works," of the *Gesamtausgabe* came out unexpectedly, at 521 pages (1936–1938). This book was immediately referred to as Heidegger's second major work. It has been translated into Russian and publishers are being sought. It is called *Beiträge zur Philosophie (Vom*

*Ereignis) [Contributions to Philosophy (of the Event)]*. We shall not rush to translate the title. This is not a lecture course, but a book Heidegger wrote clandestinely[2] when it became clear that, having resigned from the rectorate two years earlier, he would be able neither to announce such a course nor publish such a book.

In 1997, the book called *Besinnung [Mindfulness]* came out in the same Division III of the GA, i.e., outside of the lecture courses, also unexpectedly for many. The book was written—Heidegger did not use a typewriter—also clandestinely in 1938–1939.

Still more. In 1998 the unpublished work, *The History of Beyng* (des Seyns), a manuscript from 1938–1940, appears as volume 69 of the GA.

In 1999 *Metaphysics and Nihilism* comes out, in the same Division III, written in 1938–1939.

In 2004 volume 70 from Division III, "On the Beginning," written clandestinely, is expected—or has it already come out?—it is 1941. Both of Heidegger's sons would soon be enlisted in the army and sent to the Eastern Front where they would fall into the hands of the Russians.

1941–1942: Heidegger continues to give lectures, but, aside from them, he also writes clandestinely one more book whose name even experts learn of with surprise: "The Event"; not to be confused with "Of the Event," which Friedrich-Wilhelm von Herrmann is still preparing for volume 71 of the GA.

1944: Heidegger is released from teaching, as a professor not useful to the Reich, and sent to dig ditches; either then or during the time of his last lectures he writes "The Paths of the Beginning" which is also being edited now by von Herrmann as volume 72 of the GA.

The international [scholarly] community is troubled. The Forum international d'Évora pour la traduction des oeuvres de Martin Heidegger organizes international conferences and translation workshops. The first of seven books, written clandestinely, is already in English and Polish; the Russian has been mentioned above; the French, Italian, Japanese and Portuguese are under way. A colloquium for the Forum in Lausanne at the end of May 2004 was called: "The Second Principal Work by Martin Heidegger: *Beiträge zur Philosophie (Vom Ereignis).* Interpretation and translation."

In his talk at the colloquium, "How I translate *Beiträge*," François Fédier drew attention to the fact that this word, commonly used in academic work (in Russian a *contribution* or simply *On the problem . . .*), exists in a letter by Hölderlin to his friend Ebel from 10.1.1797:

I believe in the coming revolution in attitudes and ways of imagining that will make all that was hitherto blush with shame. And Germany is perhaps capable of contributing a great deal to it.[3]

The letter, unknown up until that time, was first published in the journal *Euphorion* in 1933. While considering a name for his book over a three-year period, Heidegger could not have failed to recall Hölderlin's phrase. Since the *Beiträge* obviously do not deal with the personal contribution of Professor Heidegger to philosophy, Fédier suggests that we read both parts of the title together: *Contributions to the Philosophy of the Event*. The entire significance of the title turns on the final word, important for Heidegger; in his own copy of *The Letter on Humanism*, addressed to Jean Beaufret, there is the marginal note: "After 1936, Ereignis is the word that directs my thinking." The simple translation for Ereignis is *event*. Jean Beaufret sometimes used the word éclaire, *lightning, flash, insight*. Fédier now suggests avenance, not attested in French dictionaries but easily grasped. It is related to événement (évènment) *event*, close to the triumphant avènment *advent* (in the mass), *accession* (to the throne), *beginning* (of a new era) and looks like the noun derived from avenant, *pleasant, charming*, and *fitting, appropriate*. Fédier's goal is roughly to show in what way one has to seek out Ereignis; he emphasizes that the Heidegger of this period does not occupy a position, he is all movement.

For Heidegger's thought is not an event if only because he cannot rashly claim that it is the unique Event. It [his thought—JL] is fitting because it is in harmony with the ceaseless rhythm of beginning. And it is such, since it comes to emergence, i.e., imposes itself thanks to the soft strength of its advent.[4]

2. *Being and Time* (1926)[5] does not constitute a sharp break with what Heidegger had done before. Even the rustic romanticism of the prose and poetry of the young Heidegger does not prevent our attributing to them the fundamental concepts and structure of this book. The effect of imposition without a gap occurs here thanks to the fact, frequently mentioned by Heidegger himself, that *Being and Time* belongs to the philosophical tradition and its language. Conversely, the effect of congruence is not achieved and the mutual imbrication of structures is not possible between *Being and Time* and *The Contributions to Philosophy*

*of the Event*. The issue concerns introducing into philosophy what has not gained a footing in its history. The theme of another beginning for thought reveals itself. "The past means nothing, the beginning is everything," says Heidegger in his lecture course, *The Fundamental Problems of Philosophy* from the winter semester of 1937–1938,[6] referring to the fact that what has been left out, the unsaid and unwritten at the classical beginning of thought—above all, the richly meaningful unthought of the Greeks in their term, *alētheia*—is more important than what is written and known; and he sets us the task of figuring out what has *not* been done.

The philosophy of the *Beiträge* dispenses with the features of method. Moreover, Heidegger insists that to the extent philosophy still remains paraphrase, remembrance of what has hitherto been thought and the structures developed to that end, it has missed itself. The entrance into the rut of an accessible general conceptuality, when it has become possible for each to teach philosophy to each, has become the end of philosophy. It has proved to be sufficient for the collapse of philosophy that the original essence of truth, the unconcealed, has been simplified into correctness. In *Being and Time* the philosophy of the lecture room is presupposed and sharply felt; in the *Beiträge* it turns out to be worse than problematic: a dead end. Heidegger steps onto an untrodden path.

Attention to the corpus of Heidegger's books, written clandestinely during the war years, is understandable given the general sense of philosophical decline over the last decade. The necessity for a new beginning now seems clearer than 60 years ago. But the theme of another beginning, developed in the *Beiträge* and later, cannot be grasped by conventional research approaches. The corpus of works for 1936–1944 outside the lecture courses is difficult to connect to any fields of thought. The rubrics, phenomenology, fundamental ontology, do not apply to them. The rubric of existential analytics—we are beginning to see now what a transformation in it is taking place. On the other hand, Heidegger speaks of God, the last God, the coming God, the godding (*bozhest-vovanie*) of the gods, but it is clear that there is no hope of applying to any of this the accepted theological categories. Announcing the impossibility of teaching, [or] the transmission of philosophical thought, the learning of another beginning, Heidegger all the more decisively insists on the school of founding, discipline, insistence, thoroughness; the school coincides now with the proper matter of philosophy.

Let us consider several details of the change that occurred. *Being and Time* has a transparent structure, which makes it suitable for explanations, commentaries, polemics and affords a lot of possibility for schematization, re-ordering, systematization, even the development of the material; imitations of this book are easy, and there are many of them. A detailed division into sections separates the moments of methodological preparation from the analysis, its step-by-step progress; the transition from the analysis of the whole of beings (the world) to the whole of existence (time) forms a clear border. To the contrary, a measured order is totally absent in the *Beiträge*. The same rubrics repeat themselves frequently in the various parts of its division into chapters. The basic division (1. Look ahead, 2. Response, 3. Accompaniment, 4. The Leap, 5. The Grounding, 6. The Future Ones, 7. The Last God, 8. Being) does not permit elucidation of the organizing structure. The topics of the new Heideggerian thought demand departure from a system of conceptual coordinates, forbidding the projection of their movements into measured space. Concepts now illuminate themselves (flash) with the spreading out of the all-defining event, Ereignis, which from its essential novelty excludes system, no matter how one may seek to classify it. All is ruled by the absolute first beginning. The three principal aspects of Ereignis, namely illumination (the genuine etymology, from the eye [*das Auge*]), the return to one's own (the folk etymology through one's own [*das Eigene*]), and fullness (the completeness of the event) also do not form a structure in the sense of a Hegelian triad; this is a trinity of similar things because the revelation of what is proper to one's self is both illumination and completeness.

At the same time the difference between the style of the *Beiträge* and that of *Being and Time* allows us to see the full dimension of the earlier work. The expressions, *existential analysis, analysis of being-there (vot-bytie), presence* or, as I sometimes translate it in the current essay, here-and-now-being, *die existentiale Analytik des Daseins, Analytik des Daseins,* are common coin. They are understood unequivocally: apparently what is complex undergoes analysis. Dasein, by general consent, possesses a structure. Presence[7] is above all *in-der-Welt-sein*, being-in-the-world; it is always *Mitsein*, being with others (if Levinas did not notice this, not all readers bypassed paragraphs 25–27 of *Being and Time*); furthermore, Dasein is care, *die Sorge*, and, as such, literally churns out of itself the most complex structures, throwing itself into the ready-to-hand and the present-at-hand, into what it chooses to squander itself; analysis complicates. From this perspective, is a non-analytic approach to Dasein possible?

We shall ask, however: Does Dasein really have a structure?

Keeping with *Being and Time*: in the text of this very same book we find Dasein without structure such that everything concerned with the analytic of Dasein pertains only to its fall (*Verfall*) in which Dasein ceases to be itself. Taken by itself presence is not composite, just as the soul is absolutely simple in all classical thought. The analytic of presence itself is, strictly speaking, impossible.

> Anxiety (*uzhas*), as one of presence's existential possibilities together with the presence that discloses itself in it, provides the phenomenal basis for explicitly grasping presence's primordial totality of Being.[8]

> . . . that entities within-the-world are not "relevant" at all. Nothing which is ready-to-hand or present-at-hand within the world functions as that before which anxiety is anxious. The totality of involvements of the ready-to-hand and the present-at-hand disclosed within the world as such is of no consequence; it collapses into itself. The world has the character of complete insignificance.[9]

> The complete insignificance which makes itself known in the *nothing* and *nowhere* [Bibikhin's emphasis—JL], does not signify the absence of the world, but tells us that innerworldly beings are of so little relevance in themselves that on the basis of this *insignificance* of what is innerworldly, only the world itself in its worldhood obtrudes.[10]

For total presence, the world does not become a whole on account of simplification down to one part, but on account of liberation from the structure imposed upon it by the interpretive net as it is unpacked (a felicitous term of V. V. Nalimov).

Being seized by anxiety unlocks originally and directly the world as world. One does not initially—say, through reflection—turn away from innerworldly beings and come to think only the world, before which anxiety then arises, but only first via anxiety as a disposition that will open up the *world as world*. This does not mean, however, that one thinks the worldhood of the world.

One fully ceases to think even Dasein, which becomes pure possibility.

> In presence anxiety reveals *being* in its fullest capacity to be, i.e., as *freed* for the freedom of the selection and choice of itself. Anxiety puts presence in front of its *being freed for* (propensio in . . .) what is proper to its being as a possibility, that it always already is.[11]

What is known as the analytic of presence applies only to public presence. In its essence presence is pure possibility, or, turning to the language of the *Beiträge*, the pure beginning before it gets squeezed into some sort of traditional pattern.

The analytic of original presence is impossible because of its simplicity, and also because at the level of existence presence is invisible.

> . . . in factical anxiety uncanniness is [not always] understood. The everyday manner by which presence understands its *not-at-home–ness* is a falling turning away, "extinguishing" this not-at-home-ness. Yet the everydayness of this flight shows phenomenally that anxiety belongs to the essential structure of presence's being-in-the-world as an existential that is never superfluous but *essential* in itself as a mode of presence's facticity, i.e., its disposition. The calming and assimilative being-in-the-world is a mode of the uncanniness of presence, not the other way round. *Not-at-home-ness must be grasped existentially-ontologically as a more fundamental phenomenon.*[12]

Ek-sistence is stepping out of oneself, and not essentially if it occurs either as presence's falling down (into the irresponsibility of being outside history) or up (in an elevated image of thought). Where Dasein has fallen out of itself, it is no longer present itself, it is unobservable and cannot be described. Heidegger is not a philosopher of existence because he is preoccupied with the essence of presence; the analysis of existence in *Being and Time* is merely an excursus; more important is that until the fall of presence it takes place not in stepping out from itself but in its staying in, *Innestehen*. The ontological difference between the fall into the being of beings (entities) and the focus on being, which Heidegger writes as *Seyn*, constitutes his entire philosophy. Falling for Dasein is more natural than walking a tightrope. The acrobat has developed as complete a discrimination as he can so that he might walk on the tightrope without falling. Even if only observing, we involuntarily participate in his act, in any case we empathize.

At the very beginning of the *Beiträge*, while describing the name of the book, Heidegger speaks of the difficult transition from metaphysics to eventful (*seynsgeschichtliches* ["being-historical"—JL]) thought. One may speak still only of an attempt. If the attempt succeeds, it cannot resemble "research" in the previous manner.

> The thinking to come is a *path* of thought, on which the hitherto altogether concealed realm of the essential occurrence of beyng is traversed and so is first cleared and attained in its most proper character as an event.[13]

To wish even to write a book so that the transition from metaphysics to thought might take place in it will not succeed. For this it is necessary that the essence of Being (*Seyns*) has taken hold of thought and unsettled it. Such unsettling (*Erzitterung*) liberates the power of the hidden mildness, the godding (*obozhestvlenie*) of the god of gods, from where—from the soft conciliatory nearness to the rising divinity—originates the hint for here-and-now being (*Da-sein*), pointing towards Being; it originates the founding of the truth of being. The present is not scheduled.

Reading *Being and Time* in its full dimension, each moment in the development of existence may be considered as the projection of the original simplicity of presence onto the variety of things (*veshchnoe mnozhestvo*). Despite Heidegger's detailed explanations of the preposition "in," the term, "being-in-the-world," especially in translation, sounds to many like the introduction of the one into the other. In light of the absolute simplicity of presence we understand with geometric clarity that it has no parts to distribute into something different; let us recall the classical point, which cannot touch any other point due to its simplicity, nor enter into it, nor create space, such that the point, strictly speaking, is a singular whole. The relation of presence to the world in which it is may be only one of identity. The existential das Man (people) has to be grasped as an aspect of this original "in," i.e. by taking into account the inseparability of the fall of presence from the phenomenon of das Man. The fall loses its negative moral sense and comes together with that of thrownness (*Geworfenheit*), which constitutes the essence of presence (*Dasein*) in that beginning where it has not yet entered into explained space and, accordingly, is unable not to search for directions. The theme of one's ownmost (*Eigentliches*) permeating *Being and Time*, that gave Theodor Adorno cause to mock the "Jargon of Immediacy" (*Jargon der Eigentlichkeit*), will turn out to be a step towards the thinking of the event as appropriation (*Er-eignis*) via the appearance of the god of gods in its intimate depth (*Innerlichkeit*).

Most of all, the transition from *Being and Time* to the other beginning is prepared by the concept of the moment (*Augenblick*) developed in the second part of this book. It seems that the human being, having fallen into the being of beings, has stretched itself or, as Heidegger says in one of his essays, has stretched its legs out into space once and for all. What is spatially ready-to-hand in the world (para. 22), the explanation spread out in time (para. 32), disappears in the reference and sign given in time and space (para. 17). But, after this at first glance seemingly irreversible dispersion, presence returns to its simplicity thanks to resoluteness, which steps beyond the framework of beings (para. 62). The flow of time unlocks such a thing as the moment. Just as presence, originally simple, spreads out into ek-sistence, so do the past, the present, the future turn out to be merely ek-stases of time, doubles based on the moment. In the moment time reveals its face; the essence of the past turns out to be what has become, that of the present what is immediate, that of the future what is to come. What has become is present in the moment to no lesser degree than the present (the immediate); the one and the other, what has become and what is, are linked in the present that will not be tomorrow, but already is in this flowing moment. The moment in all of what has become and what is aims toward the future.

The moment, achieved in its simple collectedness, becomes the place of the other beginning. Conversely, the history of existence, having fallen into time, when what has become fades into the infinite past [and] the present has dissipated in the ungraspable immediate moment; and yet the present, even if completed and drowned in the indeterminacy of the future may stretch out for a long time.

Here *we* must grasp the beginning of European thought and consider what has been achieved and not achieved by it because *we* stand at the end—at the end of this beginning. And this means: we stand before *a decision between this end* and its decay which may last for centuries more—*and the other beginning*, which may be merely a moment, the preparation for which demands, however, a patience which "optimists" and "pessimists" alike do not yet possess.[14]

3. We are going to clarify the distinction between metrics and topics (our terms). The former places what it considers in a system of coordinates. The latter, on which we are focusing, is not distributed within a ready-made space, but is articulated fundamentally such that all draws from it in the final account. Like the tree Schopenhauer observes, it ceases to be "one of" and nests within itself the whole world. The trajectory of historical movement, beginning in antiquity, is approaching its end. From whence it does not follow that the other trajectory begins by itself. The task of our historical being is unknown, and the only thing accessible to us is to prepare for the thought that will open it; we are its *poets*, seekers.[15] Philosophy now is already itself *another*; it does not move within a system of coordinates, but disperses their system. To dispense with metrics is difficult. It demands a leap into what is not yet. Heidegger opens up in the *Beiträge* the university of presence or, what is the same, the university of the mood (disposition). On the one hand, the unthinkable distance of the last God sets the parameters of this mood, while, on the other hand, it is the mysterious nearness of what is far. Belief (*Glaube*) opens up extreme distance and sees that nothing is closer to this distance than human beings. Fright, silence, shame (the disgrace of disagreement regarding the mystery)—these are the lessons of the new school.[16] In antiquity with its attitude towards the harmony of body and soul, the main things necessary for duty in the polis, with its opposition between the free minority and the despotic masses, were benevolence, fairness and courage. For our time it is more important to perceive the need of Being.

This time is closed to the needs of humanity, tied up in a variety of relations with beings and only with them. A situation has taken shape where nothing satisfies anyone. The necessity immediately to take measures against this lack leaves no room for the need of another, forgotten kind. Natural resources are being exhausted catastrophically. Whoever now will dare to say that the primary need is not to feed the people; it is not for the philosopher to open people's eyes to the crude but irrefutable truth: One is what one eats (*Man ist, was man ißt*)?

Who are we? Are we these people absorbed in their needs? Or are we simply the "human being" as such? The human being exists historically only, and when she does not participate in history then it belongs to her privatively. Are we then a people? The question—What is a people?—is more difficult than—Who are we? In searching for who we are, we need not go far. The question invites us to return (*die Kehre*) to ourselves. We cannot answer: "We are entrepreneurs, workers, watchmen, soldiers, merchants."[17] In my daily concerns I threw myself into the mastery of beings (*sushchim*); to think about oneself demands something else—what matters is Being. When in relation to some successful person or organized people one hears confident voices regarding complete self-realization, one has to understand them as a kind of self-assurance. This is, however, different from thinking about oneself. The human being—here the task is essentially different from some sort of successful functioning. My entire essence tells nothing about itself and cannot be described. To the question—Who are we?—there is no answer outside of obtaining what is my own, Er-eignis, the return to ourselves as that which is, i.e., as all. Whoever gives herself to thinking of this kind inevitably runs up against (52) all broadly developed forms of activity that arrange, protect and satisfy needs.[18] Philosophy will never be immediately understood; it will always meet with resistance no matter what the case, and it is better that philosophy not count on being understood—cold indifference is worse.

Try, however, not to ask this uncomfortable question—Who are we? Who will protect us from the ready-made knowledge that we are body, soul, and spirit and must live on these levels for our whole lives? What the body, the soul, and the spirit are will be explained to us. A thousand-year-old tradition will tell us what personality, genius, culture, people, and the world are. These are answers hallowed and accepted for centuries, and often ignorance of the correct answers to these questions gets punished. Heidegger refers to the answers that made the most noise in his own time: the people and race; Marxism. Both answers aimed at mastery over the world. Marxism has no relation to Judaism nor to Russianness; Russianness is barely touched by ideological infection; "If anywhere there lies dormant an undeveloped spirituality it is in the Russian people." Bolshevism is a Western, European possibility: the uprising of the masses, industry, technology, the extinction of the peasantry, the rule of rationalism as a general leveling.[19]

Terrible decisions, terrible answers. More terrible still is that they frighten our contemporaries less than the matter of thinking about ourselves. In the foregoing answers there is at least the usual landmarks, but in the latter there are none. And yet we must come to ourselves; the path to salvation, i.e., to the justification of the West leads only through the question—Who are we?

Another question—Who are the gods?—is connected with this one. The only believers are those who ask about who we are. Here Heidegger does not have just any confession in mind, but rather the "essence of faith, understood as the essence of truth."[20] The accepted way is to consider the truth a matter of knowledge but not faith; the place of faith is where knowledge cannot reach. For example, I believe in the message but I cannot convince myself of its truth. Knowledge drops the message and belief catches it. But how is knowledge of the truth of being possible? It is a clearing (Lichtung: one may think of a glade in the forest, of space on a stage, of lifting the anchor) where Being reveals itself in its essence as a conserving concealing of itself, Sichverbergen. In the clearing being is only visible as unfathomable. How to *know* such a truth? Only by sticking to it as unfathomable. To view the mystery in the truth is to believe. One may of course decide that being is merely a generalized concept of what exists, that there is no unfathomable being, no mystery for which no one has an answer. Heidegger's answer rests on picking up the future task in the question itself. Asking questions is our faith. By ceasing to hold oneself on the level defined by the parameters of depth, the abyss, the mystery [and] freedom, we lose faith.

> *Questioners* of this sort are the original and genuine believers, i.e., those who with absolute seriousness seek truth itself and not only what is true; those capable of deciding whether the essence of truth will be realized or whether this realization will seize us who know, believe, act, create, in short, who are historical.[21]

The original faith is more difficult than religious faith, which provides something to lean on: the sacred book, the icon, the bread which one takes in one's hand and eats, becoming divine by grace, if not by nature. The courage to stand without ground is not necessary for religious belief. For those who question—Who are *we*?—there is no ground other than the certainty of the mystery since "questioning is the direct realization of being and knows by experience the *inevitability* (*Notwendigkeit*) of the unfathomable."[22]

Who is the God of this faith? The latter relies on the unavoidability of the abyss, feels that we will find ourselves only in the abyss, and is certain that human beings will be capable of these depths; this is how far human freedom stretches—and here the Russian word (*svoboda*) is better than the German since it reminds us of what is ours (*svoë*).

Whoever is capable of this distance (*razmakh*) will begin to find God inadequate. This takes place when a human being is totally seized by what seizes her spirit; what seizes deeper and spiritually as well; seized by freedom and its unfathomable mystery. When she becomes capable of the unfathomable depths, God begins to be inadequate—not as a ground in the emptiness but in the sense that God can no longer be anywhere than in this *beyond-the-border*. Where the human being persists in questioning the abyss, there must be God as well; it suffices for belief to know that there can be no more worthy place for God.

Does this mean that human beings are equal to God? The un-measured and immeasurable aspect of the strange meeting place with Him preclude comparisons. The place of the event and the abyss of freedom and the depth of one's own are all extreme; the place of the meeting is not scheduled and drowns in deep silence. On the other hand, both the meeting and the higher being God are the beginning of speech, the beginning of the world.

From this still pale portrait of the landscape in which we find ourselves, it is clear that God is called the last not in temporal order but in depth. He is the last to the degree by which the human being is seized by her ownmost and nearest and at the same time he is the last as the farthest left to us in terms of the range of our persistence and perseverance. He is the last also because he cannot be overstepped; it is impossible to speak about him as long as he does not resolve our silence. Faith says that, seized in the extreme, human beings must be capable of such a depth when the last God passes by in silence, where no voices are audible, in immeasurable depth. Only by being absorbed there, in untouched silence, presence first finds its genuine voice, at first the voice of silence, the foundation of speech. When it begins to speak on this basis, it is not possible to tell whether the human being adequate to God is speaking or the God that has become inadequate for human beings. The unlimitedness of freedom suggests the one's own leans toward God. A unique extremity is demanded of human beings, so that they are adequate to the last God, and of ungrounded freedom so that God might settle into it.

The question—Who are we?—is the other side of the question—Who are the gods?—but not so that some sort of leveling takes place between the former and the latter. Something else takes place, questions fold one upon another, persistently turn to us and do not suggest answers; on the contrary, they are more likely to exclude them because, genuinely understood, they call us back from every ready-made discourse to a foundational discourse in the silence of the early quiet.

The historical human being needs nothing more than such a return. The word *need*[23] sounds negative, forcing one to think about deficiencies, even about evil. Prosperity is secured by an uninterrupted flow of useful things in addition to what is already to some degree accessible and demands now at the very least maintenance of the earlier level. Progress is concerned with increasing well-being. A clear and final (*bez budushchego*) perspective opens up; all efforts are directed toward *still* more than what already is.[24] And if human beings do not belong to what already is? What if our essence consists in what is not yet and never was? Shall we hasten to protect with all our strength the state we have already attained? No. We refer, then, to need as what compels us to explore and question. It will lead us. We will be upset if, having slept deeply, we wake up once without need. We will not expect new achievements from progress that will satisfy our existential (*bytiinuiu*) need; the contrary is more likely, need will be put aside or it will be forcibly forgotten in well-being. Existential need demands from us that we become different people. It leads us to the strange and unknown. One will rarely be ashamed to speak of natural needs. The shame mentioned above as fright-silence-shame will give barely a reason to speak of existential need. I do not admit that I need something else than all others in our general need because I fear disrupting with my discourse what at the moment I can still only be silent about.

Between need and need there is no peaceful coexistence. Having calmed one need, it will not do leisurely to take on another. For Alexander of Macedon (our example), while standing above Diogenes and his barrel, the crying need of the latter was obvious; Alexander could have lightly answered with agreement Diogenes' completely reasonable request about aid for continuing his philosophical studies, but he heard the request differently.

Fright, silence, shame, while preventing us from speaking about existential need, do not go together well with servility, do not prevent Heidegger from saying that the pursuit of things happens because of the abandonment of being; they do not prevent our diagnosing a limited degree of abandonment, while the masses, feverishly engaged in the enormous task of giving order to themselves, are not able to realize their hidden desire for self-extermination. Existential need takes upon itself the audacity of doubt that all generally cultural activity is still necessary and dares to say that there is no genuine necessity in that activity, that we have calmed ourselves too fully inside of the mechanism of culture and that we are inadequate not only for being but for any genuine cultural matter as well. Between need and need there is so little agreement that to give oneself over to the experience of silence looks like a *sacrifice* amid the general forgetting of being.[25]

The abandonment by being has made it so that all around we see only objects. Behind them need spreads like a shadow because there are too many of them, like distances that need to be shortened, or they are too small, like plots of land that need to be widened. Useless objects that we need to get rid of become a need too. All turns on the face of need. When the organized masses manage things and give order to them, the need is to maintain system—it will often be a cultural machine as well. The certainty that a general orderliness is possible as a ground for science and technology demands that beforehand the need is made plain so that we may have before our eyes an open field of operation; in this manner certainty enters into the general course of need. As to the question—Who are we?—there is no clearing (*prosvet*) left: faced with needs we are the ones dealing with them. The one focused on the matter simply does not need to question about who he is taking himself to be. We who are questioning—Who are we?—will be only a hindrance. We will be asked to report about what we are doing, to explain which economic needs of the people we are meeting with our activity.

Where indubitable knowledge about what is correct directs every action and inaction what is the point of asking the question about the essence of truth (the unconcealed)?

And where this knowledge about what is correct applies to actions, who would want to appear ridiculous by asking useless questions about some essence?

The heedlessness [of the human masses existing amid the variety of their avowed needs] occurs by obscuring the essence of truth as the foundation of presence in *being* and the creation of *historical being*.

Resources do not suffice, nor does God, the *need* for things (*sushchie*) and the *need* for being—Why are they generally referred to by the same word? Are they in the end one and the same, only hidden in the one case and open in the other? The essence of the truth (*istina*) is at once revealing and concealing?

4. The German word *Wahrheit* is etymologically linked with the important idea, to this day still current in the Anglo-Saxon world, of

certainty and solemn promise. In other languages, the branches of the same root are Lat. *verus* and Russian *vera* ["belief"—JL]. Since religion was understood as law, the Church Slavic *vera* had a powerful legal meaning; it was preserved in the adjective "true" in the sense of "reliable." A person who blindly believed everything was called an "alawaari" in old German; nowadays this words means silly or *stupid*. The development of this meaning is exemplarily that of the French chrétien fixed in mountain dialects of the eighteenth century as chrétin. When we in Russian say *correct, correctly said, how would it be possible to approach more correctly* [*verno, verno skazano, kak by tut bylo vernee postupit'*], we are closer to German Wahrheit than when we say *istina* or *pravda*.[26] All three Russian words illuminate sides of Wahrheit; each in its own way indicates that the issue concerns something that is difficult to attain. Clearest of all, the barrier surrounding the truth is perceptible in the Greek, *alētheia*; the meaning of truth is created here by the addition of the privative particle to the root with the meaning of *forgetting, slipping away, hiding, the unnoticed, a hole in memory, a hole in consciousness*. Alētheia is an ancient word; with a different accent it is often applied in Homer to speech, to an utterance and means something like *I say without dissimulation*, as if the first possibility for everything said is to lie. Heidegger does not understand how the Greeks, after a thousand years or more of using this word, could not have thought of its depth.

The verb, *lanthanō* means to slip one's attention, *to be forgotten*, often with the evil sense of to hide, to deceive, to do everything so that no one will notice. The most notable feature of this Greek word is that it does not draw a distinction between what I did not notice or what I tried to do without being noticed. If we reflect upon it, I am not able really to hide something from others that I do not hide from myself. *Lanthonō poioun ti*—in equal measure I do not myself notice what I am doing and that I do something unnoticed. The person wanted to give something to another, but *elathe auton mē dounai*, did not himself notice that he gave nothing; he gave nothing by accident. In the middle voice the word means *to forget*; and A. F. Losev heard alētheia as what one must not forget. True, for this idea Greek uses another syntax with the alpha privative.

No matter what the explanation, a reminder about the secret, the hidden, what has slipped our attention, the collapse into oblivion, remains in the undisputed Greek name for truth.

The truth of being is the event in which and as which its essence melts, revealing itself, its realization. And it [the event] is at once the realization of the truth as such. In the turning point of the event the realization of the truth is at once also the truth of the realization. And this convertibility itself belongs to being as such.[27]

In what way do we get information of a similar kind from Heidegger's text? The answer is harsh: information will not be demanded of us at all. The event is not such a thing as one might devise through thought. It is not thinkable. We are not concerned with a system of views. Why then a clearing in the woods, the creation of clarity around a mystery, a lifted anchor, releasing a boat into the water, why Lichtung? Again the harsh answer: What does your—Why?—stand on? What ground does it have? May it have another ground than in the truth? But the truth is the experience of the mystery and the clarification of it as such, i.e., above all, and in the final account, the revealing of the mystery as inevitable, as the ultimate need.

Is the realization of being really only its becoming overgrown (encrusted [*obrastanie*]), being surrounded by beings? Is this not rather the failure of being? Such a realization of being, when it first emerges as itself in distinction to beings, is unusual for metaphysics; in the best case, when metaphysics does not consider being as an abstraction from beings, it returns to ancient *phusis*, giving birth to nature, the source of beings. Beings here remain the only ground on and from which construction begins.

Let us attempt to overthrow, indeed, simply crumple up this picture so comforting for metaphysics. All that Heidegger thought through up to this time, especially in *Being and Time* comes into play here. There is no being developed before us by nature, God or being, such that we determine ourselves by means of it. We have no more freedom to stretch our hand out to beings than the roots of a tree do to stick out of the earth. From the beginning of our species (*rodovogo*) and personal existence we have grown with all our roots in the earth in a tenacity that we do not even suspect. In distinction to trees we are introduced into a world of which we know no more than we do of the earth. Sobering up as we awake, we see little for ourselves here and then no more freedom of movement than roots have in the earth. We are thrown into what has taken form before and without us. Yet none other than the force of the energy of thrownness itself throws us into what we have been thrown into. But do we really throw ourselves into beings, things, objects because all these finished things already are? Who has told us that? We have been taught that they are and are called metaphysics, religion, politics, political journalism. Does common sense not speak in the same way? And yet it does not. Common sense is closer to disbelief in explanations of the world and meditations concerning "the many mysteries that surround us." The truth that we are thrown is hidden above all by discussions (*soobshcheniami*) about it.

In the collision of civilizing narratives (*raspisanii*), where one proclaims its truth or where the truth is given over to various opinions, will the philosophy of the other beginning advance yet another explanation? No. It speaks of the ground which it seeks, returning from any given account of beings to recall that we, as ones who are thrown, do not remember when we knew nothing at all. Thrown into the strange, the enigmatic—we are ourselves the enigma. It is not necessary to think that in the philosophy of the other beginning as in existentialism one expects of human beings decisions made in the void; whoever has thought that has missed what is closest. We are thrown and thus brought out into an exclusive relation to everything. To hold to the uniqueness of our position, to be able to maintain ourselves in its indeterminateness without rushing to conclusions, is to look mystery in the face. Beings, metaphysics assures us, are, i.e., they are in some sense finished. On the contrary, Being is always only realizing itself. It emerges in the event, which is always momentary and, in a flash, creates sites, *Stätte*, where God passes by and once again evades us.[28] Is a ground for beings then possible if the clarity of the mystery is sought not in order to shroud it but to open its mysteriousness? No—it is only about the realization itself, the creation of sites that are never outside the mystery. The earlier understanding of being: a surplus of beings, phusis. The other beginning prepares the realization of being itself in the event.

How may people who have grown roots in the earth participate in the event? By not leaving their situation and by accepting it completely. The region to which they throw themselves is the very same one in which they are thrown—it is the closest and narrowest.[29] By not choosing what to throw itself into, pure presence lifts up all its thrownness and carries it. Naked acceptance becomes its entire task. Standing in the midst (*Inmitten*) of what may now be called beings gives it the chance, provided it does not avoid its rootedness, to become a clearing (*Lichtung*) of this dense environment. The latter lets go its anchor, becoming groundless (*vzveshivaet'sa v bezopornosti*) and thereby shows its truth. The mystery is not outside of beings, understood as what we are thrown into; in the clearing of the event beings return from their obviousness · (*ob'iasnennost'*). A step is made not to the side because of crowding, into the position of the observer, but into the weight [of things]. In the most extreme lack of security is revealed the range of human freedom when the human being is capable of finding in the abyss a ground. To drown in the midst of beings and to be the place of the clearing there, returns beings to their unfathomable depth and serves as a place for the mystery.

> The truth is [. . .] the unfathomable center that trembles in the passing by of the last God and in this way becomes the remote ground for the founding of the presence that creates.[30]

Is thought really at work here? No. Here the site where human being can begin first reveals itself. What, the one consisting of body, soul, spirit? We do not yet know this. We know only that without being seized by freedom (we may understand Ereignis through *freedom* as the return to what is ours) the truth will not reveal itself. It is not that thought does not suffice but that what concerns us is the early space where no one had yet established what thought was. "One cannot force freedom through the pressure of logical thought, Ereignis ist nicht denkmäßig zu erzwingen."[31] You cannot force the event in thought, or, more accurately, so: All thought, beginning with its own possibility, has given over responsibility for itself to the groundless *in the midst of.* It has no points of reference from within itself.

While writing "Ereignis" Heidegger read Hölderlin and could not have avoided thinking about the absolute impossibility for the poet to protect himself with the divine dictation, *Dichten,* under which he wrote. The impotence of the poet and the philosopher are identical here. The nearby heights of poetry seem very close.

Being is concealed, hides itself, guards itself in its inaccessibility. The metaphysical tradition in the course of the whole European philosophical school leans toward a positive understanding of truth (alētheia), seeking in it an approach to the mystery. The constant companion of philosophy, theology, on the contrary, located itself in a negative understanding of divine truth, the ungraspable, unapproachable, unnameable. But here it turns out, however, that theology knows an enormous amount about what is referred to as the ungraspable, moreover it knows this with conclusive dogmatic certainty. That there is an argument inside the mystery, indeed, that the mystery is a struggle, a battle, der Streit in the sense of Heraclitean war—this elicits at first dismay on the part of the theologian, then he recalls his dogma and with a condescending smile corrects us: well, let us assume; the invisible war, the one between the Lord and Satan. Is God not the All-Ruling, pantocrator? Is this war then not genuine, an appearance, a theatrical representation of war?—here the honest theologian may only answer that we have touched on a question that has been discussed for millennia and has not yet been resolved. He will send us off to a library of books on this theme, after the reading of which the same questions will remain with us. For this reason theologians do not correct a leaning to the optimistic understanding of alētheia. It [alētheia] has lost its alpha privative; more accurately, the philosophical school has turned the inaccessibility of the truth into a field for thought.

> The matter does not come to the question about *unconcealment* (of the mystery) and the concealing of its genesis and ground [. . .] aletheia loses [. . .] much of its original depth and groundlessness.[32]

Civilization is carried away with organization (*Machenschaft*). It was able to do a lot. Now almost everything appears to be done. Rational thought (representation) restlessly develops its possibilities in order to impose itself on the last remaining islets of non-rationalized being. It seems it lifts itself by that very fact above itself, but in fact it plants itself under the level from which it was originally seized by a direct apprehension of things as a whole.

> Thus, degrading itself, reason precisely on that account reaches an apparent mastery (on the basis of self-humiliation). This apparent mastery must someday collapse, and the coming centuries will realize this collapse, but inevitably with the constant increase of "rationality" as the "principle" of general organization.[33]

Alternate projects of civilization again propose organization, [though] more revolutionary and radical. An ever more rational structure is proposed with still more confidence in the power of reason and still less preparedness to encounter what overpowers reason in beings, things, materials, including human resources. The mystery in any case is subject to clarification.

As a ground for what? In the final account—for being. In being Heidegger also seeks a ground. What is the difference? For reason being *is*; in the cosmos, in chaos, in molecules it emerges as a reliable ground because it exists. Give science only one ground, agreeing that beings are; science will construct everything on such a ground. Thus for postmodern theoretical physics it is enough that something is; any mathematical formalism will find an application to actuality, arising only from the pure fact of being. For Heidegger this is not being; being is *not* this. It does not exist, but realizes itself exactly as our here-and-now being, Da-sein, is adequate to be seized by the abyss. What organizers call being is counterfeited to fit their main task—the complete organization of all beings.

5. A constructive dialogue between totalizing organizers and thought is not possible. Heidegger insists that, in terms of the absolute necessity and order of the first need, one must go mad.

> [. . .] there is not yet an understanding of what is necessary and seized by it. Our presence itself (*Da-sein*) is achieved only through a displacement (*Verrückung*) of human being as a whole, i.e., arising from thinking about the need of being as such and its truth.[34]

To go mad means to stop standing and building on the basis of rational representations. Reason cannot organize the event with any of its forces. Truth is not in its judgments.

Errance has gone too far. The deep need commands us to get to work all the more since it [the need] is sensed by hardly anyone. Why has being been forgotten? From a lack of talent, style, sharpness of mind on the part of thinkers, writers, planners, predictors and organizers? The question about truth seems fenced off from truths because thinkers have not left the position of thought [have not gone mad—JL].[35]

The realization of truth as the deepest and most intimate characteristic is *historical, geschichtlich*.

The history of truth, of the flashes and transformations and foundations of its essence, consists solely in rare moments widely separated from each other.

Quickly, almost under the hands of the investigators themselves, these moments turn to stone. In his diary Wittgenstein records:

Everything that only yesterday was still flowing and promising form, froze today from the morning on into a mix of metal and slag and could not soften again. Heidegger too, who said to an American graduate student: You don't like the fact that at each of my lectures you appear to be a paltry initiate to my philosophy? And I feel the same way every morning. Instead of the momentary freedom of the event, melancholy seeps in in the form of the "eternal truths" that are still not understood as a momentary gift. For 2500 years the truth has been understood as homoiōsis, adequatio, the correspondence between different concepts and things. As if someone—being? God?—were already set up so that all that remained were the details of the puzzle, to bring the bricks in the mind into correspondence with the bricks of reality, and truth would be in our hands. It was not likely always so; but if it will always be so?

> Do we not stand at the end of such a long epoch of the hardening of the essence of truth and then at the threshold of a new moment of its hidden history?[36]

Yet what can this new moment be, moreover, since it is also hidden? Will the event really not slip away again? We must never step back from taking hold of the truth, at standing without a ground. The truth, like being, is not static but is a process realizing itself. Only so does it arise historically, in the momentary event, the time-space (*der Zeit-Raum*) of the truth that then hardens into infinite time and space.

At the same time the hardening of the truth is not fatal. On its side, besides a momentary flash, there is something else as well: forbidding equivocation, an unpredictable torpor; each moment of truth is like an invisible seed in the earth that may ripen. It produces a surplus (phusis) as the ancients understood being. Here hiddenness, refusal, delay, stubbornness, silence are no less necessary than during the event of truth. The refusal of the seed: it falls into the ground in order to provide later on.

> The truth: the ground as abyss. The ground is not: *from whence*; but is in something as what belongs to it. The abyss: as time-space (*Zeit-Raum*) of struggle (*des Streits*); the struggle as the battle between earth and world, because the relation of the truth to beings![37]

The dark earth in which we have all our roots does not speak. The world, into which we are set forth, cannot look into the earth and name her; for, at the first encounter, all still merely *is*, as, for example, "this is my body here." Gradually the world begins to clarify itself. We have not rushed to explain it, for the greater the clarity of truth, the more thoroughly visible the mystery of the earth and world. The search for a ground in the earth will deceive us, since we have closed our eyes to the fact that we ourselves are earth. In order to rely on the world, we would have to know from the start where it is. We see only its parts. The ground remains invisible. The truth opens us to resoluteness, disposing us to stand in the groundlessness of the abyss.

The disposition, it seems, is the most elusive of all things to rely on. It is considered impossible to construct anything on its basis. Likeliest of all, I will not rush to show my disposition, will not begin to divulge it. At the same time this quality of disposition is necessary above all for the encounter with such a thing as the truth of being. The furtiveness of the disposition is appropriate to the truth. Was the One Who said of himself "I am the truth" not inside this mystery? Here, as usual, Heidegger is moving squarely within theology. Nonetheless he never deals with it, not for reasons of formal purity but from his unwillingness to enter a region, which, next to Revelation, makes too broad use of knowledge with an unknown origin. It is more sober to ask:

> How meager is our knowledge of the gods and yet how fundamental is their realization and dispersion in the open concealment of presence, in the *truth*?[38]

The answer to the question is assumed. Then, i.e., in an understanding of the degree of our ignorance of the gods, Heidegger continues: What will the experience of the realization of the truth say to us? There is no answer to this question due to the difficulty of remaining silent, i.e., of working out a sufficiently careful discourse. What has been sown will not remain secure, if it will be spoken. To speak accurately of the truth is no easier than correctly to remain silent about it.

Anatoly Akhutin sees in the struggle (*Streit*) over truth a positive reference to legal dispute, dialogue. One of Heidegger's pseudo-definitions reads:

> *The essence of truth is the clearing for its self-concealment.*[39]

Confrontation manifests itself here before any dialogue begins; it lies in the opposition of one to another, the clearing of the mystery and vice versa. The deeply confrontational essence (*das innig-strittige Wesen*) begins with our argument with ourselves concerning whether Being is worthy of questioning. There are always two paths before us. On the one hand, the clearing is a neutral voice, permitting us to see from our side the opposing side, from the perspective of the subject toward the object, revealed for understanding and incorporation (*osvoenie*). The other is a clearing, on the contrary, to the degree it is inseparable from the mystery, that it is also the illumination of the mystery in each being; here we are ready to note, encounter and accept the refusal of beings to reveal themselves; then they reveal anew each time the inaccessibility of their freedom. We then comport ourselves as the freedom of beings commands, we await the discovery of that freedom, we help it, we create it, protect and allow it to function on its own. The clearing spreads out together with the diffusion of the mystery.

The fusion of the mystery with the clearing is achieved only in conflict because the empty clearing is right next to it, cutting us off from beings which do not affect us from afar and to which we have become accustomed without believing that we have become accustomed to them. We, perhaps, reflect on them and will even begin to experience them as an outsider, but aesthetic experience cannot go further. The subject cannot allow itself to be ruled, it is not the slave of its disposition. There is war between an empty clearing and something else, where the mystery rushes forth to us, seizing us.

Self-concealment overcomes the entire clearing, and only when this takes place, when the "here-and-now" is entirely seized by argument in its secrecy, may it be fortunate enough to step out of an indeterminate and thus obscure region of re-presentation, ex-perience and make an attempt at persistent here-and-now *being*.

Where is the distinction between being and beings here which, it would seem, is always important for Heidegger? We do not spot it behind the unfathomable depth of *every* being. Thus a composer succeeds in making via history a random, fugitive physics of sound. Being is not in the object observed on the other side of the empty clearing; it shines through in the mystery where the truth hides itself. Only when the hidden mystery begins to shine through so that it collects in and around itself all that we create, originate, do, what we sacrifice, when the openness of the clearing turns on the side of the hidden, displacing all that was locked up in apparent objectivity, only then does the world arise out of strewn about parts and therewith—thanks to the "simultane-ity" of being and beings—the earth allows itself to be known.

> The truth is thus never only the clearing, but realizes itself as concealing that is equiprimordial with the clearing. Both, clearing and concealing, are not a pair, but the realizing of one thing, the truth itself [. . .] Every question about the truth that does not look so far ahead of itself, remains a thought having come too short.[40]

As if it were for the subject looking upon beings from its side via the neutral field of the empty clearing, the matter also concerns the clarification of the objective truth in the fight against its distortion. A well-understood subject does not even rely in this process on its own mind but on the mind of God, the creator of the universe. But precisely the belief in the reliable mind of the Creator requires that one consider beings to be co-created by God. The necessity of seeing in beings a co-creation precludes access to the mystery of self-sufficient being other than in the form of the Trinity which seems to the theologian, as has already been said, too well known. The unfettered mystery without the intervention of the divine grace, fairness, omnipotence cannot be a being here. The co-creation of beings strove earlier to find its causes. A glance about beings with their causes (origins, beginnings) is succeeded by various versions (variants) of Christianity, and of science, differing from religion. Anti-creationism instead of divine creation constitutes an evolution that faintly precludes an approach to beings aside from representations as to their causes.[41] The mystery of self-sufficient being here and there is addressed in several kinds of explanation; it is assumed only in the notion of God as law-giver or in the distant first beginning. One's look is directed away from beings, it drowns in the divine heav-ens or in theories about the emergence of the universe. And if reality weighs on us like a heavy, unmovable beast (Sartre), then this will be called literature or psychology or pathology for which in turn reasons will be found.

6. Here are two different projects: to give a chance to the mystery of the hidden God—or to set aside in time and space everything that is not falsified by causal explanation. The perspective of causal explanation is attractive but ends up collapsing into a bad infinity of causes. In *Being and Time* much of the rejection of truth as representational correctness

is still attenuated by its proximity to what it rejects. The *Beiträge* transitions to a direct ground based on how truth is realized in its essence (*v suti*). For Heidegger the sole support is now in the unfathomable mystery. If only Ereignis would not become another term in the philosophical factory, a theme of interpretive analysis; if only it would not cease to serve as an instrument of the only necessary thinking, made necessary by the extreme need of our existential abandonment.

The clearing of concealment designates not taking away the concealed and its recovery and transformation into the unconcealed, but precisely the foundation of an unfathomable foundation for the *mystery* (the delaying refusal).

> In my previous attempts to sketch out the essence of truth [. . .] when it came to definitions like: presence exists both in truth and in untruth, this position was immediately understood in terms of morality or a world-view, without grasping what was decisive in philosophical thought, in the irremovable quality of this "both" as the ground of the essence of truth, without grasping the primordiality of untruth in the sense of concealment (and not as some lie).[42]

Now the main effort is turned to holding oneself inside the clearing of the mystery; this disposition to restraint becomes the primordial ground. The return to presence (here-and-now-being)—is not another step among those that the philosophical school teaches; the whole human essence must be displaced, as was said above, i.e., by going mad.

Does this mean, however, that now we must venture to sketch out the essence of truth as the clearing of the mystery and prepare a shift of human beings to pre-sence?

> The shift from that position in which we find ourselves: from the immense emptiness and devastation that have seeped into the already long unrecognizable tradition without standards and, crucially, without the will to question, and the desert—the hidden abandonment by being.[43]

The *not* (*das Nichthafte*) belongs directly to the truth, not in the sense that it is missing something, but in the sense of a resisting slipping away that in the clearing shows itself as the inaccessibility of the mystery. It would be easier to avoid this insight and stand on established truth. It is true, that we then suddenly become uneasy for some reason inside an unending task of explanation, justification, foundation. Putting truth into the subject, we feverishly organize in our isolation. What if we throw ourselves not into this task but into what we are thrown into—into the strangeness and not-organized-by-us-ness of the earth and the world? But if we give ourselves over to their mystery as it slips away, where is our freedom? Or is there freedom only in the return to our own, what always was closest and what no one can take away from me? There arises a tight union: our presence belongs to Being, just as Being belongs to our here-and-now; we begin to become adequate to fitting ourselves into the extreme, and so, the last God.

*October 2004*

Translated by Jeff Love


# NOTES

Translator's note: The article reproduced here in English translation is based on a seminar held by Bibikhin from October 5 until November 2 of 2004, roughly a month before his death on December 12 of that year. The article is a considerably abridged version of the text of the seminar. Where Bibikhin (or Anatoly Akhutin) has translated Heidegger's German, I have generally followed the translations with occasional minor modifications. All the notes, excluding those explicitly identified as my notes, reproduce those given in the original article, with German editions given first, then the corresponding English translation.

1. Translator's note: The two German Nietzsche volumes first appeared in 1961.

2. Translator's note: Bibikhin uses the Russian phrase, *napisannii v stol,* literally, "written for the table/drawer," to indicate a kind of writing well-known in the Soviet Union as a "writing for oneself," meaning that one would not be able to publish such a text for fear of censorship or reprisals of a more dangerous sort.

3. "Ich glaube an eine künftige Revolution der Gesinnungen und Vorstellungsarten, die alles bisherige schamrot machen wird. Und dazu kann Deutschland vielleicht sehr viel beitragen."

4. "Car la pensée de Heidegger n'est pas un événement, ne serait-ce que parce qu'elle ne saurait prétendre, de façon insensée, être L'Événement unique. Elle est avenante, c'est-à-dire se modulant sur le rythme incessant de l'avenance. Et elle l'est en tant que bel et bien avenue, c'est-à-dire appareillante grâce à la douce véhémence de l'avenance."

5. Translator's note: The first German edition of *Being and Time* appeared in 1927.

6. Martin Heidegger, *Grundfragen der Philosophie: Ausgewählte "Probleme" der "Logik"* GA 45 (Frankfurt am Main: Vittorio Klostermann, 1984), 123. [*Basic Problems of Philosophy*, trans. Richard Rojcewicz and André Schuwer (Bloomington: Indiana University Press, 1994), 107].

7. Translator's note: Bibikhin translates *Dasein* in various ways, but the most frequent translation is the Russian *prisutstvie*, most readily translated as "presence."

8. Martin Heidegger, *Sein und Zeit* (Tubingen: Max Niemayer, 1953), 182. [*Being and Time*, trans. John Macquarrie and Edward Robinson (New York: Harper and Row, 1962), 227].

9. Ibid., 186/230.

10. Ibid., 187/231.

11. Ibid., 188/232.

12. Ibid.,189/234.

13. Martin Heidegger, *Beiträge zur Philosophie (Vom Ereignis)* ed. Friedrich-Wilhelm von Herrmann (Frankfurt am Main: Vittorio Klostermann, 1989), 3. [*Contributions to Philosophy (of the Event)* trans. Richard Rojcewicz and Daniela Vallega-Neu (Bloomington: University of Indiana Press, 2012), 5].

14. Heidegger, *Grundfragen der Philosophie*, 124/108.

15. Heidegger, *Beiträge zur Philosophie*, 11–12/11–12.

16. Ibid., 14/14.

17. Ibid., 49/39–40.

18. Ibid., 53/42–43.

19. Ibid., 54/44.

20. Ibid., sec. 237.

21. Ibid., 369/291.

22. Ibid., 370/291.

23. Translator's note: Russian *nuzhda,* "need" or "necessity," translates the German *Not*, which is a fundamental word for Heidegger in the 1930s and is variously translated in English as "plight," "distress," or "urgency." I have kept the simplest Russian translation, though the range of the Russian word is as broad as the German.

24. Ibid., 112–13/88–89.

25. Ibid., 114/90.

26. Translator's note: The difference between the two Russian words for "truth," *istina* and *pravda*, can be interpreted in a very Heideggerian manner to correspond to the difference between truth and correctness as Heidegger sets it out both in "On the Essence of Truth" and "On Plato's Doctrine of Truth."

27. Ibid., 258/203.

28. Ibid., 260/204.

29. Ibid., 327/259.

30. Ibid., 331/262.

31. Ibid., 235/185.

32. Ibid., 332/263.

33. Ibid., 336/266.

34. Ibid., 340–41/269.

35. *Soiti s uma* means literally "to go out of one's mind," and, thus, translates Heidegger's "Ver-rückung" quite tendentiously but not inaccurately.

36. Ibid., 342/270.

37. Ibid., 346/273.

38. Ibid., sec. 224, beginning.

39. Ibid., 348/275.

40. Ibid., 349/275.

41. Ludwig Wittgenstein says that we no longer believe in the holy Trinity, but the God-cause (of science of course) squarely and securely occupies its place.

42. Ibid., 352/278.

43. Ibid., 356/280.

## Chapter 14

# Heidegger, Synergic Anthropology, and the Problem of Anthropological Pluralism

Sergey S. Horujy

Irrespective of all *Pro et Contra* reverberating in heated discussions about the *Schwarze Hefte* and other episodes of Heidegger's political biography, his thought continues to be an ineluctable component of the world philosophical process. What is more, it holds its own special place in this process. The current philosophical situation can be characterized as a changing balance of two opposite trends or vectors, de-ontologization and re-ontologization, which, respectively, deny or accept the ontological difference, the fold of being and the essent. Although the mainstream of the process is now more in favor of the first trend, the other one is also permanently present and ineradicable. And the Swabian Sage is recognized as a kind of symbol of this ontological trend, the voice of being itself and the plenipotentiary of ontology as such. In Russian philosophy one can also find both these trends; and in addition, there was always here some intense interest in Heidegger, in spite of (but partly due to) the fact that there was no visible tradition of Heidegger studies. The unconditional leader of these studies, Vladimir Veniaminovich Bibikhin (1938–2004), was almost a lonely figure. The few Heidegger scholars worked separately, and one cannot say that there ever existed such a thing as the "Russian community of Heidegger scholars."

As for myself, I was neither a Heidegger follower nor a specialist in his work, but at the same time this work was never out of my scope. At any period of my work there were some Heideggerian ideas or themes, concepts, paradigms, that turned out to be relevant. This set of relevant Heideggerian subjects changed radically with time. And in most cases that relevance did not mean simply acceptance and adoption; it included disagreement and urged one to articulate a different position. It was a refreshing and stimulating effect, which means that I am much indebted to him. In this text I am going to present a few pages of the long story of my benefits from his wisdom.

*\*\*\**

It is worth starting with brief reminiscences about Heidegger's appearance on the philosophical scene in Moscow in the 1960s. They are quite personal and do not touch on the life of Soviet institutional philosophy so that one could say that they present a wrong perspective. However, in that period of mild late-Soviet totalitarianism there was a kind of deterritorialization of philosophy: While the imposing machinery of official Marxist-Leninist philosophy had very little to do with love of wisdom (being the ideological basis of the totalitarian machine), free thought tried to survive on neighboring territories of underground and semiunderground culture. These territories included mostly private studies not planned for publication, discussions in private settings and in the smoking rooms of big public libraries, and meetings of unofficial philosophical circles. These circles were rare and small since any regular meetings outside the orbit of ideological control were dangerous. Sporadically some texts not belonging to the ideological mainstream succeeded in being published, and any such publication was received as a big event.

As for Heidegger, the first texts that introduced him to the general public in the early sixties were articles by the young and bright Piama P. Gaidenko, one of a group of young unorthodox philosophers who tried actively to evade the official dogmatism and restore links with modern European culture. The articles were somewhere between introductory narrative and professional analysis, and became immediately and widely read and discussed. A little later, in the mid-sixties, Heidegger was much discussed in a peculiar circle, one of the oddities of Soviet life at that time. It was the philosophical circle launched by students of the physics department of Moscow State University. I was one of its organizers. Our philosophical erudition was embryonic, but nevertheless our circle was for several years one of the main philosophical spots in Moscow. The reason was simple: physicists, especially nuclear physicists, were then a privileged category considered of prime importance for the Soviet state. In this milieu ideological control was reduced to a minimum so that our circle was the closest Soviet analogue of Hyde Park Corner. In addition, physicists enjoyed respect from liberal and unorthodox intelligentsia, who supposed them to be free-thinking and well-advanced intellectually. Due to these two factors, nearly all intellectual leaders having liberal ideas came willingly to our circle to present their views. Heidegger was mentioned by many, but knowledge of his work was as a rule very superficial. Gaidenko was the main exception to this rule, and the other exception was Valery Skurlatov, a young physicist who turned to philosophy and partly to politics with a far-right bias. A fantastic rumor had it that he was one of the leaders of Russian fascism. No such thing existed then in the Soviet Union, but still in his lectures on Heidegger, Valery told us with enthusiastic approval that, at the opening of the academic year 1944, the aging philosopher canceled his lectures, called his students to the defense of the fatherland, and enlisted as a volunteer.

Access to Heidegger's texts was a big problem. Public libraries did not have them, while academic libraries had just a few and demanded special permissions. Thus he remained mostly talked about, but not read, and discussions of his work with the detailed analysis of concrete texts were extremely rare. However, I had some modest possibility to have books from abroad and I used it mostly for Heidegger; in particular, I got *Sein und Zeit, Holzwege*, and some half a dozen brochures like *Brief über den Humanismus* and *Was ist Metaphysik?* I studied them zealously and having decided soon (too soon) that I understood the Heideggerian vision of being and humankind, I wanted to share this understanding with friends and companions from our unorthodox philosophical milieu. It was probably in 1970 or close to this date. Our circle had stopped its work already, and so we arranged a kind of workshop in my small flat. There were about a dozen participants, quite a lot for an informal home meeting with a not-too-popular theme; Piama Gaidenko was present, and my friends Anatoly Akhutin and Vladimir Bibikhin (whose lifelong relationship with Heidegger was just starting to emerge) took part actively. Besides presenting my view of fundamental ontology, I tried to establish some links between Heidegger and Russian religious philosophy.

For several years such links were the main concern in my relationship with Heidegger. It was almost inevitable for Christian thought in the Soviet Union to have big expectations with regard to the Russian philosophy of the Silver Age, which included many remarkable figures and was forbidden by the Bolsheviks. Sharing these expectations, I reflected on how this tradition could have a new lease on life in a new age. As Heidegger was one of the cornerstones of this age, such reflections led necessarily to the theme of the relationship of Russian religious philosophy with his thought. Thus I started to reconstruct the interface of these two philosophical worlds. Here I shall point out just a few principal contents of it.

- Taken as a whole, the philosophical movement of the Silver Age demonstrated many features of the overcoming of metaphysics, the trend advocated actively by Heidegger.
- As I tried to show, the principal vectors of this overcoming included the turn to phenomenology conceived in a wide sense as the processing of a phenomenal base by means of a certain philosophical method. In this wide sense, fundamental ontology and such Russian philosophies as those of Pavel Florensky, Lev Karsavin, and Simeon Frank could be considered as taking part together in the phenomenological turn of modern philosophy.
- Of course, there is one more common feature, obvious and mentioned by many: the orientation of Russian thought to existentialism, again in a wide sense of taking categories of existence and problems of the conceptualization of human existence as a basis. In this aspect, existential analytics and such Russian philosophies as those of Lev Shestov, Nikolai Berdyaev, and even Vasily Rozanov—why not?— could be considered as participating together in the existential turn.
- More concretely, there is the far-reaching parallel between Heidegger's paradigm of *Kehre*, an apparent turning back necessary for the advancement of philosophical thought to its destination, and George Florovsky's conception of neopatristic synthesis, the permanent (re)turn to the living experience of the Church Fathers necessary for the advancement of theological thought to its destination. Both paradigms or conceptions state in fact the same principle: in order to grasp philosophical or theological truth, philosophical as well as theological thought must each permanently restore its tie with its

primordial source, its *Archē*. Of course, the source is different in the two cases, for Heidegger it is Greek and chiefly pre-Socratic philosophy, while for Florovsky the works and the living experience of the Greek Church Fathers; but still both thinkers promote the same *archeological* mode of thinking. One should stress that in Christian theology this particular mode belongs to Eastern Christian (Orthodox) discourse only (it is implied by the Orthodox principle of loyalty to the patristic Tradition).

However, the most essential resemblance of this discourse and Heidegger's thought is not within the orbit of Russian religious philosophy. It is the close parallel between the core of Heideggerian ontology, the principle of the ecstatic stepping-out into the clearing (*die Lichtung*) of being, and the Orthodox conception of deification, *theosis*, which means the perfect union of all energies of human being with the Divine energies. It is indeed an important point of resemblance having many implications, but the conception of *theosis* was practically unnoticed by the philosophy of the Silver Age. It started to be studied in detail only later, in neopatristic and neopalamite theology and also in my synergic anthropology (SA).

Summing up, this interface turned out to be not too promising. It was not rich enough to make realistic my suggestion that the dialogue with Heidegger could be the basis for the cardinal modern upgrading of Russian philosophy. As a whole, I found the philosophy of the Silver Age too strongly connected with classical metaphysics to make such upgrading possible, be it with Heideggerian or other ways and means. I found also that there was a considerable distance between this philosophy and Eastern Christian discourse—that is, the basic fund of ideas, paradigms, and attitudes characterizing the mentality and spiritual experience of Eastern-Orthodox consciousness. Russian religious philosophy wanted to give philosophical expression to Eastern Christian discourse, but in reality it paid too little attention to its phenomenal base, its living experience, and left aside many important components of it (*theosis* being a typical example). As a result, modern philosophy, which wanted to take into account and to include into its orbit Eastern Christian spiritual experience, could not emerge in the old line of Russian religious philosophy. What was needed was rather *ein anderer Anfang*.

\*\*\*

Further stages of my dialogue with Heidegger developed on the ground of my SA. This dialogue contributed a few essential elements to its framework, although in its general character the project of SA is not in the Heideggerian line at all. In its methodology, it is more Husserlian and partly Cartesian since it implements the strategy of the "smallest rescued bit" (this is what Husserl called the strategy of Descartes who unfolded an entire epistemology starting with a single absolutely reliable cognitive act). SA starts with the thorough analysis of a special domain of anthropological experience chosen according to the criteria of "epistemological transparency" and "anthropological full-dimensionality." Then it extends this "rescued" (i.e., completely processed epistemologically) domain, advancing gradually to the whole ensemble of anthropological experience. The starting domain is the experience of the Eastern Orthodox ascetical and mystical practice (Hesychast practice). My reconstruction of Hesychast anthropology shows that this domain satisfies both criteria. It represents Hesychast practice as a specific practice of the self, in the sense of Michel Foucault, in which the adept shapes his constitution by means of making himself or herself open or unlocked for the encounter with Divine energies (energies of a source having a different mode of being). This paradigm of a human constitution shaped in the unlocking of the human being, which includes the encounter of his or her energies with other, ontologically different energies, is the key element of Hesychast practical anthropology. This ontological unlocking of human being is called synergy (Greek *synergeia*), and the achievement of the encounter of the two energies opens the way to their perfect union, *theosis*. My reconstruction shows that the paradigm of synergy becomes the generating principle of a full-dimensional and self-consistent description of a certain anthropological formation actualized by the person in Hesychast practice.

Then we begin to extend the starting domain, basing ourselves on the observation that many notions and principles of Hesychast anthropology are very general and can be used for the description of other domains of anthropological experience as well. The most important of them is the principle of anthropological unlocking: I saw that it is an extremely general anthropological paradigm, which has lots of very different representations besides ontological unlocking (synergy). In particular, there is a special type of unlocking, which takes place in extreme experience (French *expérience-limite*: experience, in which humans get to extreme limits of their consciousness and existence so that contact with the Other that/who is beyond those limits becomes possible). In this special unlocking, the constitution of the human as such takes shape. I show that in all ensembles of anthropological experience there exist three and only three representations of such constitutive unlocking, and this "unlocking in extreme experience" is the universal paradigm of human constitution. Each of the three basic representations determines a certain full-dimensional and full-bodied anthropological formation and as a result, SA can be characterized as a pluralistic "anthropology of unlocking." Three basic formations are called, respectively the Ontological Human (constituted in the ontological unlocking), the Ontic Human (constituted in the unlocking to some ontic Other, e.g., the unconscious) and the Virtual Human (constituted in virtual anthropological practices).

It is evident from this brief description that right from the start SA enters a close but ambivalent relationship with Heidegger's discourse. The generating principle of SA is the unlocking, which is the well-known Heideggerian category: the term *die Erschliessung* used in *Sein und Zeit* corresponds literally to Russian размыкание used in SA and English *the unlocking*. The discourse of the late Heidegger does not use *die Erschliessung*, but it includes instead a cluster of terms with closely related meanings. Even the key notion *Dasein* belongs to this rich discourse of the unlocking: According to Heidegger, *Da* in *Da-Sein* points to the fundamental unlockedness of Dasein. Evidently, all this discourse represents a common ground of Heidegger's philosophy and SA, although the concept in question is interpreted in a quite different way. These different interpretations have been compared in detail in my book *Diogenes' Lantern*.[1] Simplifying for the sake of brevity, one can say that the unlocking has two different directions or two modes, inner and outer, respectively, the interiorizing unlocking (separation, differentiation) of inner contents of the self and the exteriorizing unlocking of Dasein as a whole, beyond its limits and toward the encounter with being. In *Sein und Zeit* the outer mode is almost imperceptible and the unlocking is considered almost exclusively in its inner mode; but in the late Heidegger the role of the outer mode becomes quite significant. In particular, the key paradigm of the "stepping-out into the clearing of being" corresponds evidently to the outer mode of the unlocking. On the other hand, in religious discourse the outer mode of the unlocking is strongly prevalent. As for spiritual practices, Hesychasm and SA, these discourses combine and cultivate both modes; in particular, the

*Organon* of Hesychast practice,[2] which includes the most sophisticated procedures for monitoring and transforming one's inner reality, can be considered as a very detailed canon of the inner (as well as outer) unlocking.

In general, the discourses of unlocking in Hesychasm and SA, on the one hand, and Heidegger, on the other hand, are different, but do not directly contradict each other. Their comparative analysis in *Diogenes' Lantern* is not exhaustive by far, and there are still many open questions. For example, an important component of the Heideggerian discourse of unlocking is the analytic of the call (*Ruf*) and the "challenge of being" (*Anspruch des Seins*). Its parallel is the discourse of prayer in Hesychasm and the discourse of the "ontological mover" in SA. It would be interesting to extend the comparative analysis to these subjects.

On the other hand, the principal characteristic of SA is its pluralism. In cartographical terms, the territory of the human includes here three basic parts or topics inhabited by the Ontological, Ontic, and Virtual Human. This pluralism is in sharp contradiction with Heidegger's view of the human (let us avoid the formula "Heidegger's anthropology" since anthropology had a pejorative meaning for him). All our parallels between Heidegger and SA concern ontological topics only, because only the Ontological Human actualizes the ontological difference (the difference or the fold, *die Zwiefalt,* between being and the essent,[3] *das Seiende*) and corresponds to the Heideggerian thesis "man and being belong to each other." As for the ontic and virtual formations/topics, not only are they absent in Heidegger's philosophy, but their existence is completely impossible there.

This situation leads us to somewhat more profound problems. The Ontic and the Virtual Human are constituted in certain anthropological practices and their topics are domains of such anthropological experience, which has nothing to do with ontological unlocking. We shall call it *unontological experience.* Since these formations are absent in Heidegger's philosophy, it means that this philosophy either ignores unontological experience or interprets it in some other way representing it as belonging to the Ontological Human, the only formation admitted by Heidegger. As a matter of fact, both variants take place. Heidegger ignores the experience of virtual practices (in his time they were only beginning to appear). As for the experience of the Ontic Human, it is also ignored partly and partly interpreted as related to the Ontological Human.

Below we discuss the principal problems concerning the relationship between Heidegger's view of humankind and our pluralistic anthropology, we shall first consider the ontological topic. The principle of ontological unlocking is close to Heidegger's ecstatic paradigm of human constitution; but it is interesting that, besides the resemblance, comparative analysis discovers also diametrical opposition, a kind of structural antisymmetry, between the two paradigms.

\*\*\*

Our reconstruction represents Hesychast practice and other spiritual practices, like yoga and Sufism, among others, as a stepwise process of human self-transformation, in which one changes gradually the set of all one's energies, somatic, psychic, and intellectual, in order to achieve a certain goal or *telos*. In contrast to the practices of the self studied by Foucault, the *telos* of any spiritual practice is meta-anthropological— that is, it does not belong to empirical being, and its achievement demands ontological unlocking. The way of the practice is divided into clearly distinct steps, and in the case of Hesychast practice the complete ladder of these steps is subdivided into three big blocks. Here I mention only those elements that are relevant for our comparative theme.

1. The initial block is the Spiritual Gate or *metanoia,* "change of mind," the stage, at which human beings perform a radical critical reassessment and reappraisal of both their outer and inner worlds. This reappraisal generates the rejection of worldly life and prompts the decision to break with this life and take the road leading to the *telos*.
2. The adept discovers that due to the meta-anthropological nature of the *telos* the ascension to it is an ontological unlocking, which demands some special activities collecting all a person's energies together and directing them to extreme limits of the horizon of human experience and existence in order to contact the *telos*, which is beyond these limits. The key activity is the forming-up of the union of certain special forms of prayer and attention. As found empirically by Hesychasts, such union acts as a kind of "ontological mover": The prayer, which is made incessant with the help of attention, embraces all the levels of the human being and, drawing

in all said energies, directs them to the *telos*. In this way synergy is achieved.

3. By virtue of synergy, at the higher steps of the Hesychast Ladder, the ascension to the telos is chiefly carried out by Divine energies. These steps are already approaching theosis, the complete union of human and Divine energies, and hence some fundamental changes of the human being begin here. According to Hesychast experience, such changes touch, first of all, the sphere of one's perceptive modalities: The emergence and formation of new perceptive faculties take place. The important feature of these changes is that they in no way resemble the "mystical dissolution" of one's personality and identity in the Absolute. In Hesychasm the spiritual ascension is a dialogical communion with God, and its telos, theosis, is conceived as personal being-communion, in which all a human's personal features are preserved though in a certain transcended form.

Now the basis for the comparison of this practice with existential analytics appears when we notice in the economy of Heidegger's Dasein the structure of a certain stepwise ascension similar (to some extent, at least) to the Hesychast Ladder. Again, we shall describe this structure in its principal elements only; its detailed reconstruction is presented in *Diogenes' Lantern*.[4]

To begin with, we recall that *Sein und Zeit* establishes the opposition of the two modes of temporalization, the authentic and the inauthentic, unfolding this opposition into the full-bodied ontological opposition of two modes of Dasein. Heidegger avoids axiological discourse, but it is quite fitting for characterizing his opposition. The poles of this opposition are not of equal value at all. The authentic mode concentrates in itself everything ontologically genuine and desirable: the "possibility of one's authentic existence (*Existenz*)," totality and integrity, freedom, and so forth. The inauthentic mode is characterized by a vast assortment of negative predicates and properties of all kinds: forfeiture (*Verfallen*), cowardice, concealedness, self-forgetfulness, losing itself, craving for shirking, hiding, deviating, and so on. On the other hand, it is in this wretched mode that we ourselves are, mostly and to begin with; it is our *everydayness*. As for the authentic mode, it is not given and not available to us. Such is the initial configuration of things, but this configuration is to be changed.

The existential analytic proclaims the ontological task and destination of Dasein: It must become aware of its inauthentic being-toward-death in its inauthenticity, reject this mode of being and build-up the foundations, *die Grundverfassung*, of a different mode, the authentic being-toward-death (which is "the most extreme possibility of *Dasein*"). The task means that one must cut a path through the inauthentic mode of being to the authentic one. This is an ontological path, *Dao*, if you wish, and it is proper to describe it by means of the vertical metaphor, as the way of the ascension. (This metaphor is not alien to Heidegger's discourse: It is exploited by him, as in the concept of *Kehre*.) The "way of spiritual ascension" is the usual formula for the ontological process in spiritual practices, in particular, in Hesychasm. Then we notice further points of resemblance with structures of spiritual practice. The path to the authentic being-toward-death or the "existential ascension" is a certain transformation of Dasein, which must be performed by Dasein itself, which means that the "existential ascension," like spiritual practice, is a self-transformation. Next, this transformation is a directed process, the advancement to a certain predestined state (authentic being-toward-death), just as spiritual practice is the advancement to its predestined goal or *telos*. Taken together these two properties imply that the "existential ascension," like spiritual practice, is an anthropological practice belonging to the category of practices of the self, in terms of Foucault. Moreover, in Heidegger's discourse the "existential ascension" is ontological in the full sense of the word so that its goal is *ontologically* different from its initial state, like the *telos* of spiritual practice. Summing up, we conclude that in the field of anthropological practices there is full structural isomorphism between spiritual practice and the self-transformation of Heidegger's Dasein to the mode of authentic being-toward-death.

Now we must proceed from outer to inner structures and compare the conceptualization of the "existential ascension" to that of spiritual practice. At first the parallel continues; the advancement to the goal of "existential ascension" is also a stepwise process, the big blocks of which solve problems a bit similar to those described in the list above. First of all, all the strongly pejorative descriptions of everyday Dasein have very much in common with the ascetic discourse of *metanoia* and denunciation of the "world" and worldly life. Next, in the central part of the path the problem is to set up some "ontological mover," which could secure actual progressive advancement to the goal. Looking from this viewpoint, we find that the existential analytic indeed includes certain existentialia, which perform such a dynamic function; in the first place, it is the existentialia of conscience (*Gewissen*) and resoluteness (*Entschlossenheit*). Their activation means that the overcoming of the inauthenticity of Dasein has begun. According to Heidegger, resoluteness is connected with anxiety (*Angst*), and due to this connection the "existential ascension" proceeds to the concluding stage.

Anxiety plays the decisive role at this stage. It is in anxiety that Dasein comes back to itself and becomes aware of itself in its finitude. "Being-toward-death is essentially anxiety"[5] and during all the "existential ascension" to authentic being-toward-death the evolution of a human's relationship with anxiety takes place. At the initial steps, anxiety is destructive; it takes away all forces of consciousness and brings it to the brink of paralysis and collapse. But at the further stages resoluteness and conscience change its effects radically; when humankind's consciousness acquires resoluteness and conscience, anxiety becomes a fruitful factor for it and begins to push the ontological transformation on to its goal, which is authentic being-toward-death. It can be said in the discourse of spiritual practice that *the "existential ascension" is carried out by the energies of anxiety.* And we notice an important property of these energies, which augments the parallel with spiritual practice considerably. In Heidegger's ontological discourse it is the primordial nature (*die Ursprünglichkeit*) of anxiety, while in the psychological dimension, it is its spontaneity: Anxiety arises as if on its own, and it is independent of human will and reason. Dasein does not control and manage anxiety; it can only take it into account and conform to it in some way or another. Hence it follows that in the "existential ascension," the energies of anxiety are acting as certain energies, independent of Dasein and having some source beyond its horizon. It means that they represent an analogue of Divine energies in spiritual practice, and as for their source, the *telos* in terms of spiritual practice, it is obviously death as the actual facticity, my already-come-death, which is beyond the horizon of my experience, but is constitutive for it. It is also "nothing" as an ontological principle, namely, the "eliminating nothing," *das nichtende Nichts*, according to the analysis of the connection between anxiety and nothing in *Was ist Metaphysik?*

Now the parallel is complete. We have demonstrated the full structural isomorphism of Heidegger's "existential ascension" of Dasein to authentic being-toward-death and spiritual practice. But then we notice that this new representation of the paradigm of spiritual practice is very specific. In Hesychasm spiritual ascension is directed to God and being in its fullness; the *telos* of Hesychast practice, *theōsis*, is the perfect union of all human energies with Divine energies, which begins to be approached when a synergy, the collaboration with Divine energies, is achieved. However, the "existential ascension" is directed to the anticipation (*Vorlaufen*) of death and authentic being-toward-death, and the actual advancement to its goal begins, when due to conscience and resoluteness the collaboration or *sui generis* synergy with (energies of) anxiety is achieved. The *telos* of this specific practice can be character-ized as anxiety, death (in its bare facticity, as my already-come-death) and nothing (as the eliminating nothing). In comparison with spiritual ascension, the "existential ascension" turns out to be a practice, which is also ontological (i.e., directed to a different mode of being), possesses the same stepwise ascending structure, but arranges "synergy with anxi-ety," cultivates the experience of nothing and has anxiety, death, and nothing as its *telos*. My analysis in *Diogenes' Lantern* complements this comparison, showing that the practice described by Heidegger includes also psychological and emotional components of spiritual practice. Thus the resemblance to spiritual practice is not only structural; one can say that what the thinker describes is a true full-dimensional spiritual practice, the *telos* of which is of a directly opposite nature, however. And it all makes us conclude that the *existential analytic represents the direct opposite, the inversion of spiritual practice.*

This is not the final conclusion, however. In the full context of Hei-degger's work, the existential analytic is complemented by the descrip-tion of the ontological and anthropological situation from a different position, not in the prism of falling and forfeiture. His later texts present the destination of Dasein as the "ecstatic stepping-out into the clearing of being." It is also an ontological ascension, but this time it is directed to being and not to anxiety and nothing. Of course, the discourse of the clearing of being does not contradict that of the existential analytic. Taken together, they correspond to an ontological paradigm, which is often discussed by Heidegger in his late period. It is the paradigm of salvation at the very last moment, at the brink of peril: Dasein masters the breakthrough to being after getting closest to nothing. Usually he discusses it in the context of the poetry of Hölderlin since he finds its best expression in the famous line from *Patmos*: Where there is danger, there grows also salvation. What Heidegger does not mention is that this paradigm is also one of the chief ontological principles of Kierkegaard (it is at work, in particular, in *The Concept of Dread* and *The Sickness unto Death*). But in fact its first appearance is neither in poetry nor in philosophy: It is in The New Testament, in the account of the destiny of Dismas, the Good Thief.

\*\*\*

Here we shall consider in more detail how Heidegger treats the experience, which SA attributes to the Ontic Human. The dialogue of SA with the philosopher turns now into a dispute, and a conflict of interpretations takes place. As said above, the experience of the Ontological Human has one principal distinction: In this experience the ontological difference is actualized—that is, the human being actualizes his or her relation to being as different from the essent. There is nothing like that in the experience of the Ontic Human, whose constitution, structures of consciousness, and behavior take shape not in the stepping-out into the clearing of being, but in the encounter with the ontic Other, the main representation of which is the unconscious. Heidegger recognizes and takes fully into account the existence of the experience, in which the ontological difference is not actualized and not manifested in any way. However, he develops a special strategy, a special logics and discourse, to make it possible to integrate such experience into his monistic anthropological conception. He postulates that the human constitution is strictly ontological, or shaped with the help of a specific relationship of the reciprocal dependence with being; but the ontological nature of this constitution remains masked or hidden in most human practices. These practices do not obviously show the connection of the human with being so that being does not manifest itself explicitly in them. *Despite the indissoluble bond of the human with being, being remains concealed in most human practices*. This is the key thesis, which becomes the basis for the big theme and rich discourse of concealedness/unconcealedness (*Verborgenheit/Unverborgenheit*).

The main thing is that there exist various degrees of concealedness. Unconcealedness, the pure apparition of being, is nothing but Truth = Wahrheit = Unverborgenheit = Alētheia. Figuratively speaking, this is the upper, positive end of the scale; but our problem is to understand what precisely takes place at the opposite, lower end, where concealedness reaches its maximum. According to Heidegger, concealedness is always there in some way and degree or other, since its presence is implied by the unconcealedness itself in its "essential form." The relationship in the dyad concealedness/unconcealedness is deeply ambivalent: What we see everywhere is the dominance of concealedness in lots of its forms and manifestations, but nevertheless concealedness is firmly subject to unconcealedness and being, which always keep priority and primacy: "The forgetfulness of being is allowed by being itself."[6] There is any amount of forms and predicates of concealedness, including all phenomena of falsity, appearance (*Schein*), illusion, distortion, deception, the striving after hiding, running away, shirking, being shielded, and so forth. In fact, the greater part of the existential analytics of *Sein und Zeit*, being the analytics of *Dasein im Verfallen*, "in the forfeiture," belongs to the discourse of concealedness. Concealedness especially grows and deepens in the existence of "*das Man*" rendered as "people" in the Russian translation of Bibikhin.[7] Here we are already near the most extreme concealedness. Dasein is here captured in "everyday being" and "first of all it loses hold of itself and hides itself (*sich zunächst verfehlt und verdeckt*)."[8] In *Parmenides* (1942–1943) and *Heraclitus* (1943–1944), Heidegger characterizes this extreme concealedness in other terms, introducing a specific conceptual personage: "the *lathon*, concealed, concealing itself and locking itself out . . . *Lathon* means the polar opposite to what is expressed by the word *Alēthēs*."[9] *Lathon* is a kind of the incarnation and concentrated expression of concealedness, in which the latter reaches its culmination. A priori such a figure could represent rudiments of a new anthropological formation not related to being anymore. But Heidegger does not interpret his *Lathon* in this way; he considers it as a simple epiphenomenon having no prospects of autonomous existence and status. In the final pages of *Parmenides* Heidegger presents a special description and discussion of the extreme limits of concealedness. Reaching these limits, the human being

forgets completely about being so that being becomes blurred in front of him turning into a kind of the essent as a whole, which defies definition. As a result, being is identified with the essent or is abolished as a certain empty notion. By virtue of this, the difference, which forms the basis of all differences . . . that is the difference between being and the essent is completely abolished and with the help of man . . . it turns into something, which is simply not taken into account. But nevertheless *being remains there*, if only in the mode of existence of the essent as a whole hardly reflected upon.[10]

We see that Heidegger's position is always double-edged: On the one hand, he admits the strong and radical forgetfulness and concealedness of being, but on the other hand he absolutely insists that any "abolishment of being" cannot break and eliminate the tie of human and being. This tie is the principal and ineluctable part of the very definition of the human, and the programmatic text *Brief über den Humanismus* states firmly: "Man belongs to his own essence only as long as he listens to the demand of being. . . . Man is the neighbor of being."[11] An important consequence of the ineradicable nature of this tie is that concealedness is always reversible (in principle, at least); and Heidegger stresses repeatedly that extreme concealedness can suddenly change into a resolute stepping-out into the clearing of being.

Evidently, this position contradicts the positions of SA, and so SA presents a criticism of it. Basically we do not dispute the Heideggerian discourse of concealedness, but we point out some disputable elements on its periphery. Let us consider more closely what happens at the limits of concealedness, where it reaches its peak. According to Heidegger, the complete abolishment of the ontological difference and the complete absence of any manifestations of the relation to being in human consciousness and experience still does not mean the actual absence of this ontological relation. "Being remains there." Heidegger states it insistently and repeatedly, and this statement is of no small importance for him, but what are the real grounds for it? Reviewing its context in Heidegger's discourse, we see clearly that the main ground is just his idea of the human, which is wholly and thoroughly ontological. Since this idea generated and nourished the entire prodigious Universe of Heideggerian thought, it is very convincing, but in spite of this in its nature it represents an anthropological postulate.

In addition to this postulate, Heidegger propounds also a certain concrete argument in favor of the statement in question. He says that the relation to being remains because there is the idea of the "mode of existence of the essent as a whole," even if this idea is only slightly reflected upon. This is a disputable argument. What we are ready to accept is that the human mind includes a certain intuitive idea of "the essent as a whole" which is or is not reflected upon to some or other extent. This intuitive idea emerges since the human mind is endowed with logistics including the ability to conduct inductive and deductive operations. It is indeed a universal intuition, but it develops in the epistemological plane and has no ontological dimension. Thus it cannot be used as an argument in favor of the ineradicable nature of the tie of the human and being. On the other hand, the idea of the "mode of existence of the essent as a whole" is a very different idea! If I think that the essent as a whole may have some special mode of existence, I assume *eo ipso* that there are different modes of existence, and this *ontological* assumption cannot be considered as ineluctable and characteristic of the human mind as such. Thus Heidegger is absolutely right that the idea or intuition in question is already a vague reflection or embryonic form of the ontological difference. However, if the former idea is universal, but not ontological, the latter is ontological, but not universal; and the result is that Heidegger's argument is unsound.

Thus we consider Heidegger's thesis that the human always preserves his or her tie with being as only a postulate, which has no sound proof. We do not accept this postulate and formulate an alternative position, according to which the complete absence of any ties with being as distinct from the essent is perfectly possible. SA describes two basic paradigms of human constitution and two corresponding anthropological formations (respectively, the Ontic and the Virtual Human), which do not actualize the ontological difference. Anthropological experience, in which these formations are constituted, can be called unontological, because it does not involve any relationship with being as different from the essent. It follows from this definition that all the domains of unontological experience are domains, where Heidegger's thesis "being remains there" is surely invalid. This situation makes it necessary to ask a few questions.

First, we must consider how our discourse of unontological experience is related to Heidegger's discourse of concealedness. In terms of Heidegger, the former discourse describes the experience in which any relation to being (as distinct from the essent) is absent; while the latter describes the experience in which being is concealed, and its concealedness grows gradually, but nevertheless it always "remains there." In terms of SA, the former discourse describes the ontic topic, the latter the ontological topic, and especially those parts of it that are in a certain sense drawing nearer to the ontic topic with its absence of ties with being. It means that the discourse of concealedness makes it possible to describe more precisely the relationship between the two topics. Uniting both discourses, we can trace what happens to the onto-logical dimension of anthropological experience in the transition from the ontological topic to the ontic one.

According to Heidegger, there is no such transition and no ontic topic. Being can become more and more concealed since there are countless forms of concealedness, including the most radical ones, in which the relation to being is completely imperceptible; but all these forms belong to the ontological topic, which exhausts the whole field of anthropological experience. We noticed, however, that Heidegger did not prove that being always remains there, so this key thesis is only a postulate. Rejecting this postulate, SA presents a different vision of the limits of concealedness.

By definition, the Ontological Human is constituted in the actualiza-tion of the ontological difference. However, according to the discourse of concealedness, there are parts of the ontological topic in which this actualization diminishes more and more, coming right up to its disap-pearance. On the other hand, this disappearance can never become really and fully complete. Although the growth of concealedness can continue indefinitely, this process is always reversible, and one can expect that one day a reversal will suddenly take place.[12] Contrary to this position, SA finds that there are domains of unontological experience in which the ontological difference is not actualized at all and the human does not have any relation to being (as distinct from the essent). This experience belongs to the Ontic Human (we do not discuss the Virtual Human in this text, just for brevity's sake), who has a different constitution shaped not in the ontological unlocking, but in the ontic one. Hence there is a border dividing the two anthropological topics, and what happens at this border is the transition from the concealment (of being) in all its forms to the actual and complete elimination or just bare absence. At the same time, a change in the human constitution takes place, correspond-ing to the transition from the Ontological Human to the Ontic Human. Since this transition is an event, in which the ontological dimension of anthropological experience and of the human constitution is lost, it is proper to call it the *event of deontologization*. Coming back to the notion of Lathon, we can say that in the event of deontologization, Lathon turns into the full-blooded and autonomous figure of the Ontic Human. One should stress that, unlike the growth of concealedness, it is not a gradual and continuous process. There are two radically different paradigms of the human constitution, and the replacement of one of them by the other should be conceived as a discrete and distinct act, a kind of a leap. An adequate metaphor is phase transition in physical systems, like the freezing of water. A more philosophical metaphor is the notion of the "all of a sudden" (*to exaiphnes*) introduced by Plato in *Parmenides* and meaning something "that leaves its state in an imperceptibly small time."[13] This platonic notion is used by Heidegger as one of characteristics of the event, *das Ereignis*. One can find also other predicates shared by *das Ereignis* and our event of deontologization, and one can say that this event of the loss of the relation to being is in a certain sense the polar opposite to *Ereignis*, a kind of anti-*Ereignis*, if you will.

The next important question concerns concrete forms of unontological experience (experience of the Ontic and the Virtual Human). What are these forms and how are they treated in Heidegger's philosophy? Of course, the two unontological formations cultivate plenty of the most diverse forms of anthropological experience. Here we shall consider only two examples, that is, two experiential domains, but they both are large enough and the relationship of Heidegger's thought with them is interesting and important. The first of them is the experience related to the phenomena induced by the unconscious—that is, patterns of the unconscious such as neuroses, manias, phobias, and the like. As the second domain we shall take anthropological practices of totalitarianism.

In the context of SA the unconscious emerges as one of the representations of the ontic Other. In the unlocking that actualizes the relation to this Other, the human is constituted as a certain subformation of the Ontic Human, which can be called the *Freudian Human*. Our discourse of ontic unlocking treats the unconscious as a source of certain energies located beyond the horizon of consciousness and inducing definite patterns of consciousness and behavior. (Such treatment is in accordance with the usual dynamic description of the unconscious. Cf., e.g.: "Contents of the unconscious, heavily loaded by energy, strive for coming back to consciousness and manifesting themselves in behavior [the return of the repressed])."[14] The constitution of the Freudian Human takes shape in the actualization of the relation to this "source beyond-there," exactly in the same way as the constitution of the Ontological Human takes shape in the actualization of the relation to being/God. However, the structure and dynamics of ontic unlocking and patterns of the unconscious are radically different from the mechanisms of ontological unlocking. The latter mechanisms, corresponding to the paradigm of synergy, have the character of the stepwise ascension; *grosso modo*, they can be called ecstatic and considered to be essentially the same as the mechanisms of the Heideggerian "ecstatic stepping-out into the clearing of being." As for the dynamics of the unlocking for the unconscious, it is determined by the phenomena of repression (*die Verdrängung*) and the development of induced patterns. There is nothing ecstatic about these dynamics of induced phenomena. They are topological dynamics determined by effects of the damage of the connectedness of consciousness, and the corresponding processes are mostly of cyclic, but not ascending, character. The basic patterns of the unconscious implementing such topological and cyclic dynamics are classified and studied in psychoanalysis on the basis of a wealth of empirical material. These studies of repressed and induced phenomena put at our disposal a rich pool of experience, which is surely unontological.

Now how is all this experience treated in Heidegger's philosophy? The key property of the Freudian Human is that he or she implements the paradigm of human constitution—namely, constitution in the unlocking for the unconscious—that is an alternative to the constitution of the Ontological Human, which is the constitution in the ontological unlocking. Evidently, this paradigm is an alternative also to Heidegger's vision of the human, which admits the constitution in the actualization of the ontological difference only. Hence it follows that, be it explicitly or implicitly, Heidegger denies the constitutive principle of the Freudian Human and the very existence of it as a *bona fide* anthropological (sub-)formation. The closest and most substantial contact of Heidegger's thought with this subformation was developed in the context of the friendly relationship between Heidegger and Swiss psychiatrist Medard Boss and, chiefly, in the Zollikon Seminars conducted by them both in 1959 to 1969. Even in these texts, which emerged due to this relationship (they were published by Boss), to say nothing of other texts by Heidegger, he does not go into a detailed discussion of Freud's conceptions and very rarely mentions either Freud or the unconscious. However, there are many running comments, which touch upon almost all principal points of these conceptions, and all such remarks are radically critical. In our context, for the greater part they can be divided into two groups: First, Heidegger criticizes basic Freudian notions, ideas, and viewpoints, and points out their cardinal distinctions from his own positions; second, he presents his own interpretation of phenomena studied by Freud and in psychoanalysis. Taking into account that patterns of the unconscious represent really and fully unontological experience, one can expect that the remarks in this group may be based on disputable and shaky arguments.

To start with, Heidegger gives a negative judgment about psychoanalysis as a whole. It is in the same line as his criticism of humanistic disciplines in *Sein und Zeit*:

> Psychology and psychoanalysis are schools of thought emerging on the basis of representations, which are especially inclined to block thought, because one can "explain" everything in the world by means of the reduction to unclarified subjectivity. . . . Psychoanalysis . . . treats man as a thing, turning him into the "liability to drives" (*Triebhaftigkeit*).[15]

According to Heidegger, psychoanalysis is based on methodology, which tries to explain everything by means of simple causal relations. This methodology is taken from the natural sciences and, in the first place, from mechanics, and it is grossly inadequate for grasping the human. Then, getting to the concrete, Heidegger briefly, but sharply criticizes all the "four fundamental concepts of psychoanalysis" (to use Lacan's formula), the unconscious, the drive, repetition, and the transference.

The unconscious is for him an artificial concept, which is introduced *ad hoc*, in order to secure the possibility of a completely causal description of the entire domain of psychic phenomena. Freud postulates the "overall explicability of the psychic" and "since it is absent 'in consciousness,' he must invent the 'unconscious'" to restore the continuity of causal links. And Heidegger always stresses that this postulate of all-embracing causality "is not taken from psychic phenomena themselves, it is a postulate of modern natural science."[16] The criticism of the concept of the drive presents similar arguments:

> The drive (*Trieb*) is always an attempt at explication. However . . . one always tries to explain with the help of drives something which first was not considered at all. Attempts to explain human phenomena based on drives have the methodological character of a science, the subject domain of which is not human at all, but mechanics. Hence it is doubtful in principle whether it is possible to say something about the human as such by means of a method, which proceeds from non-human objectness.[17]

Evidently, the last critical consideration here refers not only to drives, but to all psychoanalysis. As for transference, Heidegger simply denies this phenomenon: "It is completely senseless to talk about 'transference.' There is nothing that one has to transfer."[18] However, his arguments in favor of such a position are restricted to a brief and not too convincing remark: He just points out that according to existential analytics, being-there is characterized by disposition *(Befindlichkeit)* and, due to the fact that we always have some or other *Befindlichkeit*, the latter is automatically transferred by us to everybody, whom we meet and contact. Clearly, this remark means only that the existential analytic has its own analogue or substitute for the notion of the transference, which is *die Befindlichkeit*. But transference in psychoanalysis has a rich economy, which integrates it into many patterns and processes related to repression *(die Verdrängung)* and producing unontological experience. Heidegger's discourse of dispositions does not discuss these patterns and processes, and so his remark shakes their psychoanalytical interpretation in no way. The last of the four concepts, repetition, is not discussed explicitly, but there is no doubt that this concept is also not accepted by Heidegger, because psychoanalysis defines and describes it by means of the same mechanical and energy paradigms, in other words, "psychodynamics," which Heidegger rejects.

In most cases Heidegger's criticism concerns methodological and epistemological aspects of psychoanalytical discourse, and usually it is justifiable; Heidegger's culture of theoretical thought is incomparable to that of most psychoanalytical studies. However, psychoanalysis is essentially an experiential discipline having a huge phenomenal base. This base represents a vast pool of information about psychic phenomena, including systematic and verified observation data on their development and dynamics. It is empirical and descriptive phenomenology, which is for the greater part independent of general theories by Freud and others. Thus, when it discovers specific patterns and mechanisms characteristic of unontological experience and incompatible with the experience of the Ontological Human, this experiential evidence remains mostly unshaken by Heidegger's theoretical critique. Besides this critique, Heidegger presents his own interpretation of some phenomena as an alternative to the psychoanalytic one. But usually these phenomena are not connected with the principal patterns of the unconscious, like neuroses and the like, which belong to the domain of the pronounced unontological experience. And in rare cases, when

Heidegger decides to tread on the ground of such experience with his uncompromising ontologism, he is not too successful.

One typical example is his treatment of phenomena of repression (*Verdrängung*). According to Heidegger: "The phenomenon of repression can be grasped in its specific nature only if it is considered from the very beginning as an ecstatically intentional attitude to the world: to things, living beings, the people of one's circle."[19] This attitude is stated as the universal principle: "Again and again it deals with the same basic phenomenon: instead of psychic mechanics or dynamics, one should reveal and describe an ecstatically intentional attitude to the world."[20] Of course, an "ecstatically intentional attitude" is what corresponds exactly to the Heideggerian paradigm of human constitution in the stepping-out into the clearing of being. But most phenomena of repression studied in psychoanalysis are connected with patterns of the unconscious that do not implement this ontological paradigm and demonstrate typically not ecstatic, but cyclic behavior. Ecstatic and cyclic constitutive paradigms are sharply different, and hence the statement that all phenomena of repression correspond to the ecstatic paradigm contradicts experiential data.

Summing up, we conclude that although Heidegger presents just epistemological and methodological criticism of many concepts and principles of psychoanalysis, his philosophy did not destroy or shake its phenomenal foundations. Thus it does not prove that the Freudian Human does not exist. The existence of this anthropological (sub-) formation, contradicting Heidegger's vision of the Human, can be considered as a well-verified fact.

Anthropological experience in the conditions of totalitarianism is another domain of pronounced unontological experience. However, we cannot analyze how Heidegger treated this domain in the same way as we analyzed his treatment of the Freudian Human. Unfortunately, the anthropology of totalitarianism is not yet developed, and Heidegger also was not concerned with it. But instead he lived under a totalitarian regime and hence he had *volens nolens* some knowledge about its anthropological practices. Now, notwithstanding the absence of a full-bodied anthropology, one can make some initial observations and judgments about these practices. They were very specific: They included mass murders of an unprecedented scale, and this fact alone is sufficient in order to draw important anthropological conclusions. Evidently, practices of mass murder cannot be cultivated by the Ontological

Human who is constituted in the unlocking for the encounter with being/God or, in the Heideggerian terms, in the ecstatic stepping-out into the clearing of being. Here we shall not discuss their anthropological diagnostics, or the problem, which is that anthropological formations perform such practices. We simply note that these practices are not just different from those of the ontological unlocking, but opposite to them, as sharply opposite as one can imagine. The term "deontologization" is fully adequate with respect to them. But for Heidegger the actualization of the ontological difference, which is nearly synonymous to ontological unlocking, is the only and universal mode of human constitution. It means that *the anthropological situation, in which the thinker lived and participated during the Nazi period, represented a striking counterexample to his philosophy.*

This is an inner conflict. Let us try to describe and understand it. There is no need to retell the well-known course of outer events. My subject now is strictly the anthropological aspect of the notorious theme "Heidegger and Nazism." To begin with, one can note a general fact: All Heidegger's experience of the Nazi years did not arouse in him any doubts about his vision of the human and did not lead to any noticeable changes in this vision. In particular, one cannot see in Heidegger even a shadow of the idea that the anthropological practices of Nazism did not just deviate from the "ecstatic stepping-out into the clearing of being," but also cannot be treated in the discourse of the concealedness of being, and the cornerstone of this discourse, the thesis "being remains there" (conceived as "the human being's relation to being remains there") cannot be valid for them. On the contrary, he rejects this idea and although the rejection is not made pronouncedly, it is unmistakable and firm. In so far as such a rejection can only be based on the negation of plain factual reality, we are a bit struck at first. But soon we discern a certain logic behind this position.

It is the logic of hard and uncompromising ontologism; hyper- or over-ontologism, if you will. Since "being remains there," it implies unequivocally that the Germans always continue their mission, which is to be "watchmen of being" *par excellence*, preferable to all other humans except ancient Greeks. But what about mass murders, which represent openly and shockingly unontological experience? The hyper-ontological answer is obvious: Since "being remains there," these practices cannot exist. The facts that are reported as such practices are misinterpreted, it was something else, some regrettable accidentals, for which there can be lots of reasons (including some nasty qualities of the Jewry). Thus the position of Heidegger is that of a true philosopher, for whom the essence of phenomena (revealed by his philosophy) is more important than their appearance.

To be more precise, this steadfast position had a certain evolution. It is well-known that Heidegger went through a period of great enthusiasm for National Socialism, and this enthusiasm had its anthropological aspect too. In this period (the early period of the Nazi regime) he repeatedly characterizes the "National-Socialist revolution" by ontological formulas such as "the great turn of being," "the revolution of all human being," and the emergence of "revolutionary reality, which is not just empirical reality." In his discourse such formulas imply that some change of the relationship between humankind and being also took place; the great turn of being cannot but be *eo ipso* an anthropological turn. And this anthropological turn presented itself to Heidegger as an unprecedented breakthrough to being for human beings, a kind of collective, nationwide stepping-out into the clearing of being: the effort and the act, which could be only individual before (the notion of the clearing first appeared in *Vom Wesen der Wahrheit* in 1930). This anthropological/ontological side of his position is especially stressed by his biographer: "Heidegger perceived the revolution of 1933 as . . . a breakthrough into the open space, which was open before to individual philosophical questioning and thinking only. . . . [He] interpreted the revolution as a collective escape from the cave [the cave of Plato's myth —SH]. . . . The people find the truth at last and ask the question of being."[21] The utopian idea of collective being as a shared drawing into and staying in the truth of being was connected with Heidegger's idealized construct of Ancient Greece as a special mode of being; but also it seems very natural in the prism of Russian historical experience. In Russian thought there was a similar idea long since known as the idea of *sobornost'*, the harmonious spiritual community. It is very easy to suppose in the light of such ideas that the awakening of the nation during great upheavals has a genuine ontological and religious dimension. And in the epoch of the Russian revolution it was exactly this logic that pushed many intellectuals to become supporters of the Bolsheviks.

Thus Heidegger enthusiastically thought at first that the Nazi movement would bring forth the anthropological breakthrough, the achievement of an unprecedented new stage in the relationship of humankind and being. This anthropological enthusiasm did not last long, however;

it was soon succeeded by a more weighed and balanced attitude. Heidegger continued to believe that by its origins and essence, in spite of all defects and side effects, the movement had a strong, creative, and fruitful core. This core could not and did not produce the anthropological breakthrough, but still it had some anthropological merits. In *Introduction to Metaphysics* (1935/1953) he writes of "the works that are being peddled nowadays as the philosophy of National Socialism but have nothing whatever to do with the inner truth and greatness of this movement (namely the encounter between global technology and modern man)."[22] Safransky points out that the part in parentheses was added when the author was reworking his lectures of 1935 for publication. It means that this part tells us what Heidegger wanted to single out as the great truth revealed to us by Nazism, in 1953, long after its fall. It is by no means an unimportant *anthropological* truth concerning the constitutive relationship of the modern human with global technologies. Thus we conclude that at least till that time Heidegger continued to consider the Nazi movement as an anthropologically positive and productive phenomenon.

What is more, during the entire Nazi period the thinker kept unchanged the national component of his vision of the human—namely, the idea that the Germans represent a kind of anthropological avantgarde, that they have a special anthropological/ontological mission, which is similar to that of the ancient Greeks and means that they are destined and capable to be "watchmen of being" more than all other humans. In the lectures on Heraclitus he writes:

> The essence of truth was revealed to the West . . . in Greekness (*das Griechentum*). . . . In the destiny sent to it [Greekness] there is nothing past or obsolete . . . there is only the future, which is not decided yet, and we, the Germans, are the first and, very likely, the only ones for the long time to come, who can and must think towards it.[23]

Anthropological primacy and the mission of the Germans are stated here with perfect clarity, and the lectures include many similar statements. But the meaning of these texts can be grasped fully only if we take into account their date, 1943–1944. At this time the Germans are most actively busy with the realization of the Nazi programs of the elimination of people and entire nations, and all the territory, which is accessible to them, is turned into the scene of mass murders. Yes, the "encounter between global technology and modern man" takes place here too, and the most innovative and advanced results of this encounter are gas chambers. Heidegger's colleagues from the German universities created incredibly efficient gases: A mere seven kilos of Zyklon B were sufficient to kill one thousand people. Auschwitz, the most successful factory of mass extermination, succeeded in killing more than 4 million people. . . . It so happened that I first saw Auschwitz a few years ago, when I was studying *Heraclitus*. And when I was standing in front of the famous gate with the slogan *Arbeit macht frei*, I had suddenly a clear impression that something was missing there. The Soviet past has firmly imprinted stereotypes of the totalitarian landscape in my consciousness, and I quickly realized that on either side of the gate there should be beautiful streamers with the words about the Noble Mission of the Germans. With Heidegger's words quoted above.

It is indisputable that mass murders, which lasted for years and killed millions and millions of people, are nothing but an *anthropological catastrophe*. The catastrophe is two-sided: On the one side, it involved millions of murdered victims and on the other side, tens of thousands of butchers and millions of their assistants. The second side needs an anthropological interpretation because practices of mass murders are so special that they surely imply profound changes in structures of personality and identity and the paradigm of human constitution. Which anthropological formation produces them has not yet been found, but it is obvious that the Ontological Human has nothing to do with them, and in Heideggerian terms, they cannot correspond to any forms and degrees of the concealedness of being. In spite of his strongly apologetic attitude to Heidegger, Bibikhin also considered the experience of totalitarianism as "experience, which yields to clarifying comprehension in no way, by no approach and with the help of no forces whatever."[24]

Now, what is the answer of Heidegger's philosophy to this catastrophe? First, he does not say a word about it although he lived through it and among its actors. Second, he states that during all the Nazi period there were no anthropological changes, and the Germans always remained faithful to humanity's anthropological/ontological destination. Third, in all periods of his work he stuck firmly to his conception, according to which the human constitution can be shaped in only one way, namely in the actualization of the ontological difference.

Clearly, it is an inappropriate answer. Practices of mass extermination *do* contradict Heidegger's conception. And it means that the encounter of Heidegger as an anthropological thinker with Nazism resulted in his professional failure.

Thus, paraphrasing the popular sentence on "theology after Auschwitz," one can say that Heidegger's hyper-ontologized vision of the human became impossible after Auschwitz. More precisely, this vision is incomplete since it does not consider unontological experience and moreover it becomes incorrect, when Heidegger postulates that "being remains there," or that only ontological experience is possible. We have considered two domains of unontological experience, respectively, patterns of the unconscious and totalitarian practices of mass murder, with which Heidegger was concerned, though in different ways. Our discussion causes us to dispute Heidegger's positions. At the same time, it shows that the variety of anthropological experience is most adequately approached from the positions of anthropological pluralism.

## NOTES

1. Sergey Horujy, *Diogenes' Lantern* (Moscow: Institut Filosofii, Teologii i Istorii Sv. Fomy, 2010), 426–448.

2. The Organon, which is the core of each spiritual practice, is the complete set of rules prescribing the preparation, control, correction, and interpretation of its experience. See Sergey Horujy, *Toward a Phenomenology of Ascesis* (Moscow: Izdatelstvo Gumanitarnoi Literatury, 1998).

3. *Das Seiende* has been rendered in English in many ways, of which none is indisputably good (an entity, a being, what is, that which is, etc.). The version that I choose was first used in the translation of *Einführung in die Metaphysk* by Ralph Manheim: Martin Heidegger, *An Introduction to Metaphysics*, trans. Ralph Manheim (New York: Anchor Books, 1959).

4. Horujy, *Diogenes' Lantern,* 448–72.

5. Martin Heidegger, *Sein und Zeit* (Tübingen: Max Niemeyer Verlag, 1967), 266.

6. Martin Heidegger, *Heraclitus* (St. Petersburg: Vladimir Dahl, 2011), 467.

7. Heidegger, *Sein und Zeit*, section 1, chapter 4.

8. Ibid., 130.

9. Heidegger, *Heraclitus*, 219; Martin Heidegger, *Parmenides* (St. Petersburg: Vladimir Dahl, 2009), 110.

10. Heidegger, *Parmenides*, 326–27.

11. Martin Heidegger, *Time and Being* (Moscow: Respublika, 1993), 208.

12. This is the idea of the turn, *die Kehre.* Cf.: "The turn transforming peril into salvation will happen all at once. In this turn the light of the essence of being will suddenly appear." Heidegger, *Time and Being,* 256.

13. Plato, *Parmenides,* 156d.

14. Jean Laplanche and Jean-Bertrand Pontalis, *Dictionary of Psychoanalysis* (Moscow: Vysshaia Shkola, 1996), 71.

15. Martin Heidegger, *The Zollikon Seminars: Protocols, Conversations, Letters,* ed. Medard Boss (Vilnius: EGU, 2012), 354, 249.

16. Ibid., 285.

17. Ibid., 247.

18. Ibid., 240.

19. Ibid., 377.

20. Ibid., 376.

21. Rüdiger Safransky, *The German Master: Heidegger and His Time* (Moscow: Molodaya Gvardiya, 2005), 320, 336.

22. Heidegger, *An Introduction,* 166.

23. Heidegger, *Heraclitus,* 253.

24. Vladimir Veniaminovich Bibikhin, *Energy* (Moscow: Institut filosofii, Teologii, i Istorii Sv. Fomy, 2010), 247.

# Index

Boehme, Jacob, 167
Bollnow, O. F., 127
Bolshevism, 17, 305, 349; *Black
    Notebooks* on, 15; Christianity
    and, 29n37; in Russia, 15, 256
Boss, Medard, 344
boundaries, 264–65
bourgeois, 14
*Brautmystik*, 161
Brentano, Franz, 140, 274
*The Brothers Karamazov* (Dostoevsky),
    40–42, 45–46, 48, 51, 259,
    271n14
Bultmann, Rudolf, 93n125

*Capital* (Marx), 13, 229–30
captivation, 211–13
capture, 207–8, 210–11
care: call of, 38, 46; conscience as, 38;
    in Dasein, 35, 44, 299–300;
    DII on, 81; everydayness and,
    228–29; Goethe on, 68–69;
    of soul, 150; taking flight, 78;
    temporality of, 229
causality, 99, 345
center, of existence, 292–93
Christ: Dostoevsky on, 31–33, 45–46,
    49; Hölderlin and, 31–32; as
    human, 161; Michalski on, 159–
    60; Nietzsche and, 159, 161
Christianity, xii; Bolshevism and, 29n37;
    eschatology of, 47; evil in,
    6–7; God in, 7; Michalski
    on, 163; mortality and, 11;
    Platonism and, 9; salvation in,
    11–12
Chvatík, Ivan, 135n50
Cicero, 52n5
Civic Forum, 246n79
*Civilization and Its Discontent* (Freud), 76
civilization, organization in, 314–15
civil society, 181
clearing: as being, 195–97, 348; Dasein
    in, 337; of event, 313; of
    mystery, 317–18, 320; thinking
    and, 195–97; truth in, 312–13

Cold War, 252
communism, 20. *See also* Bolshevism;
    Soviet Union
Communist Party (CP), 231–33
community, 252
concealedness, 338–43, 348. *See also*
    everydayness
concealing, 44, 313, 318, 320
concept, 214, 299
conscience, 38–39, 43, 336–37
*The Contributions to Philosophy*
    (Heidegger), xiv, 9, 29n37, 47,
    255, 304; *Being and Time* and,
    295–99, 302, 319–20; Bibikhin
    on, 260–63; decisive moment
    in, 35; on future ones, 45;
    on monotheism, 283–84; on
    realized eschatology, 47
conversation, 184
Corbin, Henry, 279–80, 288–89
correctness, of histories, 9–11
CP. *See* Communist Party
creation, 261–62
Creator, 319
crime: Ereignis of, 40; of Raskolnikov,
    36–39, 42
Crimea, 95–100, 253
*Crime and Punishment* (Dostoevsky),
    34, 36–37, 39–43, 48. *See also*
    Raskolnikov (character)
Czechoslovakia, 119–22, 227–28,
    231–32, 241, 243n14;
    existentialism in, 226;
    language of, 134n23;
    philosophy in, 225, 233, 242.
    *See also* Communist Party;
    Patočka, Jan

Dasein: abyss and, 315; *anthropologische
    Differenz* and, 281; in
    apocalypse, 173; in *Being
    and Time*, 300, 331, 334,
    339; being-in-the-world of,
    141; Being of, 9, 19–20, 25,
    140–41, 239, 277, 281; as
    being-toward-death, 66–67,

# About the Contributors

**Vladimir Bibikhin** (1938–2004) was a translator from many languages, assistant to Aleksei Losev, and a Russian philosopher whose lectures at Moscow State University have gained almost legendary status. He translated *Being and Time* into Russian.

**Alexander Dugin** is a Russian philosopher, political scientist, and political activist. Author of more than thirty books, including *Foundations of Geopolitics*, four works on Martin Heidegger, and the multivolumed *Noomakhia* series, he is also the founder of the Eurasia Movement and editor-in-chief of the Russian conservative television channel Tsargrad TV.

**Horst-Jürgen Gerigk** is professor of Russian and comparative literature at the University of Heidelberg. His academic teachers were Dmitrij Tschizewskij (Russian literature), Hans-Georg Gadamer (philosophy), and Paul Fussell (American literature). His most recent publications are a Dostoevsky monograph and a study in the theory of literature: *Lesendes Bewusstsein. Untersuchungen zur philosophischen Grundlage der Literaturwissenschaft* (2016).

**Ludger Hagedorn** is head of the Patočka Archive and Research Program at the Institute for Human Sciences (IWM) in Vienna. He obtained his doctoral degree from TU Berlin, after studying philosophy and Slavic languages. His main fields of research include modernity and secularization, phenomenology, political philosophy, and history of ideas. His most recent publication is *Religion, War and the Crisis of Modernity*, volume 14 of *The New Yearbook for Phenomenology and Phenomenological Philosophy*, coedited with J. Dodd (2015).

**Sergey S. Horujy** was born in 1941 in Skopin, Soviet Union, graduated from the physics department of Moscow State University in 1964, was baptized by the priest Alexander Men in 1968, and worked in Steklov Mathematical Institute of the Russian Academy of Sciences until 2006. He obtained his PhD in 1967 and habilitation doctorate in 1976 and has published about one hundred articles plus one monograph in axiomatic, algebraic, and conformal quantum field theory. Since the 1980s he has worked on James Joyce, publishing translations of the novel *Ulysses* and all earlier prose by Joyce in addition to a monograph, Ulysses *in a Russian Mirror* (1994). Since the 1960s he has also worked in philosophy, which was on an underground basis until the fall of the Bolshevik regime. After writing studies in Russian religious philosophy, he began to develop his pluralistic anthropological conception called "synergic anthropology" based on the experience of spiritual practices, beginning with Eastern Orthodox Hesychasm. In 2005, he founded the Institute of Synergic Anthropology and in 2015 launched the international anthropological journal *Diogenes' Lantern*.

**Alexander Kluge** is a major contemporary German fiction writer, social critic, and filmmaker.

**Daniel Kroupa** was born in Prague in 1949. He switched from studying electrical engineering to philosophy under Jan Patočka. He dropped formal studies in 1970, began teaching philosophy in private in 1979, and held other, unqualified jobs up to 1989. He signed Charter 77 and participated in dissent activities. From 1989 to 2004, he was active in politics as a member of the (successively) Czechoslovak, Czech, and European Parliaments; from 1998 to 2001, he was also a party leader in ODA, "Civic Democratic Alliance." In 1995, he finished his undergraduate study of philosophy at Charles University (Prague), and in 2008 he obtained his PhD at Palacký University (Olomouc) for a dissertation on the concept of ideology. Since 2005 he has been teaching philosophy and politics at the University of J. E. Purkyně in Ústí nad Labem.

**Piotr Kubasiak** has studied Catholic theology at the Pontifical University of John Paul II, in Cracow, and at the University of Regensburg. Currently he is a PhD candidate in fundamental theology at the University of Vienna, with the doctoral thesis "Between Existentialism and Politics. Europe and History in the Thinking of Krzysztof Michalski." He is also Bronisław Geremek Junior Visiting Fellow of the Institute for Human Sciences in Vienna.

**Jeff Love** is professor of German and Russian at Clemson University. He has published two books on Tolstoy, *The Overcoming of History in War and Peace* (2004) and *Tolstoy: A Guide for the Perplexed* (2008). He is also cotranslator of Schelling's *Philosophical Investigations into the Essence of Human Freedom* (2006) and editor of *Nietzsche and Dostoevsky: Philosophy, Morality, Tragedy* (2016).

**Michael Marder** is IKERBASQUE Research Professor at the University of the Basque Country, Vitoria-Gasteiz, Spain and professor-at-large at the Humanities Institute of Diego Portales University in Santiago, Chile. His most recent books include *Pyropolitics: When the World Is Ablaze* (2015); *Dust* (2016); with Anaïs Tondeur, *The Chernobyl Herbarium* (2016); and, with Luce Irigaray, *Through Vegetal Being* (2016).

**Inessa Medzhibovskaya** is associate professor of liberal studies and literature at the New School for Social Research and Lang College in New York City. She is the author of *Tolstoy and the Religious Culture of His Time*, a study in the genre of the long intellectual biography, and of over forty journal essays and book chapters on literature (focusing mainly on Russian authors and philosophers), ideology and education, and the interplay of philosophy, religion, politics, and literary aesthetics. In addition to forthcoming volumes on Tolstoy's philosophy and its impact in the twentieth and twenty-first centuries, she was most recently commissioned to prepare the first comprehensive anthology of Tolstoy's thought in English, a busy project now underway.

**Michael Meng** is associate professor of history at Clemson University. He is the author of *Shattered Spaces: Encountering Jewish Ruins in Postwar Germany and Poland* (2011). He is currently writing a book on death, history, and salvation in European thought.

**Krzysztof Michalski** (1948–2013) was founder and rector of the Institute for Human Sciences (IWM) as well as professor at the University of Warsaw and Boston University. He was editor of the journal *Transit: Europäische Revue*. He obtained his PhD with the thesis "Heidegger and Contemporary Philosophy" (1974, published 1978), and earned his habilitation in 1986 with "Logic and Time. An Attempt at a Phenomenological Analysis." Among his numerous publications are *The Flame of Eternity* (2007) and *Understanding Transience* (2011).

**Josef Moural** studied mathematics and philosophy at Charles University, Prague (RNDr. 1987) and participated in underground philosophy and classics seminars in Prague before November 1989. He taught philosophy at Charles University (Prague), Central European University (Prague), King's College (London), and the University of California (Berkeley), and held research positions at the Jan Patočka Archives (Prague), the Center for Theoretical Study (Prague), the Institute for Advanced Studies in the Humanities (Edinburgh), and the Institut für die Wissenschaften vom Menschen (Wien). Currently he teaches philosophy at the University of J. E. Purkyně (Ústí nad Labem). His PhD dissertation was titled "David Hume's Metaphilosophy"; his *Habilitationschrift*, "Ancient Skepticism, Its Forerunners and Its Heirs."

**Andrzej Serafin** is assistant professor at the Institute of Philosophy and Sociology of the Pedagogical University in Cracow. He is editor of the philosophical journal *Kronos*. He is a Polish translator of Plato (*Symposium, Epinomis*), Jacob Taubes (*Occidental Eschatology*), and Rilke (*Letters on Cézanne*). He obtained his PhD with the thesis "The Concept of Truth in Heidegger's Interpretation of Aristotle" (2016). He is currently working on a translation of *Timaeus*.

**Vladislav Suvák** studied at the Faculty of Arts, University of Pavol Jozef Šafárik, Prešov, and the Faculty of Arts, Charles University, Prague, obtaining his MA in 1992. He obtained his PhD in 2000 from Comenius University, Bratislava, with the thesis "The End of Metaphysics and Plato." He has been senior lecturer of the history of philosophy at the Institute of Philosophy of Prešov University since 2002. He has published *Diogenis fragmenta/Diogenove zlomky*, an introductory study of, translation of, and commentary on Diogenes's fragments, coauthored in Slovak with Jaroslav Cepko and Andrej